A Union Indivisible

CIVIL WAR AMERICA

Peter S. Carmichael, Caroline E. Janney, and Aaron Sheehan-Dean, editors

This landmark series interprets broadly the history and culture of the Civil War era through the long nineteenth century and beyond. Drawing on diverse approaches and methods, the series publishes historical works that explore all aspects of the war, biographies of leading commanders, and tactical and campaign studies, along with select editions of primary sources. Together, these books shed new light on an era that remains central to our understanding of American and world history.

MICHAEL D. ROBINSON

A Union Indivisible

Secession and the Politics of Slavery
in the Border South

The University of North Carolina Press *Chapel Hill*

This book was published with the assistance of the Fred W. Morrison Fund of the University of North Carolina Press.

© 2017 The University of North Carolina Press
All rights reserved
Set in Arno Pro by Westchester Publishing Services
Manufactured in the United States of America

The University of North Carolina Press has been a member
of the Green Press Initiative since 2003.

Library of Congress Cataloging-in-Publication Data
Names: Robinson, Michael D., 1979– author.
Title: A union indivisible : secession and the politics of slavery
    in the border south / Michael D. Robinson.
Other titles: Civil War America (Series)
Description: Chapel Hill : University of North Carolina Press, [2017] |
    Series: Civil War America | Includes bibliographical references and index.
Identifiers: LCCN 2016051605 | ISBN 9781469633787 (cloth : alk. paper) |
    ISBN 9781469633794 (ebook)
Subjects: LCSH: Secession—Southern States. | Slavery—Political Aspects—
    Southern States—History—19th century. | Southern States—Politics and
    government—1775–1865. | Southern States—History—1775–1865. |
    United States—History—Civil War, 1861–1865.
Classification: LCC E459 .R58 2017 | DDC 973.7/113—dc23
    LC record available at https://lccn.loc.gov/2016051605

Jacket illustration: Detail from *Union*, painted by T. H. Matteson and engraved by H. S. Sadd
    (courtesy of the Library of Congress, LC-DIG-pga-03232).

For Katherine

Contents

Illustrations, Map, and Tables

Acknowledgments

This book originated as an investigation of why Kentucky, a state that to me seemed so similar to the states that eventually seceded, remained in the Union, and in time the project grew to encompass the entire Border South. During the research, writing, and editing of the book, I often wondered if I had bitten off more than I could chew. The encouragement, support, and advice of a host of friends, loved ones, and colleagues sustained me through moments of doubt and helped me realize that although daunting, expanding the scope of the project was a worthwhile endeavor. It is my great pleasure to get to thank them for all that they have done.

My greatest scholarly debt is owed to William J. Cooper Jr. of Louisiana State University. Bill coached me through the process of tackling a historical problem head on and provided his undivided attention to the project from start to finish. I constantly relied on his incomparable knowledge of the American South, his eye for detail, and his gracious nature as the book took shape. Bill's wit, wisdom, and benevolence have shaped my approach to the historian's craft in numerous ways; both the book and I are better products because of him. His guidance and friendship are equally treasured.

Paul Paskoff taught me the importance of utilizing quantitative data to substantiate an argument, and this book bears his imprint. It was a tough lesson for a particularly hardheaded pupil, but I must thank Paul for his guidance. Over many cups of coffee, Paul helped me to frame my evidence and clarify my argument. I greatly value his friendship and his willingness to scrutinize my conclusions and support my work. Gaines Foster always found time for me despite an enormously crowded schedule as dean of Louisiana State University's College of Humanities and Social Sciences. His meticulous analysis of the manuscript and incisive comments always probed me to think about how I framed a sentence, or utilized evidence, or made an argument. Gaines set the bar high and showed me the value of service and selflessness in academia.

Nathan Buman, Chris Childers, Geoff Cunningham, Katie Eskridge, Michael Frawley, and Adam Pratt helped me formulate many ideas and offered valuable feedback on early drafts of the manuscript. I learned a great deal from them, along with David Lilly, Spencer McBride, Kate Seyfried, Terry

Wagner, Andrew Wegmann, and Jason Wolfe, all of whom made my time in Baton Rouge better. The families of Bryce Abernethy, Steve Bagley, Joe Blackwood, Joe Browning, Phil Daye, Charlie Dickerson, Jonathan Garrett, Danny Hunt, Chris Owens, and Charles Ross have provided their share of laughs and good times along life's road. The fond memory of bygone days spent with those friends has often sustained this transplanted Carolinian who now lives on the Gulf Coast.

My colleagues at the University of Mobile have been great sources of inspiration. Matthew Downs and Lonnie Burnett are exemplary colleagues, offering sound advice and tireless support. Their good humor, tutelage, and friendship make it a joy to teach history to young people. Retired dean of the College of Arts and Sciences Dwight Steedley encouraged me to complete this book from the moment I stepped on campus, and I thank him for his support. Julie Biskner, Cassidy Cooper, Cindy Godwin, Ted Mashburn, Doug Mitchell, Gyromas Newman, Jamie O'Mally, Jeremy Padgett, Aimee Var, and Joe West might have little interest in American history, but they make coming to work fun. I value each of their friendships.

Other historians have taken time out of their busy schedules to read drafts, provide commentary, and offer encouragement. Dan Crofts and James Oakes each read an earlier draft of the project and provided many useful suggestions that helped me refine my thinking about the topic. Matthew Mason, William Garrett Piston, Rachel Shelden, Elizabeth Varon, and Michael Woods have challenged me to think carefully about the secession crisis and inspired me through their own work. Chris Fonvielle of the University of North Carolina–Wilmington and William C. Harris of North Carolina State University have provided unstinting aid throughout my career. I consider Chris a dear friend and always enjoy our conversations about history, sports, and the *Andy Griffith Show*. Aaron Sheehan-Dean, editor of the University of North Carolina Press Civil War America series, has been of enormous assistance throughout the lengthy process of turning a manuscript into a book. Aaron has been a tireless champion of this project, taking time out of his busy schedule to read several drafts of the manuscript and provide important feedback. Editor Mark Simpson-Vos has been a joy to work with and always had an answer for my numerous questions. I especially thank Mark for having faith in my work. Lucas Church, Jessica Newman, and Stephanie Wenzel also made producing this book an enjoyable experience. Ashley Moore and Annette Calzone combed through the manuscript and saved me from several embarrassing mistakes. An anonymous reader for the University of North Carolina Press carefully read the manuscript and offered insightful suggestions that improved the book in myriad ways.

Several institutions provided financial support and assistance as I conducted research, including the Filson Historical Society, the Hagley Museum and Library, the University of Chicago Library, and the Louisiana State University Department of History and Graduate School. A special thanks to the many archivists and program directors at the various repositories I visited for all your help tracking down materials.

My parents, Dudley and Rosalin Robinson, instilled in me a love for learning at a young age and have supported me without reservation during my time in North Carolina, Louisiana, and Alabama. They, along with my sister, Heather Price, and the rest of my extended family, have sustained me in more ways than they will ever know; I can only hope to emulate their sterling examples of affection, love, and stewardship in the future. My in-laws, Rev. Jack Sawyer and Carolyn Sawyer, have welcomed me into their family as one of their own and offered spiritual, intellectual, and material support, for which I am most thankful. The people of Eastern Shore Presbyterian Church in Fairhope, Alabama, have been supportive of my intellectual pursuits and have embraced my family with open arms; I cherish the many relationships that we have formed with our church family.

Finally, I owe a mountain of thanks to my wife. When I started this project, Katherine and I were good friends. Now that I am wrapping it up, we have been married for nearly four years. She has stood beside me and offered love, encouragement, enlightenment, and strength, and she always knows how to bring a smile to my face. Her unfailing love means the world to me, and I dedicate this book to her.

I am grateful to all the people who helped make this book possible, but the work herein is my own and I accept full responsibility for any of its shortcomings or deficiencies.

A Union Indivisible

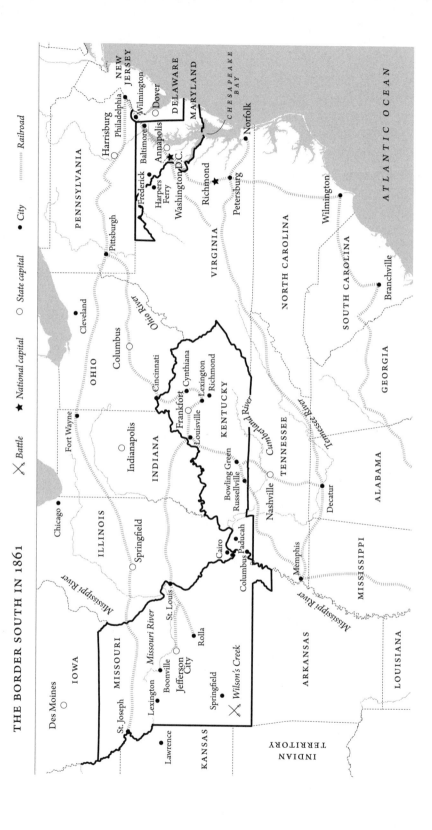

THE BORDER SOUTH IN 1861

× Battle   ★ National capital   ○ State capital   • City   ⋯⋯⋯ Railroad

Introduction

Where Is the Great Statesman? Henry Clay's Republic

Shortly after dawn on Independence Day, 1857, a bustling throng descended on the Lexington Cemetery, a quaint burial ground nestled in the heart of Kentucky's Bluegrass region. Brilliant sunlight shimmered in the cloudless blue sky and cast a fitting air over the assemblage, which had congregated to celebrate the life's work of Henry Clay, Kentucky's famed statesman. Bunting, flowers, and flags adorned many homes in tribute to the republic's birth and to memorialize Clay, a son of Lexington who had labored throughout his career to bind the disparate sections of the nation into an indivisible Union. Five separate brass bands regaled the crowd with patriotic tunes, and around the middle of the morning, local militia companies and fire brigades led a procession through town to a large stage that had been erected next to Clay's spartan gravesite. On the platform sat Clay's family, his friends and associates, and his political heirs. They had come to Lexington to lay the cornerstone of a monument that would commemorate the life of the Bluegrass State's favorite son and provide the departed doyen with a resting place worthy of his eminent political career.[1]

Five years prior, Clay had been laid to rest in the cemetery after a lifetime of public service to a nation that he had witnessed grow from a loose association of former British colonies hugging the Atlantic Seaboard to a sprawling transcontinental colossus stretching to the Pacific Ocean. By the time of his death in 1852, few other Americans had left such an indelible mark on the republic. Clay occupied several important political posts, from Speaker of the House of Representatives and long stints in the United States Senate to secretary of state, but also experienced the pain of defeat as an unsuccessful candidate in three separate presidential contests. He had few equals as a political manager. As the architect of the Whig Party, Clay used his considerable political acumen to build a formidable organization that challenged Andrew Jackson's Democrats in the rollicking arena of antebellum politics. His conservative approach to America's mounting concern with the spread of slavery and his penchant for sectional compromise grew out of his unique geographic locus in the Border South state of Kentucky, situated on the boundary between freedom and slavery. In the last three decades of his life, Clay anxiously observed the radicalization of sectional politics and witnessed mounting divisions between the free and slaveholding states, which threatened to upset the vibrant nationalism that had been forged in the nation's infancy. At odds with his grandiose vision for an enduring Union, Clay had on three occasions taken the lead in overpowering sectional impulses and cobbling together compromises that rescued the republic from the brink of disunion and possibly even civil war. "I know no South, no North, no East, no West, to which I owe my allegiance," Clay proclaimed on the floor of the Senate during one of those sectional crises. "My allegiance is to this Union and to my own State." His countrymen labeled Clay "the Great Compromiser," and scores of Border South moderates considered his political outlook gospel.[2]

After a short ceremony commemorating the placement of the cornerstone, the crowd repaired to the Lexington fairgrounds, where one of Clay's disciples, Robert Jefferson Breckinridge, delivered a stirring address. Mindful of the turbulent political environment of the 1850s, he admonished his fellow border Southerners to take up the mantle of the Great Compromiser and strive for national unity and the preservation of the Union. "Let us preserve [Clay's republic] by every mutual concession, and every proof of exalted forbearance," Breckinridge intoned, "remembering how poor and how low are all secondary considerations, when compared with the peace, the freedom, the independence, the union, the glory of our country."[3]

The crowd listened intently to his words, for the name Breckinridge carried as much weight among Kentuckians as did Clay's. Breckinridge's father, an associate of Virginia political luminaries Thomas Jefferson and James Madison, had left the Old Dominion and settled in Kentucky in the 1790s, where he quickly became a leader of Jefferson's political followers in the state legislature. Robert inherited his father's passion for politics, but after one term in the Kentucky assembly, he opted to enter the ministry. He rose to great heights in the Presbyterian Church, pastoring a congregation in Baltimore before returning to Lexington in 1847 to shepherd the town's First Presbyterian Church. During his career Breckinridge earned a reputation for his eloquent sermons and perceptive musings on matters both spiritual and political. In 1853 he left the pulpit, founded Danville Theological Seminary thirty-five miles southwest of Lexington, and served the college as both a professor and a public intellectual. Political moderation became Breckinridge's watchword: he refused to believe that the Bible sanctioned slavery and thus called for its gradual elimination in America but, paradoxically, he himself owned thirty-seven bondspersons in 1860. The shrill cries for immediate abolition that emanated from Northern rostrums unnerved the conservative Breckinridge, who worried that such a program would endanger the Union and produce social anarchy in the South.[4]

Although few white border Southerners endorsed Breckinridge's plea for gradual emancipation, many agreed with two of his key political principles, which he had inherited from Clay: his attachment to the Union and his conservative racial outlook. By the time he delivered his Independence Day oration in 1857, the widening sectional divide had left the Border South states of Delaware, Kentucky, Maryland, and Missouri in a precarious position. Most inhabitants of this northernmost outpost of slavery had throughout the antebellum period relied on conservatives like Clay to join hands with other moderates, smother the fires of sectional discord, and preserve the Union with the South's peculiar institution unmolested. Since Clay's death, ominous signs of another crisis loomed. The Whig Party foundered shortly after its architect passed away, and the Republican Party, a Northern political organization that sought to place a fatal chokehold on slavery by preventing its spread into the western territories, had risen in its stead. The antislavery Republican Party, which enjoyed rapid growth in the free states, represented the sum of all fears for many white Southerners. The slavery question also placed inordinate strain on the Democratic Party, which by 1857 had split into sectional wings over the issue of the peculiar institution's introduction in Kansas. A proslavery South Carolinian had bludgeoned a Massachusetts abolitionist on the floor of the Senate; antislavery and proslavery forces had spilled one another's blood on the plains of Kansas; and the Supreme Court only emboldened Republicans and slavery apologists when it used a Missouri slave's suit for freedom to pontificate that Congress could not prohibit the introduction of slavery in the territories.[5]

Breckinridge, though enthusiastic about the future, understood that the worsening political climate required statesmanship on par with that of the departed Clay. As he scanned the lineup of public functionaries who had joined him in the ceremony, Breckinridge felt sure that someone would step into the void left by the passing of the Great Compromiser. On that Independence Day, he shared the stage with several laudable candidates, including his own nephew John C. Breckinridge, vice president and a leader among the Southern Democrats, and James Guthrie, a railroad magnate and former secretary of the treasury under Democratic president Franklin Pierce. One man, however, stood out above the rest: John Jordan Crittenden, a white-headed statesman and devoted Whig whom Clay had personally groomed for such an occasion. "And where is the great statesman for whom is now in store, the great glory of doing for us *once* what he *thrice* accomplished?" Breckinridge queried as he reached the crescendo of his speech. As the edifice of the Union threatened to collapse in the late 1850s, border Southerners anxiously pondered Breckinridge's rhetorical question.[6]

CONDITIONS RAPIDLY DETERIORATED in the three years following Breckinridge's plea. By December 1860, the nation had become enveloped in a full-fledged crisis. In the aftermath of Republican Abraham Lincoln's election in November, South Carolina boldly left the Union; before Lincoln's inauguration, six additional slaveholding states from the Lower South seceded and joined with the Palmetto State to create their own government. The rash decision of the Deep South states left the other eight slaveholding states in an agonizing predicament: should they too sever their ties to the Union and join the nascent Confederate States of America, or should they work to secure a compromise that might produce a final settlement of the malignant slavery issue and bring the wayward states of the Cotton South back into the Union?[7]

The strain of the fractured nation proved particularly distressing for the people of the Border South. The overall percentage of enslaved persons in relation to the total population in the Border South paled in comparison to the percentage in the eleven states that eventually composed the Confederacy, yet the comparative frailty of the peculiar institution produced among white border Southerners anything but a willfulness to relinquish control over the fate of their bondspersons. Unionists in the region exerted enormous energy to convince their neighbors that secession would accelerate the extinction of slavery, whereas maintaining an allegiance to the old flag, with all the constitutional and legal protections it afforded slaveholders, would best ensure the longevity of the peculiar institution. Border South Unionists constantly pointed out that disunion would forfeit the Fugitive Slave Law, the authority of the Supreme Court, and Southern power in Congress. Unionist Francis Thomas, a former governor of Maryland, complained that secessionists in the Lower and Upper South had "abandoned every position, every safeguard in the Government that has been thrown around this institution, by deserting their posts in the Senate and the House of Representatives." Thomas and likeminded white borderites, who failed to regard secession as a shield for the Old South's social bedrock, embraced what other historians have labeled proslavery Unionism. "The very men who clamored against the contraction of the limits of slavery," Thomas growled, "have themselves destroyed all those safeguards" by exiting the Union.[8]

Border South Unionists viewed Clay's conciliatory precedent as a blueprint for action in the secession crisis. They sought to preserve Clay's republic, where moderation had overawed extremism from either quarter. "We occupy the middle ground," a Kentucky Unionist informed Lincoln, "and generally we are as much opposed to the fire eating southern disunion gang as we are to the Ultra abolitionists in the North."[9] Proslavery Unionism had long been the foundation of mainstream Border South political thought, and during the crisis that commenced with John Brown's October 1859 raid on Harpers Ferry, Virginia, and culminated in the Civil War, Unionists employed everything at their disposal to convince their neighbors that Clay's proven approach would again rescue the nation from disaster.[10] They worked assiduously to secure a compromise; they appealed to conservative Northern allies for assistance; they used legislative legerdemain and outright chicanery when they deemed it essential; and they relied on military force as a last resort. In sum, Border South Unionists by the end of 1861 had fought and won a battle in which victory was neither preordained nor facile. As 1862 dawned, the prospects of compromise had scattered, but borderland Unionists had convinced enough of the electorate that the federal government waged war to preserve the Union, not to "overthrow and destroy their domestic institutions upon which their very existence depends."[11]

Border South Unionists managed to link the perpetuity of the Union to the permanence of slavery, though often during the secession crisis the likelihood of their success seemed dubious. Contemporaries persistently observed that despite the strident efforts of Unionists, the Border South was poised to join the secession movement. "A strong conservative sentiment tends them [the Upper and Border South] to the Union; a natural sympathy with the seceding States draws them in an opposite direction," Massachusetts intellectual Edward Everett discerned in February 1861. "If the Border States are drawn into the Southern Confederacy the fate of the country is sealed," Everett fretted.[12] Some disunionists in the Lower South felt assured that the Border South would join the roster of the Confederacy. Judah Benjamin of Louisiana predicted that by the end of 1861 even tiny Delaware would sever its ties to the Union and extend the Confederacy's reach to the outskirts of Philadelphia. Although Benjamin's prophecy failed to materialize, many Confederates refused to give up on the secession of the Border South. Even in early 1862, after federal troops had occupied significant portions of the region, a Lower South propagandist predicted that the Border South's latent sympathy for secession would soon ferment into a powerful tonic for disunion. "Give to the loyal men of the border arms and munitions of war, give them material aid to repel the intervention of the invader," he advised, "and we believe they will crush out the pestilent toryism now daily growing into more formidable proportions under the shadow of federal power."[13]

Onlookers compared the Border South to a fulcrum that held the fate of the fractured nation in the balance. Politically attuned Americans understood that the secession of the Border South would alter unquestionably the balance sheet of the war. Nearly 2.6 million white persons lived in the Border South in 1860, which equaled almost half of the white population of the eleven Confederate states. Baltimore and Saint Louis operated as critical hubs of commerce and industrial production and included a heterogeneous population consisting of free blacks, enslaved persons, German and Irish Catholics, and a sizable working class. Agricultural and mineral resources, including a profusion of grain and livestock, gave the Border South a more diverse economic complexion than the other slave states. Major transportation arteries, including the Ohio and Mississippi river systems, along with the Baltimore and Ohio Railroad, crisscrossed the region and connected it to the Upper North and the Lower South. Few people failed to grasp the political and material value of the Border South.[14]

Although contemporary Americans understood the stakes of the Border South's secession, historians traditionally have devoted scant attention to the region as a collective entity. Hindsight provides great clarity about the final outcome of the Civil War in the Border South, but it also tends to obscure the unpredictable path that border Southerners traversed during the secession crisis. From the vista of 1865, Delaware, Kentucky, Maryland, and Missouri had all staved off secession and become essential contributors to the Union war effort. From the vantage point of 1860, however, the Border South's future appeared nebulous. Louisville editor George Prentice captured the angst of border Southerners and their unknown destiny weeks after Lincoln's election: "Let the Border States but stand firm in this trial, and we believe the Union, fast anchored by their calm wisdom and unshaken patriotism, will ride out triumphantly the tempest of fanaticism and of treason now sweeping widely across the public mind. Let them falter, and the Union freighted not only with their happiness and glory but with the richest earthly hope of the race, will certainly go down, beyond the reach of the diving-bell or plummet."[15] One only need look to the Border South, Prentice argued, to discover the essence of the national crisis.

Only recently have scholars fixed their attention on the Border South and its role in Civil War–era politics.[16] Several important studies of individual Border South states exist, but these investigations are primarily concerned with trends within the confines of one state rather than across the region.[17] Viewing the secession crisis from a region-wide vista illuminates the importance of interstate cooperation among Unionists, the lengths to which those Unionists went to keep their states true to the federal government, and, most significantly, the vital importance of slavery and compromise to the region's inhabitants. Such an approach also reveals that many white border Southerners either supported or looked favorably on secession. Although the Border South is sometimes portrayed as an impenetrable bastion of Unionism during the secession crisis, fire-eaters had made inroads into the region and converted some white borderites to the disunion faith. During the winter of 1860–61, a great fear arose among Unionists that many Border South fence-sitters might slide into the secession column. Unionists and secessionists alike realized the potential for disunion sentiment to spread briskly throughout the region. Fire-eaters from both within and without the Border South made concerted efforts to fan the flames of sectional animosity and transform conditional Unionists into committed secessionists. This reality roused Unionists into action; had they remained idle, the Confederacy may have swelled to fifteen states, further complicating the federal government's onerous mission to restore the Union.

The task before Border South Unionists was a most complicated one. The middle ground that tethered the North and South together during the antebellum period always relied on mutual concessions, but as the crisis of 1860–61 unfolded, the likelihood of a peaceful settlement diminished with each passing day. When the Thirty-Sixth Congress gathered in Washington, DC, in December 1860, politicians as diametrically opposed as Texas fire-eater Louis Wigfall and New Hampshire abolitionist John P. Hale ironically worked toward the same end. Radical operatives in both sections hoped to derail all compromise efforts that would solve the issue of slavery's extension into the territories. These radicals had two vastly different visions of the future: Southern nationalists envisioned an independent slaveholding confederacy, while abolitionists anticipated a United States without the degrading yoke of slavery. Conservatives, moderates, and conditional Unionists—who formed the vital center of the Border South electorate and yearned to avoid war if at all possible—looked to the past and approached this crisis as had their forebears. They wanted assurances that Republicans would not interfere with the institution of slavery in the South and sought a final accord that would forever put to rest the political quagmire over slavery's extension.[18] In essence, they craved a compromise at a point when the chances for sectional cooperation had grown remote. Border South moderates minced no words when describing the consequences if either of the radical outlooks gained traction. The absence of a settlement meant war, and as the fault line between the sections, the Border South would encounter unspeakable desolation and devastation.

Kentucky senator John Crittenden, leader of the Border South Unionists, understood the demands of the vital center and worked assiduously in Washington

John Jordan Crittenden (1786–1863). Kentucky politician and protégé of Henry Clay who led the Unionist offensive in the Border South during the secession crisis. Library of Congress.

and through a network of likeminded politicians to piece together a compromise package aimed at neutralizing the secession movement, preventing war, and extinguishing the territorial issue once and for all. Although Congress dismantled his compromise plan and some historians have labeled Crittenden a failure, the story that unfolds in the following pages casts a different light on Clay's protégé.[19] Crittenden and his coterie of Unionists managed to keep the possibility of compromise alive, even when Congress adjourned in March 1861. His continued efforts to settle the slavery issue signaled to border Southerners that all hopes for compromise had not been dashed. Once the war commenced, Crittenden shifted his approach and endeavored to limit the federal objective to the preservation of the Union, not the destruction of slavery. The labor of Crittenden and his associates prevented most conditional Unionists from making the transition to outright support of disunion. Keeping the possibility of compromise afloat and assuring white border Southerners that the primary goal of the war was reunion, not emancipation, prevented the tide of secession from washing over the Border South. This Unionist offensive put Border South secessionists on the defensive and gave Crittenden and his allies the upper hand during the crisis.

Scholars have long divided on the probability of compromise during the secession crisis. Several experts contend that the North and the South had grown so estranged by 1860 that no settlement could resolve the differences over slavery that eventually plunged the nation into war. Other historians, however, claim that the window for a peaceful settlement remained open during the secession winter.[20] Viewing the crisis through the lens of border Southerners demonstrates that a sizable contingent still believed compromise was a viable option as late as the spring of 1861. White borderites were the ultimate realists when it came to anticipating the potential destructiveness of a civil war, but due to the efforts of Crittenden and his Unionist companions, they strongly believed that the window for a political settlement on the slavery issue remained open and would prevent the outbreak or, after Fort Sumter, the escalation of that war. Hindsight reveals the implausibility of compromise at this juncture, but one cannot fault border Southerners for their wishful thinking. They lived in the shadow of Clay and in a region steeped in a political culture of consensus building that had spearheaded settlements in prior crises, and as such their words, hopes, and thoughts about the likelihood of compromise merit serious consideration.

Even after Unionists gained leverage with their offensive, fire-eaters clung to the notion that each of the Border South states might secede. Secessionists labeled compromise a base surrender to the antislavery Republican Party and warned of the inherent dangers of adhering to the Union. At times they managed to blunt the progress of Unionists and convinced some white border Southerners to work for disunion or to join the Confederate Army. Many people felt caught between these two extremes and opted for the unique approach of neutrality. Both camps fought a hotly contested political battle in the Border South well into 1861; not until the end of the year could Unionists claim a grueling victory. In the interim, border Southerners endured a clash between Unionists and secessionists that shattered families, divided communities, and left deep scars that took decades to heal.[21]

This study seeks to capture the pervasive apprehension that hung over the Border South from John Brown's raid in October 1859 through the end of 1861. The story proceeds chronologically and covers the political struggles that unfolded throughout the region. Attention is also devoted to Congress, where Crittenden and his allies made an impressive, albeit fruitless, attempt to resurrect the ghost of Clay and reach another sectional compromise. The tactics and political discussion of Unionists and secessionists are investigated closely to demonstrate the enormous effort that was required to prevent the secession movement from overwhelming the Border South. The larger conversation included debates over the future of slavery in the West, questions about sectional identity, and disputes over partisanship, urbanization, immigration, economic growth, and modernization. These issues tugged the Border South in contradictory directions during the secession crisis, but the keystone to the triumph of Unionists lay in their argument that the Union could best protect and perpetuate the peculiar institution. This particular brand of proslavery Unionism that resonated with white border Southerners reveals the complexity of politics during the Civil War. Rather than viewing Civil War–era politics as a binary that pitted antislavery Unionists against proslavery secessionists, the crisis in the Border South illustrates that many Americans occupied a political middle ground that confounds such neat characterizations. Many Unionists within the Border South constructed their allegiance to the republic in the belief that they and likeminded conservatives throughout the nation could keep antislavery politicians at bay and prevent slavery's demise. To them, radical Republicans seemed just as dangerous as fanatical fire-eaters. The events of 1859 to 1861, however, unfolded rapidly and changed the nature of the nation's political middle ground, especially once the war commenced. The protean quality of the crisis forced white border Southerners to reassess their commitment to the Union, stoked new worries about the safety of slavery in America, and manufactured a profusion of responses, some of which were unique and others which mirrored the choices of Unionists elsewhere throughout the South. Understanding how and why these states remained in the Union provides insights to the many shades of political thought that existed at the middle of the nineteenth century between the polarities of radical abolitionism and proslavery disunionism.[22]

The tacticians on whom this study focuses were overwhelmingly white men, and their contemporaries considered them elite in terms of property ownership. The grassroots political activism of women, free blacks, and enslaved persons falls outside the parameters of this particular work. Despite the fact that large segments of the population were denied access to the ballot box, antebellum politicians regarded their political system as the most democratic in the world. Political elites labored diligently to build mandates among the electorate, and the maneuvers of these politicians provide insight into the social, economic, and cultural world that all Americans—white or black, slaveholder or nonslaveholder, planter or yeoman, farmer or mechanic, native or foreign born, free or enslaved, man or woman—inhabited. Although this study concentrates on antebellum America's established political actors, census data and quantitative material complement evidence from manuscript collections, newspapers, and government records to capture the complexity of the secession crisis in the Border South. A democratic political culture thrives on debate, discussion, and dissent, and the secession crisis in the Border South illuminates both the positive and the negative aspects of Civil War–era politics.

Many contemporaries considered Virginia one of the border states, and the course of the Old Dominion exerted a powerful influence over the entire South. Border Southerners of all political persuasions made key alliances with Virginians, and those coalitions receive a fair share of attention in the present work. Since several fine studies have covered the secession crisis and internal divisions within Virginia, the state has not been placed in extended comparative perspective with Delaware, Kentucky, Maryland, and Missouri. The formation of West Virginia, which antedated the secession crisis and extended beyond 1861, has been investigated elsewhere and serves only as a point of reference for this study.[23]

This study covers a large region, and as such, it exposes a great deal of intraregional variation, especially between the eastern states of Delaware and Maryland and the western states of Kentucky and Missouri. This investigation treats the Border South as a corporate entity in order to understand the larger political trends that swept across the region during the secession crisis, but at some points internal distinctions and peculiarities are highlighted to demonstrate the diversity of this massive area. Saint Louis's German community, for instance, harbored feelings about slavery and the Union that were very different from those of tobacco planters on Maryland's Eastern Shore.[24]

Finally, a word on terms used throughout the narrative. *Radical*, often freighted with multiple meanings, refers to contemporaries who sought to achieve political objectives outside of the mainstream conventions of the period. The term has been applied to secessionists, abolitionists who pursued the eradication of slavery immediately and without compensation to slaveholders, and those who welcomed the prospect of war. The term *fire-eater* refers to secessionists; not all fire-eaters prescribed the same means to bring about disunion, and the different strands of fire-eater sentiment are discussed in greater detail in chapter 4. Likewise, the term *Unionist* and *Unionism* had many diverse meanings, especially in the Border South. Unionists in the region expressed a desire to remain in the old republic, but their degree of commitment to the Union varied along a spectrum that ranged from conditionalists, who endorsed secession in the absence of a compromise settlement or if the federal government attempted to force the Confederate states back into the

Union, to unconditionalists, who vowed to stand by the old flag at all costs. The spectrum of Border South Unionism also receives greater attention in chapter 4. The term *hardliner* relates to political actors who rigidly refused to compromise during the secession crisis. An influential group of Republicans adopted a hardline stance during the months after Lincoln's election, and their refusal to abandon the party's core antislavery principle had far-reaching implications for the Border South, as did the hardline posture of zealous secessionists. Lastly, *conservative* and *moderate* are used interchangeably in reference to Americans who sought to avoid war through compromise. They espoused a willingness to allow for concessions that would perpetuate the Union, even if it meant extending the life of slavery. In sum, conservatives and moderates operated as the antithesis of hardliners. The labels of *conservative* and *moderate* encompass a wide range of political thought, with some conservatives viewing the protection of slavery as of utmost importance and others viewing the slavery issue as an inconvenient distraction that had gained purchase in the hands of firebrands, thus making their usage fluid. Though imperfect, these terms help to characterize nineteenth-century political approaches and should not be confused with their present-day iterations.

Each of these groups shaped and shifted the contours of Clay's republic during the secession crisis. As 1862 dawned, Border South Unionists could congratulate themselves for keeping their region loyal to the United States, but as the war became more ferocious, they slowly realized the massive changes the conflict wrought. The sinews of war upended Clay's republic and unknowingly started the nation down the path to a new America shorn of the peculiar institution. Border South Unionists may have triumphed over secessionists with promises that the Union would protect slavery, but they could not win a fight against time. Some Americans looked to the future with grave misgivings and others excitedly embraced change, but without a doubt secession and war inaugurated the demise of Clay's republic.

As the sun dropped below the Kentucky foothills on Independence Day in 1857 and the inhabitants of Lexington took down the bunting and folded their flags, Robert Breckinridge took comfort in the power of his speech honoring the Great Compromiser. Before long, however, his confidence in the durability of the old republic turned to foreboding. The secession crisis tested Breckinridge's political allegiances, his vision of America's future, and his relationship with members of his own family. Only later, after four hard years of Civil War brought about the destruction of American slavery, would he realize that his oration that day had really been a eulogy for Clay's republic.

CHAPTER ONE

A Representation of Almost Every Interest and Pursuit in the Union

The Border South on the Eve of the Secession Crisis

Abraham Lincoln's election on November 6, 1860, provoked an array of reactions across the United States. In bustling cities and sleepy rural hamlets across the North, partisans of the Republican Party congratulated themselves. Caught up in the postelection euphoria, many Republicans believed that their success at the polls had once and for all crushed the Slave Power that had over the last thirty years riven the Democratic Party and gnawed at the vitals of the federal government. "The space is now clear for the establishment of the policy of Freedom on safe & firm grounds," Republican Salmon Chase forecast. Savoring their victory, youthful Wide Awakes—Republican political operatives who had campaigned for Lincoln—paraded through city streets, blissfully unaware that many of them would soon march off to war. Yet sullen Northern Democrats and Constitutional Unionists watched on with grave concern. Far from subscribing to Chase's upbeat projection, the election's losers predicted that the success of the sectional Republican organization would destabilize the republic. The cacophony of the Republican revelry, however, muffled the misgivings of Lincoln's Northern opponents in the immediate aftermath of the election.[1]

Far to the south, the election produced a different type of merriment. Fire-eaters, who had labored unsuccessfully during the previous decade to push the South out of the Union, considered the Republican victory a godsend. After a careful inspection of the election returns, these disunionists crowed that the time for action had arrived. Lincoln, whom the fire-eaters painted as the leader of a fanatical abolitionist organization, had won but 39 percent of the popular vote yet handily defeated his opponents in the Electoral College. What future did the South have in a Union under the thumb of the Republicans, who would in short order eradicate slavery? How could the long-venerated Union protect the South when Northern numerical superiority ensured defeat in every subsequent presidential election? To disunionists, the election marked a point at which the South had forever lost its voice in national politics. While they outwardly prognosticated doom, fire-eaters inwardly smiled at the Republican triumph because they calculated it would bring many erstwhile moderate Southerners into the secession ranks.[2]

While Republicans in the North lauded the prospect of a new Union liberated from the Slave Power and fire-eaters in the Lower South toasted a bright future of independence from Yankee domination, millions of citizens in the Border South felt the arresting strain of these countervailing forces. John Pendleton Kennedy, a novelist and one-time Whig politician from Baltimore, acted as did most white border Southerners: although dismayed, he calmly and carefully deliberated the crisis. Five days after the election, Kennedy secluded himself in his study and began preparing "a tract or discourse directed to the consideration of the present alarming state of affairs in the country." Kennedy mused and scribbled for just over a month, taking the occasional break for a game of billiards or to entertain visitors in his parlor. In mid-December he sent the finished product to three conservative newspapers, his confidants John Jordan Crittenden of Kentucky and Alexander Boteler of Virginia, and the governors of the border states.[3]

Kennedy's tract elucidated the perilous position of the Border South, perched on the boundary between slavery and freedom and stretched thin by affiliations with both sections. Kennedy, however, proclaimed that the Border South would not be cowed by fire-eating demagogues from the Cotton South or abolitionist agitators within the Republican Party. Like all Border South Unionists, Kennedy pleaded for all Union-loving persons across the nation to respond to the crisis with studied contemplation. Rather than falling victim to "the wickedness of Northern fanaticism, and the intemperate zeal of secession," the author advocated a convention of the border states to discuss possible terms of conciliation and compromise.[4]

While preparing his pamphlet, Kennedy carefully analyzed data about the Border South's economy and society. Unlike the Lower South, which he labeled "one vast cotton field," Kennedy presented the Border South as a region marked by great economic diversity. "The Border States exhibit within their area a representation of almost every interest and pursuit in the Union," he postulated. Commerce and industry flourished alongside agriculture because of rich mineral wealth, a dynamic population, and teeming cities. If his proposed convention could not settle the grievances between the North and the South, Kennedy went so far as to suggest that his region had all the materials to create its own independent nation free from the "disorders and distractions of the time."[5]

A brief investigation of the society, economy, and politics of the Border South in the 1850s illustrates a flaw in Kennedy's logic. Although he accurately reflected the prevailing desire of many white borderites to stay aloof from the raging sectional crisis, Kennedy overstated the likelihood of noninvolvement and understated how the events of the preceding decade had inescapably sewn the region into the conflict. Despite a diverse socioeconomic arrangement and a robust two-party political system, the presence of slavery in the Border South forged strong bonds with the rest of the slaveholding states. Slavery cast a shadow over all facets of life in the Border South, albeit a different one from that cast in the eleven states that eventually formed the Confederacy. Even in the Border South, a region with far fewer slaves than the rest of the South, the tentacles of slavery conditioned the way white people thought about their response to the secession crisis. The very fact that Kennedy felt compelled to compose an essay that boasted the merits of the Union indicates that by the winter of 1860–61, secession sentiment had infiltrated this erstwhile Unionist bastion.

SITUATED AT THE VERY heart of the nation, the Border South became an inexorable participant in the political crisis of the 1850s. While heated political debates over the extension of slavery and the enforcement of the Fugitive Slave Law widened the chasm between the sections, though, most white border Southerners acted with remarkable restraint. Periodic outbursts of violence occurred along the lengthy border that encompassed the Mason-Dixon Line, the Ohio River, and the perimeter of Missouri, a liminal space where free and slave soil overlapped, escaped enslaved persons sought safe haven, and slave catchers performed their reprehensible duty. Small-scale hostility at times erupted into significant violence, which has led some historians to paint the Border South as a crucible of relentless conflict during the 1850s. For some scholars, the 1851 riot in Christiana, Pennsylvania, brought about by a Maryland slave owner and federal agents who attempted to reclaim a group of African American fugitives, and the bloody clash along the Missouri-Kansas border as a result of the passage of the Kansas-Nebraska Act, serve as antebellum microcosms of the Civil War and explain the irreparable sectional breach that led to armed conflict in April 1861.[6]

Despite many documented cases of enslaved people escaping to the North and the occasional outbreak of violence in the 1850s, white border Southerners more often than not experienced amicable relations with their neighbors across the boundary between slavery and freedom. Violent episodes received plenty of attention because partisan newspaper editors realized their political value. Sensational accounts of tumult, however, often misrepresented daily life throughout the Border South. Of the entire region, only Missouri's western border experienced widespread, consistent violence during the decade. Scholars have demonstrated that even along the Kansas-Missouri border, muckraking journalists often sensationalized or exaggerated their reports for political effect.[7]

Family members, friends, and business associates of white border Southerners lived just across the border, and in many instances they shared a moderate political outlook.[8] Population figures from the 1860 census illustrate the ties between the Border South and the free states and territories adjoining them. By 1860, nearly 4 percent of the native population in the states of New Jersey, Pennsylvania, Ohio, Indiana, Illinois, Iowa, and Kansas Territory had been born in the Border South. This percentage may seem small, but one must consider that 61 percent of the population in the Lower North had been born in the state or territory where they currently resided. Therefore, nearly one out of every ten persons native to the United States but not born in the Lower North state where they resided in 1860 had been born in the Border South. Moreover, the more southerly counties in these free states, especially those west of Ohio, included higher concentrations of natives of the Border South. Natives of Delaware, Kentucky, and Maryland most often migrated to the Lower North states or Missouri. Transplanted Missourians usually moved farther westward to California or Texas, but the third-largest group leaving the state in the 1850s went to Illinois. While this borderland witnessed violence during the 1850s, it also saw the strengthening of intersectional kinship ties and economic networks. The people who lived along the border generally sought the construction of harmonious relationships, devoid of sensationalism and rife with the unspectacular normalcy of everyday life. Even the strongly pro-Southern *Louisville Daily Courier* conceded that Indiana, Ohio, and Kentucky "have really no conflicting interests. There should be no rivalry between them, but a generous emulation as to which shall outstrip [the others] in the race of glory and greatness."[9]

Commercial relationships buttressed the pervasive inclination toward amity between the Border South and Lower North. The economic hinterland of large Border South cities like Baltimore, Louisville, Saint Louis, and Wilmington stretched across the sectional divide. Likewise, large cities in the Lower North such as Cincinnati and Philadelphia had similar intersectional ties and operated as economic sponges for Kentucky and Delaware. By 1860, several railroads connected the borderland, and both regions were resolutely committed to keeping the Ohio and Mississippi Rivers open to commercial traffic.[10] One historian claims that rail connections in the western Border South and Lower North displaced southerly river-borne commerce and reoriented the export economy of Kentucky and Missouri northward. Though overstated, the assertion does suggest that the transportation revolution energized trade relations between the Border South and the Lower North in the 1850s.[11]

The metropolises of Baltimore and Saint Louis, along with less populous Louisville and Wilmington, gave the Border South an urban complexion that on the surface made the region appear more like the Lower North than the rest of the South. The average population of the largest cities in the Border South, 115,621, dwarfed the mean population of 32,026 for the largest cities in the Middle and Lower South, and came closer to matching the Lower North's average size of 156,564. These large cities in the Border South, however, should not distort the full panorama of the region's socioeconomic landscape. Frank Towers notes that the South's largest cities were "glaring multicultural and industrial contrasts to the homogeneity of rural life" and points out that fewer than 9,000 persons lived in the second most populous towns of Maryland and Missouri, whereas the secondary cities in the North often accommodated at least 20,000 inhabitants.[12]

Nevertheless, the presence of these immense metropolitan areas impacted the socioeconomic makeup of the Border South. While recent scholarship corrects the long-standing assumption that the South experienced little industrial and commercial growth prior to the Civil War, as a whole the states that formed the Confederacy lagged behind the rest of the nation.[13] The Border South's major cities included large-scale industrial concerns such as textile mills, meat and seafood packing plants, machinery operations, brickmaking factories, shipbuilding companies, and carriage manufactories.[14]

Baltimore and Saint Louis, and to a lesser extent Louisville and Wilmington, attracted a more diverse labor pool than the rest of the South. Natives of other countries made up nearly 10 percent of the Border South's population in 1860, and the number of border Southerners born outside the United States nearly doubled during the 1850s, placing the region in unison with trends in the free states and the Upper South. The Lower South, however, failed to keep pace with this tendency. Nearly 57 percent of all foreign-born residents in the entire South in 1860 lived in the Border South; of the eleven future Confederate states, only Louisiana, with cosmopolitan New Orleans, came close to having a comparable foreign-born element (see Table A.1).[15] Baltimore and Saint Louis both attracted thousands of immigrants from Germany and Ireland, and, particularly in Saint Louis, the German community became an influential political bloc. The presence of sizable Irish and German groups, along with their proclivity to Catholicism, resulted in an upsurge of nativism and mob violence in Border South cities. The American Party had a strong and lasting presence in each Border South metropolis, and these cities, like urban areas in the North, seldom escaped violence during elections. Border South ethnic tensions boiled over in one of the deadliest political riots of the antebellum period when in August 1855 nativists clashed with German and Irish voters in Louisville. After a vicious campaign in which Democrats and Americans hurled insults at one another, scattered altercations on Election Day escalated into a full-scale riot that resulted in twenty-two deaths. Baltimore and Saint Louis endured similar, though less destructive, disturbances in the 1850s.[16]

In addition to a large foreign-born population, the Border South contained the largest proportions of free blacks in the nation. In the aftermath of the American Revolution, the manumission of enslaved persons occurred more frequently in the Border South than the rest of the South, which established a solid foundation for a burgeoning free black population in the nineteenth century.[17] Industrial occupations and service professions in Border South cities provided economic opportunity for free blacks, who generally faced bleak prospects elsewhere. Although free blacks endured second-class status, the lure of available jobs and the safety of kinship networks allowed for an increase in the total number of free African Americans in the Border South during the decade preceding the Civil War. The region's 118,027 free blacks in 1860 accounted for 47 percent of all free blacks in the South and one-quarter of all free blacks in the nation. More free African Americans lived in Maryland than any other state in the Union, where they composed roughly 12 percent of the overall population. Moreover, free blacks made up about 18 percent of Delaware's total population.[18]

In the 1850s the proportion of free blacks to the entire Border South population dipped by just under 1 percent, a figure that meshes with the general trend throughout the South. Free African Americans faced a proscriptive onslaught during the decade as white Southerners sought to fortify their slave society. State legislatures flirted with the idea of expelling or enslaving free blacks, whom white Southerners feared might incite slave rebellions or assist enslaved people attempting to escape bondage. The legislatures of Delaware and Maryland, for instance, required free blacks to sign annual labor contracts in an attempt to control what whites considered a potential fifth column. Chafing at these constraints, some free blacks relocated to the North, which accounts for the slight decline in their proportionate numbers. Yet the fact that more free blacks did not leave the Border South points to a striking reality. Legislation in several free states prevented African Americans from settling there or required blacks to post a bond upon their arrival. African Americans discovered conditions in the North little better than those they left behind, which left the Border South's free black population with few alternatives other than to remain.[19]

The vast majority of the Border South's free blacks were clustered in Delaware and Maryland. Very few free blacks populated Kentucky and Missouri, states that had been organized long after the initial settlement of the Eastern Seaboard and where the proportion mirrored the rest of the South at less than 1 percent of the total population. White settlers carried slaves to these western outposts of the Border South to exploit their labor in agricultural pursuits. The long process of manumission in the eastern Border South, where many farmers had transitioned from tobacco cultivation to the less labor-intensive production of cereal grains, did not take root along the western border. During the 1850s acres of unimproved farmland shrank by 2 percent in Delaware and remained static in Maryland, whereas unimproved acreage increased by 5 percent in Kentucky and an astonishing 102 percent in Missouri. These numbers indicate that a wealth of farmland remained untapped in the west, whereas agriculturalists in the east had for generations responded to exhausted soil and a surplus of slaves either through manumission or the interstate slave trade. Many manumitted slaves in Maryland and Delaware settled in Baltimore or Wilmington, but a similar process had not occurred in Kentucky or Missouri. As a result, Saint Louis did not have a free black community on the same scale as Baltimore. Legal proscriptions on free black settlement in Missouri also stalled the growth of the state's free African American community.[20]

Teeming cities with polyglot populations gave the Border South a Northern feel, which did not go unnoticed by some sectional zealots in the South. Radicals like Georgia's Henry L. Benning called slavery a "doomed institution" in the Border South. He believed most Border South slaveholders, who confronted the vanguard of Northern abolitionist pressure, wished to get rid of slavery as quickly as possible. In time, Benning feared, the Border South would fall into the orbit of the free states, further endangering the slaveocracy's political power. The paranoia of Benning and likeminded sectional radicals has led some scholars to conclude that the Border South had undertaken a northward sectional trajectory during the late antebellum period. William Freehling contends that the region's location, climate, and economy led the Border South down a path that would ultimately result in a free labor society on par with the Lower North, a process quickened by the outbreak of war in 1861. Too often, however, historians have allowed urbanization, the qualms of

Southern nationalists, and the Civil War's disruptive impact to overshadow the reality that white border Southerners profited from and were stridently committed to slavery.[21]

Nervous fire-eaters and arch-Unionist Kennedy together employed similar regional stereotypes to make contradictory points. Kennedy sought the preservation of the Union while Benning schemed to dismantle it, but both alleged an enormous chasm "divided [the Border and Lower South] from each other by nature and incompatible conditions." The Deep South was marked by a monolithic economy wholly dependent on slavery and staple crop production; the Border South, by contrast, extended "over a broad domain studded with flourishing inland towns" and included "the best indications of the progress of a State to wealth and power" because of its economic diversity. In short, Kennedy and the fire-eaters allowed the region's urban areas to distort their view of the wider Border South. A gaze beyond the outskirts of Baltimore, Saint Louis, Louisville, and Wilmington reveals an overwhelmingly rural region that differed very little from the Upper South.[22]

Most inhabitants of the Border South made their living off the land. The census of 1860 indicates that 47 percent of all free persons in the Border South who provided occupational information listed farming (either as farmer, planter, or farm laborer) as their primary means of employment. Had enslaved persons and children been included in this calculation, the number would have far exceeded a majority of the working population in the region. Laborers composed the second-largest single occupational category in the Border South, and they accounted for just 12 percent of the free working population.[23] Table A.2 further illustrates the overwhelmingly rural nature of the Border South. Farmland composed nearly 59 percent of the total square mileage of the Border South, which stretched from the worn-out soil of the Chesapeake to the rocky hills of the Ozarks in southwestern Missouri and in between included pockets of especially fertile areas such as the Kentucky Bluegrass and Missouri's Boon's Lick. This percentage closely resembles figures for farmland in the Upper and Lower South and demonstrates the Border South's rural complexion. In the 1850s, the number of farms in the Border South increased by almost 30 percent, outstripping farm growth in the Upper South (nearly 18 percent) and the Lower South (23 percent) in the same span. Only the Old Northwest states of Michigan, Minnesota, and Wisconsin, along with Iowa, experienced a greater percentage increase in farms than did the Border South in the 1850s.[24]

The variety of crops produced and the size of farms in the Border South distinguished the region from the staple crop economy of the Lower South.

Borderland farmers planted tobacco and hemp, but these staples did not dominate overall agricultural output. In 1860 Kentucky trailed only Virginia in pounds of tobacco produced, while Maryland placed fourth and Missouri seventh nationally in tobacco production. The Border South yielded nearly 40 percent of all tobacco grown in the United States in 1860, which underscores its importance to the region's economy.[25] Kentucky and Missouri led the nation in the production of hemp, a crop normally manufactured into ropes and bagging. Agriculturalists in the Lower South often relied on hemp bagging to gather their cotton crop, which reinforced intraregional economic ties. The scale of hemp operations paled in comparison to the outfits of cotton, sugar, and rice barons in the Deep South, but it represented a major component of western Border South agriculture.[26] Border Southerners also cultivated enormous amounts of wheat and cereal grains. Kentucky stood tenth and Maryland eleventh in bushels of wheat produced, while Missouri placed fifteenth. All of the Border South states experienced an increase in the amount of wheat produced during the 1850s. Of the fifteen Southern states, only Virginia harvested more wheat than Kentucky.[27] Bounteous yields of corn, potatoes, and livestock supplemented tobacco, hemp, and grain output and provided greater agricultural stability in the Border South than in the Lower South.[28]

Tobacco and hemp cultivation did not require enormous tracts of land as did sugar, rice, and large-scale cotton farming, so farmers operated on a smaller scale in the Border South than did agriculturalists in the Upper and Lower South. The average farm in the Border South sat on 220 acres, compared to 322 acres in the Upper South and 501 acres in the Lower South. The diverse agricultural output, coupled with the labor demands of the crops grown, resulted in smaller farms along the border. Thus, the average Border South farm was half as large as Lower South farms and significantly smaller than those in the Upper South.[29]

The people living and working on the land of the Border South overwhelmingly hailed from slaveholding states, which strengthened intraregional bonds. Native Southerners composed 89 percent of Kentucky's free population and nearly all of these people were born in the Border or Upper South. Missouri had the lowest percentage of native Southerners; only 70 percent of its inhabitants came from the South and nearly 69 percent were born in the Border or Upper South. The statistics for Delaware and Maryland (82 percent born in the South) closely resembled one another. In the eastern Border South, eight out of ten free persons had been born in the Border or Upper South.[30] Kinship and business ties fortified connections both within the region and between the Border and Upper South in a similar fashion to those that fused the Border South to the Lower North. Inhabitants of the Border South positively understood these connections. A Missouri politician employed familial imagery when he declared Kentucky "the mother of Missouri, and Virginia, her grandmother." Throughout the secession crisis, several border Southerners commented on the powerful connections between the Border and Upper South and predicted that their states would follow the lead of Virginia in response to Lincoln's election.[31]

Deeper scrutiny of nativity figures for the Border South reveals how the region found itself straddling the gulf between the North and the South. Large portions of the native population in Delaware, Kentucky, and Maryland had been born in the state in which they currently resided. Only about 45 percent of Missouri's freeborn population had been born in state, a reflection of its later settlement and the lure of manifest destiny. Removing the in-state native population, however, unearths some intriguing population trends. Under this formula, more persons born in the North, especially the Border North states of Illinois, Indiana, New Jersey, New York, Ohio, and Pennsylvania, lived in Delaware (66 percent) and Maryland (61 percent) in 1860 than did persons born in the South. On the other hand, Kentucky (72 percent) and Missouri (64 percent) contained more people born in the South under this formula. This suggests a large flow of people from North to South in the eastern states of Delaware and Maryland and the opposite in the western states of Kentucky and Missouri. These figures shed light on the knotted Unionist and Confederate sympathies that white border Southerners tried to untangle during the secession crisis.[32]

Above all else, though, the institution of slavery gave the region its Southern identity. Slavery undergirded the society, economy, and culture of the Border South, and the peculiar institution conditioned the political climate of the borderland up to and through the secession crisis. Although fewer persons were held in bondage in the Border South than in the other slaveholding states, white border Southerners were no less adamant in their insistence that the federal government had to protect the peculiar institution and that the future of slavery lay in their own hands, not those of outsiders. In an observation that could apply to the rest of the Border South, a Louisville editor noted, "Slavery is interwoven with all her institutions, and laws, and customs, and social habits. Her people could not do without it if they would, and they would not if it were practicable. Slave property is a leading element of the wealth, as it is of the greatness, of Kentucky."[33]

Table A-3 provides data on slavery in the South during the 1850s. The slave population of the Border South increased by nearly 10 percent over the decade, a similar trend to the Upper South, which grew by 15 percent, but nowhere close to the 31 percent hike in the Lower South. Missouri witnessed an increase in its slave population that rivaled that of the Cotton South states, but the figures for Delaware and Maryland alarmed Southern nationalists who worried that abolitionists had made inroads in the Border South. Both of the eastern states lost slaves during the 1850s; no other state in the South experienced an overall decline in slave population during the same interval. The influx of free persons far outpaced the growth of the slave population in the Border South, too. The overall percentage of slaves in the total population diminished more greatly in the Border South than the rest of the South, a fact not lost on uneasy Southern radicals.[34]

The development of antisouthernism in Northern politics doubtlessly stoked the exaggerated fears of Southern nationalists. The flowering of the Republican Party, which promised to restrict slavery from the territories once it gained control of the federal government, led some nervous Southerners to conclude that their antislavery enemy had made significant inroads in the Border South. Historians note that discussions about emancipation advanced further along the border than elsewhere in the South and cite this as evidence of slavery's shaky foundation in the region. The Maryland legislature launched a state-funded colonization project in the 1830s; Kentucky's constitutional convention of 1849 debated implementing a gradual emancipation program; Missourians Thomas Hart Benton and Frank P. Blair Jr. called for free soil in the territories; and Kentucky's Cassius Clay spearheaded an outspoken antislavery coterie.[35]

These examples, arrayed against the Lower South's deafening silence on emancipation, paint a picture worthy of Southern radicals' apprehension. Yet just as urbanization blinded fire-eaters and scholars to the region's rural basis, these antislavery discussions misrepresent the true political trajectory of the Border South. The 1850s actually witnessed political entrenchment on the slavery issue in the Border South, as white border Southerners refined proslavery Unionism to shield the peculiar institution from external attacks. Rather than abandoning a system of bondage in the 1850s, white border Southerners enhanced their protective mechanisms for slavery.

The diminution of Delaware and Maryland's slave population in the 1850s aroused the concern of proslavery sectional radicals. The trend seemed almost natural in Delaware, with its miniscule slave population, but the decline in Maryland, a state that had more slaves than Arkansas, Florida, Missouri, or Texas in 1850, was a sore spot for Southern nationalists who feared the concomitant loss of proslavery political power that loomed on the horizon. Politicians in Maryland, however, refused to let this process go unchallenged and sought ways to fortify and revive slavery in the Old Line State. Prior to 1851, the state's constitution included a provision that allowed the legislature to enact a statewide emancipation program if both houses of the general assembly agreed to the policy in two different sessions. Even this tangled path to emancipation seemed unsafe to white Marylanders. Approximately 61 percent of Maryland's voters authorized a new state constitution in 1851 that explicitly forbade the legislature from abolishing slavery. The 1851 constitution also counted slaves as whole persons for legislative apportionment, giving the densest enclaves of slavery disproportionate political power. The state's new constitution showed a resolve to perpetuate, rather than eliminate, slavery in Maryland.[36]

In Maryland the American Party, made up primarily of former Whigs, faced stiff challenges from Democrats, many of whom sounded no less shrill about protecting slavery and its racial protocol than their fellow party members from the Deep South. By the end of the decade Democrats had unseated the traditionally dominant Whig/American coalition and controlled the state legislature. Democrat Curtis W. Jacobs, himself an owner of twenty-one bondspersons, in 1860 crafted legislation that prohibited individual manumission and required the state's free African Americans to hire themselves out on a renewable basis. The House of Delegates amended the legislation, keeping the prohibition on personal manumission intact but replacing the hiring-out policy with a provision that gave free blacks over eighteen years of age the alternative to enter into slavery voluntarily rather than signing an annual labor contract. The bill, which applied only to eleven counties in southern Maryland and on the Eastern Shore, passed the House by a tally of 38–14 but failed miserably in a required popular referendum. That such a harsh measure designed to place free African Americans in shackles passed the legislature so easily indicated the presence of a powerful political element in Maryland that bore a resemblance to strident proslavery factions across the Lower South. The rejection of the measure by the citizens of Maryland's densest slave counties, though, signaled the electorate's predilection for a milder response to the slave question.[37]

White Kentuckians also took measures to protect slavery during the 1850s. The delegates to the state constitutional convention in 1849 who hoped to place slavery on the path to extinction found their wishes dashed. Proslavery forces in the convention closed ranks and pushed through a constitutional provision that prevented the legislature from taking direct action on slavery. In effect, the new constitution made slavery a "permanent fixture" in Kentucky and, according to historian Harold Tallant, led to a near disappearance of "mainstream antislavery politics and public debate on emancipation." Prior to the constitutional convention, the Kentucky legislature showed its proslavery hand when in February 1849 it overturned an 1833 law that prohibited the importation of enslaved persons to the state. The repeal demonstrated some white Kentuckians' desire to expand their slaveholdings through purchase rather than natural increase. Fearful of the deleterious influence freed persons might have on the enslaved population, the legislature by 1851 required all manumitted slaves to leave the state. These measures clearly indicate that some Kentucky politicians sought to protect and nurture slavery in the state.[38]

As in Maryland, the Democratic Party in the 1850s made inroads in Kentucky, an erstwhile bastion of Whig strength. By the end of the decade, Kentucky had become "thoroughly Democratic," an incredible achievement in a state that had been dominated by arch-Whig Henry Clay and his acolytes. By 1860 Democrats controlled both houses of the legislature and elected a governor. Not all Democrats embraced a hardline proslavery stance, but some were willing to stake out an approach reminiscent of that of Lower South radicals. Despite these Democratic advances, most white Kentuckians still preferred a measured response to heated sectional issues. The conservative Whig tradition proved remarkably durable even in the face of Democratic triumphs and would rise to the surface during the secession crisis.[39]

No other Border South state possessed as powerful an opposition to proslavery politics in the 1850s as did Missouri. Democrat Thomas Hart Benton, an influential ally of Andrew Jackson, dominated the Missouri political scene for much of the antebellum period. In the 1840s, however, Benton opposed the annexation of Texas, and in 1847 he declared that slavery should not spread into the territories, which caused a major rift in the Missouri Democracy. In spite of Benton's potent appeal, state politics tilted in a proslavery direction in the decade preceding the secession crisis. In January 1849 Claiborne Fox Jackson, a former Benton lieutenant, introduced a set of resolutions in the Missouri legislature that forthrightly denied Congress's power to legislate on slavery in the territories. The Jackson Resolutions were a catalyst for Democratic divisions in the 1850s, as moderate Democrats and free-soilers gravitated toward Benton and pro-Southern Democrats coalesced under the leadership of Jackson and David Rice Atchison. A small but influential bloc of

Whigs found themselves swimming in a sea infested with two breeds of Democratic sharks. Historians look to Benton's free-soil foray and his protégé Frank Blair's construction of a Republican organization in Saint Louis as a sign of antislavery appeal in Missouri. Nevertheless, Jackson's pro-Southern wing gained the upper hand during the decade and placed the Bentonites on the defensive. Only in Saint Louis did free-soilers taste success, and even there it was limited. After he took his stand on slavery, the Missouri legislature unceremoniously refused to send Benton back to the United States Senate, where he had been ensconced for nearly thirty years. In his stead the legislature sent proslavery Whig Henry S. Geyer to Washington. Benton's free-soil proclivities derailed his political career. He later spent one term in the United States House of Representatives but lost subsequent contests for Congress, the Senate, and the governorship of Missouri.[40]

Jackson and his followers spent the rest of the decade vanquishing an opposition made up of former Democrats, Whigs and Americans, and the tiny Republican contingent in Saint Louis. The state's proximity to Kansas added a sense of urgency to politics and kept the slavery question persistently before the electorate. Although Blair became the only Border South Republican elected to Congress in 1860, his victory was not an accurate barometer of public opinion in Missouri. Most white Missourians found the Republican Party repugnant because of its sectional cast and antislavery bent. They asked the same questions as did politician John D. Coalter: "If [Republicans] abhor our institutions, how long a step will it be before you abhor us? If you abhor slavery, how long before you abhor slaveholders?" Even Benton refused to endorse the Republicans in the presidential election of 1856 because he worried their agenda might endanger the safety of the Union.[41] Most white Missourians searched for restrained responses to the sectional conflict, but they absolutely demanded that outsiders not interfere with slavery in the state. Like the rest of the Border South, Missouri politicians worked to place the peculiar institution on safe ground during the 1850s. Some, like Jackson, shuddered at the prospect of a free Kansas and sounded the tocsin of disunion. During the secession crisis, these sectional hotspurs learned that they had far overstepped the boundaries that many white Missourians had drawn.

Antislavery sentiment garnered little support even in Delaware, a state with a tiny slave population. The legislature considered an emancipation program several times in the 1840s, but each time a faction of Democrats from southern Delaware narrowly defeated these proposals. After the defeat of an emancipation bill in 1849, politicians put the issue to rest and never seriously debated it again in the 1850s.[42] Unlike the rest of the Border South, Delaware did not require freed slaves to leave the state. In 1852, however, the legislature clamped down on free blacks, denying them the right to attend political meetings, to own or possess firearms, to vote or hold office, or to testify in criminal cases in which a white person witnessed the crime. The Democratic Party controlled Delaware politics, and several political luminaries, led by Senator James Asheton Bayard, espoused a strong pro-South position. "The lower portion of this state . . . is ultra Slavery, and Bayard panders to that feeling," one spectator observed. The Republican Party attracted followers in Wilmington during the 1850s, but the organization often prioritized economic issues and soft-pedaled the slavery question to gain adherents.[43]

That antislavery politicians experienced a modicum of success in the Border South leads some scholars to classify all white border Southerners as receptive or indifferent to emancipation. In reality, Border South antislavery politicians manufactured a buzz that far outweighed their limited political impact. Aside from Saint Louis voters sending Blair to Congress, the Border South electorate refused to tolerate politicians with questionable records on slavery. Blair's story is exceptional when arrayed against other Border South politicians. He successfully ran for Congress as a free-soil Democrat in 1856 and, once in Washington, pushed for compensated emancipation in Missouri and the removal of the state's freed persons to Central America. Blair's plan never came to a vote in the House, but it did contribute to his narrow defeat in a reelection bid. An undeterred Blair charged his opponents in Missouri's First District with fraud, won his case, and in 1860 was awarded his old seat in Congress. Both elections featured three candidates; in 1856 Blair's opponents captured 56 percent of the vote, but in 1858 they racked up nearly two-thirds of the ballots. In a victorious bid for Congress in August 1860, Blair's challengers once again won 56 percent of the overall vote. Blair never won a majority in any of these elections, and his plurality diminished immediately after he introduced his emancipation program. Moreover, he benefited from a large contingent of Germans in his congressional district who supported the antislavery Republican Party. His approach to the slavery question seemed radical to most white Southerners, especially the voters of his district. Unconcerned with the moral implications of racial slavery, Blair hoped his colonization scheme would free Missouri's white population from competition with slave labor, foster economic progress, and springboard him to national prominence.[44]

Blair's antebellum record was checkered, for he advocated a modest solution to the slavery problem that made most white border Southerners uncomfortable. Political aspirants in the Border South who moved beyond colonization to more radical solutions for ending slavery had negligible political sway. Cassius Clay, who, unlike Blair, encouraged fostering alliances with abolitionists, never sniffed electoral success in Kentucky. "Whatever the fact may be," a friend of Clay reminded him, "you are regarded by the world as one of the extreme men."[45] White border Southerners had little patience for extremism, as Clay's ally John Fee found out firsthand. Subjected to mob violence and even threatened with death for his denunciations of slavery from the pulpit, Fee defiantly continued to deliver his abolitionist message throughout Kentucky. He established an antislavery community in Berea, Kentucky, in 1854, and soon began distributing Bibles to enslaved persons. Kentuckians begrudgingly tolerated Fee's activities until John Brown's failed slave insurrection at Harpers Ferry, Virginia. In December 1859, an armed posse demanded that Fee and his followers leave the state immediately. The governor of Kentucky ignored the Bereans' plea for state protection, which prompted them to relocate to the free states. Fee's case indicates that the region's desultory sufferance for extremism had evaporated by 1860.[46]

Thus, even in a region marked by smaller quantities of enslaved people and slight slaveholdings compared to the future Confederate states, discussion of ending slavery far more often invited contempt than approval. Although more of the white population in the Upper and Lower South was involved with slaveholding and owned larger concentrations of enslaved persons (see Table A.4), white border Southerners shared with their more southerly neighbors a predilection for the racial and social control brought about by the peculiar institution.[47] The muting of antislavery voices, along with the energy expended to construct constitutional and political protections in the 1850s, demonstrates the depth of white border Southerners' commitment to the preservation of slavery.

White borderites recoiled at any proposition that would bring about the demise of slavery. Although just 15 percent of white border Southerners owned enslaved persons, the slave system presented the larger white community with several advantages. Nonslaveholders hired out enslaved persons to fulfill labor needs, relied on slave labor to perform skilled tasks such as blacksmithing and carpentry, and often aspired to own bondspersons. Historian James L. Huston notes that by 1860 many white border Southerners reaped greater profits commissioning enslaved persons in manufacturing and industrial concerns than they did employing free labor. Huston's findings underscore the flexibility and the possibilities of slavery's future in the Border South.[48] While the slave trade removed enslaved persons from the region, it also proved lucrative for many white border Southerners. The harrowing practice of splitting up black families often enriched slaveholders, slave traders, and the transportation outfits that carried out the trade. The voracious appetite for slave labor in the Lower South fostered potent intraregional economic ties and amplified the Border South's economic stake in the slave system.[49]

Beyond economic considerations, white border Southerners relied on slavery to reinforce rigid racial barriers. The prospect of removing slavery invited all kinds of speculation about the place of free African Americans in society. Proportionally more free blacks lived in the Border South than elsewhere in the country, and this already significant contingent would mushroom with emancipation. When they envisioned a future without slavery, white borderites shared the racial paranoia of Lower South radicals. "The black race will be in a large majority," a Georgian speculated, "and then we will have black governors, black legislatures, black juries, black everything." Without slavery in place to order society on racial grounds and silence potential class tensions, border whites believed their world would become unhinged. In such a future, blacks would compete with whites for jobs and place, erasing the racial divisions so integral to herrenvolk democracy. White border Southerners longed to avoid this eventuality at all costs.[50]

Because of slavery's social, economic, cultural, and political underpinnings, white border Southerners searched for the best means to safeguard the peculiar institution. Although increasing numbers of whites in the Lower and Upper South saw disunion as the unsurpassed method to preserve slavery as the 1850s progressed, most white border Southerners continued to place their confidence in proslavery Unionism. A growing number of white border Southerners beat the drum of disunion during the decade, but few people marched to their cadence. Not until the Harpers Ferry raid and the election of 1860 would inhabitants of the Border South seriously begin to contemplate the feasibility of secession. Even in the midst of the secession crisis, disunionists found it difficult to assail the powerful hold of proslavery Unionism in the Border South.

The debate over the Compromise of 1850, the Kansas-Nebraska Act and the consequential dispute over the meaning of popular sovereignty, clashes over fugitive slaves and personal liberty laws, the Lecompton Constitution, and *Dred Scott v. Sandford* had so thoroughly poisoned sectional relations that many Northerners and Southerners by 1859 viewed one another as enemies rather than fellow citizens. White border Southerners felt the pinch of these strained relations, but proslavery Unionism led many to the conclusion that secession was nothing more than a fool's errand. The proslavery Unionist

approach relied on three core components: a Congress that refused to med-
dle with slavery in the states; a federal government that enforced the Fugitive
Slave Law and protected the interstate slave trade; and influential Northern
allies who assisted in preventing sectional extremists from taking command
of the ship of state. White border Southerners worked to maintain this delicate balance in order to guard slavery from potential threats.[51]

Proslavery Unionism had been tested during the 1850s but proved quite
durable. Because of its proximity to alluring free territory, no region of the
slaveholding South was as vulnerable to the permanent escape of enslaved
persons as the Border South. The census counts 803 fugitive slaves in 1860,
but some scholars have revised the number upward to as many as 5,000 es-
capees annually. All historians agree, though, that the Border South bore the
brunt of runaways to a much larger degree than the Lower or Upper South.[52]
As such, border Southerners counted on the federal government to enforce
the Fugitive Slave Law in good faith. After careful study, Kentucky Unionist
Joseph Holt acknowledged the federal government had done just that. "It is
this law, effective in its power of recapture, but infinitely more potent in its
moral agency in preventing the escape of slaves," Holt declared, "that alone
saves the institution in the Border States from utter extinction." Secession
meant forfeiting this protection; as a result, the Border South would "virtually have Canada brought to her doors in the form of Free States." "Under
such influences," Holt predicted, "slavery will perish rapidly away in Kentucky, as a ball of snow melts in a summer's sun." In Holt's eyes, the Union and
the federal government provided a critical shield to slavery that the Border
South could not forego.[53]

Because federal legislation was a key component of proslavery Unionism,
white border Southerners had to trust in alliances built with likeminded
politicians in the North who helped block their adversaries from steering
the national government toward antislavery measures. What historian William J. Cooper labels the politics of slavery had remarkable staying power in
the Border South. The politics of slavery, practiced by the Democrats and
Whigs until the 1850s, relied on national coalitions in which the Northern
wing of a party acquiesced to Southerners on slavery-related issues.[54] The
travails of the 1850s left many people in the Lower South suspicious of all
Northern politicians, which undermined the politics of slavery for that subre-
gion. The debilitative effect of a decade of arguing with Northerners about
slavery, along with the meteoric rise of the Republican Party, convinced many
people in the Deep South that slaveholders had lost all of their allies in the
free states. For them, only one alternative remained to protect slavery and the

South: secession.[55] In the Border South, on the other hand, most whites kept the faith in their Northern partners, whom they trusted to do battle with the Republicans and keep the federal government from backsliding on its protections for slavery.

The resiliency of the politics of slavery in the Border South generated a strong aversion to extremism, whether it originated in the North or the South. For instance, when in 1860 a Republican senator introduced a memorial that called for the repeal of the Fugitive Slave Law and the eradication of the interstate slave trade, a Maryland newspaper editor took notice. "The substantial quality of republicanism is its exclusive sectionalism," he wrote, "and nothing could be more surely destructive of the Union than this." The editor heaved a sigh of relief that a coalition of non-Republican senators from both the North and the South managed to table the memorial, a sure sign of the effectiveness of the politics of slavery.[56] Likewise, white border Southerners abhorred the rashness of fire-eaters who wanted to bully the rest of the South into secession. In the mind of proslavery Unionists, Southern radicals would only help Northern extremists in their quest to end slavery. A Kentuckian observed that secession "repeals the fugitive slave law, it makes personal liberty bills in the free states valid: it accomplishes just what the abolitionists desire, the exemption of the free states from any countenance to slavery."[57] White border Southerners shared the desire of other Southerners to preserve slavery, but they recommended a vastly different solution to the problem.

By 1859, white border Southerners truly felt caught in the middle of the sectional conflict. The economy, society, and politics of the region fostered ties in both directions and imbued the Border South with a strong attachment to the Union. In general the Democratic Party enjoyed success across the Border South in the 1850s, but strong partisan competition remained a key facet of the political matrix. Measures had been taken during the decade to provide unassailable protections for the peculiar institution, which tethered the fortunes of the Border South to the future of slavery. Politicians and voters looked for allies as the country geared up for the presidential election of 1860. At the very least, those allies had to accept the Border South condition that the federal government would dependably execute the Fugitive Slave Law, protect the interstate slave trade, and leave all questions about the future of slavery to the individual states where it existed. White borderites tried to avoid lengthy discussions about the extension of slavery into the territories, which they found detrimental to sectional accord. They felt these arguments had been rendered moot by the Supreme Court's *Dred Scott* decision, an opinion handed down by one of their own, Chief Justice Roger B.

Taney of Maryland.[58] Some members of the American Party even envisioned the possibility of rebuilding the old Whig coalition by uniting with moderate Republicans who would purge their organization of its radical sectional element in an effort to beat the Democrats in 1860. In October 1859, however, John Brown's raid at Harpers Ferry, Virginia, produced a political earthquake that tested this delicate Border South Unionist outlook. Its tremors rumbled deep into the secession crisis and injected a Lower South–like militancy into political discussions that Border South Unionists found difficult to stifle. As the secession crisis gathered momentum, many white border Southerners, moored to both the North and the South by the economic, social, and political realities of the 1850s, questioned whether the hallowed Unionist impulse that John Pendleton Kennedy brilliantly captured in his essay could endure the towering breakers on the horizon.

CHAPTER TWO

We Are Approaching a Crisis Pregnant with Immense and Momentous Results

The Long Shadow of John Brown's Raid, October 1859–April 1860

Edward Bates surveyed the political landscape in early 1859 and, unlike many Americans, the Missourian remained optimistic about the republic's future. Born in the last decade of the eighteenth century in Virginia, Bates came to Missouri in 1814, read law, and established a successful practice in fledgling Saint Louis. Bates quickly made the transition from frontier barrister to politician, and during his lengthy career he had helped to write Missouri's first state constitution, sat in both houses of the state legislature, spent a single term in Congress, and become the unofficial leader of the state's Whig Party. Even after the Whig organization crumbled in the 1850s, Bates clung to the principles of Henry Clay's party. By 1859, his physical appearance showed the effects of a life devoted to politics. Craggy facial recesses crept out from under a flowing white beard, which Bates's opponents believed symbolized his outmoded Whiggish political philosophy. He privately opposed the extension of slavery into the territories but also fretted that the explosive issue undermined intersectional political cooperation, the keystone of a bygone era of politics. In February 1859 he wrote a public letter that denounced the Democratic scheme to bring Kansas into the Union as a slave state under the Lecompton Constitution. Bates lambasted radicals for their efforts to gain political capital by agitating the slavery question and laid the blame for the nation's sickened political environment at the feet of Democratic president James Buchanan, who stood at the head of a party dominated by Southern zealots. He sadly admitted that "the only party I ever belonged to has ceased to exist as an organized and militant body," which left former Whigs like himself longing for a moderate alternative to the sectionalized Democrats.[1]

As the nation prepared for the presidential election in 1860, however, Bates held out hope that the disparate opponents of the Democrats could unite under one banner, defeat their common opponent, and extract the vexed question of slavery from the political matrix. A circle of political associates in Missouri, who likely convinced Bates to write the letter, were even floating his name as a potential contender to head up the Democratic opposition. Bates, his backers insisted, made the perfect candidate: he hailed from the heart of the nation; he had carried himself in a dignified manner during his career; and he championed a middle-of-the-road approach to the slavery extension controversy. Bates insisted that over time slavery would naturally wither away and die if confined to the fifteen states where it existed. He called for the compensation of slaveholders who emancipated their bondspersons, endorsed colonization as a means to solve the racial riddle caused by manumission, and adamantly declared that the federal government had no right to interfere with slavery in the states. His plan for eliminating slavery included none of the rigid extremism associated with abolitionism, which strategists considered an enormous asset for drawing in conservative voters.[2]

Influential Republicans, including *New York Tribune* editor Horace Greeley and the Blair triumvirate, Francis Preston Blair and his sons Montgomery and Frank Jr., beseeched Bates to join their organization. Bates, however, shared with most white border Southerners reservations about the design and composition of the Republican Party. In his public letter, Bates proclaimed that "the agitation of [the slavery question] has never done good to any party, section or class, and never can do good, unless it be accounted to stir up the angry passions of men, and exasperate the unreasonable jealousy of sections." While appreciative of the invitation, Bates worried about the potential fallout in Missouri from joining with the Republicans, an organization that included some of the sectional agitators he so detested. He confided to his diary doubts about the Republicans, whom he feared would advance far beyond his own ideas about emancipation if they gained the ascendancy. He alleged that Missouri had started down the path to freedom "by the irresistable [sic] force of circumstances, without any statute to help on the work." Bates reasoned that other states could follow Missouri's example to avoid the deleterious consequences of politicizing the slavery question. His reservations about the dire consequences of Republican legislative activism in the spring of 1859 led Bates to make no commitment to his suitors. Instead he hoped for a revival of the Whig Party, a national coalition of moderates who could sidestep the slavery question by emphasizing economic issues. Such an approach would smother sectional differences and free the nation from eight years of bungled Democratic rule.[3]

Bates favored a quintessentially Border South response to the worsening political climate. His noncommittal stance in 1859 foreshadowed the Border South's vain attempt at neutrality once sectional tensions escalated to war in 1861. He felt the federal government should not tamper with slavery in the states where it existed, sought a solution to the slavery extension question amenable to both sections, and faithfully believed in the enduring power of the Union. Bates attempted to downplay the territorial problem, much to the chagrin of Republican hardliners, because he understood that most white border Southerners refused to vote for a candidate who made that issue the centerpiece of his campaign.[4] His supporters considered Bates the ideal presidential candidate because he could see beyond the slavery extension issue to a brighter tomorrow. Yet in reality, Bates looked backward, not forward. He reminisced of a fictional past free from distress over slavery, and this vision blinded the Missourian to the realities of the present. The slavery question had become unavoidable by the end of the 1850s. And in the autumn of 1859, the actions of a small band of radical abolitionists in Bates's birthplace of Virginia ensured that all white border Southerners would have to confront the issue they had for so long tried to dodge.

John Brown, the leader of those abolitionists, had little use for cautious politicians like Edward Bates who wished slavery to die a slow, natural death. The Connecticut-born Brown had fought to keep slavery from polluting the plains of Kansas in the middle of the 1850s, and now he turned his attention to the Southern states. His religious convictions told him that God wanted to rid the United States of the peculiar institution and that he was the instrument for carrying out this divine charge. Brown preferred swift enterprise and made preparations to punish American slaveholders for the sins of the last two and a half centuries. He aimed to incite a slave rebellion in Virginia that would spread throughout the South, liberate four million enslaved persons, and decisively topple the slaveocracy. Brown's militant approach was the very antithesis of Bates's guarded tack, but the abolitionist's actions at Harpers Ferry ironically had a momentous impact on Border South politics. Brown's invasion quickened the march toward secession, and in the Border South the raid damaged the region's normally amicable relationship with Northern conservatives. In this environment, the alternative of disunion became a distinct possibility along the border. As scholar Peter Wallenstein notes, the raid "captured the attention even of the apathetic, shook the faith of unionists, and encouraged the disunionists" of the South. The raid injected a sectionalist bent into Border South politics that Unionists strained to withstand, and it made Bates's noncommittal political formula infeasible as the nation approached the election of 1860.[5]

Brown's raid transformed the sectional conflict into a crisis and unleashed a series of events that quickly closed the window on compromise. Border South moderates fought hard to keep that window ajar, but with each passing day their options became more limited. The crisis forced many white border Southerners, like Bates, to abandon their evasive stance on the slavery question. A trace few cast their lot with the Republicans and others became avid secessionists, but the bulk of white border Southerners continued to take inspiration from Clay and held out fleeting hope that a settlement would once again save the republic. Brown's October 1859 raid inflamed the public mind and disrupted the party machinery that Border South conservatives depended on to contain the baneful effects of sectionalism. The raid turned the subsequent election of a Speaker of the House of Representatives in early 1860 into a debacle and made it more difficult for Border South moderates to mount a viable political alternative to the Democrats and Republicans.

DURING THE ANTEBELLUM PERIOD, the American lust for additional lands in the West prohibited politicians from keeping the slavery question out of the national spotlight. Democrats made the principle of popular sovereignty the party's orthodox response to this issue. With popular sovereignty, western settlers would decide the future of slavery in the territories rather than Congress. Senator Stephen A. Douglas of Illinois had hitched his political future to popular sovereignty, which he championed as a plebeian solution to an explosive political problem made worse by Washington hucksters. Let the people who live in the territories render a decision on slavery, Douglas argued, not politicians in the nation's capital. Douglas's formula, however, inadvertently allowed sectional hotspurs like Brown to appropriate the settlement of the West for their own ends.[6]

Brown drew national attention in May 1856 when he and his sons murdered several Kansas settlers affiliated with proslavery forces in the territory. White Southerners and Northern conservatives scorned Brown's methods, while some abolitionists applauded his tactics. A Missouri newspaper labeled Brown's rampage "the legitimate fruits of the Abolition press and pulpit, who have stirred up the worst passions of a portion of their people against another portion of the country, and done [this] with a reckless or a willful knowledge of the dangerous consequences."[7]

Brown escaped prosecution for his involvement in what became known as the Pottawatomie Massacre, and by the late 1850s he had begun to solicit money, munitions, and men to strike a grand blow at slavery not in the territories but in the slaveholding states. A handful of prominent abolitionists subsidized his ambitious scheme, though Brown found it difficult to enlist many recruits. He rented a farmhouse in July 1859 on the Maryland side of the Potomac River; three months later a mere twenty-one warriors had assembled at Brown's headquarters. Brown chose Harpers Ferry, Virginia, just five miles away from the Maryland farm, as his initial target. Nestled in the mountains that surrounded the intersection of the Potomac and the Shenandoah Rivers, Harpers Ferry housed a federal arsenal and the junction of two major railroads. Brown anticipated that once his band took the town, enslaved persons from the surrounding countryside would flock to his standard. He planned to distribute pikes and firearms to the escaped slaves, swelling his ranks from twenty-one to twenty thousand. As his legion gained momentum, Brown reasoned, the peculiar institution would crumble under its weight.[8]

On October 16, 1859, Brown led his outfit to Harpers Ferry, where they captured the arsenal with relative ease and waited for the anticipated onrush of enslaved persons. His men committed a colossal blunder, however, when they stopped a train on the Baltimore and Ohio Railroad but later let it proceed. The engineer alerted the railroad company's president that some sort of armed insurrection was under way at Harpers Ferry. Word spread rapidly throughout the countryside and when Brown surveyed the town on October 17, he discovered no army of escaped bondspersons, but instead droves of white militiamen bent on subduing the uprising. President Buchanan ordered a small force of regular soldiers to the scene, which arrived around ten o'clock that night. Brown refused to surrender, so his men barricaded themselves in the town's engine works and held out until the following morning, when federal troops stormed the building. The insurrection ended as quickly as it had begun. Five of Brown's soldiers slipped away, but when the smoke cleared, another ten lay dead or mortally wounded. Brown and seven of his lieutenants were captured and clapped in manacles to await trial. Authorities soon after searched Brown's rented farmhouse and found a collection of letters that outlined his scheme for the pan-Southern insurrection. The letters confirmed the worst fears of white Southerners: an abolitionist had attempted to upset their carefully ordered society by pitting enslaved persons against their masters. Kansas-style frontier violence had been introduced in their own backyard, fewer than sixty miles from the nation's capital and eighty miles from the South's largest city, Baltimore. Most white Southerners breathed a sigh of relief that Brown failed and that no enslaved people had joined his plot, but a pall of anxiety lingered over the South. A Baltimore editor could only assume that Brown and his followers were "the victims of that social and political error with which a large proportion of the northern mind is indoctrinated and imbued."[9]

Border South moderates often emphasized during the 1850s that abolitionists represented a miniscule portion of the Northern population. As governor of Kentucky, John Jordan Crittenden visited Indiana in 1850 during the height of the sectional controversy over whether to allow slavery on lands acquired as a result of the Mexican-American War. Welcomed in Indianapolis by large crowds, Crittenden noticed the "particularly fraternal kindness & affection" exhibited for Kentucky, a welcome sign in the midst of the charged sectional atmosphere. Crittenden assured a Kentucky associate that Indianans sought "compromise & amicable settlement of all slavery questions." While in Indianapolis, the Kentuckian could not resist the opportunity to "talk right plainly to them about Abolition, & the mischiefs that its meddlesome & false humanity had brought & was tending to bring upon the Country."[10]

White border Southerners had always been leery of abolitionists, but throughout the 1850s they had entrusted moderate Northerners like Crittenden's Indianapolis audience to relegate those radicals to the political margins.[11] Nearly a decade later, Brown's raid at Harpers Ferry threatened to destroy the intersectional bridges of moderation that Crittenden and his allies had raised. White borderites expected to hear a litany of condemnation aimed at Brown from their conservative Northern friends, and plenty of free state moderates criticized the abolitionist's actions shortly after his capture. An Ohio newspaper, for instance, asked "the people of the free States [to] put down the class of politicians who belong to the school of Slavery Agitators," and one of Crittenden's associates in Boston told him of a large meeting at Faneuil Hall where the attendees roundly censured Brown.[12]

But as more details of the plot became available, many white Southerners became blinded in a fit of rage. They ignored the disapproval of Brown and instead trained their attention on Northern voices that condoned the abolitionist's actions. "Day after day," a Baltimore editor lamented, "we have the cumulative evidence, furnished voluntarily by the press and the pulpit, that John Brown is in fact the representative man of a very large class of people of the North, and that he is the object of their constant concern and sympathy."[13] The raid, undertaken so close to the Border South, temporarily upset the intersectional fraternity that had become the hallmark of antebellum borderland politics. The absence of universal Northern denunciation of Brown's deeds provoked some otherwise Border South moderates to reevaluate the safety of slavery within the Union.

While Brown awaited trial in a Virginia jail, white border Southerners pondered the ramifications of the plot. Hester Davis, the wife of a Maryland politician, regretted that a search of Brown's headquarters turned up not only firearms and "javelins for the use of the negroes" but also letters from Northern women supporting his exploits. She believed some of the correspondence came from Quakers and worried about the ominous consequences. If Northern women, even pacifist Quakers, supported such violent measures, Davis deduced, then the rest of the population in the free states surely approved of Brown's actions. Fearful that the Harpers Ferry raid was the opening salvo of a massive abolitionist assault, she demanded that her husband carry two loaded revolvers on an upcoming business trip. After her husband left for Baltimore, a neighbor's son slept at her Montgomery County house to protect the family in the event of another attack.[14] Months later Virginia intellectual George Fitzhugh accurately gauged the lasting impact of the raid on white Border South women: "Our wives and our daughters will see in every new Yankee face an abolition missionary."[15] The raid produced a tense atmosphere nationwide, but in its aftermath white border Southerners felt particularly vulnerable.

A Missourian attending West Point admitted that Brown's raid tested his faith in the ability of the Union to safeguard slavery. "I am decidedly a conservative man . . . and am in favor of promoting the well fare and future prosperity of our whole Union," the cadet wrote. "But I am from a southern state and am not willing for these northern fanatics & pirates to come upon our southern soil and deprive us of our most valuable property."[16] Brown's undertaking clearly amplified Border South paranoia about slave insurrections and the federal government's ability to guard against future abolitionist incursions. Reservations about the effectiveness of proslavery Unionism sprang forth from unnerved white border Southerners, a marked contrast to the overriding mind-set of the preceding decade. That so many Northerners appeared to sympathize with Brown stoked fears of future abolitionist incursions in the exposed borderland.

The warnings of western Missourians, who had become quite familiar with prolonged violence caused by the slavery issue during the 1850s, seemed prescient to white border Southerners in the aftermath of Harpers Ferry. Slaveholders in western Missouri had long complained about the activities of abolitionists like Brown and James Montgomery, the leader of militant free-soil forces in Kansas. In 1858 the state legislature appropriated funds to defend against Montgomery's band of abolitionist raiders, who often crossed the border, absconded with enslaved persons, and destroyed Missourians' property. Prior to the Harpers Ferry raid, leaders of Missouri's state militia and many white border Southerners dismissed western Missourians' complaints as an overreaction. Brown's Virginia excursion, however, taught the rest of the Border South that western Missourians had not sounded a false alarm. Fearful that free African Americans might serve as liaisons between

Northern interlopers and the enslaved population, the Missouri General Assembly authorized legislation that forced free blacks to enter slavery or leave the state. Governor Robert M. Stewart, a pro-Union Democrat, vetoed the bill, but his executive override did not diminish the fact that the Missouri legislature took extreme steps to protect slavery in the wake of Brown's raid. Although he felt the bill designed to rid Missouri of free blacks too reactionary, Stewart shared the legislature's belief that white border Southerners could not remain idle and allow outsiders to destabilize slavery in the region. He signed a bill in December 1859 that reorganized the state militia in the hopes of more effectively guarding Missouri from abolitionist invasions.[17]

The palpable terror that western Missourians lived with quickly made its way eastward. Mounting numbers of white border Southerners affirmed the contention of a Virginian who explained, "The border States are the exposed frontier. Into them the underground railroad insinuates its emissaries, who steal a part of our slaves and poison the minds of the balance."[18] Kentucky governor Beriah C. Magoffin, a Democrat who took office a month before the raid, discussed the implications of abolitionist activity in the Border South at length in his first message to the state legislature. He reminded his constituents that the Bluegrass State had "more cause of complaint than any other State in the Union" due to its seven-hundred-mile-long border that abutted three free states. Magoffin calculated that Kentuckians lost $100,000 annually due to the escapes of enslaved persons, and in response he recommended the reorganization of the state militia, a prohibitive tax on out-of-state peddlers— whom he feared might introduce incendiary ideas to slaves—operating within Kentucky, a repeal of a law allowing free blacks to settle in the state, and the establishment of a program to relocate free African Americans outside Kentucky. The governor hinted that he would support legislation that forced free blacks into slavery if found guilty of purported crimes such as drunkenness, immorality, and laziness. Such a law would give the state judiciary considerable latitude to enslave free blacks on trumped-up charges.[19] In response, the legislature agreed to the reorganization of the state militia system, towns and cities across the state enhanced the manpower of local police forces, and county authorities supervised more rigorous slave patrolling.[20]

White citizens in Kentucky exceeded the authorities in their response to Brown's raid. In late October 1859 a mob in Newport, just across the Ohio River from Cincinnati, stormed the printing office of antislavery editor William S. Bailey, seized his presses, and hurled the type into the river. Bailey, who disturbed his neighbors when he advocated a Brown-like crusade against slavery, defiantly resisted the mob's demand that he leave the state. His neighbors subsequently threw Bailey in jail for publishing incendiary materials. While on a tour through the North, John Fee, who had established an antislavery community in Berea, made the bold claim that the nation needed "more John Browns—not in the manner of his action, but in his spirit of consecration." Fee's injudicious remarks "called into new life the suspicion with which [Fee and his nearly one hundred followers] had been viewed," and provoked whites in Madison County to expel the Berea abolitionists from the state. Other communities followed Madison County's lead and instructed abolitionists "to leave Kentucky terra firma instanter." "We can get along without foreign interlopers," a Louisville editor snapped, "and can manage our affairs in our own way without assistance from abroad."[21]

White Marylanders also responded swiftly to the Harpers Ferry raid. Militia units from Baltimore and eastern Maryland rushed to the assistance of western Marylanders once they received word of the invasion. Brown had established his headquarters in Washington County, which in the aftermath of the raid led the county's white population to see abolitionists behind every bush. Enslaved persons composed just 5 percent of Washington County's total population, and western Maryland had far fewer slaves than the rest of the state, but the specter of a slave revolt energized the area's white population. Governor Thomas Hicks, a member of the American Party and no proslavery fanatic, allowed sheriffs and local authorities in western Maryland to arrest and detain suspicious persons on the slightest pretext. Innuendo of a forthcoming slave revolt induced the people of Frederick to outfit an armed posse that roamed the town's streets. Although the attack never materialized, the Frederick band arrested one African American for possessing a firearm. Officials in Hagerstown and Boonsboro were granted the authority to detain "all suspicious characters who may be prowling about or passing along" following the raid.[22] The state legislature appropriated $70,000 for the formation of additional militia companies to forestall future slave revolts and crafted legislation to restrict further the already limited freedom of Maryland's free black population.[23]

Even Republican Frank P. Blair Jr., whose views about terminating slavery remained far in advance of other white border Southerners, considered Brown's plot "atrocious madness & malignity." He faulted Brown not for the social chaos his raid may have caused, but for the political fallout that resulted in the Border South. Blair feared that Brown's attempted insurrection "will recoil on us as a party in the border states."[24] Suddenly, the prospects for any partnership between former Whigs, Americans, and the handful of Republicans in the Border South had vanished. Before the Harpers Ferry raid, some border Southerners held out hope that all political factions opposed to the Democrats might coalesce to beat their common opponent. Eyeing the presidential election of 1860, Samuel S. Nicholas of Kentucky urged all opponents of the Democrats to unite as the Opposition Party. Nicholas and likeminded Border South politicos presumed that abolitionists, who made up a small portion of the Republican Party, would abandon this collaborative association. Purged of the radical antislavery element, Nicholas guessed the Opposition "would become essentially national, and would easily put down the sham Democracy." The raid at Harpers Ferry sealed the fate of Nicholas's scheme, which had a remote chance of success before Brown's exploits, although a few supporters of Republican collaboration cleaved to the barren project. Border South Democrats made sure to pin responsibility for the raid on the Republicans, further diminishing the probability of cooperation. "The Democracy is turning every stone to make party capital out of it," Edward Bates astutely noted. "Very probably, they will overdo the thing and produce a reaction."[25]

Brown's raid at Harpers Ferry allowed Border South Democrats to make the claim that only they could best protect slavery in a region under attack from outside threats. Some Democrats framed all of their opponents, even conservative Whigs and Americans, as proto-Republicans bent on foisting emancipation on the Border South through the legislative process. Democratic political posturing left former Whigs and Americans with no choice but to distance themselves from the Republicans. Throughout the 1850s the Democratic Party had made inroads across the Border South by using the slavery issue as a political weapon; aside from in Missouri, which had long been a source of Democratic strength thanks to Thomas Hart Benton's dominance of the state, the growth of the Democratic Party in the decade marked a departure from Whig and American supremacy in the region. Border South legislatures were split evenly among Democrats and their opponents in 1850, but by 1860 Democrats held 62 percent of the seats in the four assemblies.[26]

The Democratic Party's ascendancy in the Border South could not match that of the other slaveholding states, where Democrats controlled 71 percent of the seats in the legislatures, but positioning themselves as the preeminent guardians of slavery resulted in impressive gains in borderland statehouses. Although their gubernatorial elections had been held prior to Brown's raid, the people of Delaware, Kentucky, and Missouri had chosen Democratic governors. Only Maryland claimed a non-Democratic executive—American Thomas Hicks—at the time of the raid.[27]

TABLE 2.1 Votes cast in congressional elections in Maryland, 1857 and 1859

Year	Democrats	% of Total	Non-Democrats	% of Total	Total Cast
1857	38,252	44.7	47,237	55.3	85,489
1859	37,658	43.3	49,370	56.7	87,028

Source: Dubin, United States Congressional Elections, 178–79, 184.

The Harpers Ferry raid occurred at the apogee of antebellum Democratic success in the Border South. Nonetheless, the case of Maryland reveals that the Democrats had not completely vanquished their foes. Only Maryland held state elections in the immediate aftermath of Brown's raid, and the results suggest that the Democracy capitalized on the resultant paranoia. Overwhelming non-Democratic majorities in the legislature disappeared in 1859; afterward Democrats gained a two-seat majority in the Senate and a sixteen-seat advantage in the House.[28] Maryland also was the only Border South state to hold congressional elections directly following the raid; the state's delegation to the United States House of Representatives remained split between three Democrats and three non-Democrats. A tabulation of the total votes in the congressional elections, however, indicates that non-Democrats outpolled Democrats by 11,712 votes in 1859. Marylanders cast nearly 57 percent of their votes for non-Democratic candidates, an increase from a non-Democratic tally of 55 percent of all votes in the 1857 elections (see Table 2.1).[29] The disparity between Democratic gains in Maryland's state government and the dip in votes cast for Democratic congressional candidates signals that non-Democrats remained a significant variable in the Border South political equation. These figures point toward a region-wide preference for a moderate response to national political questions and foreshadowed the subsequent creation of a political organization to accommodate this conservative impulse. The raid battered non-Democrats in the Border South, but even after a decade of setbacks the legatees of Henry Clay remained a potent political force.

In the aftermath of Harpers Ferry, some Border South Democrats resorted to scare tactics that closely resembled the machinations of fire-eaters in other states. Meriwether Jeff Thompson, the mayor of Saint Joseph, Missouri, and a native of Harpers Ferry, returned to his Virginia birthplace shortly after the raid and as a sign of Southern solidarity presented local authorities with a hemp rope wrought by the enslaved persons of a Missouri woman whose husband Brown had allegedly killed. While in Virginia, Thompson bought several of the pikes that Brown intended to place in the hands of liberated slaves and brought them back west to show Missourians their fate if the Republican Party gained control of the national government. Later, while confined to a Union prison during the Civil War, Thompson looked back and proclaimed, "My Southern proclivities were well known, yet, I was not, nor am I now a secessionist, 'per se,' as the Fire Eaters were called. I was then, and I am now, an 'irrepressible conflict' man."[30] Thompson split hairs when he assigned himself this label. His actions hardly differed from those of fire-eater Edmund Ruffin of Virginia, who collected some of Brown's pikes and sent them to Southern politicians and governors after affixing a note that read, "Samples of the favors designed for us by our Northern Brethren."[31] Sometime after the raid, Thompson delivered a speech and warned his fellow Missourians that Brown and the Republicans intended "to massacre millions of the happiest and freest people in the world." He admonished white border Southerners to "drive back the invading horde, before we are penned up in a few states on the Gulf coast, and the terrible consequences of a servile insurrection should burst upon us, and rapine, murder and incendiarism run riot through the land." Although far fewer fire-eaters called the Border South home than the other eleven slave states, Thompson's invective demonstrates that borderland sectional radicals harped on the same themes as their peers farther south. Through most of the decade, white borderites dismissed fire-eaters as impractical mavericks, but the outwardly favorable Northern response to the raid gave men like Thompson instant credibility.[32]

A Virginia court found Brown guilty of treason and sentenced him to hang on December 2, 1859. White border Southerners overwhelmingly agreed with the sentence. "When he was ravaging Kansas and Missouri he gave no quarter—committing murder or robbery, or running off a dozen negro slaves, with equal indifference," a Missouri paper opined, "and he ought to ask no quarter now that the law has him in its clutches." Some Border South newspapers speculated that Brown's sympathizers would attempt to rescue the abolitionist martyr, but nothing of the sort materialized. White border Southerners still remained on high alert.[33]

As Brown awaited the gallows, Northern wire-pullers realized that most Southerners would equate the abolitionist with the Republicans and damage the party's broader appeal. The weight of the attempted insurrection widened the breach between the sections, to the delight of radicals and the dismay of pragmatists who understood the necessity of intersectional amity. Observers discerned that the raid harmed Northern politicians across the political spectrum, from Republicans to Stephen A. Douglas, who had broken with Southern Democrats in 1857 over the Lecompton Constitution. "Brown has run his race and his last act has been to deal a fatal blow at the political prospects of his friend [Republican William H.] Seward and thrown a wet blanket over the shoulder of our friend Douglas and his backers," a Pennsylvanian confided to President Buchanan.[34] Republicans who sought to expand the party southward fretted, while Democrats continued to lay the blame for the raid at the feet of the Republicans and their partisan agenda to eradicate slavery. "We are damnably exercised here about the effect of Old Brown's wretched fiasco in Virginia," a Chicagoan groused. "The old idiot—The quicker they hang him and get him out of the way, the better."[35]

A stoic Brown met the gallows in early December and received "a just retribution," according to a Marylander. "So old Brown has played out his tragedy to the 5th act, and the curtain has fallen," John Pendleton Kennedy mused. "Hero or Devil?—that is the question." Most white borderites opted for the latter label, including Kennedy, whose correspondence with an associate who witnessed Brown's trial and hanging led him to this conclusion. Kennedy's confidant described Brown as "a very bold reckless man, mean hypocritical and cunning—of a low order of intellect and still lower morals." Brown's "cant about religion was mere craft," the informant explained; in truth, he felt the abolitionist deserved the label "murderer, horse thief and robber" rather than martyr for the cause of freedom.[36] White border Southerners easily convinced themselves that Brown was the devil incarnate, which left them all the more puzzled at the Northern outpouring of grief and mourning in response to his execution. Hester Davis concluded that the "Tolling of Bells, firing minute guns, sermons, prayer meetings and incendiary speeches" in the North "are not the feeling of the majority." That even a small segment of Northerners empathized with Brown proved problematic for Southern whites, though. White border Southerners had traditionally counted on a conservative consensus within the Union to buttress the peculiar institution, but now a mounting portion of the North seemed untrustworthy. Whereas white border Southerners usually exhibited a sober approach to sectional disputes, the Harpers Ferry incident and the Northern response to Brown's death led some into a delirium from which they never recovered.[37]

In the aftermath of Brown's execution, most white border Southerners yearned for a return to normalcy; unfortunately, state and national elections loomed, which meant politicians, editors, and party hacks kept the Harpers Ferry affair before the public eye. Maryland Democrats, for instance, met in December 1859 and affirmed the party's "devotion to the institution guarantied to us by the constitution, and their reprobation of the fanatical demonstrations at the North, so clearly pointing, as they do, to a determined purpose to destroy our domestic institutions, and with them the constitution and the Union."[38] Secession had entered the Border South's political lexicon, and the slim probability of non-Democrats aligning with Republicans vanished. Some border Southerners, like Henry Winter Davis of Maryland, James O. Broadhead and Charles Gibson of Missouri, and the Blair family, held on to the delusion that Edward Bates could head an opposition alliance between Republicans and former Whigs.[39] The Bates fantasy faced increasing resistance from Border South pundits, though. A Missouri editor warned that the people of the state "will never walk into the net so gracefully set, by Greely [sic] in the North, and Bates in the South."[40]

Border South Unionists hoping to combat the sectional upswing unleashed by Brown's raid realized the difficult task at hand when Congress assembled on December 5, 1859. Of the thirty-four Border South senators and representatives, 62 percent were Democrats and 35 percent belonged to the opposition bloc of former Whigs and Americans. Only one Border South congressman, Frank Blair Jr., represented the Republicans, but he had not taken his seat because of disputed election returns.[41] Border South Democrats in the Thirty-Sixth Congress ranged across a broad political spectrum, from secessionist sympathizers to unadulterated Unionists. Representatives Henry C. Burnett of Kentucky and John B. Clark of Missouri often sounded like Deep South fire-eaters when on the stump; after the commencement of the Civil War, the House expelled both men, who eventually rendered their services to the Confederate government. Senator James A. Pearce of Maryland and Missouri representative Thomas L. Anderson, on the other hand, each remained firmly committed to the Union during the sectional crisis.[42] Most Border South Democrats in this session fell somewhere between these two poles of persuasion. Though smaller, the non-Democratic bloc included several eminent statesmen who exercised a great deal of political clout. Chief among these were Kentucky senator Crittenden and Maryland congressmen Davis and J. Morrison Harris. Border South Democrats outnumbered the Opposition three and a half to one in the Senate, a sign of the ascendancy of the Democratic Party in the region's state legislatures, who at the time elected U.S. senators. Many Border South Democrats looked to Vice President John C. Breckinridge of Kentucky for leadership. Though not a senator, Breckinridge presided over the upper chamber and played an active role during this session of Congress.[43]

In the Thirty-Sixth Congress, Democrats held an overall majority in the Senate, but no party controlled the House. Republicans and Democrats claimed nearly nine-tenths of the seats in the House, but neither organization carried the requisite majority needed to choose a Speaker. This meant both organizations would need to court members of the Opposition bloc in order to elect a Speaker of their choosing. Of the twenty-nine representatives who identified with the Opposition, twenty-three came from the South, and of that number ten hailed from the Border South.[44] Thus, border Southerners made up around 37 percent of the total Opposition coalition in the House. The two dominant parties highly prized these influential votes because they would determine who held sway in the lower house of Congress. The speakership contest once again placed border Southerners in the thick of the sectional stress that threatened to destroy the republic.

The tense atmosphere on Capitol Hill proved anything but conducive to the normal Border South brand of politics that depended on moderation, conciliation, and composure. The House witnessed a protracted struggle over the election of a Speaker, a routine that rarely took more than a few meetings to settle. During this session, though, the balloting for Speaker lasted through forty-four votes and choked the business of the government to a halt. Not until February 1, 1860, almost two months after convening, did the opposing camps settle on a presiding officer. During the interim tempers flared as congressmen traded insults, challenged one another to duels, and brandished pistols in the House Chamber. The sergeant at arms found it nearly impossible to separate the irritable congressmen, whose quarrelsome attitudes excited rowdy observers in the galleries. Iowa senator James Grimes remarked that on both sides of the aisle members "are mostly armed with deadly weapons, and it is said that the friends of each are armed in the galleries."[45]

The House tallied its first vote for Speaker on the opening day of the session. Border South congressmen scattered their votes among Democrat Thomas Bocock and former Whig Alexander Boteler, both from Virginia, and Oppositionist John Gilmer of North Carolina. None of the candidates the Republicans put forward received a single vote form the Border South, an ominous sign for the party that held a plurality and needed swing votes from the Opposition group called the South Americans.[46] After recording the vote, Missouri Democrat John B. Clark fired a salvo aimed directly at the Republicans. Clark, who in 1858 had run unopposed in Missouri's Third Congressional District, submitted a resolution stipulating that no congressman who either endorsed or recommended Hinton R. Helper's book *The Impending Crisis of the South: How to Meet It* should occupy the Speaker's chair. Clark's resolution, laden with sectional overtones, elicited a mixture of applause and hisses from the partisans in the galleries. North Carolina's Hinton Helper had in 1857 published the book, which blamed slavery for Southern backwardness and the South's inability to keep pace with the free states. "Slavery lies at the root of all the shame, poverty, ignorance, tyranny and imbecility of the South; slavery must be thoroughly eradicated; let this be done, and a glorious future will await us," Helper predicted. White Southerners, so dependent on slavery for social, economic, and racial stability, considered Helper the ultimate sectional traitor. Many Republicans, however, erroneously believed Helper voiced the prevailing sentiment of poor whites in the South and considered him an ally. Over sixty House Republicans had endorsed the book and signed a letter dated March 9, 1859, that outlined a program for abolishing slavery in the South. John Sherman of Ohio, the Republicans' top choice for Speaker, had affixed his signature to the document without carefully reading the book, which cost him dearly. On the heels of the Harpers Ferry raid, Southern congressmen classified all the Republican signatories as dangerous fanatics on par with Brown. Clark's resolution signaled that border Southerners would play no part in helping the Republicans elect a Speaker who sanctioned upending slavery in the South.[47]

Clark cloaked his attack on the Republicans in the language of Border South moderation. He wished to have someone preside over the House who would respect the Constitution and show impartiality to both sections. The Constitution, Clark maintained, protected slavery, and its ultimate fate should remain in the hands of white Southerners rather than Northern abolitionists. "Whether it is sinful to hold slaves, whether slavery is a plague and a loss, and whether it will affect our future destiny, is our own business," Clark professed. "We suffer for that, and not they." The Missourian worried that Republicans would not respect the American political tradition of compromise and begged them not to "destroy the conservative sentiment—that great element which keeps the stars and stripes floating this day over this Capitol" by insisting on a Speaker who had approved of Helper's book.[48]

Clark's resolution offers a window into the unique Border South approach to the deepening sectional divide. Despite his fire-eating proclivities, Clark understood that most of his Missouri constituents eagerly sought a moderate solution to the sectional crisis. Thus, he carefully crafted his speech as a measured plea for the perseverance of the Union. Yet it also contained a veiled ultimatum to the Republicans, which freighted the speech with a sharp edge that Border South political rhetoric normally lacked. White Southerners alone were responsible for managing and making decisions about slavery's fate; he refused to hand such an important responsibility over to his political enemies. If Republicans gained control of the government, it would "raise a storm throughout this Union" and "put brother against brother, father against son." Disunion, Clark implied, would be preferable to living under the reign of Republicans. The speech and resolution revealed that Brown's raid widened the crack in the levee that white border Southerners had built to keep sectional radicalism confined to extremists in the North and the Lower South. Kentucky congressman John White Stevenson perceptively comprehended the political repercussions of Brown's raid and Clark's resolution. "It is not to be disguised that we are approaching a crisis pregnant with immense & momentous results," Stevenson admitted. "It will require clear heads & patriotic hearts—to keep together."[49]

House Republicans ignored Clark's admonition and pushed for Sherman's election. Border South representatives joined with other Southern congressmen and obstinately refused to vote for Sherman or any other Republican. Not until the twenty-fifth ballot, nearly a month into the session, did some border Southerners direct their votes toward a Northern candidate for Speaker, Democrat John McClernand of Illinois. Partisan wrangling, however, prevented the South Americans and Northern Democrats from settling on a candidate who could capture enough votes to defeat the Republicans. The impasse afforded ample opportunity for grandstanding, and some Border South moderates worried that fire-eaters in the House were using the moment to register pleas for Southern independence. A South Carolinian, "tired of guarding against secret attacks" from the likes of John Browns and Hinton Helpers, considered the speakership contest a flashpoint that would awaken the entire South to the dangers of the Union. A Georgian calculated that every member from the fifteen slaveholding states, excluding two Tennessee congressmen, condoned disunion as a remedy if the Republicans elected Sherman.[50]

Lower South radicals overestimated the fire-eating vigor of their Border South colleagues in the House, though. Most Border South congressmen reflected the conservative impulse of their constituency and strove for a solution that would preserve the Union, a marked contrast to Southern hotheads who eclipsed the boundaries of civil discourse with their verbal denunciations of the Republicans. "The Republicans keep mum—they regard that there is wisdom in silence—& I agree with them. I wish that some of our Southern friends would practice more of the maxim," Stevenson scoffed. A

Missourian likewise complained about the bellicosity of Southern radicals in Congress who damaged sectional amity with their diatribes against the Republicans. "The 'nigger,' John Brown, Helpers [*sic*] book, and the 'irrepressible conflict' are literally worn to tatters, without the slightest visible impression upon the 'Black Republican' ranks," George Caleb Bingham observed. Border South congressmen rejected the Republican candidate, but they also resisted being pushed down the path to disunion. Even though secession sentiment had crept into the borderland, most Border South politicians continued to bank on proslavery Unionism.[51]

After weeks of squabbling, the Republicans finally jettisoned Sherman and rallied behind William Pennington of New Jersey, a congressional newcomer who had not signed the endorsement of Helper's book. Southerners deemed Pennington guilty by association, however, and scattered their votes on various Democrats or Opposition men. Davis, a three-term American Party congressman from Baltimore known for his fiery temper and insatiable political ambition, had throughout the session closeted with the Republicans and urged them to drop Sherman for someone less offensive to Southerners. The substitution of Pennington for Sherman provided Davis with a pretext to modify his vote. On January 31, Davis broke ranks and switched his vote from the American candidate to the Republican Pennington. Later that day New York Know Nothing George Briggs promised to follow Davis's lead if the Marylander stood firm behind Pennington. Davis reassured Briggs of his commitment, and on February 1 the two Know Nothings cast the deciding votes for Pennington, who now had the requisite majority to become Speaker. Davis's shift stood in stark contrast to the rest of the Border South congressional delegation, all of whom held fast to their repugnance for the Republicans and cast votes for Gilmer or McClernand on the final ballot.[52]

Southern congressmen redirected their barrage of ridicule from the Republicans toward Davis for his defection. William Barksdale of Mississippi laid bare his contempt for Davis by asking for the official record of Congress to show that "the Representative of a slaveholding constituency . . . will be responsible for the election of the candidate of the Republican party as Speaker of this House." In his own state of Maryland, outraged whites hanged Davis in effigy, and the House of Delegates voted sixty-two to one to censure the Baltimore congressman for his apostasy. Even his own party organ in Baltimore predicted that Davis's alliance with the Republicans effectively ended his political career in the Old Line State. Davis had clearly overstepped the boundaries of Border South political decorum by assisting the Republicans during the speakership contest. Davis's close friend Samuel F. Du Pont of Delaware tried to soothe the Marylander, who faced social ostracism from other Southern members of Congress, in the aftermath of the vote. He suggested that other South Americans "had not the moral pluck to keep you from standing alone in this matter," and reminded Davis that although partisans would excoriate him, "Clay & [Daniel] Webster had for long times to stand much more."[53]

Davis's desertion of his fellow border Southerners should not distort the Border South's overall reaction to the speakership contest. The rest of the Border South delegation toed the Southern line and refused to submit to the antislavery Republicans, whom they viewed as dangerous agitators. White border Southerners thought along the same lines as a Virginian who called the Republicans "tadpole abolitionists [who] must in time become the genuine reptile." Yet white border Southerners also eschewed the radicalism of fire-eaters just as readily as they did the Republicans. Frustrated by the base demagoguery of Southern radicals during the speakership contest, George Pattison of Missouri commented that "there is a class of Southern fanatics, who would have been equally violent defenders of abolitionism had they been born in New England." Most Missouri Democrats, he continued, "are of course the conservative portion of the people, who deplore the fanatical agitation of the slavery subject, particularly in Congress."[54]

Both the Harpers Ferry raid and the speakership contest demonstrated that even though sectional radicalism had become a factor in the Border South's political culture, moderation remained the region's watchword. Firebrands who thought along the same lines as Clark or Davis existed, but most white borderites fell somewhere in between. "I believe there is conservatism enough in our union to prevent a dissolution—the times a short time ago looked somewhat alarming, but now the clouds are passing away & the political sky is clearing up," a Kentuckian remarked in the midst of the speakership contest.[55] Conservative politicians in the Border South harbored a less sanguine view than this optimistic Kentuckian, for they had learned firsthand the mutable nature of Unionism in the region. Cooler heads eventually prevailed and restraint once again became ascendant, but the political leanings of the region's vital center tottered in the balance. Another explosive event could very well imperil white border Southerners' preference for moderation, and the fast-approaching presidential election augured a political showdown on a grander scale than the speakership contest. As each organization geared up for the presidential election, conservatives worried about the consequences of another Republican victory.

Early in 1860, the major political parties remained in a great deal of flux. The Democrats limped toward the election of 1860 because of intraparty squabbles about slavery's place in the American territories. One wing of the party lined up behind Stephen Douglas and popular sovereignty, while many Southern Democrats had lost confidence in the Little Giant and his territorial panacea. Several Southern Democrats considered Douglas's repudiation of Kansas's proslavery Lecompton Constitution an unpardonable sin and looked for any possible means to thwart his presidential aspirations. In the wake of Lecompton's defeat, many of these Southern Democrats dismissed popular sovereignty as an antislavery Trojan horse and instead called for the party to affirm the Supreme Court's 1857 *Dred Scott* decision, which declared that Congress had no right to restrict the spread of slavery into the territories.[56]

Border South Democrats uncomfortably occupied the fault line between the party's two wings. A Kentuckian correctly described the Democracy as "split all to peices [*sic*]" in the Border South. Democratic alignments throughout the Border South depended on a vast assortment of variables, from patronage connections to local political issues, especially in urban centers like Baltimore and Saint Louis. Influential Border South Democrats, including Maryland's Reverdy Johnson and *St. Louis Daily Missouri Republican* editor Nathaniel Paschall, championed Douglas for the party's presidential nomination. Douglasites in the borderland still regarded popular sovereignty as "the most able defense of our great Southern Institution, against Black Republicanism." For many Border South Democrats, popular sovereignty and the candidacy of Douglas represented a moderate approach to the territorial issue that aligned with proslavery Unionism. "The conservative men of this Nation need a leader," a Missourian wrote Douglas, "one bold & fearless, not caring for the fire-eaters North or South."[57]

Douglas could count plenty of detractors in the Border South as well, which underscores the balkanized nature of the region and the party. Vice President Breckinridge and senators James S. Green and Trusten Polk of Missouri were a festering thorn in the Little Giant's side, and the Missouri duo missed no opportunity to disparage Douglas and popular sovereignty. Green complained that popular sovereignty left open the possibility that a territorial legislature might prohibit slavery, a direct contravention to the *Dred Scott* decision. "We ought to banish this question now and forever; we ought to hush these unnecessary issues on the subject of 'squatter' or 'popular' sovereignty," Green howled on the Senate floor. "We must strictly adhere to the decision of the Supreme Court. It is our only safety." Douglasites complained that the attacks from Green and other Southern Democrats who misrepresented the conservative nature of popular sovereignty would ensure the party's defeat in the upcoming election. The Little Giant's critics, on the other hand, smelled blood. "I, for one, am for skinning and quartering this Demagogue," one of Buchanan's associates admitted. "We must drive him from the Party or cut him in two with a platform [at the upcoming national convention]." Levi K. Bowen discerned a powerful hatred of Douglas in Maryland due to "a strong southern sentiment which regards him as unsound and dangerous," while a Missourian looked forward to derailing the Little Giant's bid for the presidency to demonstrate "that we desire hereafter not to be controlled by 'Northern Men, with Southern principles.' "[58]

Border South conservatives not affiliated with the Democrats began exploring their alternatives in early 1860. The tempestuous speakership contest convinced many former Whigs and Americans that they must create their own political organization independent of the Republicans and Democrats. A New Jersey politico claimed that members of the American Party across the North wanted "an independent Organisation [sic] all over the Union, and are looking with great anxiety to the brethren of the South, particularly to the South American members of Congress, who, it is believed have it in their power to inaugurate a great Union Party which will control the destinies of the Nation." White border Southerners served as the linchpin and power base of this nascent organization. Kentucky senator Crittenden became the new party's nominal leader, and he relied on former Whigs Kennedy of Maryland, Joseph P. Comegys of Delaware, Leslie Combs and Laban Moore of Kentucky, Missourians Hamilton Gamble and James S. Rollins, and Alexander Boteler and William C. Rives of Virginia to launch the movement. Crittenden asked Kennedy to draft an address in January 1860 that would set forth the principles of the freshly christened Constitutional Union Party. The party wished to adopt a nebulous platform that stood by the Constitution and the Union and turned back the clock to the "old times before slavery became the controlling ingredient in our politics." Delaware's George Fisher felt the new organization "will exactly suit our latitude" if it positioned itself as an alternative to the "ultra fire eating disunion democracy upon one hand and the Republican fanatics upon the other."[59]

No other political entity captured the Border South's political mentality like the Constitutional Union Party. The organization hoped its appeals to moderation and devotion to the Constitution would place it above the dangerous partisanship that had been the catalyst for extremism in the separate sections. Constitutional Unionists found their inspiration in bygone politicians such as George Washington, Henry Clay, and Daniel Webster, all symbols of nationalism triumphing over sectionalism. Moderates hoped their "new party—constitutional and comprehensive—anti-all-the-isms" would vie with the Douglas Democrats for conservative votes across the nation. Some Constitutional Unionists even imagined they could convert Douglas Democrats to their standard. "If we can revive the Old Whig spirit and unite with the large body of people who detest both of the predominant parties," Kennedy contemplated, "we may disappoint them and put a sound old fashioned statesman to the Presidency."[60] Kennedy certainly conjured up the image of Clay when he described his ideal candidate. But the very qualities these conservatives considered assets—impartiality, a nationalistic mind-set, and an evasive stance on slavery in the territories—in time emerged as liabilities. Despite their best efforts, the Constitutional Unionists and white border Southerners found it impossible to untangle partisanship from sectionalism; likewise, their reluctance to take a stand on burning issues only plunged the party and the region deeper into the conflict as time progressed. Border South conservatives who peered to the past for solutions as had Edward Bates before Brown's raid could not derail the political locomotive that chugged toward disaster in 1860.

The long shadow of Harpers Ferry ruined the already narrow prospects of the Republicans in the Border South. With the Constitutional Unionists blazing an independent course, Republicans grasped that they could attract few votes from white border Southerners. A few borderland Oppositionists warned their colleagues that a third party stood no chance of success and continued to insist that fusion with the Republicans would best foil the Democrats in the upcoming election. While working with the Republicans to elect a Speaker, Davis also made inquiries about the possibility of an electoral combination between the antislavery party and South Americans. Davis advised the Republicans to run an Old Whig from the Border South—preferably Bates—in order to capture the region's sizable moderate vote. The collective votes of Republicans, former Whigs, and Americans presented a much more powerful challenge to the Democrats than did an independent Opposition Party, Davis reasoned. He bitterly dismissed Crittenden's third-party movement as a "preposterous squad of antiques" that would split the presidential vote and hand the election to the Democrats.[61]

Some former Whigs, Americans, and Republicans in Missouri shared Davis's outlook in early 1860. The group held a convention in Jefferson City in late February, nominated Bates for the presidency, and constructed a vague platform that assailed "the systematic reopening and dangerous agitation of the slavery question by ultra political leaders" but took no particular stance on slavery's place in the territories. Rather, it merely expressed opposition to Buchanan's endorsement of the Lecompton Constitution. A Democrat quipped that the delegates "fearing to commit their candidate to any kind of a platform had to deal in generalities—So of course they said nothing of interest to any one!" Herein lay the dilemma for any Border South fusion of Republicans and Americans: most white border Southerners could not swallow a platform that expressly forbade the expansion of slavery into the territories, while Northern Republicans rightly refused to abandon their bedrock principle. Prior to the Jefferson City meeting, Bates confirmed this quandary when he acknowledged that many former Whigs and Americans in Missouri "go the length of saying that the[y] are anxious to support me, but cant [*sic*] do it if the 'Black' Republicans support me." White border Southerners continued to equate Republicanism with the radicalism of Brown, which effectively torpedoed a region-wide fusion movement in opposition to the Democrats.[62]

The tepid platform of the Missouri Opposition movement more closely resembled the doctrine of the Constitutional Unionists than the Republican Party. The delegates to the Jefferson City convention tried to occupy the middle ground, but Bates's clumsy handling of the nomination frustrated their plan. Northeastern Republicans, looking forward to the party's upcoming national convention, demanded that Bates outline his attitude toward slavery and the territories before they offered him any support. The public letter he had written in 1859—a model of the Border South's cautious approach to the sectional crisis—was too ambiguous for sincere Republicans. The Missourian initially resisted issuing a public exposition on slavery for fear that it might lead to "dissension, & possibly disruption among those who, for the general good, ought to be friends." Bates, however, eventually broke his public silence and produced a letter in which he explicitly declared his opposition to the extension of slavery into the territories, his aversion to the *Dred Scott* ruling, and his preference for the colonization of free blacks. Although he had not substantially altered his conservative approach to slavery, it was now no longer confined to private conversation or the confidential pages of his diary. Once his inner thoughts about the restriction of slavery went public, the already listless American-Republican fusion movement melted away in Missouri. "Mr. Bates has cut his throat politically, at least in all the southern states," one Missourian confessed, while a Maryland conservative complained that "his opinions are too Northern & Eastern for us." A Republican in Indiana admitted that "not a man in his right mind would pretend to think that he [Bates] could carry his own State while standing on the Republican Platform." Aside from the followers of Frank Blair Jr. in Saint

Louis, the rest of the Missouri fusion movement eventually abandoned the Republicans and joined up with either the Constitutional Unionists or the Douglas Democrats. The movement for South American collaboration with Republicans had steadily lost traction ever since Brown's raid. Bates's decision to endorse the Republican's free-soil philosophy finished off what Harpers Ferry and the speakership contest had started.[63]

As the national party conventions approached in the spring of 1860, Border South moderates momentarily relaxed. Harpers Ferry had temporarily unleashed a brand of extremism normally foreign to the Border South, but conservatives had once again regained the upper hand. Those moderates could not neglect that the timing of Brown's incursion nearly proved disastrous. The raid, followed so closely by the speakership contest and the evolving presidential campaign, had injected additional venom into the already toxic national political conversation. Most Americans now considered the election of 1860 an apocalyptic event. The disparate coalitions prepared for battle, fully cognizant that many people tied the destiny of the republic to the upcoming presidential contest. Thus, conservatives knew they could not rest on their laurels or let down their guard. Most agreed with the prognosis of a Kentuckian: "We are now a divided people—bad men have the control in most of [the] so called free States—they have passed offensive laws [and] ... they disregard the decision of the Courts. All of these troubles grow out of the slavery question—it must be settled and agitation stopped—or separation must ensue."[64] At any moment, extremists might once again jeopardize the region's Unionist impulse, a threatening sign for the health of the republic. The Border South represented an integral part of the nation's political middle ground, but Brown's raid and its reverberations demonstrated how border Southerners—who traditionally offered a voice of reason in sectional disputes—had become quite sensitive to perceived aggression from extremists. The people of the Border South looked ahead to 1860 and braced themselves for yet another momentous political clash.

CHAPTER THREE

The Wolf Is Really upon Us Now

The Presidential Race, April–November 1860

The speakership contest of 1859–60 paralyzed Congress for two long months. While senators impatiently waited for the organization of the House, Virginia's James M. Mason pressed for a congressional investigation of the Harpers Ferry raid, which opened an extended debate about slavery, Republicanism, and the antislavery movement on the floor of the upper chamber. Senators exchanged unsavory recriminations and hurled insults at one another, baldly exposing the fissures within the factious Democratic Party. Party discipline broke down, and during the debates pro- and anti-Douglas Democrats squabbled as much as proslavery and antislavery forces. All the while, Senator James Asheton Bayard of Delaware sat uncomfortably at his desk and silently watched as the slavery issue threatened to tear apart the Union and his beloved Democratic Party. Bayard privately confided that "there never was a time, when the harmony & unity of the Democratic Party was so essential to the preservation of the Union."[1]

In spite of his hand-wringing about Democratic discord, the sixty-year-old Bayard had been partly responsible for the rupture within the organization. He found Stephen A. Douglas's territorial panacea of popular sovereignty particularly repugnant because, under the Little Giant's formula, all Americans, slaveholder and nonslaveholder alike, might not enjoy equal access to the territories. Moreover, Bayard considered popular sovereignty a crack in the edifice of proslavery Unionism that would bring about slavery's eventual destruction. Bayard in 1856 worked in collusion with Judah Benjamin and John Slidell of Louisiana and Jesse Bright of Indiana to block Douglas's presidential aspirations. The cabal won the battle against Douglas in 1856, but the war within the party continued. Douglas's rift with President James Buchanan over Kansas's Lecompton Constitution exacerbated intraparty divisions on the national and local levels. In Delaware the Democracy split into two camps, with Bayard and the state's lone congressman, William Whiteley, supporting Buchanan and influential wire-puller Samuel Townsend advancing the cause of Douglas. Willard Saulsbury, Delaware's junior senator, a lukewarm supporter of the Little Giant, and Bayard's rival for control of the state party, distanced himself from Douglas as the presidential election neared.

Townsend in early 1860 managed to secure a set of resolutions at a Democratic meeting in New Castle County that advocated a rapprochement between the Buchanan and Douglas wings in Delaware in order to "help stay the action of all fanatics, from whatever quarter, who seek to weaken the bonds of Union in these United States of America." He hoped a united Delaware Democracy would support Douglas for the presidency because the Little Giant's national appeal gave the party the best chance of defeating the despised Republicans.[2]

Cognizant of the dangers of a split in the Democratic Party, neither camp was willing to find some middle ground. Bayard saw in Townsend's plea for reconciliation subterfuge; he believed his adversary would attempt to foist popular sovereignty on the Delaware Democracy and rebuffed his offer. "We will not any longer put up with the tyranny of administration men," Townsend fumed once he learned of Bayard's intransigence. "We was willing if we could do so, without sacrafice [*sic*] of principles, [to] unite with them to fight against Republicans, but we find we cannot do so." Bayard, on the other hand, had developed the impression that little difference existed "between western & north western Democrats & Republicans" and thus could not accept Townsend's plan to heal Democratic divisions within the state. If he supported Douglas and popular sovereignty, Bayard would tacitly endorse the destruction of slavery. In his mind, popular sovereignty would confine slavery to the fifteen slaveholding states and speed the pace of its demise along the border. "I am sick of Del politics & mean to stand above them," Bayard confessed to his son. He promised to exert all his energy "to see that the State does not become abolitionized or squatter-sovereignized."[3]

The divisions in the Delaware Democracy illuminate several of the problems white border Southerners confronted as the presidential election of 1860 neared. Despite the Border South's strong conservative tradition, the sectional controversy disrupted the harmony of the Democratic Party. Townsend felt that intraparty differences were so great in Delaware that Bayard and his followers would rather "see the opposition elected than a popular sovereignty Democrat."[4] Similar tensions existed within the Democratic Party in the other three Border South states. The rift in the Democracy, along with the establishment of the Constitutional Union Party in early 1860, threatened to break the nation's moderate voting bloc into fragmented pieces. Douglasites, anti-Douglas Democrats, and Constitutional Unionists competed with one another to capture the vital center of the Border South electorate and, in the process, each organization created dissension among moderate voters at a point when centrists desperately needed cooperation to keep sectional radicals at bay. A divided vote in the overwhelmingly conservative Border South actually increased the likelihood that the Republicans would win the presidency and that Lower South fire-eaters would hatch their scheme of secession, yet inflexible partisans like Bayard remained prisoners to political battles of the 1850s and refused to make concessions to their erstwhile allies. A mix of political principle, petty jealousy, and rigid superciliousness came to a head in 1860; not until after the election returns had been counted would some white border Southerners understand the full scope of the dilemma in which they were mired. Blinded by previous experiences, the high stakes of the presidential election, and their own misguided though genuine expectations of success, Border South moderates emerged from the canvass confronting a political landscape that they had desperately struggled to elude.

Bayard's hostility toward popular sovereignty also illustrates that most white border Southerners would only cast their votes for a candidate whom they regarded as safe on the question of slavery. Proslavery Unionism conditioned how white borderites, even nonslaveholders like Bayard, viewed each candidate's record and each party's platform. The intractable position of Border South partisans on the slavery issue during the election of 1860 proved ominous for the nation's political future. If tiny Delaware, with fewer than 1,800 enslaved persons, endorsed the obstinate position of Bayard, what about the rest of the South? Democrats and Constitutional Unionists jockeyed to position themselves as the best guardians of slavery and in the process they preyed on the fears of white border Southerners, suggesting that a Republican triumph would encourage an endless cascade of slave rebellions and runaways. A Republican victory would doubtlessly unleash radical forces in the North and the South and force white border Southerners to make an excruciating choice between Union and secession. The presidential canvass between April and November 1860, from the national party conventions to Election Day, reveals the depth of the Border South's dilemma: white border Southerners went to great lengths to preserve both the Union and slavery, but their course ironically unleashed forces that undermined both of these precious institutions.[5]

BASED ON THEIR careful scrutiny of the presidential election of 1856, political managers of all three major organizations understood that the border states would play a decisive role in the election of 1860. In 1856 the Democrats, yet unsullied by doctrinal disagreements on slavery's extension, defeated the nascent Republicans and the moribund American Party by carrying fourteen slave states, along with Pennsylvania, New Jersey, Indiana, and Illinois.

The Democrats won Delaware, Kentucky, and Missouri, while Maryland cast its electoral votes for American candidate Millard Fillmore. The narrow margin of the Democracy's victory in Kentucky and the loss in Maryland signaled a tough fight ahead in these traditional Whig strongholds, and the split in the Democratic Party placed the more comfortable victories in Delaware and Maryland in jeopardy as 1860 approached. Constitutional Unionists, Democrats, and Republicans all expended abundant energy in the borderland during the canvass, and each organization seriously considered candidates from the region to strengthen their respective chances with Border South voters. The Republicans, aware that nearly every white Southerner scorned their antislavery program, focused their canvass on the Lower North, while the Democrats and Constitutional Unionists hoped to capture all of the border states.[6]

Back in 1856 the Democrats had scheduled their 1860 national convention to meet in Charleston, South Carolina, the cradle of radical Southern political thought. Democrats from across the South hoped to scuttle Douglas's candidacy and his principle of popular sovereignty in one fell swoop at Charleston. Southern hardliners wanted a platform that affirmed the *Dred Scott* decision, which had secured a foothold for slavery in all of the territories, and hungered for a candidate who would acquiesce to such a territorial stance. Douglas backers knew that a tough fight awaited them in South Carolina, and as late as March 1860 some Douglasites even floated the impracticable suggestion to change the venue from Charleston to the more hospitable city of Baltimore.[7]

The Border South Democracy suffered from backbiting, sharp disagreements on policy, and divided loyalty to each wing of the discordant national organization, which resulted in a great deal of confusion on the eve of the Charleston meeting. The Border South Democracy represented a microcosm of the national party, and the problems borderland Democrats confronted illustrate how the unfolding presidential canvass propelled a region that preferred impartiality on sectional questions toward a point where the evasion of important decisions no longer sufficed.

Delaware's delegation to Charleston included Bayard and Whiteley, both earnest opponents of Douglas and popular sovereignty. Bayard privately wished for Robert M. T. Hunter of Virginia to secure the party's nomination, but figured that the Douglas opposition would likely coalesce on Vice President John C. Breckinridge. Although concerned about Breckinridge's youth and ambition, Bayard still considered the Kentuckian a better option than Douglas. Both Breckinridge and Hunter favored the ultra-Southern position on slavery in the territories, which pleased Bayard and his Delaware follow-ers.[8] Although the Delaware Democratic Convention had cast Douglas sup-porter Samuel Townsend aside when it named its slate of delegates, the herald of the Little Giant continued to make his presence felt. Townsend pressed delegate Willard Saulsbury to support Douglas and took credit for the *Wilm-ington Delaware Inquirer's* endorsement of the Illinois Democrat. Saulsbury and his brothers, whose reputation for graft and corruption preceded them, had built an impressive Democratic machine in Sussex County, and Bayard feared that Townsend might bring the easily swayed junior senator into the Douglas camp. Bayard, who served on the Charleston Convention's platform committee, planned to negate Townsend's influence and whip the rest of the state's delegation into line with his own views.[9]

Divisions in the Kentucky Democracy went beyond territorial policy. As early as 1858 the Democratic opponents of Douglas had begun to consider candidates who could supplant the Little Giant on the 1860 ticket. Two such aspirants—Breckinridge and James Guthrie, former secretary of the treasury under Franklin Pierce and current president of the Louisville and Nashville Railroad—hailed from the Bluegrass State. Guthrie's backers, including the *Louisville Daily Courier,* played up the fact that he was not associated with the Buchanan administration, which had been tarnished by the Lecompton controversy and charges of venality, and boasted of his moderate political cre-dentials. Some Kentucky Democrats, especially Douglasites, worried that the candidacy of two native sons generated petty jealousies and further strained party harmony in the state. The Kentucky Democratic Convention, which Breckinridge supporters complained had been packed with Guthrie devotees by unseemly methods, requested that the state's delegates to Charleston cast their votes for Guthrie and produced a majority platform with a plank that repudiated popular sovereignty. Some observers believed that most white Kentuckians really preferred Breckinridge or Douglas and assumed the state's delegates to Charleston would vote for Guthrie on the first ballot and then abandon him for their favorite candidate. Thus, the Kentucky delegation showed up in Charleston without a concrete plan of action in place.[10]

Cleavages within the Democratic Party affected the organization in Mary-land as well. Friends of Buchanan occupied influential leadership positions within the Maryland Democracy and controlled party machinery in the state, yet the powerful Reverdy Johnson, a former Whig who now headed the state's Douglas wing, made matters difficult for the opponents of popular sov-ereignty.[11] Johnson had in 1859 anonymously composed a lengthy pamphlet in which he used unequivocal proslavery Unionist logic to argue that popular sovereignty represented the best safeguard to Southern rights. Johnson maintained that the Harpers Ferry raid and the startling growth of the Republican Party made Democratic harmony a necessity, and he beseeched his fellow Democrats to set aside their grievances and nominate Douglas at Charleston. If the party continued down its destructive path, it would ensure a Republican victory in 1860. "The success of the Republicans will be a calamity, it is feared, beyond remedy, perpetual and fatal," Johnson estimated, and in that event slavery would surely meet its doom.[12] Johnson's philippic underscored the resonance and importance of proslavery Unionism with Border South voters, and as the campaign evolved, the other major political organizations in the borderland attempted to outflank their opponents and position themselves as the superlative wardens of slavery, though in a more moderate tone than most Lower South proslavery defenders. Johnson's pamphlet also tapped into the prevailing paranoia among white border Southerners about the motives and intentions of the Republicans. The moderate approach of white border Southerners, which had endured an onslaught by fire-eaters after John Brown's raid, would face another stern test should the Republicans triumph, Johnson warned.[13]

Johnson's appeal for Democratic unity went unheeded in the Old Line State. The Democratic-controlled legislature in March 1860 reelected James A. Pearce, a Buchanan Democrat, to the United States Senate. Pearce normally exercised a moderate political style, but administration men viewed his reelection as a victory over the Douglas forces.[14] The Maryland Democratic Convention met later that month and issued a platform that highlighted the divisions that plagued the party in the Border South. The first resolution proclaimed that the people of Maryland "are most vitally interested in the protection of slave property and in the faithful observance of all the guaranties of the federal constitution" and labeled antislavery agitation "wicked and treasonable." The convention also promised to "unite with our Southern brethren in asserting and maintaining our constitutional rights at every hazard and to the last extremity." The third and fourth resolutions, conversely, called for adherence to the Democratic platform of 1856, which included popular sovereignty as its centerpiece. The strongly worded first two resolutions revealed that Buchanan men controlled the convention, but a surprised Johnson informed Douglas that ten of the state's sixteen delegates to Charleston expressed some measure of kindliness toward the Little Giant.[15] Douglasites advised their preferred candidate that in order to curry favor with the Maryland delegates and voters, he must appear "a friend to the rights of the South—& not opposed to slavery." One Douglas follower engineered the selection of one of western Maryland's largest slaveholders to the Charleston Convention because he believed his power and prestige—both intimately tied to his ownership of enslaved persons—would "carry more weight" with voters in that section of the state.[16] Thus, even in an area with a sparse slave population like western Maryland, the peculiar institution had a notable bearing on politics. Like the Kentuckians, the Maryland delegates arrived in Charleston fully cognizant of the dangers of Democratic discord, but with no clear idea about how to proceed.

After a decade of infighting between Thomas Hart Benton's free-soil faction and Claiborne Fox Jackson's proslavery clique, the Missouri Democracy was accustomed to internal divisions. Jackson, William B. Napton, and David Rice Atchison had in 1856 wrested control of the state party away from the Bentonites, some of whom had defected to Frank Blair Jr.'s Republican machine, but Douglas could still count a large contingent of supporters in Missouri. Douglasites in Missouri worried that Jackson's approach too closely resembled the radicalism of Lower South fire-eaters, yet they despised the antislavery tenets of the Republicans.[17] "I would not trust one of them [Republicans] in my meat house after dark," a Douglas follower quipped, "much less on the slavery question." Douglas men in Missouri strongly believed in popular sovereignty as the best alternative to preserve the Union with slavery intact. The upcoming gubernatorial contest, slated for August, further exacerbated the rift in the state Democratic organization, which opened its state convention in April. "Our state, and especially the Democratic party, are in a state of indescribable confusion, and the man who escapes being dashed away upon the breakers upon the right or the left will be truly fortunate," Waldo P. Johnson observed.[18]

After three days of deliberation, the Missouri Democratic Convention adopted a decidedly pro-Southern platform that declared neither Congress nor a territorial government could abolish slavery in the territories, recommended the annexation of Cuba, blamed the Republicans for Harpers Ferry, and dismissed Northern personal liberty laws as unconstitutional and "revolutionary in their effect." Despite protests from the Douglas wing, the delegates selected Jackson as the party's gubernatorial candidate. One of Jackson's cronies considered his nomination a decided victory over the Douglasites that would "blot out the base insinuation that Missouri is preparing to desert her Southern Sisters."[19]

The selection of delegates to the Charleston Convention led to more bickering about whether to yoke the emissaries to the national meeting with voting instructions for the party's presidential nominee. The Jackson men wanted to force the delegates to vote for New York's Daniel S. Dickinson, a major enemy of Douglas and a notorious doughface whom they anticipated would grant concessions to the South if elected president. The scheme to tether the envoys with instructions failed because most of the state delegates opposed such a restrictive course of action. A majority of the delegates that the convention eventually sent to Charleston supported the nomination of Douglas, a clear indication of the Little Giant's pertinacious allure in Missouri. Thus the Missouri Democracy suffered from political schizophrenia: the platform and the gubernatorial candidate both signaled a radical streak similar to that of state organizations in the Lower South, while the delegation to Charleston primarily consisted of moderates who felt popular sovereignty offered the best protection for slavery.[20]

Delegates arrived in Charleston in mid-April, and soon the town's sultry streets and hotels teemed with men "perspiring and smoking, and engaged in mysterious conversations concerning caucus stratagems of intense interest to themselves." Bayard and his anti-Douglas Senate colleagues Jesse Bright, William Bigler, and John Slidell hoped to reprise their 1856 performance and once again arrange the Little Giant's defeat. The night before the convention opened, Bayard caroused and counted votes at his headquarters on King Street. In between meditative draws on his cigar, Bayard told a reporter that, based on his calculations, Douglas would fall short of the requisite two-thirds majority needed for the nomination. Bayard and his cabal, dubbed the Senatorial Clique, hoped the convention would settle on Hunter, Guthrie, Dickinson, or Breckinridge and even expressed a willingness to accept the Cincinnati Platform if one of their men secured the nomination. Bayard assumed that balancing a pro-Southern candidate with a moderate platform might counter the machinations of fire-eaters like William Lowndes Yancey, who came to Charleston bearing the Alabama Platform, a document that instructed the state's delegates to withdraw from the convention if the party did not produce a platform that expressly requested the federal protection of slavery in the territories.[21] While Bayard puffed away at his cigar, however, Yancey made his rounds and convinced portions of the Lower South delegations to secede from the convention "unless a resolution is adopted before the nomination of a candidate declaring in favor of Congressional protection of slavery in the Territories."[22]

The convention officially opened in Charleston's Institute Hall the next day and voted to construct the platform before selecting a presidential nominee, which played into Yancey's hands. Hopelessly divided, the platform committee deliberated for three days before submitting three separate statements to the convention. Bayard played an instrumental role in drafting the majority report, which included a declaration that neither Congress nor a territorial legislature could interfere with slavery in the territories and called for the federal government's protection of slavery therein. The majority report undermined popular sovereignty, but a North Carolina delegate confessed the two slavery-related planks "were adopted by a bare majority of the committee." Douglasites on the committee resubmitted the 1856 platform with an added pledge that the party would obey any decisions made by the Supreme Court on the territorial issue, while a third group simply submitted an unaltered Cincinnati Platform.[23]

The Border South delegates faced the uncomfortable reality that they would have to choose sides, but nothing close to unanimity existed among them. Their thoughts about the platform encompassed a wide spectrum, from the ultra-Southern position to absolute backing for popular sovereignty. Bayard and Whiteley of Delaware, for instance, gave the majority report their undivided support. Austin King of Missouri, on the other hand, "made an ultra-Douglas speech, indorsing the Northern Democracy in the most unqualified manner." King rebuked the supporters of the majority report for insisting on the protection of slavery in the territories and pleaded for unity. In the words of a reporter who witnessed the speech, King asked his Southern colleagues "not to drive the Northern Democracy to the wall, and alienate them, and thereby secure the election of [the Republican candidate] to the Presidency."[24] Such statements worried Southern hardliners, who wished for solidarity from the delegations of the slaveholding states in the event of a walkout. Unable to comprehend the vexed position of the Border South, fire-eaters like South Carolina's D. H. Hamilton scoffed at "the rascals and gulls of the South" like King who would likely stay in the convention, help nominate Douglas, and clinch his election in the autumn. The impatient Hamilton equated borderland restraint with an abandonment of the South.[25] The impetuosity of Southern radicals and their subterranean mistrust of the Border South worked in tandem throughout the secession crisis to impede the possibility of a cooperative pan-Southern disunion movement. As the Charleston fiasco proved, much to the chagrin of fire-eaters, most Border South politicians, though no less committed to the peculiar institution than other Southerners, sought solutions to preserve rather than destroy the Union.[26]

On Saturday, April 28, the convention endured additional wrangling over the various reports before adjourning until Monday. Sunday provided little rest for the delegates, as the different factions closeted with one another and tried to broker a deal to save the party. The Kentucky delegation's parlor in the Charleston Hotel became a symbolic middle ground "where genial spirits from the different sections meet to compare votes, and occasionally to test the quality of some Old Bourbon." The weekend negotiations came to naught, however, and many Democrats began to speculate that the factions within the party could not reconcile their differences. "The National Democratic party may dissolve," a Kentucky editor ruefully admitted, "and if it does the safeguard of our institutions may be destroyed, and the palladium of our Union removed from its sacred guardianship."[27] The backbiting within the party threatened to disturb the proslavery Unionism so vital to the borderland Democracy. As the weekend closed, the flustered delegates wondered if Yancey would make good on his promise to bolt.

On Monday, the Virginia delegation ratcheted up the pressure on the Border South when they joined with the Lower South and requested a plank that called for the federal protection of slavery in the territories. A showdown ensued, and Douglas's floor managers successfully substituted their minority platform for the majority report. Shortly after, Douglas supporter Charles E. Stuart of Michigan delivered "a very irritating speech, exceedingly ill-timed, unless he intended to drive out the Gulf States." In response, the delegations of Alabama, Mississippi, Louisiana, South Carolina, and Texas marched out of the convention while radical sympathizers applauded from the galleries. After this stampede, Bayard announced his withdrawal. Whiteley accompanied Bayard, but the remaining Delaware delegates stared at one another in bewilderment. A puzzled Saulsbury, like most of the remaining Southern delegates, confessed he did not know whether to stay or go. The following day a majority of the Georgia and Arkansas delegations retired from the convention, while the nonplussed Virginia, Kentucky, North Carolina, and Maryland men contemplated their next step.[28]

The raging waters of sectionalism had finally burst through the patchwork dam the Democrats had erected during the 1850s. "I have seen never more of human folly[,] imbecility[,] selfishness, and rascality than in all the rest of my life—I will never again be an actor in such conventions," Bayard fumed as he assigned blame for the party's disruption at the feet of Douglas's lieutenants. The seceding delegates assembled in Charleston's Military Hall on May 1 and named Bayard president of their convention. Three of Missouri's delegates eventually joined the two Delaware men to represent the Border South among the bolters, but the rest of the region's delegates either remained in the Institute Hall convention or returned home.[29]

Back in Institute Hall, Douglas's handlers plowed forward with the nominating process, but Chairman Caleb Cushing ruled that the party's nominee had to secure a two-thirds vote of all the delegates who had been seated when the convention originally opened. The convention voted fifty-seven times over two days, but Douglas never came close to attaining the requisite supermajority. The remaining border Southerners at the meeting scattered their votes on an array of candidates, another indication of the fragmented nature of the borderland Democracy. Hopelessly divided and at a loss for how to proceed, the convention finally decided to reconvene in Baltimore on June 18.[30]

The proceedings in Military Hall made Bayard uncomfortable. All along he had wished for Democratic unity—on his terms—and he later claimed that he withdrew from Institute Hall because he wanted that body to select a presidential nominee before writing the platform. Such a procedure would have undercut the proponents of popular sovereignty, he contended.[31] In hindsight, however, his rationale seems weak. While on the platform committee, Bayard played an instrumental part in writing the majority report that offended most free state delegates, and he appeared fully prepared to go to any length to wreck the Little Giant's ambitions. Bayard's abhorrence of Douglas and popular sovereignty provoked his rash decision to bolt, and upon sober reflection he realized that he had overreached. Few of his Border South colleagues had exited alongside him, a clear indication that although many of them loathed Douglas and his territorial principle, they preferred to work within the confines of the national organization rather than enter a convention dominated by hotheads like Yancey. A few months after the Charleston breakup, a well-placed Delawarean observed that Bayard and Whiteley had, through their impulsive decision to bolt, "killed themselves in this State."[32]

Perhaps Bayard hoped the secession of the Southern delegates would convince the Douglas handlers to drop their candidate, install a plank in the platform that called for the federal protection of slavery in the territories, and invite the bolters back to Institute Hall.[33] Bayard hinted at such a policy when on May 1 he advised the Military Hall Convention that, lacking a two-thirds majority of the entire Democracy, they could not make a nomination but only a recommendation for one. If this was Bayard's strategy, the Northern wing of the Democracy refused to take the bait, which amplified his uncertainty. Two days later Bayard professed his desire for Democratic harmony and "spoke for two hours very eloquently against disunion," after which he tendered his resignation from the convention. An Alabama delegate sneered that this meeting had been convened to save the Constitution, not the Union, which drew applause from radicals and fire-eaters. The convention then agreed to meet in Richmond, Virginia, on June 11 rather than heeding Bayard's advice for the delegates to reclaim their seats in a restored Democratic Convention in Baltimore.[34] Bayard's wavering stance reveals how white border Southerners, even those who espoused a robust proslavery outlook, harbored great suspicions about disrupting national institutions.

The Charleston debacle alarmed many Border South Democrats who looked to the party as a wellspring of proslavery Unionism. A divided Democracy effectively handed the White House to the Republicans, whose victory would encourage disunionists and place slavery on dangerous ground. Moderate Democrats across the Border South continued to hold out hope that the disparate wings of the party would patch up their differences and rally behind Douglas in Baltimore. "I am a Southern man in feeling and residence, have been raised in a Slave State fully imbued with all those warm and long cherished attachments for the institution of slavery," a Missourian acknowledged. He insisted that a vote for Douglas would best preserve the Union and protect slavery, and after the outcome at Charleston he confessed that "I am now truly in greater dread from Southern fire eaters than from Northern fanatics."[35]

While Democrats tried to make sense of the separation in Charleston, the other national organizations recognized that the Democracy's breakup aided their chances for victory in the upcoming contest. William C. Rives of Virginia determined "that the late events at Charleston have added immensely to the importance of [the Constitutional Union Party's] action & the prospect of its usefulness." John Jordan Crittenden, the figurehead of the Constitutional Unionists, noted that the new organization would benefit from its "experienced & distinguished statesmen, and they will be our security against any foolish or undesired course." Leaders of the Constitutional Union Party hoped that their unified organization would provide a voice for people who preferred "great moderation & wisdom" in political matters.[36]

Across the Border South, Douglas Democrats and the Constitutional Unionists contended for the crucial votes of the vital center. Despite their mutual fondness for moderation, though, the appearance of these two organizations in the canvass of 1860 actually splintered the middle ground and benefited extremists in each section. Henry Winter Davis had prophesied this likelihood early in the year when he pushed for a merger between Republicans and the remnants of the American Party. As Davis and Edward Bates discovered, a preponderance of Border South moderates spurned any combination with the Republicans in the aftermath of Harpers Ferry and the speakership contest, and strong partisan identification precluded cooperation between most Democrats and former Whigs.[37] Davis in the spring of 1860 temporarily set aside his Republican-American fusion plan and halfheartedly stumped for the Constitutional Unionists. He labored not so much to secure a Constitutional Union victory as to prevent the despised Democrats from winning the contest. Memories of vicious political battles against the Democracy in the 1850s kept Davis and other committed partisans from entertaining the idea of fusing with conservative Democrats. A congressman joked that Davis's "religion consists [of] hatred to democracy," and this loathing eventually pushed him ever closer to the Republicans and further out of the Border South mainstream. Throughout the canvass Davis maintained close relations with the Republicans, and many Constitutional Unionists suspected him of duplicity.[38]

The fledgling party experienced a harmonious national meeting in Baltimore, and the great bulk of the attendees, unlike Davis, exercised a genuine confidence in the success of the Constitutional Union Party. There were no unhealthy debates about territorial policy, and the new organization did not have to shoulder the weight of half a decade's worth of divisiveness and personal vendettas. The elderly leaders of the conservative organization, imbued with a keen awareness of the dangers of sectional discord, planned to attract a national following by "frowning upon every form of sectionalism & showing a catholic & equal regard for the rights & interests of every portion of the confederacy."[39] The dogma of the Constitutional Union Party matched the prevailing sentiment in the Border South: it sought to situate itself on the middle ground; the party looked to past heralds of compromise, like Henry Clay, for inspiration; and, in true Border South fashion, the organization relied on a nebulous—almost noncommittal—approach to the sectional conflict.

Despite their optimism and harmony, the Constitutional Unionists faced an onerous task. While they courted the conservative vote, deep partisan attachments made it extremely difficult to proselytize lifelong moderate Democrats who had formerly been bitter political adversaries. The Constitutional Unionists looked to resurrect the spirit of the Whig Party, but they had to chart a cautious course to avoid offending potential Democratic converts.[40] To attract votes the Constitutional Unionists had to "seek to conciliate & not to irritate," Edward Everett cautioned. "I think that both in the democratic & republican ranks there are good men,—and a good many of them,—who without any change of theoretical views are of opinions that the sectional strife has reached a dangerous length & that it is time to pause," he noted. "Why should we annoy them by dwelling upon the wrongs they have committed as members of the respective organizations[?]"[41]

The delicate approach suggested by Everett caused numerous headaches for John Pendleton Kennedy, who had been given the task of writing a Constitutional Union manifesto for prospective voters. In his original draft, Kennedy blamed the Democrats and Republicans for the sad condition of American politics, but the party's executive committee revised his work and left nothing "but a little incoherent declamation and some watery dictations which are interpolated to save the feelings of the parties it is our intention to demolish."[42] The party's determination not to offend voters exposed its greatest liability. Political organizations in antebellum America had to solicit every possible vote and utilize all available means to achieve victory. Some historians view the late antebellum period as the zenith of nonpartisan spirit in American history, but they often neglect the fact that purported nonpartisan organizations like the Constitutional Unionists had a distinctively partisan goal: to defeat the other parties in the field. Constitutional Union leaders might employ antipartisan rhetoric, but their ultimate objective—victory in 1860—was exactly the same as that of the Democrats and Republicans. As Kennedy observed, they intended to thrash their opponents; rosewater campaign tactics actually worked against this end, he correctly feared.[43] The initial campaign preference for magnanimity placed the Constitutional Unionists at a distinct disadvantage in the venomous arena of antebellum politics.

The Constitutional Unionists also confronted an age gap as they prepared for the campaign. In a society that celebrated youthfulness, the Constitutional Unionists appeared to some Americans as doddering politicians who looked to the past rather than the future.[44] Of the six men the party seriously considered as its presidential candidate, only John Minor Botts (1802) had been born in the nineteenth century. The birth of two aspirants antedated the Constitution, and George Washington was president when the other three were born. One observer commented that although the Constitutional Unionists attracted some prominent men to Baltimore, "most of them are somewhat stale in politics," while a Democratic newspaper mocked the convention's delegates as "fossilized members of the defunct Whig party."[45] Some of the potential candidates themselves complained of the enervating effect of long careers in politics. Crittenden, the party's leading presidential aspirant, instructed his associates to leave his name off the ticket. "I am tired of the life I am yet leading . . . [and] am quite prepared to retire to private life," Crittenden intoned. He preferred to operate as the party's manager—which also came with a massive, albeit short-term, workload—rather than as its candidate. Another delegate admitted that he had "come up out of his political grave" to "join the throng of the living" for the campaign, which certainly did not help the party's hoary image.[46]

The Constitutional Unionists took just two days to settle on a platform, which they labeled a declaration of sentiments, and a candidate. The declaration underscored the party's ambiguous approach to the burning political issues of the day and made no mention of slavery in the territories, the annexation of Cuba, tariff schedules, or internal improvements. With spartan simplicity, it called for the recognition of "the Constitution of the country, the Union of the States, and the enforcement of the laws." The delegates in effect asked the American people to trust the nation's future to the party of experience. The convention designated Tennessee's John Bell as its presidential nominee and gave the ticket sectional balance with the selection of Everett of Massachusetts as the vice presidential candidate.[47] Although no border Southerners graced the Constitutional Union Party's ticket, they had played a central role in organizing the party and managing the convention.

Six days after the Constitutional Unionists closed their meeting, the Republicans assembled in Chicago. Most Republicans looked toward the election with pronounced optimism in light of the Democracy's rupture in Charleston. Party managers placed great emphasis on winning the Lower North, which had been the key to a Democratic victory in 1856. Aware of the Lower North's historical penchant for moderate politics, Republicans reasoned they had to select a candidate free from the taint of radicalism. This was a bad omen for William Henry Seward, the Republican favorite entering 1860. Although he practiced a pragmatic brand of politics, Seward drew the ire of many moderate Americans for his stout antislavery record in the United States Senate during the 1850s. Centrists from the borderland had strong reservations about voting for Seward, who in their mind might upset sectional harmony by actively working to undermine slavery if elected president.[48] On the eve of the Chicago Convention, Seward's prospects for the nomination waned while those of Abraham Lincoln of Illinois intensified. Lincoln enjoyed newfound national prominence in the wake of his failed 1858 bid for Douglas's seat in the United States Senate. Though he lost the contest, Lincoln battled the Little Giant with great eloquence and tact. At the behest of party managers, Lincoln in early 1860 gave a series of speeches on the East Coast, which added to his momentum.[49]

Although his chances for the Republican nomination had "gone down like lead in the mighty waters" since the beginning of the year, Bates's handlers still held on to this fantasy when they arrived in Chicago. The Bates men doggedly maintained that if the Republicans hoped to draw any support from the

Border South, they had to choose a native son. Only Bates could "steer the vessel safely between Scylla & Charabides [*sic*]—northern fanaticism on the one hand [and] Southern Treason and Disunion on the other," James S. Rollins urged.[50] Few people took heed of Rollins's advice. Republican hardliners questioned Bates's antislavery credentials, while Border South moderates worried that if elected president, the Missourian might pander to the abolitionist element within the party. A Kentuckian lamented that the opponents of the Republicans had assailed the party's free-soil principles with such effectiveness that Border South conservatives would "support no man however pure whom the Republicans nominate."[51]

Once the Republicans gathered in the Wigwam, a hastily constructed convention hall, they quickly put to rest any notion of a Bates candidacy. In fact, the course of the convention exposed the insuperable challenges that confronted the feeble outposts of Republicanism within the Border South. Each of the Border South states sent delegations to Chicago, but some Republicans objected to them being seated at the meeting. Pennsylvania's David Wilmot questioned the plausibility of seating Southern delegates who represented states with miniscule Republican organizations. He feared that Southerners had come to Chicago "to demoralize a party, and to break it up." Border South delegates disputed Wilmot's claim, and Maryland delegate Charles Lee Armour asked how anyone could doubt his sincerity when he had risked his life while promoting the Republican cause in Baltimore. Several Northern delegates came to the aid of the Southerners and beseeched the convention to seat them so as not to appear as a purely sectional organization. The showdown produced a debate "full of fire," but the convention eventually allowed all of the Southern delegations other than Texas to take their seats.[52]

Although the Border South delegations retained their seats, the convention marginalized their influence. The Republican platform rebuked the actions of men like John Brown who invaded sovereign states for any purpose, but the seventh and eighth planks of the document sealed the fate of the party in the Border South. This portion of the platform expressed the Republican Party's intention to defy the *Dred Scott* decision and keep slavery out of the territories.[53] A Missourian immediately realized that this explicit denunciation of the extension of slavery blasted Republican prospects in the Border South. "If they had been content to say that they were opposed to the extension of slavery into free territories and to the dogma that the constitution carried slavery any where [*sic*], they could have made a lodgment in the border slave states," Jonathan Richardson grumbled, "but the Chicago platform completely sectionalized the party and is almost insulting to the South." Even

Bates fretted that the platform "is exclusive and defiant, not attracting but repelling assistance from without." Some Border South moderates pushed for a plank condoning colonization "to ward off the attacks made upon us about negro equality," but the convention spurned their suggestion.[54]

After three ballots, the convention nominated Lincoln as its presidential candidate. Bates only received a handful of votes—primarily from the border Southerners—on the first ballot, and on the subsequent two counts only the Missouri delegation remained committed to him. The Republicans seriously considered placing well-known Kentucky abolitionist Cassius Clay on the ticket as vice president, but instead settled on Hannibal Hamlin of Maine. "The mistake of putting no Southern man on the ticket will weaken our efforts in the Cause here immensely," Clay lamented.[55]

Clay's premonition rang true, especially in Missouri. Many of Bates's supporters looked elsewhere for a political home after the Chicago Convention bypassed their favorite and released an unsatisfactory platform. Rollins steered many erstwhile Bates men into the Constitutional Union camp. Less than three weeks after the Republican Convention in Chicago, the Constitutional Unionists in Missouri's Second District asked Rollins to run for Congress on their ticket. He agreed and immediately began campaigning for Bell. "In the south this is all we can do, under the circumstances," Rollins admitted.[56] Stung by Rollins's defection, Bates struggled to comprehend the objective of the Constitutional Unionists. He asked Rollins whether the new party was a genuine political organization, "or is it only (as a Baltimore paper irreverently called it) a 'Democratic Aid Society,' to serve the present emergency?" Rollins responded that Constitutional Unionists planned "to furnish a resting place, for the truly conservative elements of the country—Old Line Whigs [and] Americans—moderate men of all parties." To Rollins, Border South moderates who cleaved to proslavery Unionism were left with no other option.[57] Rollins temporarily suffered strained relations with some of his former allies who steadfastly stood behind Bates, but the voters in his central Missouri district vindicated his decision to join the Constitutional Unionists in August when they elected him to Congress.[58]

While the Republicans and Constitutional Unionists enjoyed relatively painless conventions, the Democrats attempted to clean up the mess made in Charleston. As the summer dragged on, James Bayard began to suspect that nothing would come of his earlier appeal for the Lower South delegations to return to the mainstream party fold. Even in Bayard's New Castle County, divisions in the Democracy remained rife. Douglasites and pro-South men held separate meetings and sent two different delegations to the Baltimore

Convention. The Douglas men chose Samuel Townsend and James A. Montgomery, while the other camp once again sent Bayard and Whiteley to the national meeting. Similar scenarios played out in other Southern states. After an attempt at compromise between the two wings of the party failed, Douglas operators across the Lower South decided to send new delegations to Baltimore in the hopes that they could clinch the Little Giant's nomination. Before the Baltimore meeting convened, the bolters in Charleston met in Richmond, Virginia, and decided to repair to Maryland and press for reentry into the national meeting.[59]

The Southern delegations' effort to reclaim their place made the proceedings in Baltimore just as tense as in Charleston. The competing New Castle County delegations went before the committee on credentials to plead for their seats, but the hearing devolved into a fistfight between Townsend and Whiteley. After deliberation, a majority of the committee on credentials called for the readmission of bolting delegates from Delaware, Texas, and Mississippi and the seating of the new Douglas delegates from Alabama and Louisiana. The convention voted to accept the majority report from the committee, but Douglas's managers insisted that the Little Giant receive the party's nomination. This proved too much for most of Douglas's Southern detractors, who conditioned their participation in a reunited convention upon his replacement on the ticket. Another walkout occurred, with some of the Border South men leaving and others remaining. For all the fuss they kicked up over reentry, Bayard and Whiteley once again bolted. W. B. Reed, a Kentucky delegate who stayed put, received roaring applause from the pro-Douglas audience when he declared that he and the remaining Bluegrass State Democrats "will stand with you as a wall of fire in opposing both extremes." Reed maintained that Douglas and popular sovereignty best protected the South, adding that "gentlemen who own a hundred slaves each say I am right." The convention finally nominated Douglas, while the bolters met in Baltimore's Institute Hall and selected Breckinridge to head their ticket.[60]

The presidential field was set by the end of June. The choice in the Border South revolved around three candidates: Douglas and Breckinridge of the Northern and Southern wings of the Democracy, and Constitutional Unionist Bell. Although some white border Southerners felt more comfortable with Kentucky-born Lincoln than a perceived radical like Seward, only a tiny fraction of the region's electorate seriously considered voting for any Republican.[61] Most Border South voters maintained their deep misgivings of Lincoln and the Republicans. "The abolition element of the [Republican] party will keep it sectional," a Missourian surmised, "and I am afraid to trust them on the Fugitive Slave act and slavery in the district."[62]

The Republicans could not satisfy the moderate temperament of most white border Southerners, many of whom held a balanced opinion of the larger Northern populace. Delaware's Sophie M. Du Pont noted that abolitionists made up a miniscule segment of the North's population, "a noisy & intemperate & intolerant & intolerable one, I grant you—but the South does a great wrong in classing all the intemperate & conservative North; all the men who hold the views of Washington & Jefferson & Clay &c, with them."[63] Yet white border Southerners had to choose between two conservative candidates, Douglas and Bell, which practically guaranteed splitting the vital center's vote and allowing the triumph of Lincoln. If that happened, radicals would take advantage and test the region's levelheadedness.

The August gubernatorial election in Missouri showed that the radical element in the Border South had made enough progress to get one of their own elected governor. The race included four candidates: Democrats Claiborne Fox Jackson and Hancock Jackson, Constitutional Unionist Sample Orr, and Republican James B. Gardenhire. Claiborne Jackson edged the other contestants with 47 percent of the vote, while Orr placed a close second, a sign that the embryonic Constitutional Union Party would play a major role in Border South politics. Hancock Jackson and Gardenhire trailed the front-runners by a wide margin, together winning just 11 percent of the vote.[64]

The victory of the ardently proslavery Claiborne Jackson pleased most radicals and fire-eaters, but deeper scrutiny of the election returns reveals the remarkable resiliency of the region's moderate impulse. Without a doubt, Jackson favored the Charleston bolters' stance on slavery in the territories— the struggle in Kansas convinced him that popular sovereignty could not adequately protect slavery in the West—and his political creed more closely resembled that of Yancey than that of Douglas. Fearful that pro-Southern rhetoric might alienate him from the state's moderate voters, however, Jackson sidestepped presidential endorsements while campaigning. His evasive stance on the presidential contest, coupled with a promise to support state aid to railroads, had in May earned him the backing of Nathaniel Paschall, the powerful editor of the Democratic *St. Louis Daily Missouri Republican.* Paschall, a passionate supporter of Douglas, and the radical Jackson made strange bedfellows, but the editor's endorsement boosted Jackson's sagging fortunes in Saint Louis. After the split in Charleston, Paschall presented Jackson with an ultimatum: support Douglas on the campaign trail or lose the paper's crucial endorsement. Mindful of the editor's influence, Jackson caved

TABLE 3.1 1860 Missouri gubernatorial race and slaveholding

County	% of Population Enslaved	% of Vote			
		C. Jackson (D)	S. Orr (CU)	H. Jackson (BD)	J. Gardenhire (Rep)
Howard	36.9	58.7	39.7	1.5	0.1
Saline	33.2	47.7	51.3	1.0	0.0
Lafayette	31.7	38.4	60.6	1.1	0.0
New Madrid	31.4	34.5	38.2	24.8	0.0
Clay	26.5	37.5	53.9	8.6	0.0
Callaway	25.9	43.3	52.9	3.8	0.0
Boone	25.8	40.1	57.3	2.6	0.0
Total		43.6	52.9	3.5	0.0

Sources: University of Virginia Geospatial and Statistical Data Center, "University of Virginia Historical Census Browser"; Dubin, *United States Gubernatorial Elections*, 144–46.

and agreed to stump for the Little Giant. Jackson's pandering upset some of Missouri's radical Democrats, who ran their own candidate, Hancock Jackson, in the governor's race. While campaigning, Claiborne Jackson had told audiences that he preferred Breckinridge, but now he championed Douglas in order to sustain the health of the Missouri Democracy. "Poor Claib! I pity him," a Missouri Democrat remarked. "I saw him at Jefferson City when there the other day, and he looked like he had lost all his friends."[65]

In reality, Claiborne Jackson's triumph represented no revolution in Missouri politics. Although the contest placed a dangerous sectional radical in the state's executive office, he had achieved his victory not with secessionist diatribes but with the familiar Border South formula of moderation. The conservative Paschall handcuffed Jackson, who knew he needed his support to win the race. Thanks to Paschall's endorsement, Jackson received nearly ten thousand votes in Saint Louis, whereas the Breckinridge Democratic candidate collected a little more than two hundred. Missouri held congressional elections the same day, which confirmed the staying power of the moderate mind-set. Douglas Democrats carried four of the state's seven congressional districts, while the remaining three were respectively won by a Constitutional Unionist, a Republican, and a Democrat who ran on a Breckinridge-Douglas coalition ticket.[66]

As Table 3.1 reveals, the heaviest slaveholding counties in Missouri cast nearly 53 percent of their vote for Constitutional Unionist Orr, while Claiborne Jackson won just under 44 percent of the vote. Of the seven counties with at least a quarter of the population enslaved, Claiborne Jackson won just one and polled no more than 48 percent of the vote in the rest. Clearly, many Missouri slaveholders saw through Jackson's sop to the Douglasites. Voters in Missouri's densest slave counties preferred Orr, who represented "the advance guard of the Union army of the nation." Outwardly radical candidates Hancock Jackson and Gardenhire received a pittance of votes in these counties, a strong indicator of the Border South judgment that the Union, rather than secession, best protected the peculiar institution. An August 1860 election for Kentucky's clerk of the court of appeals resulted in a huge victory for Constitutional Unionist Leslie Combs, further confirming the staying power of conservatism along the border. In the wake of Harpers Ferry and the speakership contest, and with the presidential election looming, proslavery Unionism continued to resonate with white border Southerners.[67]

Nevertheless, the Border South was not insulated from disunion sentiment. The strong reaction to alleged Northern outrages demonstrated the subterranean nature of secessionist attitudes within the region. Kentucky's Humphrey Marshall, a former Whig congressman who threw his support to Breckinridge in 1860, labeled the Republicans and Douglasites abolitionist wolves that prowled outside the peaceful homes of white border Southerners. If the wolves showed up on his doorstep, he told a crowd, he would not park in front of his fireplace and trade stories with old farmers like Constitutional Union candidate John Bell, but instead "follow to the field the young, vigorous, brave leader, whose energies and known character afforded me the hope that he would protect my property and have a proper care for my interests." Marshall admitted that he loved the Union, but he would rather see his family turned out of Kentucky if the state acquiesced in "the surrender and sacrifice of the constitutional rights of our people" under Republican rule.[68] Marshall's caustic language and implied approval of secession underscores that some former Border South moderates had transitioned into the radical camp on the eve of the election, and more would likely follow if Lincoln won.

All three of the political organizations that had a realistic chance of winning the presidential election in the Border South positioned their candidate as the strongest guardian of slavery, and the Republicans promised that, if elected, Lincoln would not interfere with slavery in the states or tamper with the Fugitive Slave Law. The other parties doubted the veracity of the Republican pledge, opening a hardy attack on the free-soil organization that preyed on white border Southerners' fears about the repercussions of a Lincoln victory. In Maryland Constitutional Unionists unleashed "violent tirades against the Republicans," while in Kentucky all three anti-Republican parties colored the Republicans as abolitionists. Anti-Republican rhetoric was stepped up in October, when Lincoln's party won state gubernatorial races in Indiana and Pennsylvania. These victories in the Lower North served as a harbinger of the party's success in that key region in November, which led to an escalation of anti-Republican prating in the Border South.[69] A Louisville paper warned that "a vote against Breckinridge is a half vote for Lincoln," and Missourians complained that Republican opponents misrepresented the party in an effort to attract voters. "Fanatical abolition addresses, and distorted paragraphs from the writings and speeches of ultra partizans are quoted in return to show than an onslaught is designed against the South," Saint Louis Republicans grumbled. The small Republican contingent in Baltimore witnessed first-hand the effect of the smear campaign. They attempted to hold a series of campaign rallies just days before the election, but each time unruly opponents scattered them with "showers of eggs, brick-bats and injurious epithets." Even the normally restrained Crittenden criticized the Republicans on the stump. The paranoid style employed by the non-Republican organizations produced panic among white border Southerners in the days before the election.[70]

In spite of their mutual awareness that a Republican victory might fan the flames of disunion, a powerful loyalty to each individual organization precluded any cooperative movement to defeat Lincoln. The political culture of the period nourished strong partisan attachments among the members of these parties that proved nearly impossible to unbind. Stubbornness, personal grudges, and political machinations also made the likelihood of fusion all the more difficult.[71] In the hopes of securing victory, the anti-Republican elements in the Border South committed themselves to a heedless campaign of fear mongering that seriously jeopardized the culture of Unionism after the election.

The arduous campaign, the rancorous infighting, and the apocalyptic auguring of fire-eaters and party hacks had by Election Day unnerved many Americans. "Thank the lord the great political struggle is at a close," a Kentuckian sighed the night before the election. "I believe that nothing but a fight will save the South. The sooner the better." The tone of the voter's prediction implies that some white border Southerners had resigned themselves to secession prior to the November 6 election. Other Border South inhabitants conceded that Lincoln would likely win, but spoke of the result in more measured, yet similarly concerned, language. "Should [Lincoln] prove to be mild & conservative the negro question would be settled," Charles Gibson of Saint Louis projected. "Should he prove the contrary, no man can tell the conse-

TABLE 3.2 Presidential election of 1860 in the Border South

State	Bell (CU)	Douglas (Dem)	Breckinridge (Dem)	Lincoln (Rep)
Delaware	3,886 (24.1%)	1,066 (6.6%)	7,339 (45.6%)	3,822 (23.7%)
Kentucky	66,058 (45.2%)	25,641 (17.5%)	53,143 (36.4%)	1,364 (0.9%)
Maryland	41,768 (45.1%)	6,080 (6.6%)	42,505 (45.9%)	2,296 (2.5%)
Missouri	58,261 (35.2%)	58,804 (35.6%)	31,312 (18.9%)	17,029 (10.3%)
Total	169,973 (40.4%)	91,591 (21.8%)	134,299 (32.0%)	24,511 (5.8%)
Combined Bell and Douglas Vote		261,564 (62.2%)		

Source: Dubin, *United States Presidential Elections*, 159.

quences." "The Wolf is really upon us now, and even in this old conservative State, a feeling of uneasiness and distrust is gradually growing up," a Maryland moderate dolefully admitted. "The people of the border states will be greatly agitated, and the secessionists further South will be in a perfect frenzy."[72] White borderites of all political persuasions unmistakably understood the probable consequences of Lincoln's victory and the impact it might have on proslavery Unionism.

The Republican strategy to convert the Lower North, a redoubt of Democratic strength in the previous two presidential elections, to their column paid dividends. Although he won less than 40 percent of the popular vote nationwide, Lincoln easily defeated his opponents in the Electoral College. He swept every free state except for New Jersey, which gave a portion of its vote to Douglas. The Little Giant finished second in the popular vote but dead last in the Electoral College; in addition to three electoral votes in New Jersey, he won Missouri. Breckinridge took every other Southern state except Kentucky, Tennessee, and Virginia, which Bell captured. The Republicans opted for a sectional approach and it showed: only in the slave states of the Border South and Virginia did Lincoln's name even appear on the ballot. In those five states, Lincoln tallied less than 5 percent of the vote.[73]

The results of the election in the Border South (see Table 3.2) demonstrate that the region was anything but a monolith. The Breckinridge forces achieved victory in Delaware and Maryland, Bell won Kentucky, and Douglas carried Missouri. A probing of the election returns, however, reveals that although partisan allegiances and internal political battles prevented consensus on a single candidate, the Border South preference for moderation remained strong. Breckinridge, who campaigned on behalf of the ultra-Southern position on slavery in the territories, won Delaware and Maryland with a plurality, and in his home state of Kentucky he captured just over a third of the vote. In Missouri he could not muster one-fifth of the total vote. In all four states combined, he received just under 32 percent of all votes cast. The other perceived radical, Lincoln, fared miserably. Although the Republicans attained more votes in the Border South than anywhere else in the slave states, they still received less than 6 percent of the overall vote in the Southern borderland.

A conservative impulse, the foundation of Border South politics in the 1850s, still existed within the region. The two candidates presented as moderates on sectional issues and who best fit the proslavery Unionist mold actually trounced the competition if their votes are combined. Together Bell and Douglas obtained 62 percent of the Border South vote. Moderates learned a couple of hard lessons as a result of the contest. First, they realized that the potent influence of partisanship divided conservative voters who could have worked together to keep radicalism at bay. A combined conservative ticket in the Border South alone would not have prevented Lincoln's election, but if the forces of moderation had promoted cooperation across the nation, the results could have differed greatly. Second, Border South moderates understood that Republicans had swept the Lower North, a region that white border Southerners had so often relied on for conservative allies. The election had been tight in some Lower North states, but in others Lincoln won by a wide margin. This caused alarm for white border Southerners who hoped to maintain conservative alliances in the North to prevent the Republicans from endangering slavery. Those who cherished a careful approach to the sectional crisis discovered that they must set aside party prejudice and work together. A Kentuckian predicted after the election that a collaborative effort on behalf of conservative principles could salve the nation's wounds by expurgating fanaticism: "It [the conservative movement] will be for the Constitution and the Union, and the overgrown children, the political charlatans, North and South, who have been engaged in destroying our noble government, will be driven so far into political damnation, that a sun beam would not reach them in an age."[74]

Proslavery Unionism hinged on the idea that the Union, not secession, best sheltered slavery. Disunion would surrender the federal government's obligation to protect slavery with the Fugitive Slave Law, abrogate key proslavery Supreme Court decisions, and relinquish the three-fifths clause, which actually enhanced the South's leverage in Congress. Most white border Southerners concurred with Abiel Leonard, owner of fifteen slaves in Mis-

TABLE 3.3 Vote for president in Border South counties with at least 25 percent of population enslaved (1860)

	County	% of Population Enslaved	Lincoln (Rep)	Douglas (Dem)	Breckinridge (Dem)	Bell (CU)	Total Cast
Kentucky	Bourbon	45.5	3	29	755	966	1,753
	Boyle	35.2	3	52	331	697	1,083
	Caldwell	25.8	3	48	618	446	1,115
	Christian	46.0	1	467	411	954	1,833
	Clark	41.5	1	60	391	959	1,411
	Fayette	44.3	5	99	1,051	1,411	2,566
	Franklin	26.7	-	37	907	790	1,734
	Garrard	34.0	21	145	195	730	1,091
	Green	26.9	2	188	367	420	977
	Henderson	40.4	5	211	498	846	1,560
	Henry	27.7	2	390	773	672	1,837
	Jessamine	39.1	3	37	559	603	1,202
	Lincoln	32.2	4	72	380	743	1,199
	Logan	33.4	3	342	169	1,490	2,004
	Madison	35.1	85	56	914	1,038	2,093
	Marion	27.6	-	904	281	475	1,660
	Montgomery	35.0	-	49	489	540	1,078
	Nelson	35.0	-	641	333	609	1,583
	Oldham	33.4	2	263	299	372	936
	Scott	39.8	-	44	1,176	734	1,954
	Shelby	40.4	-	228	594	1,176	1,998
	Simpson	28.3	-	194	319	404	917
	Spencer	35.6	-	304	94	334	732
	Todd	41.9	4	147	274	642	1,067
	Trigg	31.2	1	177	646	623	1,447
	Warren	30.7	3	615	182	1,126	1,926
	Woodford	52.0	-	16	547	633	1,196
Maryland	Anne Arundel	30.7	3	98	1,017	1,041	2,159
	Calvert	44.1	1	43	387	399	830
	Charles	58.4	6	38	723	430	1,197
	Montgomery	29.6	50	99	1,125	1,155	2,429
	Prince George's	53.5	1	43	1,048	885	1,977
	Queen Anne's	26.2	-	87	879	908	1,874
	St. Mary's	43.0	1	190	920	261	1,372
	Talbot	25.2	2	98	898	793	1,791

	County	% of Population Enslaved	Lincoln (Rep)	Douglas (Dem)	Breckinridge (Dem)	Bell (CU)	Total Cast
Missouri	Boone	25.8	12	578	652	1,671	2,913
	Callaway	25.9	15	839	472	1,306	2,632
	Clay	26.5	-	528	305	1,045	1,878
	Howard	36.9	1	939	247	920	2,107
	Lafayette	31.7	24	774	371	1,577	2,746
	New Madrid	31.4	-	117	160	223	500
	Saline	33.2	-	563	366	1,035	1,964
	Total		267	10,849	23,123	34,082	68,321
	% of Vote		0.4	15.9	33.8	49.9	
	% of Vote for Bell and Douglas		65.8				

Sources: University of Virginia Geospatial and Statistical Data Center, "University of Virginia Historical Census Browser"; Dubin, *United States Presidential Elections*, 167–71, 174–75.

souri, who called the Union "the sure bulwark of our slave property." Table 3.3 confirms the powerful appeal of proslavery Unionism in the Border South. The electorate in the forty-two densest slaveholding counties in the region cast nearly two-thirds of its vote for either Bell or Douglas. Breckinridge attracted the vote of nearly all of the remaining third of the electorate and Lincoln won just over 250 votes in these counties. A vote for Breckinridge was not commensurate with support for secession, but it did indicate a preference for a position on slavery that the region's slaveholders considered extremely hazardous. "The strongest pro-slavery men in [Kentucky] are those who do not own one dollar of slave property," a Breckinridge supporter wrote just before the election. "We would rather trust them than a thousand John Bells."[75]

Delaware's densest slave county, Sussex, where enslaved persons made up less than 5 percent of the county's total population, deviated from the general Border South trend. Sussex voters cast nearly 48 percent of their votes for Breckinridge. The moderate candidates tallied only 38 percent of the total, and Lincoln surprisingly garnered nearly one-sixth of the overall vote.[76]

Even with a strong mandate for moderation in the Border South's densest slave counties, conservatives grasped that a tough fight lay ahead. Fire-eaters clamored for the entire South to secede, and normally moderate men were now more than ever susceptible to disunionist pleas for Southern unity.

Bayard even reassessed his state's place in the Union shortly after Lincoln's election. The election results confirmed his worst fears and added to his misgivings about the South's position in the Union. "I confess, I have no hope left for the Union," he told his son, "& all we can do now is to separate peaceably if possible."[77] While they surveyed the election returns and contemplated the best method to offset the radical impulses sure to come, conservatives prayed that all of their fellow white border Southerners had not, like Bayard, thrown up the white flag, rejected proslavery Unionism, and surrendered to the apparent inevitability of disunion.

CHAPTER FOUR

What Ought Patriots to Do?

The Unionist Offensive in the Border South, November 1860–Mid-January 1861

With the presidential campaign completed and the Senate not due to convene until early December, John Jordan Crittenden in November 1860 slipped home to Kentucky for some much-needed rest. The septuagenarian Crittenden relished the opportunity to sequester himself in his Frankfort townhouse whenever his calendar provided a rare escape from boisterous campaign events, stuffy railroad cars, and crowded Washington drawing rooms. He usually spent his evenings lounging on the front steps with his family and friends, regaling the gathering with amusing anecdotes and long conversations about his beloved poplar trees that lined the front of his house. Try as he might, though, the old Kentuckian's thoughts never ventured far from politics. Even in the tranquility of his Frankfort home, the conversation eventually turned to public affairs. The deepening political impasse brought about by Abraham Lincoln's election tinged his usually cheerful visage with a gloomy sense of foreboding on this particular trip.[1]

Edward Bates remarked in late 1860 that his old Whig associate looked "older and feebler than I ever knew him," a by-product of the long hours spent organizing the Constitutional Union Party's campaign. During the late summer and fall of 1860 he stumped for John Bell from Massachusetts to Missouri at a breakneck pace, which left him exhausted. Despite all his labors, Lincoln and the Republicans now controlled the White House. To his close friends Crittenden expressed a desire to retire from public life and spend his last years in the solace of his Kentucky home. Frustrated with the highly sectionalized atmosphere in Washington, he looked forward to freeing himself from the "low party politics of the day, and the miserable scramble for place and plunder."[2]

News of Lincoln's election whipped many white Southerners into a frenzy, and political operatives in the Lower South had initiated preparations for state conventions to deliberate whether to secede. A Georgia paper forthrightly declared that the election of a Republican president meant "the Union has failed of the objects for which it was formed."[3] Crittenden shared the unease of his fellow white Southerners, but, unlike the Georgia editor, he showed no inclination to capitulate to disunionists. After all, he had witnessed firsthand his mentor Henry Clay rescue the Union from the brink of ruin on three separate occasions. Clay played an instrumental role in resolving the sectional dispute over the admission of Missouri in 1820, orchestrated a compromise to prevent a showdown between the federal government and South Carolina in the Nullification Crisis of 1832–33, and in 1850 laid the groundwork for a wide-ranging solution to the vexed question of the introduction of slavery into the Mexican Cession.[4] At each turn the American political custom of compromise had triumphed over secession. In the crisis of 1860, Americans hoped that Crittenden would fill the role of the departed Clay. Despite his deep longing to walk away from politics, his sense of duty and love for the Union drew him once more into the fray.

In response to Lincoln's victory, George Prentice, editor of the pro-Union *Louisville Daily Journal* and a close associate of Crittenden, rhetorically asked, "What ought patriots to do?" Patriots should spurn the entreaties of fire-eaters, Prentice answered, and "stand loyally and patiently in the Union under the Constitution and wield the might of the one and the checks and balances of the other to protect both." In the following months, Crittenden, Prentice, and likeminded moderates launched a Unionist offensive in order to confine the secession movement to the Deep South and to negotiate some settlement that would restore sectional harmony and forever remove the explosive issue of slavery from American political discourse. This hard-charging offensive, grounded firmly in the proslavery Unionist approach, seized the initiative from secessionists at this critical juncture in the Border South. Although the presidential campaign had drained Crittenden, he regrouped and prepared for what he thought was his final foray in Washington's political minefield. Soon enough he realized that his labors in the canvass of 1860 paled in comparison to the energy he would expend during the next several months.[5]

LINCOLN'S ELECTION PRODUCED "a perfect tempest of wrath" in the Lower South, where fire-eaters promptly set the wheels of secession in motion. Radicals in South Carolina operated as the vanguard of disunion, pressuring the state legislature to make the proper arrangements for a secession convention. Carolina fire-eaters knew they had to initiate a rapid charge to prevent a Unionist reverberation, which had stymied earlier disunion plots in 1833 and 1850. They employed the rhetoric of fear, shame, honor, and revolution to secure the meeting of a state convention on December 17, a month in advance of the scheduled conventions in other Lower South states. Fire-eaters gambled that if South Carolina took the first step, the rest of the slaveholding states would have no choice but to follow.[6]

Experience taught the Carolina radicals that their slave state brethren often got cold feet when it came to following through on promises of secession, and 1860 proved no different. Several strands of thought existed throughout the South about how best to respond to Lincoln's election. Fire-eaters pursued the most expeditious course in an attempt to capture their elusive dream of disunion. As in South Carolina, they advocated for each slaveholding state to call its own convention at the earliest possible moment, preferably before Lincoln's inauguration on March 4, 1861, and then proceed with the work of secession. This approach, labeled separate state action, gave fire-eaters the advantage of speed. Separatists plowed forward in an effort to negate the appeals of white Southerners who called for calm reflection about disunion. If they could complete the process of secession in quick order, those who broached the possibility of compromise would find themselves isolated and outmaneuvered. A Missourian rightly estimated that separatists "are more urgent than ever, taking every means to get their followers pledged to extreme measures, and to draw in and commit the timid and the doubtful, without allowing time to look to the consequences and reflect upon the bottomless pit that lies before them."[7]

Separatists planned to neutralize cooperationists and Unionists in their midst. Cooperationists promoted Southern unity; they preferred for all the slaveholding states to meet in a convention, discuss their grievances, and then decide on the best response to Lincoln's election. In cooperationist eyes, only cohesive action could convince the North of their earnestness and present a front that the federal government could not easily crush. They counted on strength in numbers and pointed to the Nullification Crisis, where the federal government cowed a defiant South Carolina, as evidence of the foolish course of separate state action. Separatists saw three major problems with the tactics of cooperationists. First, a pan-Southern convention would take precious time to organize. Once it met, the delegates might deliberate for weeks or months, sapping the wind out of the fire-eaters' sails. The separatists also worried that the cooperationist approach might not even result in disunion. After sober deliberation, unsound cooperationists might back away from secession. Finally, history informed separatists that the cooperation scheme simply did not work. In the crisis of 1850, the Nashville Convention had snubbed disunion, and in the aftermath of John Brown's raid, South Carolinians received little support from the rest of the South for a slave state meeting to discuss the possibility of disunion.[8]

Unionists also posed problems for the supporters of separate state action. These white Southerners saw no immediate need for secession and preferred to remain in the Union. Many Unionists loathed the impulsive nature of fire-eaters, especially the radicals in South Carolina. A Tennessee Unionist quipped that South Carolina "reminds of the bull that undertook to but [sic] the Locomotive off the track—courage admirable—discretion small!"[9] A wide spectrum of Unionism existed throughout the South, though historians have for the sake of clarity grouped Unionists into two major factions. Uncondi-tional Unionists vowed never to abandon the federal government and labeled secessionists base traitors. Very few white Southerners adopted such a rigid Unionist approach, but greater numbers of unconditional Unionists could be found in the Border South than elsewhere in the slaveholding states. Condi-tional Unionists were far more prevalent throughout the South, and they com-posed a large segment of the population in the Border and Upper South. Conditionalists argued that Lincoln's election served as no pretext for seces-sion and begged other white Southerners to wait and see how the first Repub-lican president would respond to the crisis. Conditional Unionists pledged their faith to the federal government as long as it did not force the seceded states to return to the Union. A policy of coercion, they warned, would likely convert them to the secessionist standard. Conditionalists also pled for con-cessions from the North on the slavery question. If they felt Northerners dis-sembled or spurned compromise, conditional Unionists were prepared to join the secessionists. For conditional Unionists, secession represented a last re-sort. The massive amount of Border and Upper South Unionists frustrated the separatists, who doubted their commitment to the cause of the South.[10]

Separatists viewed the political world in absolutes: to them all Republi-cans were abolitionist radicals, and recreant cooperationists and Southern Unionists were apostates. Nonseparatists, however, had a much more real-istic vista of the crisis. They realized that not every Republican wanted to end slavery immediately; they hoped for a groundswell of conservatism that would disarm radicals in both sections; and many exhibited a willingness to attempt sectional reconciliation. Although some separatists operated in the Border South, the overwhelming majority of white borderites fell into the cooperationist or Unionist camp. Still, this nonseparatist majority in the bor-derland should not lead to the conclusion that the region faced a crisis any less potent than in the Upper and Lower South. Political attitudes shifted greatly during the crisis, some fire-eaters shrouded their disunion proclivities behind a Unionist façade, and the slightest incident could imperil the region's mutable nonseparatist element.[11]

The fearmongering campaign tactics of non-Republicans, the election of Lincoln, and the Carolina radicals' rush to action left most white border

Southerners feeling trapped between extremes. "They [white border South-erners] are excessively provoked at the obstinacy and folly and malingering of the North and are utterly disgusted with South Carolina," a Kentuckian re-ported. Across the Border South, people of all political stripes complained that South Carolina's hasty course had forced the hand of the other slavehold-ing states. W. S. Bodley, a native of Louisville, considered the rash action of Carolina fire-eaters the consummation of a plot thirty years in the making. South Carolina radicals exaggerated every Northern affront and camouflaged every Southern iniquity in order to convert fretful white Southerners to their standard, he complained. Bodley noted that the Border South, unlike the in-sulated Lower South, had to rely on proslavery Unionism due to its proximity to free soil. The secession of the Border South actually played into the hands of abolitionists, he reasoned, because it would invalidate the Fugitive Slave Law and convince more enslaved persons to flee. Disunion "leaves the South-ern States under the cost and hazard of defending slavery as best they can with hostile neighbors and a diminished union, exposed to all ills, internal & external, which now exist and innumerable other superadded," a frustrated Bodley vented.[12]

The swift progress of disunion in South Carolina revealed a major discon-nect between the Lower and Border South. White borderland Southerners agreed that many slavery-related grievances existed, but most sought a cau-tious response to Lincoln's victory. They chafed at Deep South fire-eaters who tried to dictate their approach to the crisis. Some even charged that Lower South separatists wanted to secede hurriedly so the exposed Border South would "serve as a rampart against Northern crusaders." These border Southerners protested that Lower South radicals cared only for their own welfare, not that of the entire South. Fire-eaters, on the other hand, lamented that border Southerners dragged their feet on disunion. Virginia's James M. Mason sneered that "some of the Southern States will be tardy, & others recu-sant" on secession, while a rumor that John C. Breckinridge intended to un-dertake a pro-Union tour of the South left a South Carolinian aghast.[13] Internal Southern political divisions, which had haunted the proponents of a unified South for decades, had not vanished with the election of a Republican president. Radicals and moderates continued to harbor doubts about one an-other, which made the contradictory goals of each camp all the more difficult to attain.[14]

Even more egregious to Southern radicals, many white border Southern-ers were willing to allow Lincoln to enter the Oval Office before they made any decisions about their future in the Union. Unlike the fire-eaters, many white borderites could discern varying strands of Republicanism and hoped that perceived moderates like Thomas Corwin and Thomas Ewing of Ohio, Pennsylvania's Simon Cameron, Edward Bates of Missouri, and Francis Preston Blair Sr. of Maryland would counterbalance abolitionists. Many of these men had been allies of white border Southerners prior to the advent of the Republican Party. Moreover, the party's decision to abandon the contentious herald of the irrepressible conflict, William Henry Seward, in the election of 1860 demonstrated to some border Southerners that conservatives within the Republican Party held some sway.[15]

Some Border South Unionists tried to paint Lincoln as a conservative by arraying him against the more extreme members of the Republican Party. Unionists pointed out that Lincoln's political record did not mesh with that of the party's abolitionists, and the president-elect's friends in the borderland assured their neighbors and colleagues that he had no intention of interfering with slavery in the states. Several moderates, including Crittenden and Green Adams of Kentucky, asked Lincoln to make a public statement about his views on slavery in order to fend off secessionists and empower Southern Unionists.[16]

Prominent Border South editors George Prentice and Nathaniel Paschall opened a dialogue with the president-elect around the time of the election in the hopes that Lincoln might confirm their beliefs about his conservatism. Both men had opposed Lincoln's election but signaled they would treat the new president fairly if he published a statement vowing to uphold the Fugitive Slave Law and recommending that the free states repeal their personal liberty laws. Prentice calculated that a statement would "take from the disunionists every excuse or pretext for treason," while Paschall believed it would "keep down the excitement now pervading the South."[17] Lincoln, however, rejected their overtures and directed the editors to the Chicago Platform and his many speeches already in print for his stance on slavery. He further suggested that if newspapers like Paschall's *St. Louis Daily Missouri Republican*, "which heretofore have persistently garbled, and misrepresented what I have said, will now fully and fairly place it before their readers, there can be no further misunderstanding."[18] Lincoln meant no harm by his words, but they surely sounded anything but soothing to the editors.

Paschall and Prentice believed that a public statement from Lincoln would pacify skeptical white Southerners who sat on the fence between Union and secession and confine the disunionist impulse to South Carolina, but they misunderstood the complications such an announcement would have caused the president-elect. While a letter might have temporarily smoothed the ruffled feathers of Southern fence-sitters, it would also have opened the door to more distortion and skullduggery from secessionist radicals who would twist Lincoln's words to their advantage. Lincoln also had to worry about offending the Northern electorate that just elected him if he issued a statement on slavery. Although Lincoln was firmly committed to the party's free-soil principles, such a statement might have led other Republicans to question the new president's ability to lead the organization. Lincoln also faced the ominous task of sorting out patronage requests and cabinet appointments, which added to his busy schedule, tried his patience, and probably contributed to his terse response to the editors.[19]

Other Border South moderates harped on the fact that although the Republicans controlled the White House, the legislative and judicial branches of the federal government remained in the hands of conservatives. Several states had yet to hold elections for the Thirty-Seventh Congress, scheduled to convene in December 1861, and prognosticators estimated that the Republicans probably would not win a majority in either house. Without control of Congress, the Republicans could not pass legislation offensive to the South, Lincoln could not make objectionable appointments, and the new president would face serious obstacles when it came to dispensing patronage in the slaveholding states. Moreover, only one Republican sat on the Supreme Court in 1860, and four of the justices hailed from the South. Southern Unionists also pointed out that Chief Justice Roger B. Taney's court had effectively nullified the free-soil foundation of the Chicago Platform with the *Dred Scott* decision. Only a drastic alteration of the bench could lead the Supreme Court away from its position on slavery in the territories, and the likelihood of such a change remained remote as long as non-Republican forces controlled the Senate. These facts gave many Border South moderates persistent confidence in proslavery Unionism. "[Lincoln] is therefore utterly powerless," a Maryland Unionist imparted, "not one of his antislavery ideas can be engrafted into the legislation of the Country."[20]

Border South Unionists also suspected that the Republican Party teetered on the verge of destruction, which further convinced them that secession was unwarranted. They supposed the Republican coalition had been thrown together to win the presidency, and now that they had accomplished that objective, the disparate wings of the organization would bicker over what policies to prioritize. Party infighting would destroy the organization from within, according to Isaac Sturgeon of Saint Louis. He speculated that "within two years the Republican party will be broken to pieces & . . . the fragments can not [sic] be glued together for a canvass in '64." Likeminded white border

Southerners argued that secession would forfeit an opportunity for the Democracy or another conservative organization to overtake the Republicans in the future.[21]

The conditional nature of Border South proslavery Unionism posed problems for various political entities. Border South moderates understood the contingent nature of Southern Unionist thought, but most Republicans could discern only one variety of Unionism—unconditional. Thus, the Border South's tradition of evenhanded responses to sectional crises produced a false sense of security among many Republicans after Lincoln's election. Republicans misread the complexity of Southern Unionism and, lulled by the false confidence that unconditional Unionism reigned supreme, disregarded the inroads that fire-eaters had made even in the Border South. "We knew nothing of the South, had no realizing sense of the intensity of feeling which there prevailed; we fully believed it would all end in gasconade," a Republican later recalled. Throughout the secession crisis, Republicans had a difficult time understanding the volatility of Southern Unionism, which contributed to the worsening situation in the aftermath of Lincoln's election.[22]

White border Southerners, on the other hand, comprehended the extremely brittle nature of Southern Unionism. If radicals within the Republican Party gained the upper hand, or if Lincoln attempted to undermine the constitutional protections for slavery, or if moderate allies in the North surrendered to antislavery principles or allowed the Republicans to gain a majority in Congress, borderites warned that they would reevaluate the utility of the Union. Although Border South Unionism remained powerful after Lincoln's election, it was enormously delicate. The slightest perceived insult from Lincoln and his party threatened to transform many Border South Unionists into secessionists, a reality that many Republicans could not grasp.[23]

The fragility of Southern Unionism made securing a permanent settlement on the slavery issue of paramount importance for Border South moderates. Southern conservatives knew that if the Republicans refused to take compromise initiatives seriously, their proslavery Unionist approach would lose its luster and invite the possibility of all fifteen slaveholding states leaving the Union. A Kentuckian noted that conditional Unionists composed "the great, sound, conservative, central heart" of his state and "will struggle to the last for the Union as it was." But if the Republicans spurned a settlement, this powerful element doubtlessly would join the secession movement. The legislatures of Delaware and Missouri were slated to meet around the start of the new year, and the governors of Kentucky and Maryland toyed with the idea of calling their assemblies into special session. If the Republicans balked in Congress, it stood to reason that the Border South legislatures would follow the lead of the Lower South and call state conventions to consider secession.[24] Rumors of slave insurrections and additional outbreaks of violence on the Kansas-Missouri border only added to the hysteria in the Border South and threatened to undermine the Unionist position.[25]

The Border South occupied a most precarious position during these heady days, and Unionists across the region understood both the scope of the fight on their hands and the need for immediate combat against the secessionists in their midst. Prentice's *Louisville Daily Journal* became the mouthpiece of Border South Unionism. He counseled white border Southerners to set aside their divisive partisan allegiances and work for the common cause of the Union. Prentice called for Unionists to hold public meetings so people could engage in "political worship around the altar of their country," and encouraged the Border South to fill the role of mediator between the North and the Lower South. "Instead of being a satellite dragged at the tail and to follow the fortunes of some distant and eccentric State, she [Kentucky] is the firm centre to which they must be attracted. Massachusetts and South Carolina may fly off like excited sparks from the solid iron," Prentice intoned. "But Kentucky is not going to follow the sparks."[26]

Just like Lower South fire-eaters, Border South moderates mobilized in November 1860. In the following months, Unionists organized a plethora of meetings and rallies across the region in an attempt to dull the appeals of disunionists. John Pendleton Kennedy began composing his influential Unionist pamphlet addressed to the people of the Border South just five days after the election. In response to secessionist sermons delivered by his Presbyterian colleagues Benjamin Morgan Palmer and James Henley Thornwell, Robert Jefferson Breckinridge enlisted in the Unionist cause. Over the following months Breckinridge delivered Unionist speeches, traded oratorical blows with his erstwhile Presbyterian colleagues who advocated disunion, and oversaw the dissemination of tracts outlining the proslavery Unionist stance. Whether in print or on the pulpit, on bustling street corners or in sleepy rural villages, Border South Unionists oversaw a pitched campaign to place their views before their neighbors and defuse the appeals of fire-eaters.[27]

The Unionist campaign had great effect throughout the region, and Border South moderates initially overawed the proponents of secession with their onslaught. Unionists bombarded white border Southerners with their plea for a measured response to the unfolding crisis. Several major themes emerged in the Unionist assault and continued to exert a powerful hold over white border Southerners over the next several months. First, conservatives underscored the need for the states of the Border South to act in concert. The definition of the border states remained in flux at this early interval, for some Union polemicists also assigned the label to Virginia, North Carolina, and Tennessee. Nonetheless, Unionists time and again reiterated the collective power of these slave states and charged them with holding the line against sectional extremism from either direction. Kennedy argued that the "firmness, justice, and dignified bearing" of the Border South would make them "the authoritative and controlling power to devise and establish the foundations of a secure and durable settlement, with every provision for the preservation of Southern rights which the seceding States themselves could reasonably demand."[28] Acting in unison, the Border South had enough political power to force political concessions on the slavery issue, Unionists reasoned.

Unionists floated several suggestions about how to maintain Border South unity following Lincoln's election. Because by the end of 1860 all seven of the Lower South states had initiated the process of calling state conventions to consider secession, some moderates entertained the idea of holding a meeting of the eight remaining slave states to "fix upon a line of policy, saying to the North & South, this far shalt thou go, & no farther."[29] Other Unionists suggested a convention of both the free and slaveholding border states in order to give moderates from the Lower North a platform. The borderland summit would then present some political settlement to the rest of the nation in the hopes of silencing sectional radicals and limiting the damage done by secession. Some Unionists sought to enhance this proposal by suggesting that if the people of the Lower South or Upper North rebuffed any compromise, then the free and slave border states would create an independent, sovereign middle confederacy. A middle confederacy, shorn of the sectional radicals who had caused so much trouble, "would obviate the only difficulty in the way of settling this matter of slavery relations on a proper basis and forever."[30]

As a corollary to the appeal for Border South unity, moderates played on the strong desire for intersectional unity that had been a distinguishing feature of the region throughout the antebellum period. During the 1850s white border Southerners looked to conservative allies in the Lower North to help them blunt the thrust of radical sectionalists who used the slavery issue for political capital. Whether staking out ground for a settlement of the slavery question or talking about constructing a middle confederacy, Border South Unionists stressed that enough conservative sentiment existed in the Lower North to overwhelm Republicans and fire-eaters alike. They pointed to the results of the presidential election, where Lincoln amassed less than 40 percent of the popular vote, as evidence of a bi-sectional conservative groundswell, and Kennedy projected that 75 to 90 percent of the Northern populace would not countenance any infringement of the constitutional rights of the South. Secession instantly forfeited this influential bloc of conservatism that white border Southerners had relied on throughout the turbulent 1850s. "Nothing, therefore, can be more suicidal," Robert Breckinridge roared, "than for the border slave States to adopt any line of conduct which can justly deprive them of the sympathy and confidence of the border free States."[31]

Second, Border South moderates stressed that the people of their region would not tolerate Northern or Southern extremists dictating policy to them. White border Southerners insisted they would resist fanatical abolitionists or zealous fire-eaters bullying them into a hurried decision about their future in the Union. "We are down on both the secessionists and abolitionists believing in our humble opinions they are working for the same end but in a different manner," a Marylander intoned.[32] Border South conservatives reminded their constituents that they should not blindly follow disunionists or react precipitously to Northern radicals. Rather, they should work to confine these extremists to the margins and follow a path that best protected the Border South's self-interest. That trail, Unionists claimed, had been blazed over the previous eighty years by centrists like Henry Clay who had labored for compromise. White border Southerners incessantly conjured up images of the Great Compromiser and reminded conservative leaders John Crittenden and Stephen A. Douglas of Illinois that they must imitate the "Immortal Clay" once the new session of Congress opened in early December.[33]

During the canvass of 1860 many Border South Unionists portrayed the Republicans as the greatest threat to the safety of the Union, but in the aftermath of the election they redirected their wrath toward fire-eaters. With Lincoln legally elected, borderland moderates had to switch gears and smother the fears about the Republicans that they themselves had stoked during the presidential campaign. Now moderates stressed that the project of disunion posed the greatest threat to the Border South's self-preservation. The secession of the Border South would expose the region to inestimable dangers while protecting the Gulf South from abolitionist excursions, slave escapes, and, in the event of war, the brunt of the conflict. A Kentuckian complained that Deep South disunionists "do not stay to fight the battle but desert, & leave inestimable treasures & priceless blessings to perish behind them." "The cry of disunion comes, not from those who suffer most from northern outrage," Kentuckian Amos Kendall observed, "but from those who suffer least." South Carolina, Georgia, and Alabama lost one slave to every hundred in the Border South, Kendall argued, where enslaved persons could sense the tantalizing lure of free soil. A few bold Unionists went so far as to declare that the Border South had a completely different destiny from that of the cotton states and welcomed the idea of the Lower South's permanent separation.[34]

Historians have pointed out that fire-eaters exploited the Southern code of honor to convert their wavering neighbors to the disunionists' standard. The code rested on the contradictory concepts of liberty and slavery: a truly honorable man enjoyed unencumbered liberty, while a person without honor submitted to the will of others, as did an enslaved person. White Southerners jealously protected their honor and frequently resorted to violence if they felt another had attempted to trespass on their liberty. Southern radicals in the Deep South whipped up secession sentiment in late 1860 by proclaiming that anyone who surrendered to Republican rule lacked honor.[35] Border South moderates, however, also employed the rhetoric of honor when building their case for the Union. During their Unionist offensive, these moderates constantly painted Lower South radicals as cowards who simply used the Border South "as a barrier to protect them from the fierce abolition [element] of the North that they are arousing, but utterly impotent to avert." A truly honorable white Southerner would never shirk his duty and allow someone else to fight for him as the fire-eaters attempted to do, moderates contended. Handing one's destiny over to sectional radicals equaled a forfeiture of the white border Southerner's liberty and imbued a sense of dishonor. An Elkton, Kentucky, native noticed that Unionists in his town had confronted some townspeople who favored disunion, and now these fire-eaters no longer sported their secession cockades in public. "I hope that the wearers have become ashamed of their disunion badges," he remarked. Border South Unionists wielded honor against both the radicals in their midst and those in the North and South who might jeopardize the safety of the Union. "While [Kentucky] disdains to assume the offensive, vaunting, blustering style of South Carolina, she is no less jealous of her honor," one Border South inhabitant insisted, "and with dignity and firmness demands of the North that redress which she regards as her due."[36]

Perhaps more than any other element in the nation, Border South moderates realized the potential for war in the event of secession. Moreover, they perceived that the scope of the conflict would far surpass what many Americans imagined. A writer in *DeBow's Review*, a New Orleans–based commercial and agricultural magazine that supported disunion, considered war unlikely if all fifteen slaveholding states seceded, but also conceded that all great nations had endured civil wars. This proponent of secession fed the fears of Border South moderates when he blithely stated that if the more northerly slave states opted to remain in the Union and war commenced, they could serve as "a barrier to the access of abolition emissaries." Lower South editors in favor of secession dismissed the prospect of war or estimated that a conflict would result in few casualties, and one South Carolina fire-eater announced that all the blood shed as a result of secession would hardly fill a thimble.[37] Time and again fire-eaters promised that their course provided safety to the slaveholding states, but those who inhabited the exposed frontier of slavery questioned such assurances. Although the Border South usually enjoyed harmonious relations with the Lower North in the preceding decades, the region had endured periodic episodes of violence. The conflict on Missouri's western border, periodic confrontations over the reclamation of fugitive slaves, and the specter of slave revolts brought on by extremists like John Brown conditioned white borderites to expect the worst if a full-scale war erupted, and nothing could more quickly bring about such a clash than secession. Moderates were mindful that nearly all Northerners exalted the Union and would likely condone an armed conflict to preserve it. Kennedy vividly portrayed the outcome for the Border South should they opt to secede. He predicted "the sack of cities, the brutal and indiscriminate murder of old and young of either sex, the rape and rapine, the conflagration, the shriek of surprised families, [and] the midnight flight of mothers and children tracking their way with bleeding feet."[38]

Secession, moderates argued, produced instability and desolation for the borderland rather than safety and contentment as fire-eaters prophesied. Suffused with a realism about war that other Americans lacked, Border South moderates took to the stump to push for mediation, a course that best protected the region, rather than confrontation in the wake of Lincoln's election. A Kentuckian who advocated a sober approach to the crisis howled that the states of the Border South "do not intend that their peaceful channels of commerce shall become rivers of blood to gratify the ambition of South Carolina and Alabama."[39]

The third major theme of the moderates' campaign built on the first two. Border South conservatives insisted that the Union provided the best shelter for the institution of slavery, while secession endangered the long-term viability of the region's social, economic, and political foundation. Moderates argued that if the states of the Border South seceded, they would put the peculiar institution on the fast track to extinction. They cited a surfeit of reasons for their contention. Most importantly, secession meant the Border South would lose all the protections the federal government offered for slavery. For a region that suffered more escaped slaves than any other part of the South, relinquishing the federal government's power to capture fugitive slaves would place the institution on shaky ground. The Fugitive Slave Law, which one borderland Unionist deemed "effective in its power of recapture but infinitely more potent in its moral agency preventing the escape of slaves," had for the most part been faithfully enforced since 1850. Secession invalidated this law and brought the boundary of Canada down to the northern edge of the Border South.[40] Conservatives admitted that the power of recapture would be lost because the United States would function as a foreign nation, but they seemed far more distressed that secession would serve as an invitation for enslaved persons to escape. "What are a hundred slaves—or twenty—or more or less—worth within twenty miles of a foreign country?" a Baltimore native questioned. White border Southerners' fear about an upsurge of escapes underscores how enslaved persons utilized any leverage available to them in the master-slave relationship for their own ends. Flight operated as a potent form of slave resistance and, in the case of the Border South, it contained a sharp political edge. Moderates acknowledged that enslaved persons would easily comprehend the ramifications of secession and use the absence of the Fugitive Slave Law to their advantage; remaining in the Union, however, would prevent a northward slave exodus and the depression of slave prices. Published slave narratives, like those of Frederick Douglass— who made his heroic journey to freedom from Maryland—cultivated among white border Southerners uneasy feelings about the potential for more slave escapes should the Border South secede.[41]

Moreover, secession would convert Northern allies who pledged to uphold the Fugitive Slave Law into enemies. The realistic outlook about armed conflict in the event of disunion troubled borderland moderates because they recognized that their region would become the seat of the war. "Will not your slaves be less secure, and their labor less profitable under the new order of things than under the old?" Winfield Scott asked. If plunged into war, the Border South could no longer devote the proper resources needed to maintain slavery. Invading armies would solicit the escape of enslaved persons, and white Border South males would have to choose between protecting their families and enlisting in the Confederate cause and marching to distant battlefields. The outbreak of war would unloose all restraint and set the stage for servile insurrection on par with the Haitian Revolution. The specter of a massive slave revolt had long concerned white Southerners, and Border

South moderates warned that secession would make this harrowing nightmare a reality. The recent outbreak of violence on Missouri's western border and the rumors of abolitionist incursions gave these extravagant claims some credence.[42]

Border South moderates also pointed to the fact that if the region seceded and joined the Lower South in a slaveholding republic, the Cotton South would dominate the new government. In that case, the Border South's interests would be subordinate to those of the Gulf South. Kennedy predicted that the Lower South would push for the reopening of the African slave trade, disagree with the Border South about economic principles, and attempt to acquire additional territory in Latin America. These policies would lower the price of enslaved persons in the Border South and expedite the destruction of slavery in the region, Kennedy figured. Robert Breckinridge echoed Kennedy's warnings and bluntly asserted that if the Border South seceded, "we will have taken the most effectual means of extinguishing [slavery]; and that in the most disastrous of all possible ways."[43] Proslavery Unionism, with its many dimensions, served as a foundational component of the Unionist offensive.

Unionists in the Border South certainly did not understate the magnitude of the crisis that confronted their region. They recognized the enormous stakes at risk if the Union broke apart, and they hoped to avoid such a calamity at all costs. The final theme of the Unionist offensive accentuated this fact. Moderates argued that the federal government must not use force to bring any state that had seceded back into the Union, and if a state did exit the Union, its inhabitants should not attack federal troops or government officials. The emergent cold war between the Lower South and the federal government must not become a hot one, Unionists contended; such an outcome would ruin the chances of a mediated settlement. People realized that the geographic position of the Border South, along with its political heritage, placed the region in the vanguard of conciliation. "If [the Border South] will only assert their prerogative & assume the umpire, we shall all fall in with their decision," a Massachusetts native admitted. Any attempts at coercion jeopardized the Unionist edge, though, so moderates pled for both the federal government and Lower South secessionists to keep their weapons holstered.[44]

The Unionist campaign helped keep secessionists at bay in the Border and Upper South in November and the following months. Had moderates in these eight states simply thrown up their hands and failed to act, the seeds of disunion may have blossomed in midwinter and provoked a response from the Border and Upper South that mimicked that of the Lower South. They preached the value of the Union and the possibility of settling the slavery issue, which left disunionists disappointed and on the defensive. The campaign forced Border South fire-eaters to rely on some outside event—like a coercive stance from the federal government, or the inability of Congress to agree on a settlement, or the secession of Virginia—to spur their neighbors into action. Just as Lower South fire-eaters charted an aggressive course to push their states out of the Union, borderland moderates energetically acted to keep their states in the Union.[45]

Progress toward a compromise served as the lifeblood of the Border South Unionist offensive. The efforts of Unionists within the Border South were intimately connected to the maneuverings of politicians in the nation's capital, who held the fate of a settlement in their hands. Moderates hoped that the momentum of the Unionist campaign would carry over to Capitol Hill and result in some compromise on the slavery question that might isolate South Carolina extremists, incapacitate Southern fire-eaters, neutralize Northern radicals, and relieve the intersectional tension that threatened to engulf the nation in civil war. Crittenden traveled to Washington aware that his curtain call in the Senate would require every ounce of political acumen that he had accumulated over his long career.

Upon reaching the national capital in early December, Crittenden sensed that many of his colleagues had returned to Washington in no mood to negotiate a settlement. Democrats, Republicans, and moderates alike blamed the developing crisis on their foes, while fire-eaters and Northern hardliners showed little interest in finding some middle ground to save the republic. President James Buchanan's mouthpiece in the capital announced that the Republicans had to initiate the process of conciliation in order to satisfy the South, while the Republicans' Washington organ laid all responsibility for the salvation of the Union at the president's feet. The wide gulf between the approach of the lame duck president and the Republicans made the job of conciliators enormously difficult. Buchanan forces called for the Republicans to retreat from the party's keystone antislavery principle in their hour of triumph, while Lincoln's party declined to shoulder the blame for the national emergency and naturally refused to backpedal from the Chicago Platform.[46]

Nearly all white border Southerners felt that any effective permanent settlement on the slavery issue required the acquiescence of at least a portion of the Republican Party. Without Republican cooperation, the political battle over slavery might continue in perpetuity. Some Republicans outwardly appeared flexible on compromise, which gave Border South moderates some hope. Influential Republican editor Thurlow Weed, who also happened to serve as William Seward's political manager, had in late November proposed a settlement of the slavery issue on the basis of the Missouri Compromise. Weed suggested restoring the Missouri Compromise line, which had been repealed by the Kansas-Nebraska Act, to the territories; slavery would be allowed in all territory south of the line and forbidden north of it. Weed's close relationship with Seward offered moderates a glimmer of hope that some Republicans would at least contemplate the possibility of compromise.[47]

Congress heard Buchanan's annual message on Tuesday, December 4, and it did little to assuage the apprehension of Border South moderates. In partisan fashion, Buchanan charged that Northern abolitionists had brought the sectional crisis to its present state and chastised the Republicans for politicizing the slavery issue and feeding the misgivings of Southerners. Although Buchanan understood the dread of the Southern people, he contended that Lincoln's legal election served as no impetus for disunion. The lame duck president affirmed that the Constitution denied the right of secession, yet in the same breath he deflected all responsibility for dealing with South Carolina to Congress. Furthermore, Buchanan insisted that the federal government possessed no power to force South Carolina to remain in the Union. Beyond a recommendation that all Northern states repeal their personal liberty laws, he advised Congress to call a national constitutional convention to settle the slavery question.[48] Few people found solace in Buchanan's wavering stance on secession. Crittenden considered the president's message "a vile mass of cowardly verbiage to colour over his base surrender of the Union," and immediately began drafting a series of compromise resolutions to submit to the Senate.[49]

Crittenden understood that partisanship, an essential component of antebellum politics, could serve as an obstacle to a settlement. Just a couple of months prior, he had participated in a highly partisan political campaign that had divided conservatives throughout the nation. Politicians would have to set aside party goals and work for the common aim of preserving the Union, so Crittenden made overtures to Stephen Douglas and his Democratic followers to assist him in securing a compromise. Douglas publicly announced he would "act with any individual of any party" who sought to save the nation and asked the rest of his fellow senators to "lay aside all party grievances, party feuds, [and] partisan jealousies" for the present. Crittenden also reached out to fellow Kentuckian Lazarus Powell, a Democrat, who on December 6 introduced a resolution in the Senate recommending the creation of a committee of thirteen senators charged with finding a solution to the sectional impasse. Over the following two weeks, fire-eaters and hardline Republicans, anxious to delay or obstruct a compromise settlement, utilized stall tactics to prevent the formation of the committee. Attention swung over to the House of Representatives, where moderates hoped to make more headway.[50]

At the behest of Virginia's Alexander Boteler, the House established the Committee of Thirty-Three, made up of one congressman from each state, to consider the issue of compromise. Non-Republicans in the House charged Speaker of the House William Pennington with stacking the committee with congressmen opposed to a settlement. The Speaker placed sixteen Republicans on the committee but assigned only two free-state Democrats to the body, effectively silencing the conservative voice of the Northeast and Old Northwest. The rest of the Democrats on the committee represented each Southern state except for Kentucky, Maryland, and Tennessee, from which Pennington assigned Oppositionists. Pennington appointed two Border South Democrats, William Whiteley of Delaware and John S. Phelps of Missouri, and two borderland Opposition men, Maryland's Henry Winter Davis and Francis Bristow of Kentucky, to the committee. The Speaker named Republican Thomas Corwin of Ohio, an established moderate, chairman. Corwin faced an uphill battle due to the polarized partisan nature of his committee, though. If Davis, who had drawn closer to Lincoln's party over the past year and privately considered the panel a "humbug," voted with the Republicans and any Southerners abstained from participation, compromise proposals would have a tough time getting out of the committee.[51]

The maneuverings of the House committee demonstrated the wide gulf that separated the mind-set of Border South moderates and Lower South fire-eaters. Border South Unionists conveniently ignored the composition of the committee and instead emphasized to their constituents that the panel's formation indicated progress in Congress. George Prentice predicted that the House committee "will be the dove to pluck the olive branch and place it within the ark of our constitutional liberty and glory and independence." As long as the committee met, deliberated, and appeared to advance toward a settlement, borderland moderates could hold off the appeals of secessionists. The House referred a plethora of compromise proposals to the Committee of Thirty-Three in early December, which gave Border South Unionists additional ammunition to combat disunionists. Crittenden likely consulted with committee member Thomas A. R. Nelson of Tennessee, who at the commission's second meeting introduced a comprehensive settlement package that closely resembled the Kentuckian's subsequent proposal to the Committee of Thirteen.[52]

Davis's initial contempt for the committee softened, and on December 13 he entered a resolution calling for the revision of Northern personal liberty laws, along with legislation that altered key provisions of the Fugitive Slave Law. Davis proposed granting alleged fugitive slaves a trial by jury and paying magistrates hearing these cases a flat fee for their services. He aimed his proposal squarely at the inhabitants of the border states. White border Southerners felt that personal liberty laws impaired their property rights, which were protected by the Fifth Amendment of the Constitution. Borderland Northerners, on the other hand, protested that the Fugitive Slave Law subjected accused runaways to judicial decisions of a single magistrate—who received ten dollars if he ruled the person a fugitive and five dollars if not—rather than to the judgment of an impartial jury. Published slave narratives and the testimony of African Americans confirmed that the Fugitive Slave Law had resulted in innocent free blacks being placed in shackles and sent southward. Davis's suggestions would ostensibly add objectivity to fugitive slave cases. The Marylander intended to capitalize on the intersectional amity that white border Southerners found absolutely essential to the preservation of slavery.[53]

Southern firebrands in Washington realized that as long as moderates dangled the possibility of compromise before the voters, the South's electorate might once again waver on disunion. The same day that Davis offered his proposal, Albert Rust of Arkansas submitted a resolution that affirmed Southern grievances and implied that secession would occur if the committee could not produce a settlement. Indiana's William McKee Dunn introduced a substitute for Rust's resolution that acknowledged Southern complaints but dropped all language hinting at disunion. The Dunn resolution passed twenty-two to eight, with all of the negative votes coming from Republicans. Fire-eaters, hungry for any sign of Republican intransigence, ignored the fact that eight members of Lincoln's party also voted in favor of Dunn's conciliatory resolution and saw in the negative votes an opportunity to fan the flames of secession. That night a caucus of Southern politicians listened to Mississippi congressman and Committee of Thirty-Three member Reuben Davis fulminate against the Republicans. He presented a document that boldly proclaimed that "all hope of relief in the Union . . . is extinguished" and recommended immediate separate state secession. Twenty-nine Southern politicians signed the Mississippian's Southern Manifesto, yet not one of the signatories hailed from the Border South and only three Upper South politicians affixed their names. The introduction of conciliatory measures in the Committee of Thirty-Three deepened the divide between the various sub-regions of the South.[54]

While the Committee of Thirty-Three debated Henry Winter Davis's proposal, Crittenden on December 18 revealed his compromise package to the Senate. Crittenden's plan, comprising six constitutional amendments and four resolutions, served as the polestar for moderates in Congress and for Border South Unionists back at home. The centerpiece of the Crittenden Compromise was the reintroduction of the Missouri Compromise line. His first amendment forbade the introduction of slavery in all territory north of 36°30′ then in the possession of or subsequently acquired by the United States. South of the line, however, slavery "is hereby recognized as existing, and shall not be interfered with by Congress, but shall be protected as property by all the departments of the territorial government during its continuance."[55]

Crittenden carefully worded his territorial amendment to appease Northerners worried about Southern expansion. His stipulation for slavery south of the line omitted mention of anything about subsequently acquired territory, so it effectively applied only to the areas of the Mexican Cession that had not applied for statehood. The original wording confined slavery to a territorial cage and freed the federal government from the responsibility of protecting the peculiar institution therein. This undercut Breckinridge Democrats who had clamored for the federal government to oversee the protection of slavery in the territories and also closely resembled Weed's solution to the crisis. Historians have often overlooked the cautious verbiage of Crittenden's original territorial amendment, but contemporary fire-eaters took notice. Henry Winter Davis chuckled that the lack of a "hereafter acquired" clause for territory south of the line frustrated disunionists, whose "ultimatum is a right to carry slavery to the South pole." Southern conservatives, on the other hand, appreciated that the amendment undermined the Wilmot Proviso.[56]

The other five amendments of the Crittenden plan also dealt with the slavery issue: Congress could not interfere with slavery in areas under its exclusive jurisdiction, like federal forts and dockyards; Congress could not abolish slavery in the District of Columbia so long as it existed in Virginia and Maryland, and any future emancipation program required the consent and compensation of the district's slaveholders; Congress could not obstruct the interstate slave trade; and slaveholders who encountered obfuscation in the free states while attempting to reclaim a fugitive slave would be able to sue for compensation if they could not retrieve the runaway. The final amendment declared that no future amendment to the Constitution could overturn these provisions, nor could any forthcoming amendment grant Congress the power to abolish slavery in the states. Crittenden also included four resolutions that affirmed the constitutional legitimacy of the Fugitive Slave Law, asked for the repeal of personal liberty laws, and requested the perpetual cessation of the

African slave trade. He also asked for alteration of the Fugitive Slave Law to provide equal fees for commissioners overseeing fugitive cases and to remove the repugnant feature granting federal marshals the power to force private citizens to assist in the capture of escaped slaves.[57] Crittenden's panacea clearly offered more concessions to the South, but he viewed that region as the aggrieved party. Moreover, the compromise package demonstrated how proslavery Unionism conditioned the approach of borderland conservatives. Favorable letters from borderites poured in thanking Crittenden for his efforts, and in the following weeks citizens from across the Union flooded Congress with memorials and petitions begging for the plan's adoption.

Scholars studying the crisis have attacked the Crittenden Compromise, so warmly received by many contemporary Americans, from a variety of angles. Some historians have labeled the package infeasible and unwieldy; others have suggested no settlement could patch the sectional divide; while others have lambasted Crittenden for his lack of moral scruples in his attempt to extend the life of American slavery.[58] Overly dependent on hindsight, these views obscure the reality of the situation during the crisis. First, nothing precluded Crittenden's package from being broken into pieces as had Henry Clay's omnibus that a decade earlier eventually became the Compromise of 1850. The groundswell of support for the Crittenden Compromise during the winter indicates that many Americans still believed the possibility of a settlement quite reasonable. Finally, aside from a small cadre of abolitionists and African Americans, few Americans viewed the slavery controversy through a moral lens. As reprehensible as it seems to modern sensibilities, the plight of the republic, not of four million enslaved persons, concerned most citizens. Furthermore, Crittenden had not tethered slavery to the Union in perpetuity as some historians charge. The final amendment only forbade Congress from abolishing slavery; the individual states still had the power to eradicate the peculiar institution within their borders. That his compromise would have allowed slavery to exist far beyond its death in the final three years of the Civil War is obvious, but no one at the time knew what the future held in store, nor did most Americans have second thoughts about perpetuating slavery in the states where it existed. Border South Unionists, therefore, had every reason to remain optimistic that Crittenden's plan offered a practical, viable solution to the sectional impasse.

Despite their optimism, Crittenden and other moderates asked the Republicans to acquiesce in a settlement that challenged the keystone principle of their party. While several elements had come together to form the Republican coalition in the 1850s, the bedrock of the party centered on the prevention of slavery's extension into the West. Although some Republicans entertained the notion of compromise, this formative precept of the party had not changed. From Springfield, Lincoln admonished his colleagues to stand by the cardinal tenet of Republicanism. "There is no possible compromise upon [the extension of slavery]," he told Illinois congressman Elihu Washburne, "but which puts us under again, and leaves all our work to do over again." He advised all Washington Republicans to "hold firm, as with a chain of steel." Republican intransigence exasperated Crittenden and his followers over the following weeks, but moderates simply asked too much from Lincoln's party. Republican John Sherman candidly acknowledged that conciliatory measures "demand of Conservative Republicans a surrender of this House—their manhood—their religious & moral convictions." The territorial aspect of Crittenden's plan asked Republicans "to swallow every profession of principle they ever uttered," Henry Adams scoffed. "No real republican would ever consent to listen to it."[59]

On December 20 Vice President John Breckinridge announced the roster of the Committee of Thirteen, which included senators from various partisan and sectional backgrounds. He selected Republicans William Seward, Jacob Collamer of Vermont, James Doolittle of Wisconsin, James Grimes of Iowa, and Ohio's Benjamin Wade. Northern Democrats included Stephen Douglas, William Bigler of Pennsylvania, and Henry Rice of Minnesota. Jefferson Davis of Mississippi, Virginia's Robert M. T. Hunter, Lazarus Powell, and Robert Toombs of Georgia represented the Southern Democrats. Crittenden, the only Opposition man, rounded out the panel of eminent senators. Although Powell chaired the committee, Crittenden served as the de facto leader of the body. The committee membership covered a broad range of political thought, from the Republican hardliner Wade to the fire-eater Toombs, which increased its likelihood of success.[60]

Around the same time the Senate formed the Committee of Thirteen, fire-eaters from the Deep South made a direct appeal for the Border South to join their disunion crusade. Secession commissioners visited each of the Border South states in an attempt to cajole politicians, from governors to state legislators, to make preparations for leaving the Union. Mississippi's Alexander Hamilton Handy unsuccessfully tried to convince Maryland governor Thomas Hicks to convene the legislature into special session so it could call a secession convention. Hicks responded that as long as compromise proposals remained before Congress, he would not budge. "Let us show moderation as well as firmness," Hicks admonished Handy, "and be unwilling to resort to extreme measures, until necessity shall leave us no choice." The undeterred

Handy addressed a large crowd at Baltimore's Institute Hall, where he be-
rated the Republicans, disparaged Henry Winter Davis, and suggested that
Congress would not agree to a compromise. After a lackluster response at
Baltimore, Handy made several more speeches across the state. The tepid response led him to the conclusion that the "peculiar local situation" of Maryland, sandwiched between Pennsylvania and the national capital, forestalled
any immediate action in the Old Line State.[61]

Other Lower South commissioners sent to the Border South had a similar
experience. They quickly realized that the earnestly begun Unionist offensive
had neutralized the secession movement along the border. Not even South
Carolina's exit from the Union on December 20 could sway most white border Southerners as long as Crittenden kept his compromise afloat in Washington. Governor Beriah C. Magoffin of Kentucky told a commissioner from
Alabama that he still had faith that Northern conservatives, the long-standing
allies of Border South moderates, would work with Southerners to find a settlement. "You have no hope of a redress in the Union," Magoffin conceded.
"We yet look hopefully to assurances that a powerful reaction is going on at
the North." Magoffin did issue a call for his legislature to meet in special session on January 17, but for the present he was content to wait patiently for the
outcome of Crittenden's efforts in Washington. Another secession commissioner noted that most of the crowds he addressed in Missouri halfheartedly
responded to his pleas for disunion. "Missouri feels and realizes her critical
situation, being a border State. . . . She will move with slow and cautious
steps," the commissioner reported. A secession emissary who met with Governor William Burton of Delaware came away with the understanding that
although many people in the state sympathized with the Lower South, the
great majority favored an adjustment within the Union.[62]

While the Lower South secession commissioners made their fruitless
pitches to white border Southerners, the Committee of Thirteen convened.
At the behest of Jefferson Davis, the committee agreed that it would not report
any compromise package to the Senate unless a dual majority of Republicans
and non-Republicans on the panel voted in favor of the proposition. Crittenden suffered a setback on December 22 when the committee defeated each of
his six proposed amendments in piecemeal fashion. The proposal to extend
the Missouri Compromise line went down to defeat because all five Republicans, along with Davis and Toombs, cast negative votes. Both Davis and
Toombs wished all of the territories to remain open to slavery and believed
that restricting the spread of slavery lay outside the purview of Congress.
Moreover, Crittenden's territorial proposal still lacked a "hereafter acquired"

phrase for southern territory, which prevented the potential expansion of slavery into the tropics. The remaining five amendments had the support of all the committee members except the Republicans.[63] The committee unanimously agreed to adopt his resolutions suggesting an amendment of the Fugitive Slave Act and a permanent restriction of the African slave trade, but the Republicans blocked the other two measures. In response to the Crittenden plan's defeat, Toombs wired his constituents and advised the secession of Georgia.[64]

Over the next few days the committee considered several other compromise proposals yet reached no agreement. The Republicans offered a constitutional amendment, which the committee agreed to, that prohibited Congress from abolishing slavery in the states but made no headway on the critical territorial issue. Douglas crafted a proposal based on the Crittenden plan that utilized popular sovereignty for the territories, but it too met with defeat. Under the leadership of Seward, whose political intercessor Weed had earlier in December met with Lincoln and relayed the president-elect's views on compromise to his friend, the Republicans held firm in opposition to the expansion of slavery.[65]

The rejection of the various compromise proposals in the Committee of Thirteen threatened to wreck the Unionist offensive in the Border South. Crittenden somberly told a circle of friends that he had suffered the "darkest day of my whole life" when the panel dismissed his plan. A lack of progress could stall Unionists' momentum and provide secessionists with an opportunity to advance, which made the congressional committees a focal point for white border Southerners. The prospects of a settlement emerging from the House committee also looked gloomy toward the end of December. The representatives from Florida, Mississippi, and South Carolina, confident of secession, had stopped attending the panel's meetings, and Henry Winter Davis's proposed revisions of the Fugitive Slave Law had become ensnared in a subcommittee. Thomas Nelson's compromise proposal, which closely resembled the Crittenden plan, drew the ire of some Southerners because of its omission of a "hereafter acquired" clause for southern territory. Albert Rust of Arkansas proposed adding the clause, which mired the committee in further disagreement. Rust's suggestion was defeated thirteen to sixteen; every Republican in attendance plus Davis cast negative votes, while the other three Border South members voted in favor of the clause's insertion. In desperation Nelson substituted the Crittenden package for his own, but another quarrel over language brought the committee's labors to a crawl. In response Louisiana's Miles Taylor charged the Republicans with bad faith and indicated he would take no part in further deliberations.[66]

Although crestfallen, Crittenden refused to surrender. He arranged a meeting of border state congressmen and senators at Willard's Hotel on December 28, where Maryland's J. Morrison Harris took the lead in forming an unofficial bipartisan committee made up of five Republicans, five Democrats, and four members of the Southern Opposition. The border state committee included members from fourteen free and slave states and served as a contingency plan for Unionists. In case either of the congressional committees adjourned without a settlement, the border state committee offered another vehicle for compromise. Harris scheduled the committee's first meeting shortly after the start of the year, while Crittenden and Douglas collaborated on a telegram designed to buoy the confidence of Unionists. They utilized the language of proslavery Unionism and emphatically insisted that Southern rights would be protected in the republic. "Don't give up the Ship. Don't despair of the Republic. Let all good men rally bravely to the struggle," they counseled. Although they addressed their telegram to Unionists in Georgia, newspapers across the nation reprinted the message that Crittenden and Douglas had designed to bolster the spirits of moderates and soften the blow that surely would come when the impasse on the Committee of Thirteen went public.[67]

A couple of days later, the bad news from the Senate committee broke. Hopelessly divided, the Committee of Thirteen reported that it had reached no settlement. Undeterred, Crittenden on January 3 submitted a resolution calling for a national referendum on compromise. Convinced that a popular mandate for a settlement existed, he hoped to take the issue of compromise out of the hands of scheming politicians and vest it in the American people. Working in tandem with Douglas, Crittenden suggested that the Little Giant's compromise package from the Committee of Thirteen go before the nation in the plebiscite. Douglas shared Crittenden's confidence in the electorate and predicted that the American people would expeditiously ratify a compromise package. The plebiscite offered yet another alternative route to compromise that Unionists could utilize in case of congressional failure. These options demonstrate Crittenden's keen understanding that the hope of compromise was essential to the vitality of the Unionist offensive. As long as some means of securing a settlement remained viable, Border South Unionists had a weapon to combat secessionists.[68]

Crittenden's efforts paid immediate dividends in Delaware, where the general assembly convened on New Year's Day. In his message to the legislature, Governor Burton blamed Northern abolitionists for the present crisis but expressed his ardent desire for a settlement along the lines of the Crittenden

Compromise. The following day Burton notified the legislature that a secession commissioner from Mississippi wished to address the general assembly. The governor also recommended the legislature call a state convention, a sign that the Mississippian had some impact on Burton. H. Dickinson of Mississippi addressed the legislature on January 3 and beseeched Delaware to join in with the disunion movement. The response of the legislators exhibited the first fruits of the Unionist offensive. The House unanimously passed a joint resolution that expressed its "unqualified disapproval" of secession, while the Senate concurred by a vote of five to three. Even in the wake of the Committee of Thirteen's breakup, the Unionist campaign helped Delaware moderates maintain a resilient attitude toward secession. The legislature subsequently passed a resolution in support of the Crittenden Compromise by a wide margin and rebuffed the recommendation for a state convention, which reveals the persistent belief that all options for compromise had not been exhausted.[69]

Events in Jefferson City, conversely, showed how radicals could take advantage of congressional stasis to advance their cause. The state legislature convened on December 31, 1860, and although Alabama's secession commissioner discovered little enthusiasm for secession among most of the legislators, he found a kindred spirit in Missouri's new governor. Claiborne Fox Jackson deemed Lincoln's election "a declaration of war upon the whole slave property of all the Southern States" and longed for his state to join the secession movement. His inaugural address, in which Jackson roundly condemned the Republicans and defended the course of South Carolina, did not disappoint fire-eaters. "The first drop of blood shed in a war of aggression upon a sovereign State will arouse a spirit which must result in the overthrow of our entire Federal system," Jackson barked. The governor asked the legislature to pass measures for a state convention and recommended that all of the slaveholding states assemble and present an ultimatum to the free states on the vexed slavery issue. If spurned by the North, then the South should collectively leave the Union, Jackson reasoned.[70]

Although moderate Douglas Democrats and Constitutional Unionists controlled over 55 percent of the seats in Missouri's general assembly, radicals held several key leadership positions. Lieutenant Governor Thomas C. Reynolds, an avowed secessionist, presided over the Senate, while the House elected Breckinridge Democrat John McAfee to the Speaker's chair. The triumvirate of Jackson, Reynolds, and McAfee could twist the arms of their colleagues and endanger the state's position in the Union, especially if moderates made no tangible progress in the nation's capital. Reynolds had spent most of

December in Washington and was certain no compromise would materialize. He urged Missouri to prepare its state militia to defend against Republican coercion and plotted with other secessionists to overrun Frank Blair Jr.'s Unionist bastion of Saint Louis. To this end, allies of Jackson and Reynolds introduced separate bills to give the governor unfettered control of the state militia and to organize a police force in Saint Louis. These measures illustrate that Jackson and his minions realized the need for aggressive action to reverse the momentum of the Unionists.[71]

Moderates in the Missouri legislature did not back down in the face of the pro-secession onslaught. On January 8 the legislature recessed to observe Andrew Jackson's 1815 victory in the Battle of New Orleans. In the previous legislative session, the general assembly had commissioned famed artist George Caleb Bingham to paint large portraits of Old Hickory and Henry Clay for display in the statehouse. A native of Missouri, onetime Whig state legislator, and devoted Unionist, Bingham despised secession. At a ceremony on Jackson Day, Bingham unveiled his paintings in the House Chamber in front of a large crowd that included many state legislators and officials. The artist took the opportunity to deliver a rousing speech in defense of the Union, reading excerpts from Andrew Jackson's farewell address and praising Old Hickory for his forceful stance toward South Carolina during the Nullification Crisis. Shortly after Bingham concluded his remarks, Reynolds rebuked the artist and complained of "meddlesome outsiders and disappointed office-seekers" who would use the occasion to discredit the Palmetto State. Bingham and Reynolds thereafter exchanged heated words, and the confrontation nearly turned violent. "I cared nothing about his assumption of dictatorial airs," Bingham later explained in the *Daily Missouri Republican*. "But I regarded him as desecrating the temple in which he stood, by lauding, as a virtue, treason against my Government."[72]

The exchange between Bingham and Reynolds illustrates the passions unleashed during the secession crisis and provides a unique perspective of the Unionist offensive in the Border South. A former arch-Whig, Bingham dropped his partisan bias and praised Andrew Jackson, whom many Whigs once considered the devil incarnate, for his strong Unionist position. He even advocated cooperation with his former Democratic adversaries to keep secessionists in check. "I trust the genuine remnant of the Old Whig party united with the Douglas Democrats and Republicans will be strong enough in the Legislature to keep our state in its true position of loyalty to the Union," Bingham predicted. Desperate times called for desperate measures, and just as Crittenden, the former Whig, had joined hands with a Democrat, Douglas, in order to preserve the republic at Washington, so too did countless other Unionists across the Border South. The confrontation also demonstrates that Border South moderates would not rest on their laurels and allow radicals to gain the upper hand. Bingham used his artistry, his oratory, and his political connections to confront the Missouri fire-eaters. Finally, Bingham emphasized proslavery Unionism and argued that secession endangered both peace and the future of the peculiar institution. Follow Claiborne Jackson, Bingham warned, and all Missourians could count on desolation and the destruction of their slave property. Edward Bates echoed this proslavery Unionist viewpoint. "Disunion," he predicted, "though it may not at once destroy slavery everywhere, will weaken it everywhere, and depreciate its value everywhere, and very probably culminate in bloody abolition."[73]

The fight between Unionists and radicals in the Missouri legislature continued over the following days. The followers of Claib Jackson managed to pass a bill calling for a state convention, but moderates joined together to attach a stipulation that subjected the actions of the convention to the approval of the Missouri electorate. Should delegates to the convention vote for Missouri's secession, the popular referendum would slow the process of disunion and provide Unionists with an opportunity to launch a final counterattack against the fire-eaters. One moderate who voted in favor of the convention with the referendum proviso commented that since the House "had pared the nails and drawn the fangs of the tiger, he was willing to let it loose." Jackson and Reynolds had their convention, but the people of the state would decide Missouri's fate. The fight in Missouri highlighted the volatile nature of conditional Unionism in the Border South and how the preemptive Unionist offensive helped contain secessionist sentiment at this critical juncture.[74]

While Unionists battled secessionists in Dover and Jefferson City, Crittenden and his colleagues kept jockeying for compromise in Washington. The border state committee met in early January and after two lengthy meetings produced a compromise proposal based on Crittenden's package with a few alterations. The border state plan included a single constitutional amendment that forbade Congress from interfering with slavery in the states, while the remaining features of the package emerged as legislation. Moreover, Republicans on the committee agreed to a division of the territories on the basis of the Missouri Compromise line, but they stripped the Crittenden plan of its stipulation calling for territorial governments to protect slavery south of the line. This modification gave residents south of the line the opportunity to ban slavery prior to applying for statehood. Finally, the committee omitted all references to territory hereafter acquired in this section of the package.[75]

Republicans from the border state committee presented the plan to a party caucus on January 5 but found the rest of their organization unreceptive to the compromise package. Several Republican hardliners blasted the compromise as a surrender of principle and at the meeting John Sherman, a member of the committee, acknowledged that he could not vote for the settlement. James T. Hale of Pennsylvania, another Republican on the committee, tried to convince his party brethren of the necessity of compromise, but his colleagues stood firm. Hale also attempted to sway the president-elect, but Lincoln remained unconvinced that conciliation would satiate the Southern demand for additional slave territory. "If we surrender," an unmoved Lincoln avowed, "it is the end of us, and of the government."[76]

With conciliation efforts ostensibly at a dead end in each of the compromise committees, Crittenden on January 7 labored to bring his package directly to the Senate floor. The same day Emerson Etheridge of Tennessee attempted to present a modified version of the border state plan to the House, but Mississippi's William Barksdale objected to its introduction and the Tennessean could not secure the necessary two-thirds vote to push forward. The inability to get the compromise package before the House alarmed some white border Southerners. "Etheridge-Crittenden bill voted down. All hopes lost. Disunion inevitable," a troubled Kentuckian frantically telegraphed home to Paducah.[77]

Etheridge's failed maneuver, coupled with a worsening situation in South Carolina, forced Border South moderates to work with a greater sense of urgency. Militiamen from South Carolina had gathered along the shore of Charleston Harbor and demanded the evacuation of Fort Sumter, an installation on a manmade island in the middle of the harbor that was garrisoned with federal troops. This standoff threatened to upset the efforts of Crittenden and his colleagues. An attack from either side would surely jeopardize the national mandate for conciliation and might throw wavering Border South moderates into the disunionist column. Crittenden reiterated on the floor of the Senate that the Republicans must not take a coercive stance toward South Carolina. "If the sword is to be the only weapon relied upon," he intoned, "then woe to your Administration! Your victory will be turned to blood and ashes."[78]

Four events on January 9 complicated matters for Crittenden's forces. Mississippi joined South Carolina and seceded, ensuring that the Palmetto State had a partner in its disunion project. Mississippi's action emboldened radicals in other states, making the task of Unionists all the more difficult.

Second, Republican senator Daniel Clark dampened the prospects for a settlement when he entered a substitute resolution for the Crittenden package that declared compromise unnecessary and unwarranted. The hardliner Clark fired a salvo across the bow of moderates, though the Senate postponed the matter for the present.[79]

Third, Lazarus Powell proposed an amendment to Crittenden's territorial remedy adding a "hereafter acquired" clause to the language that dealt with territory south of the Missouri Compromise line. Powell told the Senate that Crittenden accepted his amendment and remarked that his colleague had intended to include the phrase when he initially submitted his package. Northern Democrat George Pugh doubted the propriety of including the clause because it would diminish the likelihood of the plan's passage, but Powell insisted its inclusion made the territorial feature "clear and distinct." Powell's amendment passed by a tally of twenty-nine to twenty-four, with all eight Border South senators voting in favor of his alteration. All but one of the negative votes came from Republicans, which signaled that Lincoln's party would not support the Crittenden measures since they now explicitly contradicted the cornerstone of their territorial policy. Whereas Republicans might construe Crittenden's original wording as a means to confine slavery to the arid Southwest, the new phraseology invited expansion into Latin America. No evidence suggests why Crittenden acquiesced on the phrase's inclusion, though it seems likely that senators from the Lower South pressed for the clarification. Powell's contention that Crittenden had intended to include the phrase in the original proposition seems disingenuous, since the Kentuckian had not altered the wording of the package when it was presented to each of the compromise committees or when he introduced it on the floor of the Senate two weeks later.[80]

Finally, the standoff at Charleston nearly escalated into war when at dawn on January 9 the Carolinians opened fire on the merchant steamer *Star of the West*, which Buchanan had ordered southward to reinforce the garrison at Fort Sumter. The ship retreated to the Atlantic and the guns at Charleston returned to silence, but the volley severely tested the patience of most Northerners. Samuel F. Du Pont observed that the incident had "greatly exasperated the North & coercion views are spreading." Crittenden scrambled to offset the ill effect of the news by inviting some thirty proponents of compromise to a dinner party at his residence that night.[81]

In this tense atmosphere the Unionist battle continued in Washington, yet Congress remained paralyzed. Anything but harmony existed on the

Committee of Thirty-Three, which ended its deliberations on January 14. Unlike the Senate panel, the House committee did offer proposals to the lower chamber. Unfortunately, the lack of accord on the committee resulted in several different propositions that represented the views of moderates, fire-eaters, and Republican hardliners. The House temporarily shelved the work of the Committee of Thirty-Three to allow congressmen to digest and sort out the numerous reports. In the Senate Crittenden and other moderates continually pressed for a vote on his compromise measures in an effort to gauge Republican interest in a settlement. Frustrated northern Democrats and conservatives from the Upper and Border South charged the Republicans with avoiding a vote in order to mask their unwillingness to compromise. On January 16, after the Senate voted to add the Powell amendment to Crittenden's settlement, the Republicans closed ranks and took action. They carried a resolution that replaced Crittenden's proposal with Clark's hardline declaration that the present situation merited no need for compromise. The Clark substitution passed twenty-five to twenty-three, with all eight Border South senators voting against it. Republicans registered every single affirmative vote.[82]

The Republican roadblock in Congress rippled through the Border South with distressing effect and confirmed that having a serious compromise proposal on the table was an essential ingredient of Border South Unionism. In Frankfort, Governor Beriah Magoffin on January 17 recommended that the Kentucky legislature call a convention to consider the state's place in the Union. Magoffin's hopes for a settlement had dimmed in the three weeks since he had snubbed the Alabama secession commissioner. "Thus firm in position, obstinate in spirit, and sullen in temper," Magoffin charged, "the Republicans have thwarted every scheme devised to restrain the seceding States." An erroneous secondhand report circulated that Missouri senators James Green and Trusten Polk advocated secession in the wake of the congressional setbacks, which alarmed moderates. In Maryland, Thomas Hicks fretted that if Congress did not quickly act, supporters of secession might leave him with no choice but to call the legislature into session.[83]

"I had strong hopes that the Resolutions I submitted, might be accepted as a basis, at least, for measures of adjustment & reconciliation," a chastened Crittenden confessed after his compromise had been replaced with the Clark resolution. "That hope is almost gone!" Although he admitted "everything here looks gloomy & foreboding," Crittenden and his moderate colleagues in the two and a half months since Lincoln's election had buoyed the hopes of Southern Unionists and kept fire-eaters at bay in the Border South.[84] The

Unionist offensive convinced many white border Southerners that Crittenden, Douglas, and other moderate leaders would find some means to extri-
cate the nation from the crisis. Aware that compromise would likely fester in
the highly charged halls of the Capitol, Crittenden began to explore other
options for compromise. The following months proved that Unionists in the
Border South had yet to expend all of their ammunition in the fight against
secession.

CHAPTER FIVE

Compromise May Restore the Union, but the Sword Can Never Preserve It

The Unionist Offensive, Conditional Unionism, and the Vital Center, Mid-January–March 1861

Colonel Alexander William Doniphan cut an imposing figure when he strode into the overflowing Liberty, Missouri, courthouse on a blustery late-January night to speak about the crisis of the Union. Well over six feet in height, the brawny Doniphan sported a shock of coarse red hair that, according to one observer, protruded from the top of his scowling visage "like porcupine quills." The attorney had made quite a name for himself in the thirty years since he left Kentucky and settled in Liberty, the bustling seat of Clay County at the western edge of the Boon's Lick region. Local judges and fellow barristers admitted that Doniphan's gift for speechmaking greatly exceeded his mastery of the law, but the fifty-one-year-old attorney had built an impressive practice and earned a comfortable living defending clients. Whether representing petty criminals or persecuted Mormons, he often delivered his defense with rhetorical flourish, utilizing his towering frame and rolled-up sleeves to intimidate his courtroom adversaries.[1]

When the United States went to war with Mexico in 1846, Doniphan's military acumen generated national fame that far exceeded his provincial legal renown. He guided a regiment of Missouri volunteers westward into modern-day New Mexico, oversaw the occupation of Santa Fe, drafted a legal code for the new American territory, then led his troops to victory at the battles of El Brazito and Sacramento, which cleared out the province of Chihuahua and contributed to the eventual defeat of all Mexican forces. Upon his regiment's return to the United States, one of Doniphan's soldiers published a pamphlet idolizing their commander, which went far to cement the attorney's reputation as a war hero. Americans hailed Doniphan and his volunteers as torchbearers of the citizen-soldier tradition that reached back to the Revolutionary War.[2]

His successful legal practice and experiences in the Mexican War paved Doniphan's path to three separate terms in the lower house of the Missouri legislature. Although he joined the Whig Party and despised the political program of the Democrats, Doniphan and Democratic firebrand David Rice Atchison cultivated a close relationship and cooperated with one another in an attempt to keep antislavery agitators from settling in Kansas. Doniphan espoused a moderate temperament toward most political issues, but he emphatically insisted that the Constitution protected slavery and that all Americans should have access to the western territories. An owner of five enslaved persons in 1860, Doniphan could not tolerate abolitionists who sought to violate the liberty of his fellow white Southerners. Despite his national fame, the war hero never occupied any office higher than the Missouri General Assembly and, by the winter of 1861, had quietly resumed his law practice. He kept abreast of national affairs, however, and once he learned of John Jordan Crittenden's mid-January setback in Congress, he decided to enlist in the Unionist offensive in his home state.[3]

A testament to Doniphan's celebrity, some two thousand Missourians from the surrounding countryside on January 28 braved the cold weather and snow-covered terrain to hear him speak at the Liberty courthouse. Because only about a third of the crowd could cram inside the building, Doniphan moved the meeting outside so all comers could listen and take part. The old war hero climbed onto a platform in the cold night air and with his trademark style delivered a ninety-minute paean to the Union. Doniphan extolled the virtues of Crittenden's compromise package and insisted that hopes for its passage remained alive, noting that the Virginia legislature had recently passed a resolution calling for a national peace convention that would serve as another instrument for a settlement. According to Doniphan, a show of hands at the meeting indicated that "19/20 of the crowd" endorsed the Crittenden resolutions.[4]

As he came to the conclusion of his oration, Doniphan reminded his listeners that they must elect moderate delegates to the recently called Missouri state convention. Against his wishes, the members of the meeting unanimously agreed to place Doniphan's name on the ticket. He preferred that Unionists in his district find some Democrats to send to the state convention to give their delegation bipartisan appeal, but whoever was chosen had to meet certain requirements. "Let no man be nominated who is in principle radical," Doniphan insisted. "We must keep the issue secession or compromise—and hence we must have compromise Union men so that no submission issue can be forced upon us." He understood the Border South's delicate situation and fully recognized that in order to keep the region in the Union, the hope of a settlement that protected slavery had to remain authentic. The Border South's vital center hung in the balance and, in the absence of a feasible opportunity to secure a compromise, many of the region's conditional Unionists might convert to the secession cause. During this crucial interval, compromise proposals operated as a life preserver for conditional Unionism in the Border South.[5]

Doniphan returned home that night with a hoarse voice and numbed extremities, yet the bitter cold could not dampen his high spirits. As long as new avenues to a compromise settlement remained open and white border Southerners felt confident that remaining in the Union did not imperil slavery, Unionists could isolate the secessionists in their midst. Beyond compromise, Border South Unionism hinged on the prevention of war. Doniphan and other borderland Unionists maintained that the federal government could not coerce the seceded states to return to the republic, nor should Lower South radicals inaugurate a shooting war. Either eventuality might upset the Unionist offensive and the safety of slavery in the Border South. The period between mid-January and the end of March 1861, marked by diminishing hopes of a compromise settlement and an escalating chance of military conflict, severely tested Border South Unionism. Some white border Southerners joined the secession movement and others opted for a unique approach of neutrality, but most of the region's vital center remained committed to the Union. The interval revealed the limits to which some Border South Unionists would accede, the malleability of conditional Unionism, and the remarkable durability of the Unionist campaign orchestrated by Crittenden and his colleagues.

WHILE DONIPHAN AND OTHER Border South moderates took to the stump on behalf of the Union, Crittenden continued the fight for a conciliatory settlement of the slavery issue in the nation's capital. Although he considered Daniel Clark's substitution resolution declaring compromise unnecessary an affront, the Kentuckian explored other means to circumvent Republican obfuscation in Congress. As his faith in congressional action waned, Crittenden's trust in the American people grew. Correspondents from across the country informed him that in spite of the dangerous *Star of the West* episode, most Americans still yearned for a settlement. If he could only get his proposal before American voters, Crittenden believed, the electorate would sanction it.[6]

The course of the legislatures of Delaware, Kentucky, and Missouri further convinced Crittenden that a strong mandate for his settlement existed. Delaware's general assembly on January 17 passed a resolution voicing approval of the Crittenden Compromise and instructing the state's members of Congress to "advocate the said proposition" or any other means of reconciliation. The legislature claimed this plea for compromise "reflect[ed] the will of a large majority of their constituents" and the American people. The endorsement of Crittenden's package passed the House by a vote of nineteen to two and the Senate by a tally of eight to one. The paucity of votes in opposition to the resolution demonstrated that many Delawareans had yet to give up on compromise. Even Senator James Asheton Bayard, whose cozy relationship with Lower South fire-eaters and antics at the Charleston Convention invited accusations that he was a closet secessionist, announced his support of the Crittenden resolutions.[7]

Debate in the Kentucky legislature, which met on January 17, also centered on the need for compromise. The legislature on January 24 settled on a series of resolutions that asked Congress to call a national convention to discuss the myriad compromise plans that politicians had placed before the public and proclaimed that Kentuckians preferred the Crittenden Compromise above all others. Moderates in the House defeated an attempt made by some of their secession-leaning colleagues to add language to the resolution that stated that if the Northern states rejected compromise, Kentucky would secede. Stripped of this ultimatum, the pro-compromise resolutions cleared the House by a vote of eighty-two to eight. No roll call exists for the Senate vote, but the upper chamber agreed thirty-seven to zero to the suggestion of the House to present the Crittenden Compromise as the best means to quell the crisis.[8]

The Unionist offensive managed to check disunionists in Frankfort during the early stages of the special session. Representative John O. Harrison and Senator John F. Fisk coordinated on a resolution that required the sergeant at arms to fly the American flag over the state capitol for the duration of the session. Pro-secession forces dismissed the flag initiative as "a token of submission" and unsuccessfully attempted to table the resolution, which passed both houses by a wide margin. Unionists stymied Representative James G. Leach's attempt to bring a resolution before the House that called for the newly created Committee on Federal Relations to report a bill calling a state convention. Leach had tried to cater to moderates by including a stipulation subjecting any actions of the state convention to popular ratification, but Unionists joined together and tabled the resolution by a vote of fifty-four to thirty-six. A similar initiative for a state convention stalled in the Senate, where moderates used an array of obstructionist tactics to combat this first step toward secession. Kentucky Unionists held firm and refused to follow the path of the Missouri legislature, where pro-secession forces had managed to call a convention, albeit one that the Unionists had handcuffed by subjecting the body's decisions to the electorate's approval. Moderates achieved two additional victories when they buried separate resolutions that declared secession legal and called for an alliance with the seceded states if the free states rejected compromise in the Committee on Federal Relations.[9]

The great lengths to which Unionists went to thwart a state convention in Kentucky have gone largely unnoticed by scholars of the sectional crisis.[10] Yet these moderates labored day and night to prevent the Bluegrass State from even putting the question of a convention before the people. "I doubt if our people will ever know the deep debt they owe the conservative men who controlled that Assembly, not so much for the good accomplished as for the evil prevented," Unionist representative C. F. Burnam later recalled. "Argument, persuasion, entreaty, the party lash—all means that can be conceived of, are brought into requisition," a journalist for the pro-secession *Louisville Daily Courier* scoffed. A proponent of secession lamented that moderates in the general assembly "are acting as a firm phalanx against any prompt & speedy action" by keeping alive the hopes that a settlement might yet be reached.[11]

By employing Unionist symbolism, backroom bargaining, and every conceivable parliamentary maneuver, moderates prevented Kentucky from following North Carolina and Tennessee, where both legislatures allowed for a popular referendum on whether to call a state convention. Although voters in both Upper South states rejected a convention in February, the passage of the referendum bills put in place the machinery for a quick withdrawal from the Union if any event occurred that endangered the flimsy truce between Lower South secessionists and the federal government. Had they not taken action, Unionists may have lost the momentum to secessionists and allowed Kentucky to join the Upper South states that eventually opted for disunion. Advocates of a state convention with well-earned reputations for political trickery exerted all the influence they could muster on politicians in Frankfort, but they could not open a breach in the Unionist lines. Much to the dismay of fire-eaters, Unionists had built an impressive bulwark that was difficult to assail as long as hopes for a settlement remained alive.[12]

Kentucky politicians of all stripes, however, reviled the prospect of the federal government coercing any of the seven Lower South states back into the Union. In the aftermath of the *Star of the West* incident in Charleston Harbor, several Northern state legislatures offered the federal government financial aid, supplies, and men to subdue Lower South secessionists. Some Northern governors put their states on a war footing by urging enlistments in state militias, instructing state militia officers to conduct drills, and procuring weapons and military equipment. In response, Representative G. W. Ewing crafted a set of joint resolutions expressing regret that some Northern governments had made these preparations and asking Governor Beriah C. Magoffin to warn other state executives that if Northern troops marched southward, "the people of Kentucky, uniting with their brethren of the South, will, as one man, resist such invasions of the soil of the South at all hazard and to the last extremity." Both resolutions, which highlighted the fragile nature of Border South Unionism, passed the House with ease.[13]

Fire-eater Blanton Duncan viewed himself as the catalyst for Ewing's resolutions. He admitted to a South Carolina confidant that he had whipped many Kentucky legislators into a frenzy over the actions of the Northern governments. A newspaper reporter also claimed that prior to the vote on the resolutions, one of the state legislators circulated a letter from an unnamed Kentucky congressman who suggested Crittenden had given up on compromise because of Republican intransigence. Unconditional Unionist Leslie Combs complained of Duncan's machinations and remarked that Frankfort "is full of Devils & Fireeaters—generally with hair all over their faces—as if ashamed to be seen by honest men." Combs noted that proslavery Unionism relied on "the anxious hope that the North will do justice on the Slave & Territorial questions." Duncan's scheming aside, Ewing's resolutions illustrate both the robust antipathy toward coercion among white borderites and the conditional nature of Southern Unionism. Any bellicose action from the North, especially from their critical allies in the Lower North, threatened to capsize Unionist sentiment in the Border South, and even the rumor of compromise reaching a dead end in Washington could affect borderites' attitudes about secession.[14]

Although the Missouri legislature had already decided to hold a state convention, the subject of the Crittenden Compromise did not go away in Jefferson City. Representative Mortimer McIlhany introduced a resolution that distinguished the Crittenden plan "as a fair and equitable adjustment of the troubles which now afflict the country" and instructed Missouri's congressional delegation to "use all their influence to secure [its] passage." The House placed McIlhany's resolution aside, though several politicians referenced the Crittenden package and the importance of proslavery Unionism during debate. Senator John Gullett proclaimed that although he hailed from a district with few enslaved persons, "he wanted to see slave property protected as scrupulously as any other property." Remaining in the Union and securing a compromise settlement were the best means to do this, he argued. Unionist Robert Wilson reminded his fellow politicians that if Missouri chose secession over compromise, they would surely expedite the destruction of slavery. Pro-spectively surrounded on three sides by a foreign nation, secession invited a raft of slave escapes, welcomed additional abolitionist incursions, and created an indefensible eight-hundred-mile-long border. "That institution about which we have talked so much in this hall, must in a few years disappear from our borders, should we secede," Wilson forewarned. Compromise and the Union, not secession, perpetuated slavery in Missouri, moderates argued. Citizens of Saint Louis in late January inaugurated a petition drive and in a few days collected over twelve thousand signatures in favor of the Crittenden package.[15]

In Maryland, Governor Thomas Hicks continued to resist the entreaties of those who wanted him to convene the legislature in special session. Eleven state senators even signed a circular letter requesting the governor to call the legislature, but Hicks remained unmoved. An unconditional Unionist reminded Hicks that Democrats, many of whom sympathized with secession, controlled both houses of the legislature and thus would speedily pass a convention bill. Under Maryland's constitution, he noted, the executive lacked the veto power, which increased the odds that a convention bill would pass. With this in mind, Hicks refused to budge and asked the people of Maryland to rely on "the sober second thought of the masses," especially Northern conservatives, who would align with the Border South on the quest for conciliation. Rumors of secessionist plots to carry Maryland out of the Union also strengthened Hicks's resolve to keep the legislature from assembling.[16] Hicks stayed in close contact with Crittenden and kept the Kentuckian abreast of developments in Maryland, where he detected a strong mandate for compromise and an equally sturdy concern about congressional deadlock. He told Crittenden that obdurate Republicans and inflexible secessionists "remind me of a pair of bull year-lings with the heads butting together and pressing agt [against] each other[,] each striving for the mastery." If only they listened to the electorate, Hicks reasoned, these politicians would grasp the prevailing impetus for a settlement. A Baltimore merchant likewise observed "a strong Union feeling here, but no disposition to aid the government agains [sic] the South."[17]

When the Crittenden measures stalled in the Senate in mid-January, Hicks briefly considered calling the legislature into session. The pertinacious stance of the Republicans, along with rumblings of an assassination plot aimed at Hicks, rattled the heretofore poised governor. Pennsylvania governor Andrew Curtin, a Republican, sent a goodwill delegation to Maryland to demonstrate solidarity in the effort to battle secessionists, but Hicks refused to receive it. The governor told the Pennsylvanians that Maryland could handle its own affairs and added he "was a Southerner and a slaveholder, and that his whole feelings and interests were identified with the South." The fate of compromise in Washington had a controlling effect on the vital center in the Border South, and even stout Unionists like Hicks had second thoughts about their approach to the crisis during the dark days of mid-January. Shortly thereafter, however, Hicks recommitted himself to holding the line against those who wished for the legislature to assemble.[18]

Two phenomena helped moderates across the Border South regain their confidence in the prospects of compromise. First, in late January the idea of a convention of the states started to gain traction. As early as December, Magoffin had proposed a meeting of all the slave state governors to "arrest the secession movement, until the question as to whether the Union can be preserved upon fair and honorable terms, can be fully tested," but the Kentucky governor received a lukewarm response from other executives. With the compromise effort apparently stillborn in Congress, a growing number of Americans advised a national gathering. In the middle of January, Crittenden got each member of the Kentucky congressional delegation to endorse a telegram to Magoffin asking him to appoint five politicians to meet with officials from Virginia in Washington for the purpose of finding a solution to the national impasse. Convinced that partisanship and demagoguery inhibited a settlement in Congress, many moderates vested their hopes in a national convention made up of dispassionate, clear-headed statesmen who would willingly work toward a realistic compromise.[19]

The Virginia legislature took the lead in the push for a national convention and in mid-January passed a resolution inviting every other state in the Union to send delegates to Washington on February 4. The general assembly submitted a slightly altered version of the Crittenden Compromise as a basis for negotiations and dispatched emissaries who pled with leaders in Washington and South Carolina to refrain from reckless action that might provoke violence. Unionists across the Border South quickly latched on to Virginia's call for a peace convention. The legislatures of Delaware and Kentucky swiftly passed resolutions to participate in the convention and each state sent committed Unionists from various partisan backgrounds to the Washington meeting. The proposition faced greater difficulty in the divided Missouri General Assembly, but on January 31 the legislature settled on its delegates. With the legislature out of session in Maryland, Hicks took it upon himself to assign his state's participants in the Washington Peace Conference. Opponents of Hicks howled that his decision to send commissioners without legislative fiat represented a usurpation of executive power, but the governors of six other states also sent delegates without consulting their legislatures.[20]

Of the twenty-three men who represented the Border South at the Washington Peace Conference, eleven belonged to the Democratic Party and ten to the Opposition. The party affiliation of two delegates is unknown, but no Republicans represented the Southern borderland at the convention. These eminent border Southerners, including Alexander Doniphan, James Guthrie, Reverdy Johnson, and Henry Clay's son James B. Clay, were on average fifty-five years of age and owned around eleven enslaved persons. Ten of these delegates, however, owned fewer than five or no slaves at all, while five of the emissaries had reached planter status. Nearly all of the Border South delegates had been born in the Border or Upper South, though one originally hailed from South Carolina and another from Pennsylvania. Their age, wealth, attachment to slavery, and familiarity with the Border South meant that these men plainly understood the importance of finding a solution to the crisis that protected slavery.[21]

While the nation waited for the Washington Peace Conference to convene, Crittenden and his colleagues persisted in their effort to get Congress to consider some compromise plan. He successfully managed to get the Senate to reconsider its January 16 vote to substitute the Clark resolution for his plan, which revived the possibility of a congressional settlement. To throw in the towel on Capitol Hill would have provided Border South disunionists with greater leverage and confirmed to many white Southerners the fire-eater argument that the South had no future in a Republican-controlled Union. Severn Teackle Wallis, an outspoken Baltimore politician with secessionist proclivities, caustically warned a Maryland Unionist "that in the absence of such concessions on the part of the North, the dismemberment of the Republic is a foregone conclusion, & nothing will be left to us, here, but a choice of adhesion to the one or the other of its fragments." Moderates anticipated that a compromise agreement would allow borderites to avoid, or at least delay, making a decision between Union and secession.[22]

Although Crittenden managed to get his compromise proposals back on the Senate calendar, he failed to persuade moderate Republicans to break ranks and support his plan. Just as Unionists had employed obstructionist measures in the Border South legislatures to derail the initiatives of radicals, Republicans in Washington utilized parliamentary procedures to stall a second vote on the Crittenden package. Republicans brought an array of other matters before the Senate and the few remaining Southern radicals in the upper house sustained the delaying tactics in an attempt to disrupt any progress toward a settlement. Stephen A. Douglas watched helplessly and fumed that "it is no longer worth while to conceal from ourselves the fact that the extremists on this side and on the other side are in concert, from different motives, to defeat a settlement." Even though he could not procure a vote on his resolutions, Crittenden had seen to it that radicals could not entomb the issue of compromise. He successfully bridged the gap between the substitution of the Clark resolution and the meeting of the peace commissioners in Washington by repeatedly pressing for consideration of his measures. Once the peace conference opened, Crittenden relaxed his campaign for deliberation of his compromise package, but promised to renew his efforts after the meeting concluded. His strategy buttressed the Unionist offensive and kept secessionists from winning over large segments of the Border South's vital center.[23]

In the House of Representatives, the chances for a comprehensive settlement appeared to break down. Debates of the six separate reports from the Committee of Thirty-Three commenced on January 21 and continued ad nauseam throughout much of the remainder of the session. "The Committee of Thirty-three neither saved the Union nor their own reputations," a newspaper correspondent grumbled in the midst of the unending discussion of the different proposals. During the often vituperative deliberations, several Border South congressmen admonished their colleagues to vote rather than talk. Every day that Congress remained inactive provided fire-eaters with additional grist and increased the likelihood that some border Southerners would abandon the Union. A few House Republicans showed a willingness to discuss the possibility of compromise in early February, including Illinois congressman William Kellogg, who submitted his own settlement package that extended the Missouri Compromise line westward. Stalwarts cracked the party whip, however, and brought these Republicans back into line. The party faithful would go no further than accepting Thomas Corwin's suggestion for a constitutional amendment that protected slavery in the states. Kellogg faced a figurative Republican firing squad for introducing his package; one observer in Illinois regarded the congressman as "politically dead in all parts of the state but among democrats."[24]

Abraham Lincoln's stance on compromise had not changed significantly in the two months since Congress convened. Still ensconced in Springfield, the president-elect maintained his public silence on the unfolding national crisis and brushed off the mountain of entreaties from white border Southerners who asked him to make a statement about the slavery controversy. The petitions of a few influential Border South moderates, however, did provoke Lincoln to relent ever so slightly. Earlier in December Nathan Sargent, an old acquaintance of Lincoln, met with a handful of politicians in Washington to discuss the crisis. During the meeting Senator James A. Pearce of Maryland admitted that although a public statement from the president-elect would have little impact in the Lower South, it "would have a powerful effect in the Northern slave states, and might arrest the epidemic now so fearfully & rapidly spreading." Crittenden and Kentuckian Green Adams also informed one of Lincoln's emissaries that a public statement outlining the nuance of the president-elect's position on slavery in the states as opposed to the territories would smother the disunion movement in the Border and Upper South.[25]

President James Buchanan subsequently sent Duff Green, a Kentuckian and a formerly powerful newspaper editor, out to Springfield in the hopes of convincing Lincoln to issue a letter that sketched his intentions toward the South. Green placed the Crittenden resolutions before Lincoln, who replied that he could not accept an extension of the Missouri Compromise line because it would leave the root of the territorial issue unresolved. Although "he intended to sustain his party in good faith," Lincoln added that he would acquiesce to the will of the people if they chose to add an amendment to the Constitution. Green apparently convinced Lincoln to compose a letter in which he outlined his belief that no change to the Constitution was necessary, but that he would not interfere with the amendment process if the American people consented to the alteration. Furthermore, the president-elect copied directly from the Chicago Platform the Republican position that each state had the sovereign right to "control its own domestic institutions according to its own judgment exclusively."[26]

Lincoln consented to the publication of the letter under the condition that six of the twelve senators from any of the Deep South states aside from South Carolina also affix their signature to the document. He placed the communication in the hands of his trusted Republican lieutenant Lyman Trumbull, not Green, and instructed him to deliver it only if he felt it would do the party no harm. Although Green apparently received the letter, he did not make its contents public. Speculation about Green's reticence to publish the letter revolves around two possibilities: he held back because of Lincoln's "unwillingness to recommend an amendment to the constitution which will arrest the progress of secession" or because he could not procure the signatures of six Southern senators. Green did file a report of his visit to Springfield in the *New York Herald* and commented that once in office Lincoln would meet several demands of the South—from taking no action against slavery in the District of Columbia and federal property in the slaveholding states to keeping the interstate slave trade intact—but noted on the issue of slavery in the territo-

ries that Lincoln was "firmly and unequivocally resolved to make no concession." While Green painted Lincoln in a favorable light, his testimonial did
little to pacify nervous white Southerners.[27]

From outward appearances, Lincoln seemed to have quarantined himself
in Springfield, idly counting the days until his inauguration. In reality he labo-
riously pored over correspondence from Washington, entertained an endless
stream of visitors, and sifted through a mountain of recommendations for
cabinet appointees. The composition of his cabinet became an engrossing
issue because it would likely indicate the political trajectory of his administration. Would he fill his official family with hardline Republicans and radical
abolitionists, or would he opt to staff his cabinet with moderates? This question carried momentous weight among white borderites, who utterly depended on cooperation from Northern conservatives to preserve slavery. For
the inhabitants of the Border South, the composition of Lincoln's cabinet
served as a barometer of the Republican stance on the South and would likely
impact the vital center's outlook on Union or secession.[28]

Lincoln twice met with Edward Bates in December and told the Missourian that he planned to include both him and New York senator William
Henry Seward in his cabinet. Bates worried that Seward's inclusion "would
exasperate the feelings of the South, and make conciliation impossible,
because they consider Mr. S[eward] the embodiment of all that they hold
odious in the Republican Party." The president-elect assured Bates that
Seward's reputation for radicalism actually cloaked a conservative outlook
and pointed out that the New Yorker had privately suggested several Southern moderates to round out the cabinet. Lincoln's declaration may have eased
Bates's mind, but the inclusion of Seward, whom one Kentuckian considered
"the most obnoxious man of all to the South," left many white border Southerners dismayed. On the other hand, many moderates welcomed Bates's addition to the cabinet. Aside from his groping for the Republican nomination
in the run-up to the Chicago convention, Bates had established himself as a
conservative on the slavery extension issue.[29]

Most Border South conservatives considered Bates the best choice of the
tiny collection of Southern Republicans. Rumors swirled that Lincoln might
assign a post to Cassius Clay, an irascible abolitionist from Kentucky, which
frightened many white border Southerners. Robert Jefferson Breckinridge
remonstrated to Lincoln that the appointment of Clay would likely tip the
balance in the Bluegrass State toward secession. "Kentucky would feel in-
sulted at having forced on her as her organ a citizen over whom she would
even prefer Seward," George Robertson remarked. Some Republicans also

mentioned Henry Winter Davis for a post in the cabinet, which generated discontent among the Border South electorate. Davis's assistance in electing a Republican Speaker of the House had not faded from memory, and most Border South voters dismissed him as a radical firebrand. Lincoln reserved a spot in his cabinet for someone from the powerful Blair family—whose patriarch, Francis Preston Blair Sr., had been instrumental in the formation of the Republican Party—and the inclusion of fellow Missourian Bates made it unlikely that Saint Louis native Frank Blair Jr. would receive an appointment. The president-elect settled on Frank's older brother Montgomery Blair, a Maryland attorney whom most people considered a moderate on the slavery issue.[30]

Lincoln's decision to include moderate Border South men like Bates and Montgomery Blair in his cabinet suggests that the president-elect hoped to offset his party's sectional cast. Still, he faced an uphill battle convincing white border Southerners that the Republicans meant their region no harm. People from the Border South considered Bates and Blair better choices than Clay or Davis, but nonetheless they were still Republicans.[31] Without some public assurance that he would not touch slavery in the states, white border Southerners worried the new president might fall victim to radicals in his party who planned "some subterranean design to wage an exterminating crusade against [the South] by all the power and patronage of the incoming administration." James Asheton Bayard voiced similar concerns and worried of the racial consequences of Republican rule. He told his son that the "inevitable result of [Republican] dogmas must be the destruction of negro slavery, and the ultimate equality of the negro and the white man." Congressman Thomas L. Anderson of Missouri laid bare the paranoia that had engulfed the Border South since Lincoln's election: "Many of our slaves are now impressed with the idea that, after the inauguration of Mr. Lincoln, they are to be free. This impression makes them restless and discontented [and] renders our homes, our wives, and our children unsafe."[32]

Lincoln's silence, the possibility of armed conflict at Charleston Harbor, and the inflexibility of Republicans in Congress together manufactured a great deal of disquietude within the Border South's vital center. Affairs in Saint Louis complicated matters for Border South moderates who, in order to sustain the Unionist offensive, wished to avoid an armed conflict at all costs. The city contained a lightly guarded federal arsenal packed with about sixty thousand stands of arms and was commanded by a known secessionist sympathizer. Frank Blair Jr. heard reports that at the behest of Governor Claiborne Fox Jackson, militants planned to seize the arsenal and distribute the arms to the state militia. Blair worried that a heavily armed state militia would embolden Missouri secessionists in their quest to push the state out of the Union. In January 1861 he organized a Union Committee of Public Safety along with his own militia unit to counterpoise the secessionists in Saint Louis. Blair named his militia unit, composed mostly of Republicans and Germans, the Home Guards to distinguish it from the state militia. Fears arose among moderates that a violent standoff in their own backyard, rather than far-off Charleston Harbor, might unravel the tapestry of Unionism in the Border South. Isaac Sturgeon warned Buchanan that if either the fire-eaters or Blair's organization captured the arsenal, "war would at once begin in this section."[33]

Fearful of an outbreak of hostilities, General-in-Chief Winfield Scott ordered Lieutenant W. J. Robinson and forty federal soldiers to Saint Louis, where they anxiously held their post while secessionist militia units mobilized around them. Captain Nathaniel Lyon marched a company of U.S. troops into the city on February 6 to reinforce the forty regulars and Blair's Home Guard. Lyon, a Connecticut-born officer with a reputation for impetuosity, wrested control of the federal arsenal from pro-secession Major Peter V. Hagner. The amplified federal contingent restrained the secessionist forces in Saint Louis for the time being, but the presence of U.S. troops alarmed the state's congressional delegation. Senator James S. Green and Congressman John B. Clark questioned why federal troops had been introduced in Missouri, and each submitted resolutions of inquiry to the secretary of war. The resolutions failed to advance in either house, but Clark caused an uproar when he pressed the matter and avowed, "I want to know whether martial law is declared in my State; whether our women and children . . . are to be met by soldiers and bristling bayonets."[34] The possibility of armed conflict in Saint Louis foreshadowed the difficulties that Unionists would have to contend with should force overcome negotiation. Furthermore, the prickly reaction of Green and Clark laid bare the contempt that many white border Southerners held for federal troops entering any part of the South, even the Unionist stronghold of Saint Louis. Any hint of coercion threatened to weaken conditional Unionism within the Border South's vital center.

Aware of the mounting frustration of white border Southerners, Republican George Palmer of New York on February 11 offered a pair of resolutions that proclaimed the federal government and the people of the North had neither the desire nor the constitutional right to interfere with slavery in the states and that Northern radicals who did not ascribe to this viewpoint were "too insignificant in numbers or influence to excite serious attention or alarm." Intended to allay the fear of border Southerners, the resolutions instead provoked the wrath of Henry C. Burnett, a Democrat from western Kentucky who embraced secession. Described as "a big, burly, loud-mouthed fellow who is forever raising points of order and objections, to embarrass the Republicans in the House," Burnett had throughout the session cast aspersions at Lincoln's party. Burnett engaged in a lengthy and rancorous debate with several Republicans about the Palmer resolutions and their party's intentions toward slavery. At the suggestion of Republican John Sherman, the language of the resolutions was simplified to declare that neither Congress nor the Northern state governments could interfere with slavery in the states. The abridged resolution passed the House by a vote of 161–0, though four Border South congressmen refrained from casting a ballot.[35]

The debate surrounding the Palmer resolutions illustrated the mounting aggravations of white border Southerners and indicated that some people had begun to reevaluate their section's place in the Union. Some, like Burnett, reaffirmed their belief that the Republicans intended to dismantle slavery and increasingly warmed to secession as the days passed and no compromise settlement emerged. Others expressed interest in armed neutrality, a policy whereby each state in the Border South would in the event of war maintain its relations with both the federal government and the seceded states. Former governor Robert M. Stewart of Missouri broached the possibility of armed neutrality upon leaving office in late December 1860, and in time other Border South politicians explored this option. A Kentucky attorney nicely summed up the approach of neutrality: "I have a good rifle of my own—and will never fight against the South[,] but I am in favor of restoring the Union." He added that he would help hang the first federal tax collector who tried to procure money from him to fund a war for the purpose of coercing the seceded states back into the republic. Reunion must come through mediation, white border Southerners insisted, not by the sword, and armed neutrality presented another possible mechanism to achieve that end. The plodding course of Congress and long-standing fears about the Republicans by February exposed the conditional nature of Border South Unionism. Many inhabitants of the Border South stayed true to the Union, but an increasing number of people began to consider neutrality a potential halfway house between a Republican-dominated Union and secession.[36]

Many Americans transferred their hopes for the perpetuity of the Union from the hamstrung Congress to the peace conference, which on February 4, 1861, opened its proceedings in Washington. The same day, delegates from the Lower South gathered in Montgomery, Alabama, to create a government of their own. Nearly everyone appreciated the irony that the two conventions—one charged with preserving the republic and the other with tearing it asunder—met on the day on which seventy-two years earlier the Electoral College confirmed George Washington as the first president of the United States. "This day will decide whether we are to have absolutely two governments," Samuel F. Du Pont solemnly reflected.[37]

A portrait of the first president stared out at the approximately 60 delegates from eleven states who assembled in the dance hall of Willard's Hotel on the first day of the Washington Peace Conference. Over the following days more representatives arrived; by the end of the proceeding in late February, over 130 delegates represented twenty-one states at the conference. Time and distance prevented California and Oregon from sending delegates to the meeting, while political wrangling in state legislatures left Michigan, Minnesota, Wisconsin, and Arkansas without representation. Iowa and Maine simply instructed their congressional contingent to represent them at the conference, but with their primary commitment to Congress, these delegations only intermittently participated in the meeting. The seven Lower South states had seceded and thus sent no delegates to the peace conference. The refusal of the Lower South and portions of the Upper North to send delegates to the conference indicated that the borderland states were much more eager to effect a settlement than the people of other regions.[38]

With the Lower South and portions of the Upper North striking a posture of defiance, conservatives hitched their hopes of a settlement to the good faith of their Lower North allies. Republican-controlled legislatures in Illinois and Ohio, however, had appointed inflexible delegates to the peace conference and Indiana governor Oliver P. Morton admitted that he favored sending representatives to the meeting not because he "expected any positive good to come from it, but to prevent positive evil." Worried that some Northern delegates might cave and agree to a settlement, Morton recommended that the other Lower North states dispatch hardliners who would "operate as a powerful restraint upon any disposition on the part of the other states to compromise the integrity and future of the Republican party." Moreover, the legislatures of Illinois, Indiana, New York, Ohio, and Pennsylvania—all with Republican majorities—indicated that although they were sending delegates to the meeting, they felt it unnecessary to amend the Constitution at present. Other states bound any action of their delegates to the approval of the state legislature. These stipulations and riders boded ill for Border South moderates who in previous sectional disputes had often counted on the collaboration of the Lower North.[39]

Former president John Tyler of Virginia chaired the Washington Peace Conference, but his presence did little to inspire the American people. At the behest of Kentucky's James Guthrie, a committee of one delegate from each state was formed to review the numerous compromise proposals before the nation and make a report on the best mode of settlement. Although the official rules of the meeting mandated secret proceedings, Guthrie and the other border Southerners on the committee surely communicated with Crittenden about their progress. The rest of the convention waited, at times impatiently, while the committee, chaired by Guthrie, closeted from February 6 until February 14. In the interim, Border South moderates implored their colleagues from the North to recognize that the success of the Unionist offensive hinged on a settlement. "Our Border State friends say we must not be deceived— Unless some adjustment is made those now Union men, will join their futures to the Southern Confederacy," an Ohio delegate noted. Davis fretted that the "assembled fogeydom" at the peace conference would only complicate matters for Congress. If the meeting broke up without a settlement, Border South fire-eaters would take advantage. On the other hand, any compromise that emerged from the convention would probably go down to defeat in Congress, which would yield the same result.[40]

While the delegates in Washington awaited the Guthrie Committee's report, Lincoln on February 11 started his meandering journey to the nation's capital. The president-elect had received invitations to stop and deliver remarks at several points between Springfield and Washington, which afforded Lincoln the opportunity to break his long-standing public silence on the national crisis. Border South moderates certainly grimaced when they read his remarks in the paper. In Indianapolis he made light of the Southern demand that the federal government not attempt to force the seceded states back into the Union, likening such a position to "a sort of free-love arrangement." A day later in Cincinnati Lincoln tempered his comments and reminded Kentuckians across the Ohio River that back in 1859 he had proclaimed that Republicans "mean to leave you alone, and in no way interfere with your institution; to abide by all and every compromise of the constitution," and to treat them with mutual respect as Americans. Lincoln assured the crowd that circumstances had not changed his viewpoint toward the South, but he concluded his remarks with the tactless warning that if the South could not see this, then "the fault shall not be mine."[41]

While Republicans in the North found Lincoln's remarks comforting, white borderites dismissed the president-elect's comments as flippant and offensive. Kentucky's Blanton Duncan read Lincoln's Indianapolis speech and believed it confirmed that the new president "is the most fanatical of his party & it is idle to hope for peace." Duncan also heard a secondhand account from a colleague who had visited with Lincoln before he left Springfield and explained to the president-elect that several resolutions lay before the Kentucky legislature expressing disapprobation at a federal policy of coercion. One of the resolutions even said that if the federal government used force against the seceded states, Kentucky would consider the act "a dissolution of all previous compacts" and make preparations to resist invasion. Lincoln allegedly responded that if these resolutions represented the true sentiment of Kentucky, "let her prepare for war." The fire-eater Duncan of course searched for any shred of evidence to make a case for the secession of the Border South, but more impartial white border Southerners also lamented the tone of Lincoln's speeches. "He approaches the capital of the country more in the character of a harlequin, dealing with the great issues which agitate and agonize the minds of thoughtful and rational men as if they were only the absurdities of a pantomime which would all be 'put to rights' by a touch of his magic wand," a Baltimore editor muttered. Alexander Doniphan took time out from his labors on the Guthrie Committee to read Lincoln's speeches and remarked, "We are constantly looking for him to ruin everything [with] his ridiculously childish display of eloquence & presidential taste and literary attainment." An angry Doniphan branded Lincoln "as ridiculously vain and fanatic as a country boy with his first red morocco hat" and dismissed the president-elect as "an ignorant, country buffoon." Lincoln had prepared an address expressly for Kentuckians on his journey eastward, but he never delivered it. The intended speech laid out his rationale for refusing to endorse compromise and stated that if the American people disliked him, they could vote him out of office in the next election. Considering how the Border South reacted to his other speeches, the statement intended for Kentuckians probably would have done more harm than good.[42]

While Lincoln's cavalcade churned toward Washington, the Guthrie Committee on February 15 finally presented its majority report to the peace conference. The proposal from the committee contained elements of both the Crittenden Compromise and the proposal put forth by J. Morrison Harris's border state committee. The package included an extension of the Missouri Compromise line and, in an effort to attract Republican support, it did not require Congress or territorial governments to protect slavery south of the line. In addition to the other familiar facets of the Crittenden plan, the majority report recommended that four-fifths of the Senate must approve any future territorial acquisitions. This supermajority requirement would diminish the likelihood of the United States acquiring more territory and stifle the sectional agitation that came with the expansion of the republic. According to one attendee, Guthrie and Reverdy Johnson of Maryland had taken the lead in ushering the majority report through the committee. Separate minority reports from the committee called for a national constitutional convention, which some moderates considered nothing more than a means for Republicans to continue their policy of inactivity, and a hardline Southern report that included a provision that clarified the right of secession.[43]

The proceedings in the Washington Peace Conference ground to a halt over the next several days as the delegates discussed the compromise proposals. The debate exposed the harsh reality that differences of opinion about slavery in the territories would likely preclude a settlement that all parties found satisfactory. Border South delegates pled for Republicans at the convention to accept the majority report in order to stave off secession in the remaining slaveholding states, but no breakthrough occurred. Although he rarely entered into the endless floor debates, Doniphan watched, listened, and became less hopeful that the convention would accomplish anything of substance. He privately complained that most Republicans had come to Washington to derail any conciliatory measures and worried that if the president-elect came under the spell of hardliners within his party, "then we may go home and tell our people to call on Gabriel to blow for the Union will be dissolved in a few days or months at most." The Missourian, who had been an integral participant in the Unionist offensive just a month before, seriously began to entertain the possibility that the Border South might leave the Union in the absence of a compromise. Some exasperated border Southerners reached a similar conclusion by mid-February, which steadily chipped away at the vital center's faith in proslavery Unionism.[44]

Lincoln arrived in Washington during the early morning hours of February 23 after hurrying through Baltimore the previous night. Rumors swirled about a possible attempt on the president-elect's life as he made his way through Maryland, and federal authorities convinced Lincoln to forgo addressing the people of Baltimore. The night of his arrival in the capital, a weary Lincoln met with several delegates of the peace conference at a reception in Willard's Hotel. Most of the Southern delegates walked away from the meeting worried because the president-elect showed no inclination to give way on the territorial issue and adamantly declared that the Constitution had to be "enforced and obeyed in every part of the United States."[45]

Three days after Lincoln appeared in Washington, the peace conference rejected the territorial provision of the majority report by a vote of eleven to eight. Lincoln's presence seemed to strengthen the resolve of Republicans in the convention. Of the Border South delegations, only Missouri voted against the report because, as Doniphan later explained, nothing less than the original Crittenden resolutions would permanently remove the issue of slavery in the territories. Missouri's negative more accurately reflected the growing frustration with the Republicans among white border Southerners than it did a longing for the original Crittenden proposition as Doniphan attributed. The convention adjourned for the night, but informal caucuses lasted into the small hours as the delegates sought some means to revive the scuttled settlement.[46]

The following night several influential delegates from the Upper and Border South held another meeting with Lincoln. Doniphan, Charles S. Morehead and Guthrie of Kentucky, and William C. Rives and George Summers of Virginia all beseeched the president-elect to comprehend "the dreadful impending danger, and entreated and implored him to avert it." Coercion, they warned, would unquestionably turn the tide in favor of secession in the Upper and Border South, but if the Republicans adopted a conciliatory stance, those eight slaveholding states would likely remain in the Union. The elderly Rives made an impassioned appeal on behalf of the Union but told the president-elect that if he opted for coercion and forced Virginia to secede, even an old Unionist like himself would go with his state. Lincoln reportedly responded with a bargain: if Rives could promise to keep Virginia in the Union, he would withdraw the troops from Fort Sumter once he entered office. Rives replied that he had no authority to make such an arrangement, but that he would continue to work to preserve the Union.[47]

Whether Doniphan and his associates had an impact on Lincoln remains mere conjecture. Nonetheless, when the peace convention reassembled on February 27, the Illinois delegation had a change of heart and voted in favor of the territorial provision, while four other states abstained from voting, which allowed the measure to pass by a count of nine to eight. With the territorial hurdle leaped, the convention quickly approved of the remaining articles of the majority report and hurried it to the Capitol for the consideration of Congress. Aside from Missouri, whose delegation abstained on the territorial provision and voted against a measure dealing with slaveholder compensation in cases where fugitive slaves could not be recaptured, each Border South state approved of every piece of the majority report, which promised to sustain proslavery Unionism. Cannons boomed as the peace conference adjourned, and one newspaper prematurely proclaimed, "Every border State has been saved . . . , and the return of the seceded States to the Union is now but a question of a short time." A Wilmington, Delaware, businessman noted that the news of the peace convention's passage of the settlement provoked a celebration in the streets.[48]

The work of the peace conference signaled headway for borderland moderates, but they were nowhere close to clinching a victory. The fate of compromise returned to Congress, whose members in the interim had made no progress toward a settlement. One observer bemoaned to John Pendleton Kennedy that congressional inertia had aggravated the situation in the Border South to the point that "the ground upon which you stand—solid as it may seem to you now, will become quicksand to swallow you & all your noble Conservatives." Moderates needed Congress to approve one of the compromise packages to avoid an erosion of support for the Union.[49]

Two events on February 18 illustrated the protean character of Unionism in the Border South. In Missouri, voters trekked to the polls and selected delegates for the state convention slated to meet in Jefferson City at the end of the month. The result of the election demonstrated the enduring power of the Unionist offensive. Conditional and unconditional Unionists smashed their secessionist competitors in the contest—not a single one of the ninety-nine delegates elected had campaigned on behalf of separate state secession—much to the dismay of fire-eaters. "Our election is over & as far as Missouri is concerned the Union is safe," a moderate exclaimed. Secessionists had made a last-ditch attempt to proliferate disunion documents in the hopes of converting voters, but they discovered that the well-established Unionist offensive easily counteracted their poorly managed onslaught. Weeks of campaigning paid dividends for Missouri Unionists, who captured 110,000 votes in comparison to 30,000 for disunionists.[50]

Despite the auspicious results of the February 18 election, Missouri's fate remained undecided. Candidates for the convention entered the field on one of three tickets: Conditional Unionist; Unconditional Unionist; and States' Rights or Anti-submission. The predominant form of Unionism among the delegates was the conditional variety, which meant that external events could easily convert these men to the secessionist camp. One scholar counts fifty-two of the ninety-nine delegates as Unconditional Unionists and the remaining forty-seven representatives as Conditional Unionists, while another assigns the Conditional Unionists with a two-thirds majority. Exact numbers are difficult to ascertain because a fire later damaged the official election returns. Although imprecise, these estimations highlight the contested nature of Unionism in the Border South. Unionists attending the Missouri convention split almost evenly among the two factions and several most likely wavered between the two blocs, which meant that a defiant Northern posture toward compromise or an explosive physical altercation in the South could easily tip the balance toward disunion.[51]

While Missourians registered their votes, the introduction of a controversial piece of legislation in the United States House of Representatives on the very same day exemplified the tenuous nature of Border South Unionism. Republican Benjamin Stanton of Ohio reported a militia bill to the House that prepared the nation's military for the eventuality of war. Southerners shrieked in protest and complained that this so-called force bill—which allowed officers to make enlistments, accept volunteers, and arm their troops— would mark coercion as the federal government's official policy. White border Southerners would have been aghast to know that two inhabitants of their region had been prime movers in the introduction of the objectionable legislation. In response to the rumored machinations of secessionists in Saint Louis, Frank Blair Jr. had written his brother Montgomery in January and asked him to communicate to his congressional contacts that a militia bill would indisputably help keep the city in Unionist hands. Davis also had a hand in the legislation, though he did try to water down a more offensive force bill. He told a friend that he "drew it & know it will do its work & got it substituted for a very offensive and impudent one." Blair and Davis, however, greatly miscalculated the Border South's mainstream attitude toward coercion. Every border Southerner in the House, aside from Davis, voted to reject or abstained from voting on the legislation, but they could not prevent the bill from moving forward.[52]

Blair and Davis failed to grasp that anything that smacked of coercion threatened to reverse the Unionist tide in the Border South. A Delawarean upbraided Davis for voting with the Republicans in favor of Stanton's bill, which she considered unconstitutional and extremely harmful to Unionism in the region, and in the House debate on the legislation, borderites unleashed a barrage of condemnation against the measure. Many Border South congressmen linked their fears of coercion to their suspicions that the Republicans would use the military to destroy slavery in the states. Two days prior to the introduction of Stanton's bill, Republican Daniel E. Somes of Maine had suggested that the people of the Border South should consent to the abolition of slavery in Washington, DC, and undertake gradual emancipation within their own borders. William E. Simms of Kentucky labeled Stanton's legislation "a bill of murder," dismissing it as "a war measure, not only made desperate in its designs, but a measure in direct violation of the Constitution." "While ostensibly you merely talk of enforcing the laws," Simms queried, "will you not avail yourself of the war you have thus inaugurated to accomplish that first and highest purpose of your party organization, the overthrow of slavery throughout the southern States?" Republicans refused to dignify the Kentuckian's charge of a "double purpose" in the force bill and moderates within Lincoln's party managed to postpone the measure, which effectively killed the legislation. Nevertheless, Simms more accurately expressed the sentiments of the Border South than did Blair or Davis. Coercion and force endangered proslavery Unionism, and most of the region's inhabitants dreaded the commencement of a civil war that would surely place the peculiar institution on fragile ground.[53]

The icy atmosphere in Congress proved anything but conducive to passing some form of compromise during the late stages of the session. One by one, the House and the Senate voted down the vast array of compromise proposals, from the Crittenden resolutions to the call for a national constitutional convention, which moderates had introduced over the course of the session. Republicans closed ranks to defeat the various settlements, while in most cases Border South congressmen registered affirmative votes for them. The peace conference proposals did not even come up for a vote in the House because moderates could not assemble the two-thirds majority needed to suspend the rules and introduce the measures. In the Senate, a haggard Crittenden begged his colleagues to pass anything and offered to replace his own resolutions with those of the peace convention. He acknowledged that the major difference between his package and the peace conference settlement was the "hereafter" clause. Crittenden explained that he had acquiesced in adding the clause because he wanted a permanent solution. Even so, he would gladly appease the Republicans by accepting the peace convention resolutions without the inclusion of the offensive clause. Despite his appeal, the Senate refused to substitute the peace conference measures for his own. In its final hours the Senate defeated the Crittenden Compromise by a tally of nineteen to twenty. Enough Republicans agreed to Thomas Corwin's proposed constitutional amendment that prevented Congress from interfering with slavery in the states to allow for its passage, but other than that, Lincoln's party held firm and prevented the extension of slavery into the territories.[54]

The Republican effort to block any compromise settlement frustrated many white border Southerners who had banked on Congress rescuing the divided nation at the eleventh hour. An observer in Delaware complained of the Republicans' "plotting and plodding on selfish and dark thoughts and deeds," while Kentucky's John C. Breckinridge expressed regret that Lincoln's party was "hardening and consolidating every day." A Marylander bemoaned the "sour, conceited numskulls who both in and out of Congress represent the inveteracy of Black Republican policy." Missouri senator James Green suggested that the intransigence of the Republicans had forced some elements of the Border South's vital center to give up on proslavery Unionism. "I believe the die is cast," Green fulminated, "that there is a belligerent feeling, diversity of sentiment, and a difference of opinion so diametrically opposite that we cannot live together."[55]

Green's words, which illustrated how some white border Southerners had by early March slid into either the secessionist or the neutral camp, surely stung Crittenden and other Unionists. In what he thought to be his final speech on Capitol Hill, Crittenden praised the efforts of his Northern colleagues, especially Stephen Douglas and Pennsylvania's William Bigler, who had worked with him to secure a settlement during the session. In an effort to reassure faltering Border South Unionists, Crittenden reminded his audience that passage of the Corwin amendment "may have some good effect, like a solitary ray of sunshine breaking through the clouds, which might show an opening in them." The Kentuckian wanted borderland Unionists to consider the Corwin amendment a first step toward a more satisfactory settlement rather than the dying breath of the old republic. Some white borderites indeed considered the Corwin amendment a lifeline to a comprehensive compromise that might come later, which prevented wholesale defection from the Unionist column.[56]

The grueling session of Congress came to a close at dawn on March 4. Later that day tired Washington politicians assembled to hear Lincoln's much anticipated inaugural address. In the speech Lincoln promised to "hold, occupy, and possess" all federal property, but also disclosed that he had no objection to the Corwin amendment. The president ended the speech with a plea for friendship and peace with the South, which resonated with many Border South conservatives. A Kentucky politician felt that Lincoln's address had done nothing to exacerbate the crisis, and he estimated that if the new president evacuated Fort Sumter, "the Union cause in the Border States of the South will be vastly strengthened." Other white border Southerners, however, took umbrage with Lincoln's message and believed it signaled a Republican determination for war. "Some think it warlike & some think it conservative," a Kentuckian scribbled in his diary after polling his neighbors.[57]

The diversity of opinion among white border Southerners illustrates the numerous degrees of Southern Unionism and underscores how Lincoln's course during the previous three months had forced some of the region's inhabitants to reassess their Unionist outlook. The moderately toned inaugural

and Lincoln's well-balanced cabinet could not offset his initial studied silence
and his barbed remarks on the journey to Washington in the minds of some
border Southerners. Lincoln's actions, coupled with Republican inaction
in Congress, led many erstwhile moderates to doubt the continued reliability
of proslavery Unionism. John C. Breckinridge's hopes for the permanency of
the Union had grown dim by March. The Kentuckian feared the Republicans
would opt for "collision and bloodshed" and suspected that, in spite of
Lincoln's claims to the contrary, the party had designs to eradicate slavery
throughout the nation. The former vice president, who earlier in the winter
had labored on behalf of a settlement, increasingly called for a peaceful
separation between the United States and the newly created Confederacy,
and warned that the eight remaining slave states were "discontented and
gloomy and trembling in the balance." As time passed, Breckinridge and
many other white border Southerners edged ever closer to a neutral or secessionist standpoint.[58]

Lincoln's course of action became a heated topic of discussion at the Missouri state convention, which on February 28 convened in Jefferson City. The
delegates chose Sterling Price, a former Missouri governor, as president of
the convention, and Unionists rammed through a resolution to move the
meeting from Jefferson City, where Governor Jackson and his circle of fire-
eaters might have a debilitating influence on wavering members, to Saint
Louis. Nearly 61 percent of the delegates owned slaves, though a solid majority of the slaveholders owned nine slaves or fewer. The mean slaveholding for
the delegates was just under five enslaved persons, which closely mirrored
slaveholding trends throughout Missouri, where 88 percent of slaveholders
held fewer than ten slaves (see Table A.5). These delegates, the vast majority
of whom had been born in the Border or Upper South, acutely understood
the critical importance of the peculiar institution to their state and region.[59]

Once they relocated to Saint Louis, the convention created a committee on
federal relations at the behest of Hamilton Gamble, a former chief justice of
the Missouri Supreme Court and brother-in-law of Edward Bates. The thirteen-
man committee included Gamble and Doniphan, freshly arrived from the
Washington Peace Conference, and promptly began preparing a report to
stake out Missouri's future course of action. While the committee deliberated, delegates entered into debate that ranged from bitter denunciations
of coercion to practical suggestions for a compromise settlement. Luther J.
Glenn, a secession commissioner from Georgia, addressed the body on
March 4 and requested Missouri's secession, but most delegates brushed off
the fire-eater's recommendations. Unionists buried Glenn's recommendation

for secession in a special committee and later postponed consideration of the issue until the end of the year, effectively killing his request. The power of proslavery Unionism remained alive among the delegates, who on March 7 adopted without a single dissenting vote a resolution of thanks to Crittenden and Douglas for their "patriotic, able and untiring efforts" on behalf of compromise. Crittenden and other Unionists had come to the realization that the fate of the remaining slaveholding states hinged on keeping a settlement package alive, and the unanimous passage of the resolution, along with the unceremonious dismissal of Georgia's secession commissioner, revealed the fruit of their labors. Even though many white border Southerners had started contemplating the idea of neutrality and secession, the resolution and vote exposed the staying power of the Unionist offensive. The resolution even indicated the embers of compromise had yet to be extinguished, additional proof that, at least in the eyes of border Southerners, Crittenden had not wholly failed in his quest for a settlement. Doniphan, though dismayed at Republican intransigence, later gave an impassioned speech on the floor of the convention. Unprepared to condone secession and "bring about a calamity that will destroy the Border slave States and the whole Union," Doniphan insisted that other avenues for compromise still remained open. "I live by hope," he declared, "and as a Union man I shall only die when hope dies."[60]

Although the convention lavished praise on the peacemakers, it heaped scorn on the Republicans. Discussion of Lincoln's inaugural turned into a platform for pro-secession delegates to position the new president as a tyrant who meant to use the military to force the seceded states back into the republic and bring an immediate end to slavery throughout the United States. James H. Moss warned that if Lincoln agreed to a policy of coercion, "the friends of the Union [in Missouri] will melt away like snow-flakes." Realizing that such language might heighten Missourians' fears about remaining in a Republican-controlled nation, Unionists managed to suspend discussion of Lincoln's inaugural and steer the meeting toward consideration of the work of the committee on federal relations.[61]

The committee on March 9 submitted its report to the convention, and the body's findings indicated that conditional Unionists retained the upper hand at the meeting. The statement from the committee captured the essence of Border South proslavery Unionism. It emphasized that although the Republicans had gained the ascendancy in national politics, the Supreme Court still served as a check on any repugnant legislation that might interfere with slavery. Further, the committee acknowledged that the federal government had always faithfully executed the Fugitive Slave Law and reminded the delegates that in rare instances when abolitionists had invaded the South to overthrow slavery, "they meet their death by the law, and that is the end of their scheme." The report affirmed that secession was unwarranted for several reasons: the magnitude of present grievances did not require such bold action; trade would dwindle in the event of Missouri's secession; and, significantly, "our slave interest would be destroyed, because we would have no better right to recapture a slave found in a free State than we now have in Canada." The committee attached seven resolutions to the report that included a promise for Missouri to continue to work toward compromise, a declaration that the Crittenden Compromise represented the best basis of adjustment, a call for a national constitutional convention to enact a settlement, and a cautionary warning that coercion would blast all hopes for a peaceful solution and provoke war.[62]

Pro-secession delegates unsuccessfully attempted to attach an ultimatum to the resolutions that stated that if the North rejected the Crittenden Compromise, then Missouri would secede. The outspoken fire-eater John Redd growled that if the rest of the delegates were willing to allow federal troops to remain in the seceded states, then they should go ahead and remove the grizzly bear from the Missouri coat of arms "and substitute in its place the fawning spaniel, cowing at the feet of its master and licking the hand that smites it." Redd announced that Missouri could stay in the Union and allow the Republicans to carry out "the extinction of slavery everywhere," or the state could join in the secession movement. Redd and likeminded radicals tried to position disunion as the best guardian of slavery, but Unionists poked holes in their argument. Sample Orr speculated that if Missouri seceded and lost all the protections of the Union, they would witness the destruction of slavery in the state within a year. "The only salvation for the institution of slavery," Orr maintained, "is her adherence to the Government that protects slavery." M. L. Linton reminded Redd that his disunion panacea would make "a Canada of every Northern State" and invite a surge in slave runaways, which would weaken the peculiar institution. Linton compared secession to "cutting off an arm to cure a wart—it is like jumping out of the frying pan into the fire."[63]

Outflanked by the Unionists, some of the pro-secession representatives changed tack and pushed for the committee's report to include a statement requesting the withdrawal of federal troops from the seceded states. Unionists softened the fire-eaters' language, which as originally worded sounded like another ultimatum, and passed a resolution that stated the removal of federal soldiers would greatly enhance the chances for peace. Unionists believed the modified resolution would still express the great desire of most white border Southerners to avoid a collision of arms without sounding belligerent or provocative. While all border Southerners did not approve of secession, they generally agreed with delegate Alexander W. Woolfolk, who remarked, "Compromise may restore the Union, but the sword can never preserve it."[64]

By March 22, the convention had passed each one of the seven resolutions suggested by the committee on federal relations. Most of the provisions cleared the convention with ease, which underscored the perseverance of a strong Unionist impulse in Missouri. Throughout the winter, moderates in the eight slave states remaining in the Union had toyed with the idea of a Border State convention, and several of the Missouri delegates warmed to this suggestion. Gamble, mindful of the need to sustain the Unionist offensive by keeping all means for a settlement alive, had been in communication with colleagues in Virginia's state convention, whose delegates also discussed the need for a meeting. Gamble engineered the election of seven delegates to the proposed Border State convention, which represented another victory for Unionists. Before adjourning, the convention agreed to meet again in December 1861 and established a committee of seven charged with the task of reassembling the body in the event of an emergency. Delegate Samuel Breckinridge privately admitted that the committee of seven had been created because "our Governor, & the state officers generally, as well as the majority of the members of the Legislature, are avowedly hostile to the Convention, & entirely in the interest of secession." Unionists worried that Jackson would take matters into his own hands if conditions deteriorated in the state.[65]

Border South Unionists could breathe a sigh of relief as the Missouri convention adjourned in late March. The previous two and a half months had been trying, but they had relegated secession to the Lower South. The Missouri convention had not taken any steps toward disunion, and Unionists in the legislatures of Delaware and Kentucky had blocked secessionists from even calling a sovereignty convention. Even though Congress had spurned a comprehensive settlement, Crittenden and his allies could point to the fact that a constitutional amendment protecting slavery in the states had advanced from Washington and now awaited ratification by the states. Moreover, the proposal for a Border State conference presented Unionists with another option for compromise. On the whole, the Unionist offensive had endured a taxing trial, absorbed the shocks of Republican and fire-eater intransigence in Washington, and maintained the hopes of white border Southerners who sought a peaceful solution to the crisis.

Yet the possibility of a clash between the federal government and the seceded states, which grew with each passing day, threatened to spoil the Unionist offensive in the Border South. Some elements of the vital center, fearful of an armed conflict and distressed by the inflexibility of the Republicans, had already lost faith in the Unionist offensive, and more would surely follow if the threat of war became a reality. "At present, the country is resting in anxious suspense, altogether uncertain of the future," a Maryland Unionist remarked. If Lincoln opted for a coercive policy, it would "instantly break down all this conservatism, and drive the whole of the Border States into a separation." Another onlooker noted that "Missouri is safe for the present. The Convention is decidedly anti-Secession; but every body is in a fever about Fort Sumpter, the question being—how can it be supplied without opening the war?"[66]

War would unquestionably jeopardize the arguments of proslavery Unionists and transform many white border Southerners into secessionists. Over the past couple of months, conservatives had helplessly witnessed some of their neighbors shift from a conditional Unionist approach to neutrality or, to a lesser degree, a preference for secession. Missourian Thomas Shackelford recalled that during the state convention, Price, the president of the body who had been elected on a Unionist platform, confessed to him in mid-March, "I believe that war is inevitable. . . . I cant [sic] fight against the South, so I must go with the Border States." After the convention adjourned on March 22, Price never retook his seat. Another Missourian watched the state convention "sacrafice [sic] Right, Principle, and every thing else for the sake of the name." "As long as there was a possibility of an amicable adjustment, I was for Union," he continued, "but now that all hope is lost, and the Union virtually disolved [sic], common sense dictates that [the Border South's] interest[s] are identified with the South." The region's vital center remained vulnerable and, without Crittenden's efforts in Washington and the relentless Unionist offensive, many more conditional Unionists would have made the transition to outright secessionists. In the upcoming months, Border South Unionists would have to find some way to prevent secession sentiment from metastasizing.[67]

Doniphan's course during the first quarter of 1861 provides a window into the shifting mind-set of many white border Southerners during this interval. His effusive optimism about a peaceful settlement, so evident when he tramped through the snow and addressed his neighbors back in late January, began to wane as he observed the Washington Peace Conference neutralize the Crittenden resolutions. Even the peace convention's transient "patchwork" had not satisfied congressional Republicans, who in March dismantled it and every other serviceable compromise proposition. For most of the Missouri state convention, the gifted orator sat in unusual silence. By the time the convention adjourned and he returned to his western Missouri home, early spring rain showers had replaced the white snow of winter and left a muddy morass. Doniphan's mood closely resembled the dark skies that opened every day and kept him housebound. In marked contrast to his Unionist speech at the state convention, he confessed that he had "no well founded hope" that the national crisis would ever improve, and now he used the poor weather as an excuse to refrain from taking the stump. In time, Doniphan "quietly folded the comforts of his home around him" and became "an idle spectator of one of the mightiest Revolutions that ever crowned the earth." The old colonel would not raise his sword against the Union, yet neither would he unsheathe it to subjugate the South. The Unionist offensive had kept the Border South safe thus far, but many white border Southerners had, like Doniphan, begun to have second thoughts about the effectiveness of proslavery Unionism as winter gave way to spring.[68]

CHAPTER SIX

If We Can't Go with the South Let Us Quit the North

War, Violence, and Neutrality, March–June 1861

Throughout the secession crisis, Border South moderates feared for the worst if an outbreak of hostilities occurred between the federal government and the Confederate States of America. War would instantly reverse all momentum for a compromise settlement, sap the strength of conditional Unionism, and force white border Southerners who had for so long sought to avoid conflict to take sides. "The moment that the first drop of blood is shed the last ray of hope vanishes, and then all the border slave States will go out," a delegate to the Missouri state convention anticipated. "You cannot stop the tide of public feeling." The Unionist offensive had by April 1861 managed to limit the progress of secessionists in the region, but an increasing number of white borderites had begun to entertain the possibility of a permanently fractured American republic. If gunshots and cannon fire replaced debate and bargaining, it seemed very likely that the Border South would cast its lot with the Confederacy.[1]

Franklin Buchanan of Maryland, a lifelong officer in the United States Navy, nervously watched events transpire during the secession winter from his post as commanding officer of the Washington Navy Yard. By the spring of 1861 Buchanan found it increasingly difficult to reconcile his devotion to the Union with his sympathy for the South. In Buchanan's mind, the Republican Party represented a mortal threat to national peace and endangered the South's peculiar institution. Himself the owner of six enslaved persons who worked as servants at his country estate on Maryland's Eastern Shore, Buchanan considered Abraham Lincoln's election and Congress's inability to secure a comprehensive settlement the last gasps of a once-glorious republic. "We can never again feel as proud of the flag we sail under, as we have felt during our naval careers," he confided to an old navy friend. Although he vowed to uphold his duty to protect the Washington Navy Yard from rebels, Buchanan had grave doubts about the nation's future and the lasting clout of proslavery Unionism.[2]

Thousands of white border Southerners shared Buchanan's sinking spirit as winter turned to spring. The Unionist offensive had buoyed their hopes while Congress was in session, but as the war clouds darkened over the nation, many Border South conservatives second-guessed the likelihood that the old republic could be preserved. John Jordan Crittenden had delivered his Senate valedictory and returned home to Kentucky empty-handed, while in Charleston Harbor Confederates trained their artillery on Fort Sumter and its garrison of fewer than one hundred soldiers. The subsequent outbreak of war at Fort Sumter and eruptions of violence in the streets of Baltimore and Saint Louis presented Border South Unionists with their greatest test. Yet the four states of the Border South reacted to war, violence, and Lincoln's call for troops to suppress the rebellion in a unique manner that underscores the lasting influence of the Unionist offensive. Unlike the states of the Upper South, all of which seceded during this pivotal interval, the Border South stayed put. The region remained on shaky ground between March and June, but fire-eaters could not breach the fortifications that Unionists had built since Lincoln's election.

It would be patently false, however, to claim that white border Southerners found the inauguration of war pleasing. Many of the region's inhabitants reacted as did Buchanan, who in the aftermath of an April 19 clash in the streets of Baltimore between federal troops and borderland secessionists felt the Border South's attachment to the Union had been forever severed. Confident that Maryland would secede, Buchanan hastily resigned from the United States Navy. The expected revolution never materialized in Maryland or throughout the rest of the Border South, though. The deterrents that Unionists had put in place, along with an increased federal military presence as a result of the violence in Baltimore and Saint Louis, prevented the Border South's exodus from the Union. As a result, many white border Southerners opted for a policy of neutrality while they weighed their increasingly limited options. A confused and embarrassed Buchanan even attempted to withdraw his resignation, but the secretary of the navy refused. While he contemplated his next step from his Eastern Shore home, the unemployed Buchanan's hatred for the Republicans multiplied. "The rascally northern interference with the institution of slavery, with which they never ought to have interfered, is the first cause, and has brought about a dissolution of our glorious union," Buchanan groused. The old mariner tried to embrace a neutral attitude during the spring, but he found his sympathy for the Confederacy growing with each passing day.[3]

Neutrality represented a distinctively Border South approach to the opening of the war. Although Kentucky, Maryland, and Missouri officially adopted a policy of neutrality for a brief interlude, many borderland inhabitants embraced a neutral mind-set that outlasted the secession crisis. Neither carefully planned nor a permanent solution, neutrality at least gave white border Southerners some added time to make decisions about their allegiances. During that interim, Unionists once again took the initiative and worked to assure their Border South neighbors that the war was being fought to reunite the nation rather than to destroy slavery. The stepped-up federal military presence proved invaluable to Unionists who once again found ways to outflank their secessionist enemies. Federal bayonets brought many white border Southerners to the stark realization that "geography has something to do with the policy of the states."[4] Many frustrated secessionists left the region to join the Confederate cause, while others, like Buchanan, waited on the sidelines and continued to evaluate the situation before making any more rash decisions. During this critical interlude, Unionists decisively gained the upper hand and refused to relinquish it for the duration of the crisis. Their achievement represented the culmination of several months of earnest labors to position the Union as the ultimate guardian of slavery.

CRITTENDEN, NO LONGER a United States senator, returned home to Frankfort in mid-March, just as the Kentucky legislature reassembled after a monthlong recess. Although greatly wearied by the grueling schedule of long Senate sessions, endless committee meetings, and late-night parlor politics, Crittenden's return to Kentucky did not signal the beginning of his dearly sought-after retirement. Kentucky Unionists, aware that the battle against Border South secessionists continued, approached Crittenden about running for Congress and leading the Unionist offensive from the House Chamber. Crittenden's presence in Washington would indicate that even with a Republican president in the executive office, the hope for compromise remained alive. "You can do more for us & yourself in the house than you can do in the Senate," a Unionist asserted. "Lincoln is a bigoted fool therefore it is more necessary you should be in Congress." Although initially reluctant to sign up for another tour of duty in Washington, Crittenden's return home convinced him that retirement would have to wait once again. With Kentucky's congressional elections scheduled for August, he had some time to contemplate how to proceed. For the present, he devoted his time and energy to organizing a convention of the Upper and Border South states.[5]

Once Congress adjourned without a comprehensive settlement, a growing number of Unionists in the Border and Upper South clamored for a meeting of delegates from the eight slaveholding states remaining in the Union. The border slave state convention had been discussed at length in the state conventions of Missouri and Virginia, the general assemblies of Delaware and Kentucky, and the Southern press.[6] Rendering the recently passed Corwin amendment as the first step in the process of conciliation, Unionists believed a convention could serve as an alternative vehicle for compromise and signal to wavering Southern Unionists that conservatives had yet to surrender to secession. "A heavy responsibility devolves upon the central states, where the great heart of the country beats," a Virginian remarked in response to the possibility of a border state conference. "May they be fully alive to their responsibilities and true to them!" In short, the border state conference would sustain the Unionist offensive with Congress out of session.[7]

Kentucky Unionists played their trump card on March 21 when they asked Crittenden to speak to the state legislature. No other personality held as much sway in the Border South as did Crittenden, and the invitation provided the leader of the Unionists with a platform that drew the attention of the national press. Five days later Crittenden delivered his address to an overflowing crowd packed inside the Kentucky House chamber. During his two-hour speech Crittenden emphasized that as long as an outbreak of hostilities was avoided, the Border South could depend on support from the conservative masses of the North. He underscored that in the recently adjourned session of Congress, thousands of Northern voters had sent him petitions and letters in approval of his compromise measures. This groundswell "showed me that the argument which had been so often used to disunite us—that the North hates the South and that the South hates the North—is not true," Crittenden proclaimed. He warned that extremists in both the North and the South had fired the passions of the people and clouded the true spirit of intersectional cordiality that still existed. Thus, Crittenden advised that the South should continue to press for its rights within the Union. "Let us struggle in the Union, contend in the Union, make the Union the instrument with which we contend, and we shall get all that we ask—all that we can desire—all that reason can warrant us in expecting," Crittenden implored in this manifesto of proslavery Unionism.[8]

He continued with a reminder that most white border Southerners had family and friends who lived in either the North or the Lower South, which made coercion utterly repugnant. The shedding of blood, Crittenden cautioned, would dash the hopes of reconciliation and instantly convert intersectional amicability into sectional hatred. Rather, both sides ought to find a peaceful means of patching the old Union back together. In his speech Crittenden conjured up the ghost of Henry Clay and referred to his mentor's efforts to preserve the Union in 1850. In his appeal for a peaceful solution,

Crittenden pointed out that the electoral process, not revolution, granted the American voter the best means of setting aside unfit political leaders like the Republicans.[9]

Crittenden's speech greatly assisted Unionists in the Kentucky legislature whose pleas for proslavery Unionism had been sustained by the possibility of a congressional settlement. Now that Congress had adjourned, Border South Unionists needed some other vessel for compromise. C. F. Burnam credited Crittenden with rejuvenating the Unionist offensive in the general assembly and claimed his speech paved the way for the passage of a resolution calling for the border state conference. Crittenden and several Unionists laid out the framework for the convention over dinner shortly after he delivered his speech. Although some pro-secession legislators attempted to disrupt their efforts, Unionists arranged for the convention to convene in Frankfort on May 27. Elections for Kentucky's delegates would take place on May 4.[10]

When Kentucky's general assembly adjourned on April 5, Unionists congratulated one another for their efforts. Although some conservatives had in the absence of a congressional settlement jumped off the Unionist bandwagon, this brief meeting of the Kentucky legislature highlighted the resiliency of the Unionist offensive. For a second time in 1861, moderates had prevented their pro-secession colleagues from ramming a bill for a state sovereignty convention through the legislature. This time, pro-secession legislators even failed to bring the state convention proposition to a vote. During this brief sitting, the Kentucky legislature also ratified the Corwin amendment to the United States Constitution, which forbade Congress from abolishing slavery in the states where it existed. While nearly every Southern Unionist agreed that this amendment addressed only a segment of the many political issues dividing the nation, they could at least view its passage as a first step toward a comprehensive settlement that would calm the nerves of vacillating conservatives. Aware that passage of the Corwin amendment might bring portions of the vital center back into the Unionist fold, Kentucky secessionists tried to block its ratification by adding various explanatory resolutions to the measure. One called for the immediate withdrawal of all federal troops in the South, while another insisted the Corwin amendment was "a declaration of rights we already claim to possess." Unionists stripped the final resolution of these riders and settled on language that expressed the shared conviction that passage of the amendment did not equate to a final settlement of the crisis. Rather, it demonstrated Kentucky's desire to avoid further agitation of the slavery issue and represented a springboard for additional conciliatory measures.[11]

Politicians in favor of disunion had come to Frankfort full of optimism, yet once again found themselves overmatched by the wiles of Unionists. Fire-eaters could, however, count one small victory in late March. The same day the legislature opened, a group of disunionists met and organized Kentucky's Southern Rights Party. Blanton Duncan orchestrated a network of Southern Rights clubs that circulated secession propaganda across the state and launched a campaign to gather signatures for petitions to the legislature in favor of calling a state convention. Nevertheless, the unfolding events in the legislative session demoralized some of the Southern Rights members and exposed the party's lack of administrative skill in comparison to the Unionists.[12]

Crittenden's presence helped offset the embryonic Southern Rights Party, which one moderate labeled a band of "Secession buccaneers." John C. Breckinridge, whom the legislature had tabbed to replace the retiring Crittenden in the United States Senate, discovered in April 1861 that his predecessor was a difficult act to follow. In a speech before the legislature on April 2, Breckinridge struggled to convince many fence-sitters to join the Southern Rights crusade. Whereas Crittenden stressed the commonalities between the North and South, Breckinridge accentuated the differences between the sections. Republicans reigned supreme in the North, he claimed, and now the federal government resembled "an alien government, the worst that ever cursed the world." He cautioned that in the recently adjourned Congress, Republicans had practiced the art of deception on the slavery issue. Even though Republicans acquiesced in the Corwin amendment, they remained firmly opposed to the spread of slavery in the territories. This, he averred, signaled a Republican design to abolish slavery "by more circuitous but not less fatal means." If the Republicans succeeded in this plot, Breckinridge envisioned social ruin for Kentucky. The former vice president did endorse the proposed border states conference, but he declared that if nothing came of the meeting, then Kentucky should join the government that best protected its people from the "combined influence of fanaticism, hypocrisy, and perfidy"—the Confederate States of America.[13]

Breckinridge's speech did little to mobilize the Southern Rights men in the legislature. He viewed the border states conference as the last straw before permanent separation, whereas Crittenden saw it as one of many progressive steps toward reuniting the nation. Although chastened by recent events, many Kentuckians still shared Crittenden's conviction that moderates in the North would cooperate with them on a compromise initiative. Both Unionists and Southern Rights adherents, however, fully grasped the mutable nature of conditional Unionism. Events outside the Border South could alter most white borderites' opinions about secession and upend the vital center's confidence in Northern cooperation, which made the border states conference all the more important. Both camps geared up for the May 4 election for delegates to the meeting and considered the contest a litmus test for the Border South's future. The Unionist offensive received more ammunition when Crittenden finally agreed to run for Congress.[14]

Since the beginning of the secession crisis, Border South Unionists had anxiously monitored two situations—one in Saint Louis and the other in Charleston, South Carolina—wherein federal troops stared down pro-secession forces. Earlier in the winter Nathaniel Lyon and a small contingent of federal regulars had joined with the Unionist Home Guard under the direction of Frank Blair Jr. and Franz Sigel, a leader in Saint Louis's German community, to keep the city's federal arsenal safe from prowling fire-eaters. Secessionists in Saint Louis made their presence known by flying disunion flags from rooftops throughout the city, including one atop the courthouse for a few days in early March. Basil Duke, a Saint Louis attorney, had organized a pro-secession paramilitary organization of about four hundred men called the Ninth Ward Washington Minute Men, which increased the likelihood of confrontation. Duke later admitted that "the chief and primary object of this organization was the capture of the arsenal," but a lack of sufficient arms and cold feet from some secessionist leaders prevented the Minute Men from achieving their goal during the winter. Moderates and fire-eaters alike celebrated on April 1 when the city's voters elected Daniel G. Taylor, who ran on an anti-Republican coalition ticket, to the mayor's office. The Republicans had controlled the mayor's office since 1858, but in April 1861 their candidate lost by a wide margin. "We have taken our position against Lincolnism," a moderate editor boasted, "and against that malignant theory of the North which declares perpetual war on the slave States and their institutions." Disunionists also rejoiced when Governor Claiborne Fox Jackson appointed Duke and several other pro-secession men to the Saint Louis Police Board. Military activity, the mayoral election, and Jackson's tinkering with the police board left the people of Saint Louis on edge.[15]

Despite the simmering tensions in Saint Louis, by April 1861 the standoff had not escalated into open warfare. Americans could not count on similar results in Charleston Harbor, where a federal force commanded by Kentuckian Robert Anderson at Fort Sumter became a symbol of defiance for Confederates and an emblem of national resiliency for Northern hardliners. For months white border Southerners of all political persuasions had bemoaned the presence of federal troops in the seceded states. Before returning to Kentucky to speak to the legislature, Breckinridge used the special session of the Senate in late March, normally reserved for confirming the nominations of the incoming president, to submit a resolution that called for the removal of all federal soldiers from the Confederacy. Unwilling to act on the resolution both because it represented a tacit recognition of Confederate nationhood and because most Republicans considered it a base surrender to traitors, the Senate cast it aside. Moderate border Southerners also wished for the removal of federal forces from the Lower South, albeit for different reasons. They understood that as long as the two sides faced off in the cradle of secession, an overzealous potshot might provoke return fire and bring about war, which would derail all hopes for a peaceful compromise settlement. Unionists in both the Missouri state convention and the Kentucky legislature had made pleas for Lincoln to remove the troops from the seceded states so that negotiations toward compromise could proceed unencumbered. Delaware's Samuel F. Du Pont, like many other committed Unionists, conceded that the evacuation of Fort Sumter would be "a bitter pill to swallow," but he figured such a course would prevent war and exponentially increase the likelihood of a political settlement.[16]

Breckinridge asked for the removal of troops so that the Confederate project could advance unimpeded, but he provided a common Border South explanation when he introduced his resolution. White border Southerners realized that the outbreak of war would plunge their region into the thick of the contest. "Those of us who live a few miles on either side of the border, if the passions of men should become aroused . . . would be engaged in it; yes, and would have to contribute our children to the unnatural strife," Breckinridge somberly predicted. A Delaware Unionist echoed Breckinridge when she remarked, "Every patriot ought to bend all his energies to prevent the commencement of civil war, for if once begun it will be applying the match to the tinder, [and] the whole land will be in a blaze." A Kentuckian lamented that if war commenced, "the beautiful Ohio would run red with the blood of slaughtered brethren." More so than other Americans, borderites grasped the destructive toll that a civil war would unleash. Their geographic position along the sectional fault line, along with flashes of episodic violence in the preceding decades, taught them that a full-blown armed conflict would place the Border South in a most vulnerable position.[17]

As handwringing in the Border South over the impending outbreak of war intensified, conditions in Charleston deteriorated. Soon after Lincoln entered the executive office on March 4, 1861, the new president received astonishing news: Anderson only had enough food and supplies to keep his garrison sustained for six more weeks. Before most Washington revelers concluded their inauguration festivities, Lincoln faced a painfully difficult decision. Should he reinforce Anderson, which would certainly provoke retaliation from the Confederate forces on the shore, and risk the commencement of war? Or should he evacuate the federal troops, avoid war, and possibly face a fractured Northern populace? Over the next six weeks Lincoln weighed his options, relying on the counsel of his cabinet, General-in-Chief Winfield Scott, and a small team of military advisers.[18]

Lincoln in mid-March polled his cabinet to ascertain their thoughts on the situation at Fort Sumter. From the beginning, Secretary of State William Henry Seward advocated the removal of Anderson's men. Several Upper South Unionists had convinced Seward that the remaining eight slaveholding states would stay in the Union only if the federal government adopted a pacific stance toward the seceded states. He reasoned that the evacuation of Fort Sumter would demonstrate to these Unionists that the administration had chosen peaceful means to end the crisis, which would smother any lingering support for secession in the Upper and Border South.[19] Missourian Edward Bates originally followed Seward's line of thinking and advised the president to remove Anderson's men from Charleston and send additional troops to Fort Pickens and other installations along the Gulf of Mexico, which held less symbolic value than Fort Sumter. Bates's Border South approach to war, the Union, and the fate of slavery contributed to his initial decision for withdrawal. He predicted that reinforcing Sumter would bring about armed conflict, which "would soon become a social war, and that could hardly fail to bring on a servile war, the horrors of which need not be dwelt upon." At the outset, only Maryland's Montgomery Blair voiced outright opposition to evacuation, which he viewed as caving to traitors. Bates, the cautious moderate, adhered more closely to the conventional opinion of the borderland, while Blair, influenced by his brother Frank's interaction with Saint Louis secessionists, thought more in terms of absolutes. Still, Montgomery Blair rationalized his stance by insisting that a firm stand at Charleston would cultivate Southern Unionism as had Andrew Jackson's response to the South Carolina nullifiers in 1833.[20]

During the following two weeks, Seward worked every angle possible to convince the president to evacuate Fort Sumter, yet Lincoln remained uncommitted. The secretary of state kept in contact with Virginia Unionists and Confederate commissioners in Washington but made the grave mistake of assuring them that Anderson's men would withdraw from the fort. Lincoln, however, finally decided in late March to resupply Anderson after General Scott suggested abandoning not only Sumter but also Fort Pickens. Lincoln could not accept Scott's recommendation to yield both forts, especially since Pickens suffered little duress in relation to Sumter. He viewed Scott's suggestion as ignoble submission, and all but Seward and Secretary of the Interior Caleb Smith now agreed with the president. In early April Lincoln prepared orders for the navy to provision Sumter. Tipped off that a flotilla had left New York City with supplies for Anderson's men, Confederate president Jefferson Davis instructed the commanding officer at Charleston to prevent the federals from restocking the bastion. Before sunrise on April 12, the Confederate batteries opened fire on the fort. After a bombardment of more than thirty hours, the federal garrison surrendered and evacuated Charleston Harbor. On April 15, Lincoln responded with a proclamation calling for seventy-five thousand troops to subdue the rebellious Lower South states. "I fear the effect of this event upon the Border States," John Pendleton Kennedy despondently scribbled in his diary. "It strengthens the secession men and may end in driving us all out of the Union."[21]

Reactions to the bombardment of Fort Sumter and Lincoln's proclamation varied from outrage and indignation to exuberant delight. In response to the news, disunionists raised a secession flag over the courthouse in Elizabethtown, Kentucky, while fire-eaters took to the streets of Magnolia, Delaware, and cheered for the Confederacy. One Kent County, Delaware, merchant adamantly refused to allow authorities to post Lincoln's call for troops inside or outside his store. While a great gulf separated the mind-set of fire-eaters and unconditional Unionists in the Border South, both groups seemed relieved that the contest had finally come. Disunionists were confident that the Border South would now follow the Lower South out of the Union, and unyielding Unionists looked forward to vanquishing the fire-eaters in their midst. "The war has begun & I am glad it is inaugurated by the act of Rebels in the State of South Carolina; if it has to be, let those who are the authors of all the trouble, reap the first fruits of the dire Calamity," an unconditional Unionist in Delaware squawked.[22]

Moderates greeted the news with a less sanguine outlook than did secessionists and unconditional Unionists. The opening of war apparently caught some Unionists off guard and left them unsure of how to proceed. A Kentuckian noted that "the Union party seem as mad as march hares, running backward & forward from one extreme of policy to the other." James Guthrie worried the attack would result in the secession of the eight remaining slaveholding states and feared that emboldened fire-eaters might even attempt to capture Washington, DC, and throw the federal government into disarray. An inhabitant of Saint Louis informed Stephen A. Douglas that until the attack on Fort Sumter he had stood firmly beside the Union, but now he would never join with the Republicans whom he charged with inaugurating the war "for party purposes against slavery." Sumter and Lincoln's call for troops produced a change in sentiment for many borderland conditional Unionists. William Nelson reported that in Louisville "the people have absolutely gone mad. Some of the best Union men are talking and acting as officers of secession meetings." Orville Hickman Browning gazed across the Mississippi River from his Illinois home and concluded that "treason and secession are rampant" in Missouri. The outbreak of war and Lincoln's proclamation tested the conditional Unionism of the Border South's vital center unlike anything up to this point.[23]

People in both the Border and Upper South understood that the action of Virginia would have a profound impact on the other slaveholding states. Virginia proudly boasted of a prestigious political lineage that dated back to the early seventeenth century, and most white Southerners revered the Old Dominion's lengthy roster of eminent statesmen. Many white border Southerners originally hailed from Virginia and naturally looked to their former home for guidance during the crisis. A prominent Virginian predicted that the Old Dominion "is so ponderous a vessel of state that she will drag all the rest of the border slave states along in her wake." An adviser to Lincoln earlier warned that if Virginia seceded, he might as well prepare for the rest of the Border South to "surrender to the demon." "If Virginia plays the fool now the whole South is lost," a Kentuckian likewise fretted. Border South Unionists braced for the worst when on April 17 the Virginia convention voted eighty-eight to fifty-five in favor of secession.[24]

Neither the Missouri convention nor the legislatures of the four Border South states were in session when on April 12 the feeble truce between the Confederacy and the federal government collapsed, which certainly benefited the Unionists. Had the Missouri convention remained in session beyond March 22 or the Kentucky legislature beyond April 5, the fears of a conditional Unionist metamorphosis to outright disunionism may have been realized. Much to the chagrin of fire-eaters, legislators and delegates had scattered and returned to their homes when the war began. Disunionists relied on brisk action; with none of the Border South legislative bodies in session, their task became more difficult. William Watkins Glenn, a Baltimore fire-eater, griped that although Virginia had voted to secede, his disunionist colleagues in Maryland did little more than talk of their indignation about

Lincoln's proclamation. Glenn recalled with frustration that the lack of "concerted action" on the part of fire-eaters prevented Maryland from riding Virginia's coattails in April. Two Kentuckians with disparate loyalties later conceded that had the Kentucky legislature been in session when the crisis at Fort Sumter came to a head, it likely would have followed Virginia's lead and called a convention. A prominent Kentuckian even believed that if the Bluegrass State opted for secession, Maryland and Missouri would have done the same. Although purely conjecture, these observers figured that Kentucky could have had the same effect on the Border South as did Virginia on the Upper South.[25]

The attack on Fort Sumter and Lincoln's proclamation tipped the balance in favor of disunion in the Upper South, where the machinery for secession had been assembled earlier in the winter. All four of the Upper South states contained significant pockets of pro-secession sentiment, which, unlike in the Border South, operated as an effective counterweight to the Unionist offensive. Prior to the bombardment, state conventions had met in both Arkansas and Virginia, though neither body had rendered a final decision about its state's future. Virginia's convention was in session at this crucial interval and wasted little time passing a secession ordinance in response to Lincoln's proclamation. In Arkansas, the governor recalled the adjourned convention and in early May it swiftly declared the state out of the Union. Although voters in North Carolina and Tennessee had spurned holding a convention in February, the groundwork had been laid for each state's exit from the Union. The Tennessee legislature in early May approved of a military alliance with the Confederacy and a month later the state's voters approved of secession in a public referendum. North Carolinians sent delegates to a state convention in mid-May, which expeditiously passed a secession ordinance. Border South Unionists, however, had through their efforts during the winter applied the brakes to precipitate legislative action. Had Crittenden and other Unionists not labored so assiduously in the preceding months, secessionists in the spring of 1861 probably would have been able to gain the upper hand along the border as they did in the Upper South.[26]

The harsh reply to Lincoln's call for troops from several Border South governors demonstrated the indignation that many borderland politicians shared. Their biting rejoinders stung the president and the Northern populace and revealed that if the Border South legislative bodies had been in session, their outrage may have resulted in uncharacteristically precipitous action. "In answer I say emphatically Kentucky will furnish no troops for the wicked purpose of subduing her sister Southern States," Beriah C. Magoffin snorted. Claiborne Fox Jackson made an even bolder declaration: "Your requisition, in my judgment, is illegal, unconstitutional, and revolutionary in its object, inhuman and diabolical, and cannot be complied with. Not one man will the State of Missouri furnish to carry on any such unholy crusade." Governor William Burton of Delaware also refused to provide troops to the federal government, although he responded to the war department in more measured language than did Magoffin and Jackson. Burton explained that Delaware law did not include a provision for a standing militia and, therefore, he could not turn any units over to the federal government. He conceded that volunteer companies existed and state law granted him the authority to commission the officers of these units, but "it is altogether optional with them to offer their service to the U.S. authorities."[27]

The jarring rebukes of Magoffin, Jackson, and Burton revealed the complexity of the Border South position. None of these Democratic executives wished to contribute troops to a war against their Southern brethren, and all three claimed that Lincoln lacked the constitutional authority to call up soldiers for such a purpose. Most white border Southerners agreed that Lincoln had overstepped the executive's constitutional bounds with his call for seventy-five thousand men to crush the rebellion. Nathaniel Paschall remonstrated that the question before the people was "whether our liberties are secured by laws or whether they are subject to . . . the mere will of despotism." Still, the Saint Louis editor held out hope that a pacific separation might occur between the warring sections. "The ties by which the Border States have been bound to the Union, and which have been displayed in many sacrifices of feeling and interest for its preservation, have been much weakened," he proclaimed. Paschall admitted that if Lincoln did not entertain the possibility of a peaceful settlement, the Border South might have no choice but to secede.[28]

While Paschall conceded the possibility of secession, he gave voice to the growing demand for neutrality in the Border South. Once the cannons opened fire at Fort Sumter, Paschall and other white border Southerners experienced greater countervailing sectional pressure than ever before. Magoffin and Burton both backed neutrality as the best response to the possibility of war. Magoffin called the Kentucky legislature into session on May 6 so it could prepare the state for the future, which alarmed committed Unionists. They had twice before vanquished fire-eaters in the general assembly who had clamored for a state convention, and now Unionists wondered if they could hold the line. Unconditional Unionists distrusted Magoffin and doubted his intentions. "He is a rebel at heart and afflicted beyond the hope of cure," James Speed later surmised.[29]

Scholars have engaged in a lengthy debate about the intentions of the Kentucky governor in the spring of 1861 and formed two camps of opinion: one group portrays Magoffin as a disunionist who hoped the adoption of neutrality would eventually push Kentucky into the Confederacy, while the other praises the governor for his efforts to keep the Bluegrass State out of the fray.[30] While enriching our understanding of Magoffin, these interpretations tend to overstate his long-term vision. The opening of the conflict blindsided Magoffin, as it did almost every other borderite. Although war had been much discussed ever since Lincoln's election, few Americans had prepared for an actual conflict. His preliminary response to the war belied sheer confusion rather than ulterior motives or patent choreography for Kentucky's future. A policy of neutrality represented a way station, not a final destination, for the people of the Border South, and Magoffin opted for it in an effort to extend Kentucky's decision-making process.

Magoffin initially sought a decidedly Border South solution to the commencement of war. In addition to advocating neutrality, he gauged the interest of the governors of Indiana and Ohio in joining him to mediate a peaceful settlement between the Confederacy and the federal government. If they could together secure a truce between the warring sections, "the passions of the people may cool in the meantime" and politicians could find some means by which "this horrid war may be stopped and our difficulties adjusted in a manner honorable to all parties."[31] In his proclamation Lincoln called for a special session of Congress to meet on July 4; Magoffin figured that preventing armed hostilities until that point would produce a mandate for a settlement. While Magoffin counted on the antebellum intersectional amity that had been so integral to proslavery Unionism, he failed to comprehend the momentous sea change in Northern public opinion after Fort Sumter. No longer did white Northerners view the crisis as merely a political question about slavery's future in the republic. With their nationalism placed on trial, most Northerners succumbed to a *rage militaire* that shattered the intersectional goodwill that had been a trademark of antebellum proslavery Unionism.[32] The bombardment at Fort Sumter "united all the free states as one man," Sophie Du Pont discerned. "What has started the North, is the sentiment of fealty to the constitutional authority of the land & the flag of our country." Across the North, politicians and editors called for the subjugation of Southern traitors. Northerners now placed noncommittal white border Southerners in the same category as bloodthirsty Confederate rebels, which left the inhabitants of the borderland confused and concerned. As a Baltimore inhabitant astutely observed, the Border South had become "the cloth between the shears." Ohio governor William Dennison refused Magoffin's invitation and proclaimed the federal government "to be wholly in the right." Indiana governor Oliver P. Morton also declined and beseeched Kentucky to side with the free states in the contest.[33]

At the same time that he reached out to the governors of Indiana and Ohio, Magoffin also sent emissaries to New Orleans to purchase arms and munitions for the state militia. The Kentucky legislature had in March 1860 passed a law to revamp the militia, which it christened the State Guard. The general assembly placed Simon Bolivar Buckner in charge of the State Guard, and by early 1861 he had organized sixty-one companies and scrounged equipment and weapons from every available outlet within the Bluegrass State. The State Guard had a decidedly pro-Southern complexion, and some Kentuckians believed that Magoffin intended to use it "to cow down the unprotected Union men" who had thus far blocked all avenues to secession. The governor realized that in order for a policy of neutrality to gain respect, the state had to arm itself adequately. His agents, however, found few available weapons in the Crescent City, and Magoffin's search for arms in the heart of the Confederacy further aroused the suspicions of unconditional Unionists, who in response urged the formation of independent militia units to counter the presence of the State Guard.[34]

Delaware governor Burton, like Magoffin, had trouble deciding how best to respond to the opening of hostilities. His refusal to commit Delaware troops to the U.S. government upset some of the state's unconditional Unionists, who felt that Burton and James Asheton Bayard's clique of Democrats planned to deliver the state to the Confederacy. Bayard, who in late March had on the floor of the Senate proclaimed that war could never mend the severed ties between the Confederacy and the federal government, took an inopportune vacation through the Lower South during April. In the aftermath of Fort Sumter, unconditional Unionists charged him with conspiring with Confederate officials. Bayard privately expressed a strong desire for Delaware to join in the secession movement, but he concluded that "unless [Virginia] and Maryland go South, we are tied hand and foot" to what he derisively labeled "a free negro republic."[35] Burton refrained from calling the legislature into special session, which concerned Unionists. While the governor wavered, volunteer militia units with differing sectional allegiances organized throughout the state. A Wilmington editor bemoaned that many of these militia outfits were composed of "secret secessionists" who hoped to bring about Delaware's secession through force. Henry Du Pont, president of the Du Pont Powder Works located just outside Wilmington, coordinated the raising of Unionist militia and complained that without the legislature in session to pass an appropriation bill, his troops would suffer from inadequate supplies and munitions.[36]

Missouri's Claiborne Jackson, unlike Magoffin and Burton, acted in a decisive manner after Lincoln's proclamation. No one questioned Jackson's sympathies or motives; he unapologetically yearned for Missouri to join the Confederacy. Jackson called the state legislature into an emergency session on May 2 so it could prepare the state for war. Militia units hummed with activity in the days following Jackson's defiant response to Lincoln, and secessionists in western Missouri captured the federal arsenal at Liberty and absconded with a stockpile of weapons and four cannon.[37] Jackson informed the president of the Arkansas state convention that the people of Missouri would not countenance living under the thumb of the Republicans. He felt the Republicans' primary goal was to eradicate slavery, and to do this they had begun "the most damnable and hellish crusade that was ever waged against any people upon earth." The halfway step of neutrality would not satisfy Jackson, who preferred "a full, complete and final separation," and predicted that Missouri would secede within thirty days.[38] Many Missourians appreciated Jackson's brash reply to Lincoln's request for troops, but the governor misread the majority opinion of his constituency. Far more white Missourians favored neutrality and thought along the same lines as a Columbia editor who recommended that the Border South "stand as wall of fire between belligerent extremes, and with their strong arms and potential counsel keep them apart."[39]

Of the four Border South executives, Thomas Hicks had up to April 1861 proven the most committed to the Union cause. The events at Fort Sumter and Lincoln's call for troops, however, led to a series of events in Maryland that placed the fate of the state in great peril. Prior to Fort Sumter, tensions ran so high in Baltimore that one inhabitant claimed that "people are afraid of their own shadow." Afterward, Baltimoreans with conflicting sectional allegiances brawled in the streets and kept the city on edge. Mindful of this powder keg, Hicks traveled to Washington on April 15 and conversed with the president, Winfield Scott, and Secretary of War Simon Cameron about the call for soldiers. The triumvirate promised Hicks that any troops raised in Maryland would either protect the national capital or stay within the Old Line State. The governor returned to Annapolis, mulled over the offer, and on April 17 agreed to the proposition.[40]

Hicks technically had not agreed to furnish any troops for the subjugation of the seceded states and had adopted a de facto policy of armed neutrality.

As a symbol of this policy, the Maryland state flag for a brief stint replaced the American flag above some public buildings. Hicks surely understood that this policy did not satisfy all Marylanders. Some Marylanders questioned his cooperation with the Lincoln administration, while others implored him to call the legislature into session so it could make arrangements for a state convention. Throughout the spring Hicks fretted that the spirit of disunion had grown so large that it might overwhelm Unionists, especially once Virginia seceded.[41]

One historian of Maryland politics considers Hicks's course of armed neutrality a ploy to buy precious time for Unionists to check the advances of fire-eaters after Fort Sumter. In hindsight, such a program seems like a neat step in the state's inevitable progression toward the Union column. Neither Hicks nor any other Unionist, however, knew what lay in store for Maryland. Even in late July, once the war had begun in earnest and federal troops occupied the state, a Baltimore native alleged that "there is no hotter secession state than Maryland and in the final enlistment she will go with the South." Moreover, Unionist John Pendleton Kennedy acknowledged in September that "here in Maryland we are only saved from the outbreak of civil conflict by the presence of the great force which now keeps the peace of the State." The governor advocated de facto neutrality because it was the most noncommittal course available and perfectly suited to a Border South state.[42]

Furthermore, the swift onrush of another crisis deprived Hicks the luxury of time or foresight. Maryland's proximity to the national capital proved inauspicious for a policy of neutrality because military units from the northeast responding to Lincoln's proclamation would have to cross through the Old Line State to get to Washington. Baltimore, a cauldron of excitement in the days after Fort Sumter, housed an interchange of the major rail lines connecting the northeast to the national capital. To reach Washington expeditiously, nearly all northeastern units would be siphoned from secondary lines onto the Philadelphia, Wilmington, and Baltimore Railroad, which terminated at Baltimore's President Street Station. These passengers had to disembark and travel a mile through the heart of the city to Camden Station, where they boarded trains bound for Washington. On April 18 angry citizens ignored a plea from Mayor George W. Brown to refrain from taunting southbound soldiers and greeted the first Northern troops to enter Baltimore with epithets, jeers, and renditions of "Dixie." The troops, nonplussed and dumbfounded by the crowd, did not respond to the provocations. Later that evening T. Parkin Scott and Ross Winans, politicians in favor of secession, hosted an impromptu convention that passed a series of resolutions calling on Marylanders "to repel, if need be, any invader who may come to establish a military despotism over us." Brown and Hicks reported the worsening situation to Lincoln and advised the federal government to find another route for soldiers coming to Washington. "It is not possible for more soldiers to pass through Baltimore unless they fight their way at every step," an unnerved Brown warned the president.[43]

Unfortunately, troops from the Sixth Massachusetts and ten companies of unarmed Pennsylvania militiamen left Philadelphia before dawn on April 19 and arrived in Baltimore at noon. Chaos descended once the approximately 1,700 Northern troops disembarked at the President Street Station and boarded horse-drawn trollies destined for Camden Station. Observers packed Pratt Street, and "as the troops kept passing, the crowd of bystanders grew larger, the excitement and—among many—the feeling of indignation grew more intense." Seven companies of the Massachusetts soldiers made it through the gauntlet unscathed, but the mob pelted the last horse-drawn car with debris and erected barricades in the street. The remaining four companies had to march through the growing mob, which now rained bricks and stones down on the troops. The frenzied throng soon added bullets to its arsenal of brickbats, rocks, and rails. Discipline among the green troops quickly dissipated; they returned fire and a full-fledged street battle erupted. Mayor Brown, Police Marshal George P. Kane, and a contingent of Baltimore policemen eventually pressed back the mob. The Massachusetts troops endured as many as thirteen deaths and three dozen wounded men in the melee. The Pennsylvania militiamen never left the President Street Station and instead scattered once the mob descended on them; some escaped by rail back to Pennsylvania. Still, three Pennsylvanians perished, more than twenty suffered wounds, and about two hundred temporarily went missing. Officials estimated that twelve civilians died during the fracas and an unknown number sustained injuries. The violence brought tears to the eyes of a Baltimore Unionist, who lamented that Maryland's "soil must be a battle field, a slaughter house, because her people . . . cannot see Northern troops pass through to war with their brethern [*sic*] of the South."[44]

The bloodletting in the streets of Baltimore weighed heavily on Hicks. Brown called a public meeting at Monument Square the afternoon of the riot in order to calm the situation and prevent further violence. Several prominent Baltimoreans addressed the excited crowd, including Mayor Brown, William P. Preston, and Severn Teackle Wallis. Nevertheless, the speakers agitated rather than soothed the crowd. Wallis notably expressed his sympathy for the seceded states and made known his desire for Maryland to leave the Union. "He hoped the blood of the citizens, shed by an invading foe," a reporter wrote of Wallis, "would obliterate all past differences, and seal the covenant of brotherhood among the people." The crowd demanded to hear from Governor Hicks, who had ensconced himself in a nearby hotel. When the governor showed up he voiced a desire for the preservation of the Union, which provoked an angry rebuke from the audience. Shaken, Hicks retreated and stated, "I will suffer my right arm to be torn from my body before I will raise it to strike a sister State." Brown, worried about the governor's safety, invited him to lodge at his house. That night Hicks, disoriented and confined to a bed, met with Brown and other Baltimore officials and apparently gave his approval for Maryland militiamen, the Baltimore police, and private citizens to burn all the major northbound railroad bridges surrounding the city to prevent more troops from entering.[45]

Hicks returned to Annapolis the next morning; two days later he finally relented and called the legislature into special session. Maryland secessionists felt that the outburst in Baltimore would provide them with the strength to push a convention bill through the general assembly when it met on April 26. They received more welcome news when on April 24 a special election in Baltimore resulted in all ten of the city's seats in the lower house going to members of the newly christened Southern Rights Party, an assemblage of erstwhile Democrats who hoped to align Maryland with the other seceded states. The special election occurred because the House in 1860 had vacated the ten Baltimore seats on the suspicion of voter fraud. The Southern Rights candidates ran unopposed in the spur-of-the-moment election, and less than a third of the voters that participated in the 1860 presidential election cast ballots on April 24. The low turnout can be attributed to the election being called less than forty hours in advance of the polling, the absence of opposition to the Southern Rights candidates, and the disarray from the April 19 riot. Still, the election represented a victory for Maryland fire-eaters and gave them high hopes as the legislature prepared to meet.[46]

A contingent of four Baltimore officials led by Mayor Brown met with Lincoln, his cabinet, and Winfield Scott on April 21 and begged them to find an alternative route for shuffling troops to Washington. The president acquiesced and decided that henceforth soldiers would travel by rail to the Chesapeake Bay, then board water transports to Annapolis, where they could once again take the railroad to the capital. General Benjamin Butler and the Eighth Massachusetts Regiment took this circuitous route on April 21 and made it to Washington with minimal interference, a testament that the bypass of Baltimore proved less provocative to the people of Maryland. In order to avoid a collision between the legislature and federal troops, Governor Hicks on April 24 moved the special session to Frederick, a town situated in the heavily Unionist western portion of the state.[47]

The Baltimore riot resulted in several significant consequences for Maryland and the Border South. First, it prodded Hicks to summon the legislature into session after months of delay. The general assembly, and especially the Southern Rights contingent from Baltimore, caused no shortage of headaches for Unionists in the following months. With the legislature finally in session, Maryland Unionists realized that they would have to intensify their offensive to keep the state's fire-eaters from gaining superiority. More ominously for Maryland secessionists, however, the riot gave the federal government an excuse to station troops permanently in the state. Once Butler's troops landed at Annapolis on April 21, Maryland did not rid itself of a federal presence for the duration of the war. "Our Pontius Pilate (Gov Hicks) without washing his hands," a disunionist fulminated, "handed our beloved state over to blustering Abe to be crucified." Federal troops augmented Maryland's unconditional Unionists and their presence intimidated conditional Unionists, the largest segment of the Border South populace, who may have otherwise converted to the secessionist standard. Finally, the riot added more ferocity to the Northern *rage militaire*, which greatly reduced the chances for bringing about a truce and solidifying a compromise. Border South conservatives found few allies in the once-ripe region of Northern moderation, the Lower North, after the altercation at Baltimore. "If Baltimore was laid in ashes the North would rejoice over it and laud the Spirit that dictated the act," remarked Andrew H. Reeder of Philadelphia. "All hope of help, and almost all hope of neutrality, from the Border States is given up by our people. The policy of conciliation which a few weeks ago had so many friends," Reeder continued, "has now no friends at all." In time the moderate impulse within the Lower North revived, but at this crucial juncture its disappearance struck a hard blow for Border South conservatives. A Kentucky Unionist remarked that news of the Baltimore riot had produced "general gloom and apprehension . . . intermixed with general military ardor" throughout the Bluegrass State.[48]

Hicks welcomed the legislature to Frederick on April 26 with an address in which he defended his response to the Baltimore riot. The governor noted that he had personally asked Lincoln that no additional federal troops cross over Maryland soil, but the president replied that he could not comply. Lincoln explained that the soldiers had come to Washington to protect the national capital, not to place Maryland under the heel of a military despotism.

After this explanation, Hicks asked the legislature to adopt an official policy of neutrality. "We have violated no rights of either section," and thus "I cannot counsel Maryland to take sides against the General Government, until it shall commit outrages upon us which would justify us in resisting its authority," Hicks declared. The governor cautioned that if Maryland embraced secession instead of neutrality, the state would become the seat of the war. In that event, Maryland would suffer economic, political, and social devastation, a familiar refrain that had been repeated by many Border South Unionists. Emboldened disunionists in the legislature ignored Hicks's recommendation and immediately pressed for the creation of a special committee to draft legislation for calling a convention.[49]

Unionists realized that, just like their brethren in the Kentucky legislature and the Missouri state convention, they faced a sturdy opponent. Democrats held a two-seat advantage over Americans in the Senate and a sixteen-seat edge in the lower house, though party affiliation did not always distinguish fire-eaters from moderates. Party lines underwent a wartime mutation from the antebellum distinctions of Democrats and Americans or Constitutional Unionists into Union and Southern Rights organizations. The Union Party had begun to form prior to the Baltimore riot, and its organizers tried to distance it from any affiliation with the Republican Party. Because so many white border Southerners disapproved of Lincoln, the Republicans, and their followers in the region like Henry Winter Davis, leaders of the movement strove to distinguish themselves from the president's party. "The Union party must sustain not the administration but the government," William Kimmell explained. To do so, Kimmell advised a nationwide coalition of the moderate followers of Crittenden and Douglas. Union Party organizers labored to make voters realize that their opposition to secession did not equal disapproval of slavery. Maryland fire-eaters attempted to smear the Union Party as handmaidens of the Republicans, "but we firmly hold to the middle national ground we have always held & we desire to conquer a peace," one leader explained.[50]

Maryland Unionists in the general assembly employed an array of tactics to stonewall the progress of secessionists. In the House they swept the proposal for a state convention into the committee on federal relations. Although Southern Rights men occupied five of the seven seats on the committee and outspoken secessionist Wallis chaired it, the group as a whole suffered from a divergence of opinion about how best to separate Maryland from the Union. Wallis insisted that it could only be accomplished by calling a convention, electing delegates, and allowing that body to render a decision. Other Southern

Rights men feared that the lengthy convention process would not result in secession, especially since federal soldiers had entered the state, and instead claimed the legislature could adopt a disunion ordinance. Unionists in the Senate took advantage of the tactical disagreements dividing fire-eaters and composed an address that assured Maryland's voters that the legislature had no authority to pass an ordinance of secession.[51]

While Unionists and fire-eaters sparred in Frederick, a period of relative calm overcame Maryland. Just ten days after the Baltimore riot, Kennedy noted that "the spirit in favor of secession in this State is very much sobered." He credited the improved atmosphere to the presence of three large camps of federal troops stationed just across the Pennsylvania border, poised to pounce on Maryland if the general assembly made a bid for secession. Fire-eaters complained that the federal troops frightened many of their colleagues who just a week earlier had promised to do all in their power to help Maryland join the Confederacy. As long as Maryland lay between the national capital and the free states, however, the federal government would use any means necessary to keep the state in the Union column. Illinois Republican Lyman Trumbull's recommendation that Unionists and the federal government "meet them [Maryland secessionists] right square in the face & we shall soon subdue them. . . . Let the blows fall thick and hard," made an impression on Lincoln. The president gave Butler the authority to suspend the writ of habeas corpus and reduce Baltimore with artillery fire if it would bring the secessionists to heel. The federal military presence, which grew over the course of 1861, provided needed support to Maryland Unionists in their efforts to reverse the tide of the state after the riot.[52]

Secessionists in the legislature soon realized the combination of federal might and Unionist resolve made their dream of disunion very difficult to attain. In early May they made a desperate attempt to gain the upper hand through circumvention. At a secret session of the legislature, fire-eaters introduced a Public Safety Bill. Ostensibly intended to safeguard the state from invasion, the bill actually undermined Hicks's executive authority by establishing a seven-person committee of public safety. Coleman Yellott, the bill's sponsor, wanted to vest the committee with the power to organize and arm the state militia, remove and appoint militia officers above the rank of captain, and provide for the defense of the state. Few people failed to see that the committee, dominated by secessionists, provided fire-eaters with the tools to procure Maryland's secession. "This is the most open and bold exposure of the machinery of secession we have yet had," a Unionist gasped. In response Unionists organized public meetings throughout the state and flooded the legislature with no fewer than forty-four petitions in opposition to the legislation in the days following its introduction, another sign of the administrative abilities of Border South moderates.[53]

Unionists in the Senate utilized every possible parliamentary tactic to prevent the Southern Rights men from ramming the Public Safety Bill through the upper house. They paralyzed the measure's momentum with a dizzying array of amendments, filibusters, and calls for adjournment. The Unionists claimed victory on May 4 when the Senate sent the bill back to committee, which one reporter considered "as equivalent to its defeat, certainly in its present shape, and unless radically modified." Whereas the fire-eaters faced internal dissension about how to proceed, the Unionists once again closed ranks and coordinated an effective campaign to thwart their enemies.[54]

Fire-eaters in the legislature discovered they had exhausted their options. Wallis, who chaired the House committee on federal relations that had been deliberating whether to call a convention, on May 9 delivered a report packed with invective. He labeled Lincoln's call for troops nothing less than a declaration of war and castigated Hicks for his tepid response to the president's proclamation and poor handling of the Baltimore riot. "Unless the American Revolution was a crime, the declaration of American Independence a falsehood, and every patriot and hero of 1776 a traitor," Wallis snarled, "the South was right and the North was wrong." Because of the governor's vacillating course since the Baltimore riot, Maryland had been trampled over by the federal military "and her name blotted out, for the time, from the list of free governments." Secessionists surely liked Wallis's language, but they did not like his recommendations. Because of the military presence, "no election, held at such time and with such surroundings, could possibly be fair or free." An election for delegates to a convention, he concluded, would not reflect the will of Maryland's people as long as the gleam of federal bayonets could be seen at the ballot box. Therefore, the committee recommended that Maryland officially implement a stance of neutrality and hold off calling a sovereignty convention at present. A few days later the legislature adopted a policy of neutrality and adjourned until June. The short session produced none of the results that fire-eaters had just three weeks prior considered within reach. Without a sovereignty convention, a board of public safety, or even legislation to arm the state militia, Maryland radicals returned home empty-handed.[55]

Maryland fire-eaters viewed Wallis's lament as nothing more than capitulation to the Unionists. "I anticipate the very worst, and when I find that I and others who are ready at all hazards to resist and fight are left in the lurch I will resign and leave the State—go into Virginia and claim the privilege of shouldering a musket in the cause of Southern rights," one Maryland secessionist scoffed in response to the legislature's inaction. The number of Maryland radicals who went southward will never be known, but the combination of federal troops and Unionists' redoubled efforts convinced many fire-eaters to abandon what they now considered a lost cause in the Old Line State. The mayor of Baltimore figured as many as twenty thousand men fled Maryland and joined the Confederacy in the wake of the legislature's inactivity, but acknowledged that this was a liberal estimate. Far more Marylanders who sympathized with the Confederacy adopted a neutral attitude and refused to take up arms for either side in the contest. "Maryland has succumbed to Lincoln, and degraded herself," a distressed diarist moaned.[56]

Federal military action in the middle of May crowned the Unionist campaign in Maryland. On May 13 Butler led his troops into Baltimore and occupied Federal Hill, and the following day he arrested Ross Winans, a Southern Rights legislator who had just returned from Frederick. Charged with treason and imprisoned at Fort McHenry, Winans had no means for legal recourse since Lincoln had suspended the writ of habeas corpus along the rail corridor from Philadelphia to Washington. Butler's action set a precedent that alarmed Maryland fire-eaters, who faced the possibility of imprisonment for flying secessionist flags, sporting the blue cockade, or speaking out against the federal government. On the heels of the legislature's adjournment and Winans's arrest, Hicks officially abandoned the state's policy of neutrality and called for four regiments to meet the terms of Lincoln's April 15 proclamation. Recruiting for the Union army began at once. Northerners and unconditional Unionists applauded Hicks's decision, while many Marylanders were dumbfounded. "It is said that Nero fiddled while Rome was burning and it appears to me that you have been fiddling as far as the welfare & safety of your state is concerned," a group of upset Marylanders protested.[57]

In Delaware, Unionists also intensified their efforts to ensure that the proponents of secession did not gain leverage. Rumors that secessionists planned to overrun the Du Pont Powder Works, along with reports of the mobilization of disunionist militia groups in Kent and Sussex Counties, spurred Unionists to action.[58] Although Governor Burton still refused to offer troops to Lincoln based on his reading of the state constitution, on May 11 he issued a pair of general orders that designated Henry Du Pont major general of Delaware's armed forces and gave him the discretion to distribute arms and munitions to volunteer units as he saw fit. Du Pont tried to strengthen the governor's order by requiring all members of volunteer companies to take an oath of allegiance to the United States before receiving any supplies. Du Pont agreed with another Delaware unconditional Unionist who remarked, "I look upon a conditional Union man as a rebellious character equal to the secessionist[s] of S Carolina." Aware of the erratic nature of conditional Unionism, Du Pont feared that weapons distributed to conditionalists might eventually be turned against his forces. Upon hearing of Du Pont's pledge requirement and the general's intention to disarm any companies that refused to take the oath retroactively, Burton rescinded his general orders. The governor claimed Du Pont lacked the legal authority to require the oath of Delaware volunteers, which he felt "would indicate a distrust of their loyalty and reflect upon them as good citizens."[59]

Although unconditional Unionists complained of Burton's hedging stance, the governor did not interfere with the organization of troops who wished to volunteer their services to the republic. The First Delaware Volunteer Infantry in May 1861 enlisted in the federal cause without any meddling from Burton. The governor loathed Lincoln and the Republicans, but he and most Delawareans valued the Union to a greater degree than many white border Southerners. Secessionist activity still occurred in Delaware, but by the end of May the Unionist offensive managed by Du Pont had left little doubt that as long as Maryland stayed in the Union, so would Delaware. "We have some bloody secessionists in this State, but they are pretty well muffled," Du Pont confidently disclosed at the end of the month. Delaware had abandoned its de facto policy of neutrality in favor of the Union.[60]

James A. Bayard discovered firsthand that many of the residents of Wilmington had thrown in their lot with the Union. Thomas F. Bayard kept his father informed of Delaware's reaction to the opening of the war as he made his way home from his vacation in the Deep South. Thomas held his neighbors in contempt because so many residents seemed reluctant to support secession and aid the Confederacy. He even advised his father to carry a revolver in case anyone attacked him for his Southern sympathies. Upon his arrival in Wilmington on May 4, Bayard faced accusations that he had conspired to pull Delaware out of the Union while on his trip. He denied these reports, noting that he had scheduled the vacation a year in advance. Shortly after his return to Wilmington, Bayard traveled to Philadelphia on business and was greeted by an angry mob of at least two hundred people. The Philadelphia police detained Bayard for his own safety, took him to the mayor's office, and helped him secure passage back to Delaware. Upon his return Bayard offered to resign from the Senate if the citizens of Delaware did not agree with his stance on peaceable separation. He remained in office at the behest of his friends, though he removed most of his family to Dorchester County, Maryland, in the wake of the incident. Bayard's experience illustrated the firm commitment to the federal government of many inhabitants of the northernmost portion of Delaware.[61]

While Du Pont exerted his energy to keep Delaware safe for the Union, Kentucky politicians watched with interest as the state's voters went to the polls on May 4 to choose their delegates to the border state convention. The outcome was a foregone conclusion, however, because the entire slate of Southern Rights candidates had removed their names from the ballot. James Brown Clay, a Southern Rights candidate and the son of Henry Clay, explained that he had withdrawn because the clash at Fort Sumter, the secession of Virginia, and the Baltimore riot had convinced him that few, if any, states would now take the meeting seriously. Blanton Duncan, who had been angling for Kentucky's secession, rejoiced that the Southern Rights men would not take part in the election. "All this [talk of compromise at the border state convention] is damn nonsense & child play," Duncan howled, "for there is no Earthly chance of restoring the Union & Kentucky is compelled to take position with the seceded states." Another Border South secessionist disparaged the idea that any good could come from the convention. He scoffed that the delegates, by holding out the false hope of compromise, would only chain "the border States as a tail to the Northern Confederacy, and thus abolitionize them all." With no Southern Rights candidates in the field, Unionists swept the May 4 election in Kentucky.[62]

Approximately three-quarters of the Kentucky voters who cast ballots in the November 1860 presidential election participated in the May elections, which indicated a fairly strong turnout.[63] The popularity of Crittenden, who headed the Union ticket, aided the Unionists, along with the fact that some secessionists had already begun a southward exodus from the state. In late April, Duncan and John Hunt Morgan recruited young men, marched them out of Kentucky, and offered their services to the Confederacy. Other proponents of secession, frustrated by Kentucky's idleness, began making their way for the Confederacy after Fort Sumter and Lincoln's proclamation.[64] The May vote, however, did not indicate an outright endorsement of unconditional Unionism. Even Crittenden expected Kentucky to adopt a neutral stance, as did many other people who voted the Unionist ticket. "Kenty is averse to this Civil War," Crittenden told his son. "And it is now, & I trust will continue, to be her determination to keep out of the strife." Another Unionist described his preference for neutrality bluntly: "If we can't go with the South let us quit the North & not be like a free negro at a Barbecue unable to speak till they have all left."[65]

The Kentucky legislature convened once again just days after the border state convention election, and its actions revealed that many Kentuckians did not want to join either side in the conflict. In his message to the general assembly, Magoffin acknowledged that secession "is now receiving the thoughtful attention of the people and authorities" across the Border South, and thus he advised the passage of legislation that would allow for a referendum on a state convention. Moreover, he asked the legislature to adopt measures to place Kentucky in a position of armed neutrality for the present. Magoffin portrayed himself as neutral in thought and deed, but in reality his initial discomfiture about the crisis had given way to a belief that Kentucky would eventually join the Confederacy. Confederate general Gideon J. Pillow met with Magoffin in late April and the governor told him that because of its proximity to the Lower North, Kentucky had to adopt a policy of neutrality for the present. "I condemn and utterly abhor his neutral policy, or rather his alliance with Lincoln," Pillow reported to Confederate officials, "but yet I am satisfied that he will ultimately break the shackles with which he is now manacled."[66]

Those shackles proved most difficult for Magoffin to unchain. Petitions for armed neutrality inundated the legislature, and most of them indicated an ardent desire to adopt such a stance in order to broker peace between the warring sections. A petition from 242 Bracken County women, for instance, beseeched the legislature to follow the example of Henry Clay, assume a stance of neutrality, and act as a mediator to bring about a settlement. "Guard us from the direful calamity of Civil War," the women requested, "by allowing Kentucky to maintain inviolate her 'armed neutrality.'" No fewer than sixty-four similar petitions reached the legislature during the brief session. Many Kentuckians clearly viewed neutrality as another avenue for peace and compromise, rather than some meandering path toward secession.[67]

During the May session the Southern Rights legislators again ineffectively devoted much of their energy to securing passage of legislation to summon a state convention. Aware that their opponents now considered armed neutrality akin to a declaration of the state's Unionism, the Southern Rights men worked to prevent an official proclamation of neutrality. Once again, they failed: on May 16 the House adopted by a tally of sixty-nine to twenty-six a resolution that called for Kentucky to occupy a position of neutrality and to involve itself in the conflict only as a mediator between the sections. The House agreed to a second resolution that approved of Magoffin's sharp rejection of Lincoln's request for troops by the wide margin of eighty-nine to four, but the Southern Rights men had foundered in their effort to convert conditional Unionists into secessionists. Crittenden explained to Winfield

Scott that the adoption of the two resolutions did not indicate Kentucky's defiance of the Union, but rather a means "to preserve, substantially and ultimately, our connection with the Union." Magoffin issued an executive neutrality proclamation four days after the House passed its resolutions. The Southern Rights men in the Senate held out until the final day of the session, when the upper chamber passed a set of resolutions in concurrence with the policy adopted by the House and the governor.[68]

Unionists in the legislature took additional steps to give neutrality teeth and ensure that neither Magoffin nor any other state officials could bend the policy in favor of secession. For some time Unionists had expressed concerns that the officer corps of the State Guard included an overwhelming majority of secessionists. William Nelson, a naval lieutenant, unconditional Unionist, and liaison for the Lincoln administration, had in April begun to raise Unionist militias throughout the state to offset the State Guard.[69] The general assembly passed a bill creating a five-man military board and vested it with the power to borrow funds for arming the state, gave it the ability to purchase munitions and accoutrements, and granted it control over the state's military preparation. Magoffin sat on the board, but the remaining members were absolutely loyal to the Union. To ensure passage, the bill left the State Guard intact, but also established the Unionist Home Guard, and required both militias to swear an oath of allegiance to the United States Constitution. With their work done, the Unionists on May 24 procured the legislature's adjournment. "Thus has ended the weakest, most worthless Legislature ever called together," a pro-secession reporter spat.[70]

Unionists in the Kentucky legislature had accomplished what secessionists had attempted in Maryland—they stripped the governor of his sole constitutional authority over the state militia—in order to achieve the contradictory objective of keeping the state safely in the Union. They ignored their constitutional scruples and even violated the neutrality proclamation when in late spring they began funneling arms and money from the federal government to Unionists throughout the state. "If we dont have [the guns]," Joshua Speed informed Lincoln, "we will in all probability have to run the gauntlet for our lives." Afraid to risk losing Kentucky, federal authorities blessed the weapons distribution program, but cloaked their involvement. Nelson managed the delivery of what Kentuckians dubbed "Lincoln guns" to the state's Unionists. Together these efforts ensured that many conditional Unionists would not slip into the ranks of secessionists.[71]

Deteriorating conditions in Missouri contributed to Lincoln's resolve to keep Kentucky in the Union column at all costs. Prior to calling the legislature into special session, Governor Claiborne Jackson and General Daniel M. Frost, a leader in the state militia, made preparations to attack the U.S. arsenal in Saint Louis, rid Missouri of the federal presence, and open the way for the state's secession. To carry out his plan, the governor realized that he must adequately arm and equip the state militia, who would no doubt confront federal retaliation. Jackson reached out to Jefferson Davis, who agreed with the governor "as to the great importance of capturing the arsenal and securing its supplies." Davis sent cannon to Jackson, who ordered the state militia to begin drilling. Frost established an encampment for the militia units under his command on the western edge of Saint Louis and named the base Camp Jackson in honor of the governor.[72]

Missouri Unionists suspected that in the aftermath of Fort Sumter and Baltimore, the governor and his pro-secession colleagues might try to push the state out of the Union. A Jefferson City Unionist assured his associates that "the Old Fox will be well watched here. His movements are carefully guarded and will be hard of detection, but we may catch him yet." In Saint Louis, Frank Blair Jr. and Nathaniel Lyon prepared for an expected attack on the arsenal, which to Missouri secessionists had assumed comparable symbolic value to Fort Sumter. Blair would not let the Unionists of Saint Louis suffer at the hands of a fire-eating mob as had occurred in Baltimore. He informed his brother that he would not condone "shilly-shally childsplay with these infamous scoundrels." "There is but one policy now," Blair thundered, "and that is vigor, vigor, vigor." With General William S. Harney, federal commander of the Department of the West, away in Washington to give the president a report on Missouri, Lyon organized four regiments of volunteers and Blair distributed weapons to the Home Guard. Unionist forces occupied the high ground near the arsenal, and Lyon established a perimeter around the building. The two unflappable Unionist leaders worked with Illinois governor Richard Yates to ship any excess arms and munitions housed in the arsenal across the Mississippi River for safekeeping.[73]

By the time the legislature assembled in Jefferson City on May 2, Saint Louis had become a volcano waiting to explode. Jackson asked the legislature to adopt a policy of armed neutrality, yet his actions in the three weeks after Fort Sumter unmistakably indicated that he wished to use the policy to steer the state toward secession. The Missouri governor shared none of the reticence of the other Border South executives. Unionists in the general assembly eventually acquiesced in armed neutrality, but stymied the initial efforts of Jackson's pawns to pass a bill placing the state on a war footing and granting the executive expansive military authority. Although the legislature met in secret session, few doubted the topic of discussion in the statehouse. "By a good many of the reckless politicians, a collision at St. Louis would be hailed as a God-send," a newspaper reporter gleaned from sources privy to the clandestine meeting of legislators.[74] In far-off Washington, DC, Edward Bates implored the Saint Louis Unionists to avoid a collision at all costs because it would result in disastrous consequences for the state's citizenry, especially slaveholders. The onset of war on Missouri soil would yield "a general stampede of the negroes, both to the north & to the south, & the state will be practically abolitionised in less than 100 days."[75]

In the heated atmosphere of Saint Louis, however, few participants thought about the long-term consequences of war. Lyon and Blair decided to take the initiative after they received word that the pro-secession men had procured arms from the Confederacy. Lyon on May 10 marched two companies of U.S. regulars and a couple of volunteer regiments into Camp Jackson and overwhelmed the meager state militia unit. Realizing that the federal forces far outnumbered his own, Frost surrendered to Lyon without a fight. Both sides had averted violence, but once Lyon began marching his prisoners back through the streets of Saint Louis, the seething tensions between Unionists and secessionists detonated. A gathering mob howled at the federal troops who escorted the column of prisoners, reserving their greatest scorn for the pugnacious Lyon and soldiers of German extraction. The scene quickly devolved into a reprise of the Baltimore spectacle: jeers and taunts gave way to gunfire and a riot soon erupted. In a spree of violence that lasted three days, twenty-eight civilians, two federal soldiers, and three state militiamen lost their lives.[76]

As in Maryland, the Saint Louis riot did not produce the outcome that secessionists desired. Upon receiving news of Lyon's foray, the legislature swiftly passed the militia bill and other military measures that Jackson craved. The governor mobilized the state militia, took control of Missouri's railroads and telegraph network, and exploited the contacts he had made as state banking commissioner in the 1850s to solicit funds for arming the state troops.[77] Most Missourians condemned Lyon's rash approach, but Jackson could not capitalize on the indignation of the populace. The tense atmosphere abated somewhat when on May 21 recently returned General Harney met with Sterling Price, the president of the adjourned state convention and newly appointed commanding general of the Missouri State Guard, and the two mutually agreed to respect the state's neutral position. Unionists, distrustful of Jackson and Price, complained that secessionists continued to commit acts of aggression. Because he feared Missouri might secede if the truce remained in effect, Lincoln arranged for Harney's removal and replaced him with Lyon.[78]

Lyon's elevation turned the tide in favor of the Missouri Unionists. In Lyon, unconditional Unionists found a man who shared their steadfast devotion to the flag. He believed two classes of Missourians existed—Unionists and traitors—and would use everything at his disposal to guarantee the state remained true. Alexander William Doniphan remarked that Lyon preferred "eating the lamb to lying down with it." Conservatives, desperately clinging to the rapidly vanishing policy of neutrality, in early June arranged a meeting between Missouri's pro-secession and unconditional Unionist factions in the hopes of preserving peace. Jackson and Price met with Lyon and Blair at Saint Louis's Planters' House on June 11 and soon discovered that Doniphan's depiction of the new commander was accurate. After hours of unfruitful discussion, Lyon coolly pointed to each of his guests and stated he would rather see them "and every man, woman, and child in the State dead and buried" than concede to state officials "the right to dictate to my Government in any matter however unimportant." Lyon turned to the governor and announced, "This means war." Astonished, Jackson and Price watched as Lyon whirled around and exited the room.[79]

Lyon's bold declaration ended all hopes for neutrality in Missouri. As in Baltimore, the riot in Saint Louis gave the federal government the pretext it needed to occupy Missouri. The federal commander prepared to march on Jefferson City, but before Lyon's troops arrived, Jackson and the state government evacuated. Lyon encountered a small contingent of state forces at Boonville and won a thorough victory in the skirmish, which forced the state government to flee to the southwestern corner of Missouri and allowed the federals to control the length of the Missouri River, a vital transportation artery. Lyon's triumph over Jackson equaled a major victory for the Unionist cause in the state; the duly elected governor of Missouri spent the rest of the war on the run from federal forces. Even prior to Lyon's challenge, the increased presence of federal troops had fortified the Unionist offensive in eastern Missouri. "The Camp Jackson affair and other events following it have operated like a poultice," a Unionist noted. "The inflammation has been drawn out of a great number of men who were heretofore rampant secessionists." George Caleb Bingham agreed, comparing the state's fire-eaters to once-ferocious tigers who had been caged by the federal troops and now "become the sport of boys who will poke them in the ribs and make merry over their insane antics." Many dark days of internecine violence lay ahead, but Lyon's late-spring stand dealt Missouri's secessionists an enormous setback.[80]

"Strayed." A pro-Union political cartoon depicting General Nathaniel Lyon and federal troops compelling the flight of Missouri secessionist forces under the leadership of deposed governor Claiborne Fox Jackson and Sterling Price. Federal force helped sustain the Unionist offensive throughout the Border South during the secession crisis. Library of Congress.

The collective shock of Fort Sumter, Baltimore, and Saint Louis seriously undercut the movement for a peaceful settlement between the Union and the Confederacy. Hopes of engineering a compromise on the slavery controversy were fleeting as well. By June only Kentucky continued to adhere to an official stance of neutrality, but even there both the Union and Southern Rights organizations either violated or circumvented the policy. Neutrality meant many things to different white border Southerners, but few people saw it as a permanent solution. Crittenden felt neutrality would help the Union cause and Jackson believed it would aid secession, but most people in the borderland saw it as a convenient approach that would delay the inevitable decision between Union and Confederacy. Still, the imperfect policy of neutrality, along with a growing contingent of federal soldiers, had produced a satisfactory result for Border South Unionists. The renewed efforts of Unionists and the intimidating presence of federal soldiers kept the Border South in the

Union during an interval when the four states of the Upper South witnessed a substantial erosion of Unionism and sided with the Confederacy. Neutrality and federal force combined as essential ingredients in the Unionist offensive, and many borderland secessionists took notice.[81]

As spring turned to summer, Franklin Buchanan watched helplessly from his Eastern Shore estate and tried to maintain a neutral attitude, but as he ruminated on the bold actions of borderland Unionists, he became increasingly disgusted. He had by the summer of 1861 drawn the difficult conclusion that secession would never materialize in the Border South. In August, Buchanan finally abandoned his neutral attitude, crossed the Potomac River, and offered his services to the Confederate navy.[82]

CHAPTER SEVEN

Every Day's Delay Weakens the Secessionists and Strengthens the Union

Secession Defeated, June–December 1861

The growing number of federal troops on Maryland soil in the spring of 1861 disgusted Severn Teackle Wallis. Descended from a wealthy Eastern Shore family, the forty-four-year-old Wallis had chosen to remain in the Old Line State, unlike his father, who had in 1837 left behind the exhausted soil of Maryland's coastal plain and headed west to the virgin bottomlands of the Mississippi delta in search of land and slaves. The younger Wallis had by 1860 established a successful Baltimore law practice, amassed a respectable fortune, and with his sharp legal mind and cosmopolitan refinement gained entrée into the city's highest social circles. A lifelong bachelor, Wallis employed two African American servants in his Saint Paul Street home but owned no enslaved persons himself. Wallis's urbane and genteel style, however, did not prevent him from taking a deep interest in the unfolding national crisis. The nonslaveholding Baltimore socialite was one of the Border South's most outspoken proponents of secession, and during the late meeting of the Maryland General Assembly, Wallis—who had been elected to the House of Delegates on the Southern Rights ticket in the wake of the April 19 riot—had been unable to engineer the calling of a state convention.[1]

Wallis's polish and charm gave way to indignation and frustration when parlor conversations turned to the future of his beloved Maryland. Known for "the sharpness of rapier-like thrusts which he gave his adversaries," Wallis in early 1861 focused his resentment on two entities: the Republicans, whom he considered a band of abolitionists bent on provoking war in order to complete their project of eradicating slavery; and Maryland governor Thomas Hicks, whom he charged with collaborating with the Lincoln administration to place Maryland under the bayonet and prevent the state's secession. A friend recalled that Wallis "hated and loathed [abolitionism] with a hatred and loathing which exhausted the resources of his unmatched vocabulary of invective." An acquaintance remembered that when stirred to speak of the Republicans, emancipation, or Hicks, Wallis unleashed broadsides that poured forth "as if from the mouth of a gatling-gun." The tall, spare, stooped Wallis hardly evinced the countenance of a firebrand, but a storm raged inside him. When talking about politics, Wallis's blue eyes seemed "now to dance with smiles and again to darken and flash with scorn."[2]

By the summer of 1861, however, the likelihood of Maryland or any of the Border South states seceding had become quite remote. The Unionist offensive had convinced most white border Southerners that the Union could protect slavery better than secession, and the elevated presence of federal soldiers and Unionist militias prevented many erstwhile conditional Unionists who had come to favor disunion from taking action. Numerous disenchanted white border Southerners adopted a neutral attitude, while some former conditional Unionists opted to leave the Border South, head southward, and enlist in the Confederate cause. Yet, just like he had done in the 1830s when his father abandoned Maryland for other opportunities, Wallis opted to stay put in his Border South home and fight for the cause of secession. A handful of other devoted fire-eaters remained in the Border South in the latter half of 1861, but they stared defeat in the face. The Lincoln administration continued to utilize force to hold on to the Border South and Unionists continued to spread their proslavery Unionist message to their neighbors. During this interval, Unionists changed the emphasis of their campaign to destroy the last remnants of disunion within the region. With the outbreak of war, Border South Unionists slowly came to the realization that the hour for a compromise settlement had passed. Instead, they maneuvered to reassure their neighbors in the last half of 1861 that the objective of the war was to sustain the Union with slavery intact, not to eliminate the peculiar institution. Despite a few bumps on the road, their campaign worked and the Border South remained true to the old flag. Ironically, the increased vigor and breadth of the Civil War inaugurated a process that would once and for all shatter the proslavery Union that Border South moderates sought so stridently to preserve.

THE SPARSELY ATTENDED border state convention, which convened on May 27 in Frankfort, indicated that with the commencement of war, many white border Southerners had begun to have grave doubts about the probability of a compromise settlement solving the nation's ills. Four Missourians joined a full slate of delegates from Kentucky and a single representative from Tennessee over the course of the weeklong meeting. Delaware and Maryland sent no delegates to the summit and few observers took time from their busy schedules to attend the proceedings. "The members themselves look as though they have despaired of doing anything," a reporter mocked.[3]

John Jordan Crittenden presided over the meeting, which after a week of deliberation unveiled a message that revealed the Unionist Border South mind-set and the importance of slavery to the region. The delegates aimed their missive at the conditional Unionists of the South and asserted the need for constitutional amendments that would "secure to slaveholders their legal rights, and allay their apprehensions in regard to possible encroachments in the future." They estimated that the passage of the Crittenden Compromise would go far to quell the anxieties of Southern Unionists, and the delegates recommended its introduction at the special session of Congress scheduled to meet on Independence Day. If no progress was made at the special session, the delegates urged the summoning of a national convention to vote on the amendments. These conservatives hoped that the passage of the Crittenden measures would not only allay Border South Unionists but also draw the seceded states back into the Union. The delegates warned of the urgent need to adopt the resolutions in order to avoid the escalation of the war. All of the delegates in attendance save Kentucky's Charles S. Morehead, who approved of neutrality, signed the statement. In a separate address to the people of Kentucky, the Bluegrass State representatives vowed to fight to safeguard the institution of slavery in the upcoming session of Congress.[4]

Few people outside the Border South took notice of the handiwork of the border state convention. Across the North and within the Confederacy most Americans felt the die had been cast and instead focused their attention on preparing for the looming military conflict. The meeting, however, did help to sustain the Unionist offensive in the Border South. Crittenden and his colleagues made it perfectly clear that despite the bellicose posturing of other Americans, they intended to maintain the fight for compromise and peace. Moreover, they declared once again that the preservation of slavery unquestionably required adherence to the Union. Scores of Border South moderates in the aftermath of the meeting took to the stump and emphasized the key correlation between adherence to the Union and the maintenance of the peculiar institution. Kentuckian Garrett Davis had met with Abraham Lincoln in late April and received the president's guarantee that he "would make no attack, direct or indirect, upon the institutions or property of any State." Unionist newspapers circulated Davis's report of the meeting in an effort to assuage white border Southerners' concerns about Lincoln's intentions. Upon returning to Missouri, John B. Henderson, one of Missouri's delegates to Frankfort, advised Unionists to issue a proclamation that echoed the border state conference message and Lincoln's assurance to Davis. "Be sure that you pledge . . . that there is no desire by the Government to interfere with slave property," Henderson instructed. "If this be done and promptly done," he continued, "the victory is won and Missouri is safe."[5]

The border state convention bridged the gap between the outbreaks of violence in Charleston, Baltimore, and Saint Louis and the meeting of Congress in July and signaled to the region's vital center that moderates would continue to push for a settlement. The rest of the nation may have given up on compromise, but they had not. Moreover, the message from the convention indicated that the Unionist leadership had a plan in place for the outbreak of war. In order to appease Border South moderates, they sought affirmation that the federal government would not interfere with slavery in the states. With federal troops on the soil of three Border South states, Unionists had to assure their neighbors that they had not come to carry off slaves. In essence, centrists once again outmaneuvered the fire-eaters by framing the conflict as one to preserve the Union, not to eradicate slavery.   .

The message of the Unionists registered with the voters of Kentucky and Maryland. The executives of each state had to push their congressional elections, usually held in August in Kentucky and November in Maryland, up to June in order to have representation when the special session of Congress opened on Independence Day. The early meeting date did not affect either Delaware or Missouri, where congressional elections had taken place in 1860. At the Union Party's state convention in Maryland, the executive committee issued resolutions that affirmed the state's commitment to the Union and called for the Border South to take the lead in mediating an end to the war. Moreover, they promised that "the Union men will oppose to the utmost of their ability all attempts of the federal executive to commingle in any manner its particular views on the slavery question."[6]

When Marylanders went to the polls on June 13, they delivered a resounding victory to the Union Party. Unionists defeated Southern Rights contenders in five of Maryland's six congressional districts and only in the Third and Sixth Districts did the Southern Rights candidates come anywhere close to beating their opponents. The race in Maryland's Fourth District, which encompassed Baltimore, pitted two Unionists against each other. There Henry May defeated Henry Winter Davis by a wide margin, another sign that white borderites harbored suspicions about politicians allied with the Republicans. An embittered Davis carped that "a combination of the secessionists with the mamby pambies of the peace party" had engineered his defeat, but upon an investigation of the overall results in the state, his attitude improved. "That ends secession in Md," Davis pithily admitted.[7]

Kentucky Unionists enjoyed similar success in their congressional elections, which took place a week after the Maryland contest. Unionists routed the Southern Rights ticket in nine out of Kentucky's ten congressional districts.

Except for the state's First District, where incumbent Henry C. Burnett defeated Unionist Lawrence S. Trimble by a wide margin, the Union Party trounced its competition. The closest race occurred in the Eighth District, where Crittenden overpowered incumbent William E. Simms, who captured only 40 percent of the vote. A pleased Nathaniel Paschall treated the Unionist victory as a sign of the dominance of proslavery Unionism in the Border South. "Mr. Crittenden draws, as we all draw, a distinction between Republicanism and the Government of the United States," Paschall observed. "We are *for* the Government, *not* the Administration—*for* the Constitution, *not* the Chicago platform."[8]

Tables 7.1 and 7.2 provide the results of the June 1861 congressional elections in the Border South. In addition, data have been culled from the 1860 federal census to compute the percentage of slaves in relationship to the overall population of each congressional district. Burnett, the only victor from the Southern Rights Party, won Kentucky's First District, where enslaved persons composed roughly 19 percent of the overall population. Four other districts in the Bluegrass State had denser slave populations than Burnett's, and in each one the Union Party candidate captured no less than 59 percent of the vote. The results suggest that for the most part, Kentuckians viewed the Union Party as the best vehicle to preserve slavery. The Maryland results reveal a closer contest in the state's district with the densest slave population; Unionist Charles B. Calvert narrowly edged Benjamin G. Harris in Maryland's Sixth Congressional District. Nonetheless, the Maryland results demonstrate a correlation between Unionism and dense slave concentrations. The 1861 congressional elections also show that some pro-Confederate Kentuckians and Marylanders had left their state, opted for neutrality by refusing to vote, or, in Maryland's case, been scared away from the polls by federal troops. The number of votes registered in the 1861 election was down almost 8 percent from the 1859 congressional canvass in Kentucky, and in Maryland the number of votes cast had dropped a striking 23 percent. The election results confirmed a Delaware observer's belief that "every day's delay weakens the secessionists & strengthens the Union."[9]

Most Border South conservatives expected Crittenden once again to lead the conciliatory forces when Congress convened in midsummer. J. B. Underwood, a Union Party candidate for a seat in the Kentucky legislature, advised Crittenden to introduce a war aims resolution during the session. If Crittenden could steer through a resolution stating that the people of the North had gone to war to preserve the Union and not to destroy slavery, Underwood believed it would soothe the concerns of white border Southerners and revive

TABLE 7.1 Results of the June 13, 1861, Maryland congressional election

Congressional District	% of Total Population Enslaved	Candidates	% of Vote
First	19.0	John W. Crisfield (U)	57.4
		Daniel McHenry (SR)	42.6
Second	6.6	Edwin H. Webster (U)	98.6
		Others	1.4
Third	2.0	Cornelius L. Leary (U)	52.0
		William P. Preston (SR)	48.1
Fourth	1.0	Henry May (U)	57.6
		Henry Winter Davis (U)	42.5
Fifth	5.0	Francis Thomas (U)	96.2
		Others	3.8
Sixth	40.4	Charles B. Calvert (U)	50.9
		Benjamin G. Harris (SR)	49.1

Note: The data for the Second, Third, and Fourth Districts are slightly skewed. The Second District included a portion of Baltimore County; the Third District included a portion of Baltimore County and the First to Eighth Wards of Baltimore; the Fourth District included the Ninth to Twentieth Wards of Baltimore. Because these data are not readily available in the U.S. Census, I simply included the raw data provided. Therefore, my calculations for the Second District include all of Baltimore County; for the Third District I included all of Baltimore County and Baltimore city; and for the Fourth District I included all of Baltimore city.

Sources: Dubin, *United States Congressional Elections*, 189; Parsons, Beach, and Dubin, *United States Congressional Districts and Data*, 64; University of Virginia Geospatial and Statistical Data Center, "University of Virginia Historical Census Browser: U.S. Census of 1860."

some of the antebellum intersectional accord that Border South moderates considered essential to proslavery Unionism.[10] Several obstacles made Crittenden's task difficult. Few Northern congressmen held a magnanimous attitude toward any Southern state, let alone the Border South, where the blood of federal troops had been shed in the Baltimore and Saint Louis riots, and many Northerners considered neutrality tantamount to disunion. "But as long as [Kentucky] tries to impose terms upon the Government to advance her own slavery interest," a Republican editor railed, "she will be regarded as seeking to secure the profits of rebellion without incurring its dangers." An Ohio colleague told Crittenden that the outbreak of violence had incensed so many Northerners that it would be unwise to introduce his compromise package once again. "The conservative men who rallied around you last winter would consider this an unpropitious moment," the Ohioan acknowl-

TABLE 7.2 Results of the June 20, 1861, Kentucky congressional election

Congressional District	% of Total Population Enslaved	Candidates	% of Vote
First	18.8	Henry C. Burnett (SR)	59.1
		Lawrence S. Trimble (U)	40.9
Second	24.0	James S. Jackson (U)	73.4
		John T. Bunch (SR)	26.6
Third	25.6	Henry Grider (U)	77.0
		Joseph H. Lewis (SR)	23.1
Fourth	17.4	Aaron Harding (U)	80.7
		Albert G. Talbot (SR)	19.3
Fifth	24.2	Charles A. Wickliffe (U)	75.1
		H. E. Read (SR)	24.9
Sixth	11.4	George W. Dunlap (U)	97.3
		Others	3.7
Seventh	18.1	Robert Mallory (U)	79.4
		Horatio W. Bruce (SR)	20.6
Eighth	36.7	John J. Crittenden (U)	59.2
		William E. Simms (SR)	40.8
Ninth	16.0	William H. Wadsworth (U)	75.9
		John L. Williams (SR)	24.1
Tenth	7.3	John W. Menzies (U)	65.2
		Others	34.8

Sources: Dubin, United States Congressional Elections, 189; Parsons, Beach, and Dubin, United States Congressional Districts and Data, 60; University of Virginia Geospatial and Statistical Data Center, "University of Virginia Historical Census Browser: U.S. Census of 1860."

edged. Moreover, the Kentuckian had lost his most influential Northern ally, Stephen A. Douglas, who unexpectedly died in early June. An Ohio Democrat claimed that Southern Unionists "heard of his demise as the death knell of their loyal hope." "I know of no man who might have been more useful in this fearful crisis," Crittenden solemnly observed.[11]

The president's Independence Day message to Congress indicated that the Republicans planned to prosecute the war to the fullest extent possible. Lincoln asked Congress to appropriate $400 million in order to equip, arm, and train an army of four hundred thousand men. The Republican-controlled Congress responded with legislation that granted even more money and men than the president had requested. A few border Southerners who sympathized with disunion, among them Henry C. Burnett, James Asheton Bayard, and John C. Breckinridge, used the session to grandstand against the Republicans and the war, which further complicated Crittenden's task. Burnett sparred with Northern congressmen and defiantly refused to vote for any war measures, which led several colleagues to question his loyalty. Bayard attacked the president's suspension of the writ of habeas corpus, likened Lincoln to the absolutist paragon King Louis XIV of France, and unashamedly made known his preference for a peaceful separation between the United States and the Confederacy. In an impassioned speech before the Senate, Breckinridge accused the Republicans of implementing a plan of emancipation under the guise of wartime confiscation. The onset of the war provided militants in both the North and the South with a soapbox, and in this frenzied environment, obstreperous shouts of zealotry often muffled the voices of moderation.[12]

The tenor of Congress convinced Crittenden that most Northerners were absolutely committed to crushing the rebellion. Without the assistance of congressional delegations from the Upper South and with overwhelming Republican majorities in both houses of Congress, the Crittenden Compromise faced an even more ominous chance of passage than it had at the previous session. Therefore, rather than expose his compromise proposals to another humiliating defeat, Crittenden instead sought to clarify the goal of the federal government in the burgeoning war. Crittenden focused on a war aims resolution because he knew that if Congress again spurned his settlement package, additional conditional Unionists in the Border South might go over to the secessionists. One observer remarked in mid-July that in spite of the recent Unionist victories in the Border South, the region still crawled with massive quantities of "mewling conditional creatures" whose allegiance hung in the balance. Rather than handing conditionalists a pretext to defect if his compromise again failed, Crittenden would avoid the question altogether. Instead, he worked to fashion the war as one to preserve the republic.[13]

Crittenden on July 19 presented a resolution similar to the one that Underwood had earlier suggested to him. The resolution affirmed that secessionists in the Lower South had brought about the war and plainly declared the preservation of the Union the sole objective in the contest. "This war is not waged upon our part in any spirit of oppression, nor for any purpose of conquest or subjugation, nor purpose of overthrowing or interfering with the rights or established institutions of those States: but to defend and maintain the supremacy of the Constitution and to preserve the Union with all the dignity, equality, and rights of the several States unimpaired," Crittenden's resolutions stated. Some hardline Republicans tried in vain to table the resolution, but

Burnett succeeded in having it divided between the portion that laid blame for the war at the feet of the seceded states and the remainder, which specified the war's aims. The accusatory clause passed the House by a count of 121–2, with only Burnett and Missouri's John William Reid voting in the negative. The House approved the second provision 117–2, with the dissenting votes coming from two Republicans. The Senate on July 24 approved Crittenden's resolution by a tally of 30–5; the four senators from Kentucky and Missouri, who felt the resolution unjustly assigned responsibility for the start of the war to the Confederates, joined Republican Lyman Trumbull in opposition to the measure.[14]

The war aims resolution briefly quelled the fears of white border Southerners, who worried that the Republican-dominated Congress would make the destruction of slavery its paramount objective. Garrett Davis predicted that the Crittenden War Resolution would "have great & salutary influence in the adhering slave states, and much influence over the public opinion of even the seceded States." The passage of the resolution, however, soon proved a pyrrhic victory. The first major battle of the Civil War took place at Manassas, Virginia, while Crittenden's resolution worked its way through Congress, and resulted in a startling Confederate triumph. On the heels of the loss, Republicans resolved to remove any impediments to a more thorough prosecution of the war.[15]

During the session a confiscation act, which would allow the federal army to seize the property of those engaged in active rebellion against the government, had been discussed widely. The measure included enslaved persons in its definition of property, which most white border Southerners viewed as a first step toward a program of total emancipation. Southern Unionists had already read of General Benjamin Butler's refusal to return fugitive slaves in Virginia, and Maryland slaveholders protested that federal troops enticed enslaved persons into their camps and prevented their owners from reclaiming them. "I beg leave to say that these grievances require immediate correction if the Government desires to protect our Rights and encourage and foster the Union feeling in the Border States," a Maryland congressman notified the president. Congress acted in spite of the opposition of border Southerners and Democrats. Near the end of the session, the bill passed the House by a vote of sixty to forty-eight with the support of only one Border South congressman—Frank P. Blair Jr. On August 5, the Senate approved the confiscation act, though none of the Border South senators voted in favor of the bill.[16] A Delaware Unionist admitted that the measure made it "hard to be obliged to fight for our nationality," while a Kentucky paper bashed the legislation as "the necessary and inevitable result of the teachings of Abolition statesmen."[17]

While Congress debated the Crittenden War Resolution and the necessity of confiscation legislation, the Missouri state convention reassembled in Jefferson City on July 22 to address the flight of the state government. Several vacant chairs revealed that many of the conditional Unionists, including convention president Sterling Price, had decided to align themselves with Claiborne Fox Jackson, chosen not to attend, or faced difficulties making it to the meeting. With a quorum in place, the convention replaced Price with Robert Wilson and established a committee of seven to consider what to do about the state government's exodus. Disagreements arose as to what authority the convention possessed: Could they actually declare the state government deposed and operate as a provisional government, or did they only have the power to call a special election to staff the vacated government? James O. Broadhead on July 25 delivered a report from the committee that proclaimed the executive office vacant. To remedy the situation, the committee recommended that the convention appoint executive officers who would govern until August 1862, when a special election for those offices would take place.[18]

Several moderate members of the convention felt that the committee had suggested too bold of a course. On July 26 the convention voted to add Hamilton Gamble, who had returned from a trip to Washington, DC, to the committee and recommit the report. Gamble overhauled certain parts of the report to make it more amenable to conservatives. The lengthy interim between elections, which one Missourian confessed appeared "as an act of usurpation by the convention," proved a sticking point. After lengthy debate over the constitutionality of these suggestions, the delegates in the end voted to vacate the state's executive offices, deposed the general assembly, and scheduled new state elections for November 1861. The convention also decided that as the proxy of the Missouri's electorate, they could fill the executive offices and establish a provisional government until the November election.[19] The next day, the convention appointed the moderate Gamble as governor and Willard P. Hall as lieutenant governor. In a brief inaugural address, Gamble pled for the delegates to work in harmony to bring peace to Missouri and the nation. Without harmony, "the scenes of the French Revolution may be enacted in every quarter of our State." With its work complete, the convention adjourned on the last day of July. "C.F. Jackson, who has proved himself so pestiferous an instrument in bringing civil war and great disasters on this State, is no longer Governor," Nathaniel Paschall triumphantly declared.[20]

Gamble's plea for unity never came to fruition, and the proceedings of the convention offered foreboding signs of Missouri's future. Whereas the convention enjoyed relative accord in its earlier session, the July meeting witnessed greater dissonance among the delegates. The stress of the war, Jackson's rash actions, and constitutional disagreements had created a fissure among the state's Unionists. About one-third of the delegates present at Jefferson City voted in opposition to each of the major policy measures the convention approved. The drastic, even extralegal, steps that the convention took pushed some conditional Unionists into the pro-secession ranks. As in other areas of the Border South, many Unionists still harbored ample reservations about the Republicans. Charles Gibson expressed great unease that their Missouri opponents might classify conservative Unionists as Republicans, which would damage Unionism in the state. Gibson told Gamble that on a recent visit to Washington he had informed Lincoln that abolitionist speeches by Republicans on the floor of Congress had done more damage to Border South Unionism than the tirades of fire-eaters.[21] Jackson and his itinerant followers played up these divisions in an attempt to attract conditional Unionists to their camp. In response to the convention's establishment of a provisional government, deposed lieutenant governor Thomas C. Reynolds publicly recommended that the state legislature pass an ordinance of secession, and on August 5 Jackson issued a declaration of independence for Missouri.[22]

The daunting presence of Union soldiers also impacted Missouri. Lincoln appointed John C. Frémont, the Republican Party's first presidential nominee in 1856 and a known political opportunist, as commander of the Department of the West. The Blair family handpicked Frémont and believed that he would collaborate with other Unionist leaders, among them Nathaniel Lyon and Hamilton Gamble, in the fight for Missouri. Frémont, however, believed Missouri fell solely under his control. He arrived in Saint Louis in late July, surrounded himself with a band of sycophants, and refused to cooperate with Gamble and the provisional government. A nonplussed observer noted that "men of patriotism, honor and probity, ready to devote their lives and property to the defense of the Union are really under the ban, while a gang of California robbers and scoundrels rule, control and direct everything." Unionists also complained that federal troops searched private homes at will and committed acts of violence against Missourians they perceived as disloyal. A distressed Missourian complained that the strong-arm tactics of federal soldiers were "making secessionists every day."[23]

Frémont considered Lyon and Blair novices, arrogantly dismissing the Unionist leaders as "military asses." Frémont's relationship with the Blairs quickly deteriorated, especially in the aftermath of the Battle of Wilson's Creek, which took place just over a week after the state convention adjourned. On August 10 the State Guard, led by former convention president Sterling Price, combined with Confederate forces in southwestern Missouri to hand the federals a stunning defeat. The brutal fighting foreshadowed the vicious nature of the war to come and buried forever Gamble's fleeting wish to avoid violence in Missouri. All told, the battle produced over 2,500 casualties, and the losses on each side exceeded those in any single battle during the Mexican-American War. Lyon lay among the dead soldiers scattered at Wilson's Creek, but during the fray an unresponsive Frémont remained at his headquarters in distant Saint Louis. The battle unleashed a flurry of guerrilla violence in western Missouri that soon engulfed most of the state. "Men begin to reason that the only hope of safety is to be neutral or join the winning side," John Poyner reported to Lincoln. "The people are divided, distracted, overawed and disheartened."[24]

Frémont's actions during the month of August compounded the growing contretemps with Frank Blair. Frémont suppressed local newspapers that questioned him, refused to grant an audience to other Unionist leaders, played favorites with the Saint Louis German community, and blamed the Lincoln administration for the disaster at Wilson's Creek. Blair fumed that the martinet Frémont seemed more concerned with keeping Union soldiers out of taverns than with stopping Price and the State Guard, who through the month of August advanced toward central Missouri. Blair's patience reached its limit on September 1, when he wrote his brother Montgomery and recommended Frémont's removal from command at the earliest possible moment.[25]

Lincoln might have chalked up Blair's exasperation to unfulfilled ambition, but a stream of complaints about Frémont's swelling hubris corroborated the Missourian's criticisms. Petty jockeying for leadership of the Unionist movement was one thing, but Lincoln took notice when on August 30 Frémont issued a proclamation that seriously impaired Unionism in the western half of the Border South. Due to an upsurge in guerrilla violence, Frémont declared martial law throughout the state and promised swift execution for any person a court-martial found guilty of disloyalty. The general included a stipulation that allowed federal troops to confiscate the property of disloyal citizens and, moreover, granted freedom to any enslaved persons owned by those inhabitants. Frémont's decree worked at odds with Crittenden's War Aims Resolution, overstepped the Confiscation Act, and signaled to wavering Border South conservatives that the Republican desire to eradicate slavery had surpassed their limited objective of preserving the Union.[26]

From the start of the secession crisis, Border South conservatives had preached that only the Union could preserve the institution of slavery. The whole foundation of proslavery Unionism rested on this assumption. Frémont's proclamation, coming less than a month after Congress had passed the Confiscation Act, greatly jeopardized the Unionist position in the Border South. A Kentucky newspaper labeled the edict "an abominable, atrocious and infamous usurpation," while John Henderson complained that thousands of Unionists in northern Missouri had gone over to the secessionists. "Say death and Union men will accede to it," Henderson groused, "but they have been bedeviled on the nigger until many of them take spasms whenever a word is said on the subject." With a stroke of his pen, Frémont threatened to undermine everything that Crittenden and the Unionists had worked for over the previous nine months.[27]

Perhaps nothing better illustrated the brittle nature of Border South Unionism than the reaction to Frémont's proclamation, especially in Kentucky and Missouri, the region's largest slaveholding states. Kentucky Unionists had claimed another victory when on August 5, nearly a month before Frémont's edict, they ran roughshod over the Southern Rights Party in the election for the state legislature. The Union Party won seventy-six out of one hundred seats in the lower house and twenty-seven of thirty-eight seats in the Senate, yet even in the hour of triumph a Louisville resident cautioned government officials against counting the state safe. He warned that many Kentuckians still supported secession and that numerous conditional Unionists sympathized with the Confederacy. Conditional Unionists "vote and talk Union," he acknowledged, but in reality "almost *every* union man considers the *South* aggrieved." "I am sure that Kentucky is only a Union State for fear of the consequences of being the seat of war as a border Confederate State," he added. Similar warnings emanated from Missouri, where N. J. Eaton commented that the state "is trembling in the balance now, & I do not know but it is too late to save it." Eaton feared that in the wake of Frémont's decree, many members of the Home Guard and the federal army would throw down their weapons, quit the fight, and hand the state over to the disunionists.[28] Kentucky's Garrett Davis admitted that "the proclamation fell amongst us with pretty much the effect of a bomb shell." "There is a very general, almost universal feeling, in the state against this war being or becoming a war against slavery," Davis remonstrated. Conservative Unionists across the region made

Lincoln abundantly aware of the proclamation's potentially disastrous impact.[29]

"There is not a day to lose in disavowing emancipation or Kentucky is gone over the mill dam," a group of Unionists wired to Lincoln's friend Joshua Speed, who owned six enslaved persons and a large farm outside Louisville. Speed minced no words when he alerted Lincoln that the emancipation edict "will crush out every vestage [*sic*] of a union party in the state." "So fixed is public sentiment in this state against freeing negroes & allowing negroes to be emancipated & remain among us," Speed calculated, "that you had as well attack the freedom of worship in the north or the right of a parent to teach his child to read." No statement better captured the essence of proslavery Unionism in the Border South. Both the State Guard and the Home Guard continued to build up their forces, which placed Kentucky on the brink of an internal civil war. On top of the deleterious effect of Frémont's proclamation, Unionists worried that William Nelson's blatant violations of neutrality might further endanger their cause. In mid-August Nelson actively recruited volunteers for the federal army and established Camp Dick Robinson in central Kentucky as a citadel for his Union soldiers. All the while, Confederate forces had assembled just across the southern border of Kentucky. Lincoln realized he must proceed carefully to keep from losing the Border South to the Confederacy.[30]

Despite admonitions from Republicans who protested that the president had alienated "the great mass of your supporters in the North in order to propiciate [*sic*] a few quasi Union men in Kentucky and Mosouri," Lincoln reined in Frémont. He privately asked the general to revise the proclamation so that it meshed with the recently passed Confiscation Act, which stipulated that only enslaved persons who actively engaged in aiding the rebellion were subject to freedom. Moreover, the legislation allowed federal courts to review any confiscations that took place under the policy.[31] When Frémont dragged his feet, the president on September 11 issued a public letter that officially modified the edict. Lincoln faced a firestorm of criticism from the radical elements of his party, but he held firm. Frémont's obstinacy forced the president to remove him from command two months later. The president informed Orville Hickman Browning, who protested his adjustment of the emancipation decree, that if he failed to act, he feared the weapons that the federal government had funneled to Kentucky Unionists would have been turned against them. He noted that one Bluegrass State Union company had already disbanded in response to Frémont's proclamation, and he ventured that Kentucky and the rest of the Border South might secede if he did nothing. "I think to lose Kentucky is nearly the same as to lose the whole game. Kentucky gone, we can not hold Missouri, nor, as I think, Maryland," Lincoln explained. "These all against us, and the job on our hands is too large for us." Lincoln, unlike many other Republicans, grasped the proslavery nature of borderland Unionism. The president made a hard-edged political calculation, but his alteration of the decree certainly resuscitated the Unionist cause in the Border South.[32]

Lincoln's adjustment of Frémont's decree paid immediate dividends in Kentucky, where the official policy of neutrality was abandoned in September 1861. Fearful that the Union army might gain a strategic advantage in the Mississippi valley if it took the riverside town of Columbus, Kentucky, an impatient Confederate general Leonidas Polk ignored the state's stance of neutrality and on September 3 ordered the occupation of the city. The Union army countered by seizing Paducah, and the legislature, cognizant of Lincoln's alteration of Frémont's proclamation, sided with the federal forces on September 18 and requested that the Confederates leave the state. The exhausting labors of the state's committed Unionists, a heavy dose of subterfuge, and Lincoln's delicate maneuvering held Kentucky in the balance, but the introduction of federal troops sealed the state's fate.[33] Union soldiers now occupied portions of all four Border South states, making the project of secession ever more fleeting. Even prior to September, observers in Kentucky and Missouri noticed that the pace of frustrated Confederate sympathizers leaving the region had escalated over the summer. Orlando Brown happily watched as secessionists in Kentucky moved "to Virginia, to Tennessee, or [to] the Devil," and J. O. Davis reported that large numbers of Missourians streamed southward to join the Confederate army. The military struggle for the western states of the Border South had just begun, but the likelihood of an official push for secession had been reduced greatly.[34]

Although many pro-secession white border Southerners had by autumn trekked southward to enlist in the Confederate army or to wait out the war in more comfortable surroundings, a scattering of the region's inhabitants refused to relent in their effort to pull the Border South states out of the Union. In September the fugitive Claiborne Jackson summoned the legislature to meet in Neosho, a town in the far southwestern corner of the state, to make arrangements for Missouri's secession.[35] Extant records do not reveal how many of the deposed legislators showed up in Neosho in late October, but it seems likely that no more than a handful made an appearance. The Senate journal for the session, perhaps as a means to obscure the scant turnout, contains no roll calls. Moreover, the names of only twelve of the state's thirty-three senators appear in the document. The House created a committee of five to determine if a quorum existed, but the panel never produced a report and the lower chamber's journal does not include a roster or roll call votes.[36]

The absence of a quorum, however, did not daunt the assertive Jackson. The legislature passed a secession ordinance over a single negative vote, ratified the Provisional Confederate Constitution, and selected members to attend the first Confederate Congress.[37] On November 28, 1861, the Confederate Congress admitted Missouri to the new nation, but the state's government spent the rest of the war in exile. It met only once more, in early 1862, but with federal troops in the vicinity of New Madrid, the legislators scattered before attending to any business. The resolute Jackson never returned to his home along the Missouri River; rather, he established the seat of his Confederate government in Arkansas, where he died in late 1862 after a battle with stomach cancer.[38] Because of the Unionist offensive, the presence of federal troops, and Lincoln's shrewd management of Frémont, Jackson's dream of a Confederate Missouri never reached full maturity, but the vicious guerrilla violence that ensnared the state for the next four years demonstrated that many Missourians shared his secessionist vision.

The story in Kentucky closely mirrored that of Missouri, with one major exception—in the Bluegrass State, a U.S. congressman, not the elected governor, led the charge for secession. Henry Burnett protested the prosecution of the war while in Washington during July and August. When he returned home to Cadiz in late summer, Kentucky's neutrality vanished and the legislature declared for the Union. Rather than remain prostrate, as did Governor Beriah Magoffin, Burnett took action. He raised a regiment of Confederate volunteers and in late October chaired a meeting of pro-secessionists held in Russellville, a small town nestled in southwestern Kentucky just miles from the Tennessee line. Burnett and the attendees called for a sovereignty convention to meet in the town on November 18. Burnett presided over the November meeting, which attracted approximately two hundred Kentuckians. The convention passed a declaration of independence, adopted an ordinance of secession, established a provisional state government, and named George W. Johnson, a planter from Scott County, governor. Burnett and former congressman William E. Simms repaired to Richmond and made an appeal for Kentucky's inclusion in the Confederacy. Jefferson Davis and the Confederate Congress complied, and on December 10 Kentucky officially became the thirteenth member of the Confederacy. As in Missouri, the Kentucky Confederate government spent most of its life fleeing the Union army. The United States Congress in December 1861 expelled Burnett, who spent the rest of the war in the Confederate Senate. Missouri and Kentucky fire-eaters had in their minds accomplished their state's secession, but the bulk of the Border South's vital center refused to sanction the legitimacy of the movement and viewed these efforts as face-saving stunts.[39]

Historians studying the antebellum South have faced the problem of identifying who, outside of fire-eaters who trumpeted the cause of disunion on the stump and in the press, endorsed secession. The voices of disunionist zealots like Jackson, Meriwether Jeff Thompson, and Severn Teackle Wallis open a window into the mind-set of Border South secessionists, and thorough analysis of election returns provides clues to the depth and breadth of secession sentiment throughout the Border South. The manuscript record offers a glimpse of how contemporaries in the Border South regarded the secessionists with whom they worked and worshiped, attended court days and county elections, shared familial ties, and, in extreme instances, fought. An inhabitant of Flemingsburg, Kentucky, remarked that "all substantial property Holders in the state are on the side of the Union—But every poor white scamp, every adventurer, every demagogue & every disappointed office seeker & slavery fanatic" endorsed secession. The Kentuckian also rehashed a scene at a Frankfort tavern, where in January 1861 an outspoken, and most likely besotted, fire-eater energetically preached the gospel of disunion from his barstool. Not all members of the barroom congregation experienced a conversion that day. During the fire-eater's tirade a substantial slaveholder interrupted and asked why the disunionist so adamantly wanted Kentucky to secede. The fire-eater responded that he desired to maintain his rights of property, to which the slave owner queried how many enslaved persons the hotspur owned. The disunionist answered that he owned no slaves, but members of his family possessed twenty-nine bondspersons. "Well sir," the slaveholder retorted, "tell your 'people' to bring their slaves to me & I'll buy every one of them & then your damnd [sic] County will have no excuse for going out of the Union."[40] A similar incident that occurred in Bowling Green supports this depiction of Unionists as well-off slaveholders and secessionists as upstarts. A wealthy Kentuckian confided to her diary in March 1861 that her youthful brother Warner fought a classmate who had chastised him for his resolute Unionism. Warner, whose family owned twenty-eight slaves, thrashed his fellow student and declared that "he would teach a low down cur who didn't know which side of the line he was born on and never owned a mule, much less a negro, how to call him a 'Yankee and Abolitionist, because he was Union.'"[41]

Anecdotal evidence from Missouri complements the portrayal of Kentucky secessionists as poorer and younger than the state's Unionists. "The old oaks, the men of property and substance" in Saint Louis supported the Union, Isaac Sturgeon detected. "The young men, the hot heads and rable [*sic*] to a great extent with few honorable exceptions of age and experience," he continued, "are with S. Carolina and for any extreme measures." Congressman John S. Phelps agreed, noting that the vast majority of Missouri secessionists in his district owned no slaves.[42] The depiction of secessionists in Maryland varied somewhat from those of western Border South fire-eaters. A Marylander claimed that the "Old 'Aristocracy'" of the Eastern Shore and southern Maryland combined with Baltimore merchants whose trade primarily went southward to form the backbone of secession sentiment in the Old Line State.[43] Delawareans often commented on the secessionists that surrounded them, but unlike elsewhere in the Border South, few contemporaries classified those disunionists as rich slaveholders or meager parvenus.

Scholars investigating the Border South have offered some conclusions that tend to support to varying degrees the generalizations about fire-eaters contained in the manuscript record. James E. Copeland uses census data and the records of volunteers for the Union army from Kentucky to map pockets of Union and secession sympathy within the Bluegrass State. He finds that most support for secession came from the western end of the state and notes that slaveholding and prosperity were more entrenched in central Kentucky, where Unionists outstripped fire-eaters.[44] In his study of election returns in Missouri, William Roed argues that no strong correlation existed between votes for John Breckinridge in 1860 and support for secession. While he reaches no firm conclusions about Missouri secessionists, Roed's discoveries support the notion that some conditional Unionists easily transitioned into Confederate sympathizers during the crisis.[45] Frank Towers utilizes census data culled from the arrest records of the April 19 Baltimore Riot to confirm the contemporary assertion that wealthy merchants took the lead in promoting secession in Maryland's largest city.[46]

In an effort to enhance the picture of who composed the secession movement in the Border South, census data have been compiled for attendees of pro-secession conventions or meetings in Kentucky, Maryland, and Missouri. For Maryland, a roster of a February 18, 1861, state convention that met in Baltimore and attracted delegates from across the state was utilized. Although the convention met without official sanction from the state legislature, many of the attendees warmly endorsed secession. Census data were recovered with reasonable certainty for 152 of the seated delegates; Tables A.6

and A.9 in the appendix provide a composite snapshot of those delegates and their interest in slavery.

Finding a sample of Missouri fire-eaters proved more problematic. The scanty journals of the deposed Missouri legislature that in October 1861 met in Neosho and drew up a secession ordinance divulged very little information about who actually attended the meeting. The journal did not include a roster of attendees and excluded roll call votes, while most of the same legislators served on the few committees created during the brief session. The avoidance of names in the journal suggests a true quorum did not exist in Neosho, but Jackson and his colleagues moved forward anyhow. Despite these deficiencies, census data were collected for thirteen of the state legislators (mostly from the Senate) and Governor Jackson. Although an admittedly sparse sample, the data in Tables A.7 and A.10 at least provide a starting point for understanding who supported secession in Missouri.

The secession convention that met in Russellville, Kentucky, in November 1861 offers a decent sample for building a composite of Bluegrass State disunionists. Extant records include a list of the signers of the state's secession ordinance, but a few issues hamper the document. A transcription of the list survives, but several of the names do not include their county of residence, rendering it impossible to locate those signers with any certainty. Also, as a means to provide an illusion of legitimacy by adding more signatures to the ordinance, the organizers of the convention apparently had soldiers and civilians, rather than true delegates, affix their names to the document.[47] Nevertheless, census data have been recovered for eighty-seven of the signers and are displayed in Tables A.8 and A.11. Unfortunately, no data were discovered that would offer a reasonably accurate glimpse of the secessionists in Delaware.

Together, the profiles of secessionists in three of the four Border South states tend to corroborate the evidence from the manuscript record. The secessionists from Maryland were older and richer than their colleagues in Kentucky and Missouri, and the vast majority of disunionists in the Border South made their living farming or practicing law. Aside from Missouri, most of the region's fire-eaters had been born in the state in which they resided in 1860. Large slaveholdings accumulated by a handful of these fire-eaters skewed the average slaveholdings upward, but the median values and the breakdown of slaveholdings in Tables A.9, A-10, and A-11 indicate that in general most borderland secessionists were not substantial slaveholders. Strikingly, a majority of the men in each of the three samples owned fewer than five enslaved persons or none at all.[48]

A comparison of the findings about these groups of secessionists with census data that Ralph Wooster compiled and analyzed for the legislatures of Kentucky and Maryland and the author's own data for the strongly Unionist Missouri state convention illustrates a few important points. A profile of the attendees at the Maryland convention closely resembled the membership of the Maryland legislature, in which the average age (44.5 years) and median age (44 years) nearly mirrored those of the delegates. Wooster found that the mean slaveholdings for the legislators stood at 9.5 (as compared to 8.4 for the delegates to the convention) and the median holding stood at one slave (in comparison to two for the delegates).[49] The Missouri legislators who attended the rump session in Neosho were significantly younger (average age of 39.4 years) than the delegates who attended the Unionist-controlled convention (average age of 45 years). Although the mean and median slaveholdings of the legislators exceed those of the delegates, one must consider the small sample size of the Neosho legislature and the fact that Governor Jackson's ownership of forty-eight slaves significantly raised the average. When Jackson's slaveholdings are removed, the average falls back to 4.5 enslaved persons, a figure smaller than the average for delegates to the Missouri convention (4.8 slaves).[50] The signers of the Kentucky secession ordinance were younger (an average age of 37.6 and a median age of 35 for the signers; an average age of 41.3 and a median age of 40 for the legislators) than their counterparts in the Unionist-dominated legislature, though their slaveholdings closely resembled one another (the legislators held 6.3 slaves on average with a median value of 2 enslaved persons; the signers owned a mean of 6.1 slaves and a median of 2).[51] This quantitative evidence suggests that proponents of secession in the Border South generally had less of an attachment to slavery than did their Unionist counterparts. These composites illustrate the strong connection between the protection of slavery and Unionism, rather than disunion, in the region and underscore why proslavery Unionism resonated with white border Southerners.

Committed fire-eaters who chose to stay in the Border South by the end of 1861 came to the glaring conclusion that the combination of proslavery Unionism and federal force had smashed their dream of secession. With Unionism triumphant in Kentucky, the keystone of the Border South, Lincoln approved of a bold approach to crush out the last vestiges of secession in Maryland. Several Southern Rights men still clamored for the legislature to adopt a secession ordinance when it reconvened on September 17, which worried the federal administration. Lincoln authorized the arrest of several pro-secession political figures to head off any last-ditch attempt to carry

Maryland out of the Union. Under the direction of General John Dix, federal troops on September 13 detained twenty-seven members of the state legislature, Congressman Henry May, Baltimore mayor George W. Brown, and the editors of several antiadministration newspapers and confined them to Fort McHenry. "The 'Hotel de McHenry' is becoming quite fashionable and popular," a Maryland Unionist laughed in response to the rash of arrests.[52]

In the small hours of September 13, Severn Teackle Wallis felt the hard hand of war himself. Federal soldiers surged into his Baltimore home, rifled through his personal belongings, clapped him in handcuffs, and whisked him away to Fort McHenry. Locked in his cell, Wallis protested that he and his colleagues had been arrested on mere pretense. Over the coming months he used his pen to unleash a salvo of invective at Lincoln and the Republicans for abrogating the civil liberties of Marylanders and bending the war to their abolitionist designs. "You allowed the victims to languish, for nearly a year and a half, in prison after prison, to which they were dragged—you emancipating negroes, the while, by the thousand, as the President now is, by the million," Wallis fulminated in a letter to Republican senator John Sherman. Yet for all his venom and for all his self-assurance that he occupied the side of right, Wallis and his fire-eating colleagues had suffered an irreversible defeat. By the second year of the Civil War, their energy had been transferred from the movement for the Border South's secession to extended discourses on what they perceived as Republican constitutional violations.[53]

As the war increased in intensity, Republicans and unconditional Unionists shrugged off Wallis's complaints. Secretary of State William Henry Seward reportedly responded to objections about arbitrary arrests in the Border South with a harsh rejoinder: "I don't give a damn whether they are guilty or innocent. I saved Maryland by similar arrests, and so I mean to hold Kentucky." As Wallis and other Border South fire-eaters discovered, Unionists utilized every tool available to ensure the region did not slide into the secession vortex. Missourian Abiel Leonard captured the resolve and resourcefulness of Border South Unionists: "We must cut down the secessionists in this State or they will put us down—it has come to this issue at last, and we must meet the issue boldly, and not with words, but with acts and pretty strong ones too, if we would succeed."[54]

By the end of 1861 the Unionist offensive and federal forces had left Border South fire-eaters prostrate and defeated. The hard labors of Unionists had convinced most white borderites that although their hopes for compromise had been dashed, adherence to the Union offered the best means to preserve the slave-based society, economy, and culture of the Border South. Borderland inhabitants who doubted the durability of proslavery Unionism had fled the region, felt the mighty hand of federal power, or been cowed into silence and left with nothing more than the fading anticipation of future Confederate deliverance. As autumn turned to winter, Wallis languished in a dank cell with nothing more dangerous than his pen and acerbic wit, a fitting symbol of the demise of the secession movement in the Border South.

Conclusion

Pursued to the Last Extremity:
Henry Winter Davis's Republic

Robert Jefferson Breckinridge's tone had changed drastically in the four and a half years since he delivered his oration at the dedication of the Henry Clay National Monument in Lexington, Kentucky. A likeness of Clay now rested atop a 120-foot-tall limestone shrine, but by December 1861 the Great Pacificator's statue no longer kept watch over a unified nation. The cancer of disunion had during the interim spread into the Border South and even into Breckinridge's own family. Several of the men with whom he shared the dais at the 1857 Independence Day ceremony had cast their lot with the Confederacy; two of Breckinridge's sons and a son-in-law eventually enlisted in the Confederate cause; and in December the United States Senate expelled his nephew John C. Breckinridge for his Confederate leanings, prompting him to ─ offer his services to Jefferson Davis. In 1857 Robert Breckinridge extolled Clay for his lessons of "forbearance, brotherhood, and mutual concession for the common liberty." After the opening of the Civil War, however, forbearance and brotherhood had given way to a rugged determination to see the project of disunion destroyed at all costs. The Presbyterian minister promised that the American people would "put an end to the traitorous dominion of the cruel and perfidious class minority" that had brought about the conflict. A wartime ardor to annihilate traitors, even his wayward family members, supplanted Breckinridge's antebellum plea for conciliation.[1]

By the end of 1861, Border South Unionists had accomplished a hard-fought political victory that often goes unnoticed. Customarily obscured by the secession of the Lower South, Fort Sumter and the Upper South's procession out of the Union, and the massive buildup of armies in the corridor between Richmond and Washington, the fight in the Border South was no less perilous that these other closely studied events. The battles took place in the halls of Congress, the legislative chambers of statehouses, and smoke-filled backrooms; on the stump at country barbecues, tidy county courthouses, and seedy taverns; on the crowded cobblestone streets of Baltimore, Wilmington, and Saint Louis; in the craggy hills of southwestern Missouri; and along the dusty roads that traversed the interior of Kentucky. John Jordan

Crittenden oversaw the Unionist campaign to defeat secession in the Border South, and though his dream of compromise went unfulfilled, he and his colleagues managed to relegate disunion to the Upper and Lower South. Unionists worked tirelessly to keep the hope of compromise afloat, which prevented many white border Southerners from making the outright transition to the fire-eater camp. Once the guns of Fort Sumter and the tumult of Baltimore and Saint Louis blasted the fleeting opportunity for a peaceful settlement in the summer of 1861, Unionists changed tack and sought to convince their neighbors that preservation of the republic, not the destruction of slavery, remained the primary goal of the federal government. The protracted exertions of Crittenden and other Unionists, along with their growing dependence on federal might in the last half of 1861, demonstrate that contemporary white borderites in no way believed their region was predestined to remain in the Union. Throughout the crisis proslavery Unionism had been utilized to hold the line against fire-eaters, and not until the end of 1861 could Unionists consider the Border South safe from secessionist threats.

The Unionist victory emboldened some white border Southerners and embittered others. For Robert Breckinridge and many other Unionists in the Border South, by the end of 1861 the great American tradition of compromise seemed as lifeless as Clay's bones, which lay entombed under the Lexington monument he had consecrated in 1857. They joined the ranks of unconditional Unionism and sought to vanquish their foes by any means necessary. These men agreed with Joseph Holt, who had gradually reached the conclusion that "the treason confronting the nation, with the cancer of slavery, of which it was the accursed progeny, could be extirpated only by the surgery of the sword." Still other Unionists clung to the ephemeral notion of neutrality, hopeful that war would cease before it escalated to once-inconceivable levels. By 1862, conditional Unionists faced the painful task of choosing an allegiance. The vast majority of white border Southerners, unlike Breckinridge, agonized over this decision. A tormented Kentucky mother spoke for many borderites in response to her son's jubilant celebration of the Confederate victory at the Battle of Bull Run. "To me the news of victory on either side is distressing for we are all brethren & I did still hope for compromise," she sadly remarked. Some conditional Unionists remained committed to the old flag as long as the war's objective did not stretch beyond reunion, others tried in vain to stay out of the fray, and still others joined the Confederacy once it became apparent that the federal government had placed the peculiar institution in its crosshairs. "How this state of things breaks up the family ties, carrying scorn to so many happy homes," a Louisville woman lamented in the summer of 1861.[2]

Calculating the amount of Border South conditional Unionists who abandoned the Unionist cause is a difficult enterprise. Scholars have estimated the number of border Southerners who fought for the Union or the Confederacy, but poor contemporary record keeping and the absence of vital documents lend a certain level of doubt to the viability of these figures. Furthermore, many white border Southerners who joined the Confederate armed forces enlisted in states other than their own, and the figures neglect whole swaths of the population, such as women and the elderly. Nonetheless, enlistment approximations provide a context for understanding the Unionist offensive in the Border South. Table A.12 provides a breakdown of estimated troop enlistments from each Border South state and compares these numbers to the overall 1860 population of white and black (both enslaved and free) men age twenty to fifty-nine. Approximately 29 percent of all white men aged twenty to fifty-nine enlisted in the Union army, while some 14 percent of all white men of the same age joined the Confederate army. The data suggest that twice as many white border Southerners opted to fight for the federal army, an indication of the effectiveness of the Unionist offensive. Over 40 percent of enslaved and free blacks of the same age group enlisted in the Union army, which illustrates strikingly the devotion of African Americans to the cause of freedom.

Former conditional Unionists who went over to the Confederacy often did so after tormenting deliberation and reflection. Once they made their choice, though, these newly minted Confederates zealously defended their decision. In late 1861 George W. Johnson, who split his duties as governor of Kentucky's Confederate state government in exile with soldiering in General Albert Sidney Johnston's Confederate army in Tennessee, showed no hint of his erstwhile preference for peace and neutrality. Full of enthusiasm and envisioning a short war, he boasted to his wife, "I expect to be with you much sooner than Lincoln and his minions may desire." His prognostication about the war and his dismissive attitude toward Unionist strength soon proved erroneous. During a vicious fight against federal forces that included a large contingent of his Kentucky neighbors at the April 1862 Battle of Shiloh, Johnson suffered grisly wounds to his thigh and abdomen. He died two days later, an ominous foreshadowing of the internecine violence that devastated the Border South throughout the war.[3]

The voices of the participants exhibit the high stakes involved in keeping the Border South tethered to the Union and underscore how close these four states came to secession. Writing after the war, Basil Duke calculated that without the federal occupation of Saint Louis, Missouri would have joined the Confederacy, substantially altering the outcome of the Civil War. "I was convinced then, and believe now," Duke wrote, "that it would have eliminated all danger of failure [for the Confederacy]." Unionists across the Border South went to great pains to foil their secessionist foes, certain that if they relaxed for even a moment, disunionists might gain the advantage. "If those who favored the Union had been less active and vigilant, there is no reason to believe the State would have been declared out of the Union," Kentuckian Thomas Speed reminisced. In the spring of 1861 Garrett Davis summarized the tenacity with which Border South Unionists worked during the crisis. "We will remain in the Union by voting if we can, by fighting if we must, and if we cannot hold our own," Davis confided, "we will call on the General Government to aid us."[4] Had these Unionists remained idle and allowed the Border South to secede and join the Confederacy, the federal war effort might very well have been ruined at the outset. Border South Unionists, however, doggedly labored to place the fulcrum of the Union in a position where the lever of victory in the Civil War tipped decidedly in favor of the United States.

Abraham Lincoln came to understand the strategic importance of keeping the Border South in the Union, and once he did he listened attentively to the Unionists who explained the precarious and nuanced nature of proslavery Unionism. Scores of Border South Unionists warned the president that the very success of their offensive hinged on convincing the inhabitants of these four slaveholding states that the federal government would not interfere with the peculiar institution. Through 1861 Lincoln, mindful of the significance of keeping these states loyal, attempted to limit the war to the preservation of the Union and exposed himself to ridicule from the radical wing of his party. While white border Southerners continued to cast a suspicious eye on Lincoln, his revision of John C. Frémont's emancipation edict and decision to sack the noncompliant general revealed the president's absorption of the critical precept of Border South Unionism.[5]

The president boldly employed federal military power to prevent the Border South's defection from the Union, but on the subject of slavery Lincoln acted with restraint. The Crittenden War Resolution, protests over the confiscation of enslaved persons, and the outcry over Frémont's proclamation convinced Lincoln that broad swipes at slavery would unquestionably undermine the progress that Border South Unionists had made. Arraying census data for the Border South men elected to the Thirty-Seventh Congress against the census data of those chosen to sit in the Provisional Confederate Con-

TABLE C.1 A comparison of Border South congressmen and senators in the Thirty-Seventh U.S. Congress and the Provisional Confederate States Congress

Nation	Mean Slaves Owned in 1860	Percentage Who Owned No Slaves in 1860
United States	13.2	20.0
Confederate States	6.7	47.1

Note: The numbers for the U.S. congressmen and senators do not include those members who either resigned to join the Confederacy or were expelled because of doubtful allegiance. These data include only those who remained attached to the Union cause. Census data were located for thirty of the thirty-three U.S. politicians and seventeen of the eighteen Confederate politicians. The U.S. politicians hailed from all four Border South states, whereas the Confederate politicians came only from Kentucky and Missouri, the two Border South states officially recognized as a part of the Confederate States.

Sources: US Census of 1860, Slave Schedules; "Biographical Directory of the United States Congress"; Warner and Yearns, *Biographical Register of the Confederate Congress*, appendix 3.

gress further establishes the link between slavery and Unionism in the Border South. Table C.1 illustrates that Unionist Border South congressmen owned, on average, nearly twice as many enslaved persons in 1860 as did the border Southerners sitting in Congress in Richmond. Furthermore, nearly half of the representatives in the Confederate Congress owned no slaves; only one-fifth of the Unionists fit this category. The region's politicians and electorate unmistakably comprehended the correlation between Unionism and slavery in the Border South. William S. Harney underlined this connection in the spring of 1861 when he warned a Missourian that if the state left the Union, it would lose every protection that the Constitution and federal law vouchsafed to its slaveholders. "The protection of her slave property, if nothing else," Harney advised, "admonishes Missouri never to give up the Union."[6]

Not until November 1861, with state elections completed and federal troops occupying portions of each of the Border South states, did Lincoln feel comfortable enough to broach the sensitive question of emancipation. The president sent out feelers to two Delaware Unionists, who, after a discussion with Lincoln, pressed members of the general assembly to enact a program of gradual, compensated emancipation. Lincoln hoped to use Delaware, with fewer than 1,800 enslaved persons, as a laboratory for Border South emancipation. The president wished to avoid constitutional entanglements and believed the experiment in Delaware, where the proposed project of emancipation would last until 1893 and slaveholders would be indemnified $400 for each enslaved person they owned, might catch on in the rest of the Border South. Moreover, to offset concerns about social unrest, Lincoln suggested sending the freed slaves to the Caribbean or Africa. Even at the end of 1861, though, Border South Unionists adamantly refused to embrace Lincoln's conservative emancipation program. The devout Unionist Hamilton Gamble, who had been handed the governorship of Missouri by the state convention, spoke for many Border South conservatives when he responded to rumors of Lincoln's emancipation proposal. "If he should yield to the malignant influence of those black hearted and insane abolitionists I have no longer hope for the restoration of peace and order," Gamble barked. "In such a war I can take no part." The Delaware legislature agreed with Gamble. Lincoln's intercessors could not muster support among the state's legislators, and the bill for compensated emancipation never received formal introduction in the general assembly.[7]

By the beginning of 1862, few of the region's inhabitants were prepared to part voluntarily with the peculiar institution. Even in the northernmost outpost of the South, where areas of sparse enslaved populations outweighed pockets of dense slave concentrations, slavery commanded an authoritative influence over the region's politics, society, culture, and economy. This truism animated the Unionist offensive from its inception in November 1860 and continued to resonate with the white populace of the Border South. Few white borderites, even those who owned no slaves themselves, could imagine a future without slavery, and most remained firmly convinced that if emancipation occurred, its responsibility lay with the individual states, not the federal government. Lincoln's abortive efforts in Delaware illustrated that in early 1862 these states refused to embark on such a journey.

In the spring of 1862, Sophie M. Du Pont, who harbored great reservations about the legality and social consequences of emancipation, asked her close friend Henry Winter Davis what he thought about the prospect of abolition. He agreed that emancipation at present violated the law of the land, but disagreed with her misgivings about the outcome. In his usual position far in advance of the Border South mainstream, Davis considered immediate emancipation just and necessary. "The rebellion has ensured this result—which two years ago no one would have been justified in saying was likely to occur in five hundred years," Davis forecast. "There may be suffering—inconvenience [and] confusion—but no injustice."[8]

Hardly any white border Southerners agreed with Davis in 1862, but his prophecy came true. Ironically, as conservative Border South Unionists and slaveholders like Robert Breckinridge called for the war "to be pursued to the last extremity," they also unbridled the forces that would undermine slavery, the institution they sought to protect by remaining in the Union. Large

Henry Winter Davis (1817–65). Baltimore politician and proto-Republican who often found himself far in advance of the Border South political mainstream. Library of Congress.

battles, guerrilla warfare, marching armies, the liberation of bondspersons in the Confederacy, and the flight of enslaved persons over the course of the war substantially weakened the peculiar institution across the Border South. American slavery received its deathblow in 1865 when Congress passed and three-fourths of the states ratified the Thirteenth Amendment. Unsurprisingly, two Border South legislatures tenaciously clung to the proslavery Unionist mind-set and refused to approve the amendment. The Delaware legislature finally acquiesced during the administration of William McKinley, thirty-six years after the conclusion of the Civil War, while Kentucky held out until 1976.[9]

During the secession crisis Border South Unionists cautioned that war, once commenced, would alter forever the landscape of the region. "Our fields will be laid waste, our houses and cities will be burned, our people will be slain, and this goodly land be re-baptized 'the land of blood.' And even the institution, to preserve or control which this wretched war was undertaken," the delegates to the border state conference in the spring of 1861 accurately predicted, "will be exterminated in the general ruin."[10] Henry Clay's statue in 1865 peered out over a scarred, transformed, and remodeled land, one that his Border South heirs had seen on the horizon and vainly tried to resist. The Clay sculpture cast its gaze longingly to the past, but the gravestones of Union and Confederate soldiers in the cemetery below marked a watershed in American history. Unionists had kept their states in the Union, but the exigencies of civil war had irrevocably destroyed proslavery Unionism and Clay's America. Whether they were willing to accept it or not, white border Southerners now lived in the republic of Henry Winter Davis.

Appendix

TABLE A.1 Percentage of total population foreign born

State or Region	Year		
	1850	1860	10-Year Change
Delaware	5.7	8.2	2.5
Kentucky	3.2	5.2	2.0
Maryland	8.8	11.3	2.5
Missouri	11.2	13.6	2.4
Border South	7.0	9.1	2.1
Upper South	0.9	1.5	0.6
Lower South	3.1	3.4	0.3
Entire South	3.3	4.4	1.1
Entire North	14.3	18.8	4.5
United States^	9.7	13.1	3.4

^ The national data only include information for the thirty-three states in 1860. The territories of 1860 are excluded from national data, and the 1850 census had no data for Oregon.

Sources: University of Virginia Geospatial and Statistical Data Center, "University of Virginia Historical Census Browser: U.S. Census of 1850" and "U.S. Census of 1860."

TABLE A.2 Percentage of land in farms in 1860

Region	Sq. Mileage in Farms (Improved and Unimproved)	Total Area (Sq. Miles)	% of Total Area in Farms
Border South	70,293.65	119,883.64	58.6
Upper South	133,004.49	205,416.59	64.7
Lower South	180,239.80	543,203.16	33.2
Lower South without Florida and Texas	136,076.90	228,346.69	59.6
Entire South	383,537.94	868,503.39	44.2
Entire South without Florida and Texas	339,375.04	553,646.92	61.3

Sources: University of Virginia Geospatial and Statistical Data Center, "University of Virginia Historical Census Browser: Agricultural Schedules, Census of 1860"; square mileage attained from www.quickfacts.census.gov/qfd/index.html.

TABLE A.3 Slave population of the South

State/Region	Slave Population		% Increase/ Decrease	% of Total Population Enslaved		10-Year Change
	1850	1860		1850	1860	
Delaware	2,290	1,798	-21.5	2.5	1.6	-0.9
Kentucky	210,891	225,483	6.9	21.5	19.5	-2.0
Maryland	90,368	87,189	-3.5	15.5	12.7	-2.8
Missouri	87,422	114,931	31.5	12.8	9.7	-3.1
Border South	390,971	429,401	9.8	16.7	13.7	-3.0
Upper South	1,047,635	1,208,758	15.4	29.9	29.2	-0.7
Lower South	1,761,668	2,312,352	31.3	46.7	46.5	-0.2
Entire South	3,200,274	3,950,511	23.4	33.3	32.3	-1.0

Sources: University of Virginia Geospatial and Statistical Data Center, "University of Virginia Historical Census Browser: U.S. Census of 1850" and "U.S. Census of 1860."

TABLE A.4 Slaveholdings in the South in 1860

State/Region	% of White Population Slaveholders^	Slaves Owned by % of Slaveholders				
		<5	5–9	10–19	>20	>100
Delaware	3.2	81.1	14.7	4.3	0.0	0.0
Kentucky	21.0	57.0	25.3	13.6	4.0	0.0
Maryland	13.4	60.8	20.5	12.5	6.3	0.1
Missouri	11.4	64.4	23.5	9.9	2.2	0.0
Border South	14.9	60.2	23.8	12.2	3.8	0.0
Upper South	23.9	50.2	24.0	16.4	10.5	0.3
Lower South	34.7	43.2	22.5	16.1	16.6	0.9
Entire South	24.5	49.0	23.3	15.4	12.0	0.5

^Computed by multiplying the number of slaveholders by the average family size (5) and dividing by the total white population.

Source: University of Virginia Geospatial and Statistical Data Center, "University of Virginia Historical Census Browser: U.S. Census of 1860. Slave Schedules."

TABLE A.5 Slaveholdings of the delegates to the March 1861
Missouri state convention

Slaves Owned	Number	Percentage of Total Delegates
0	39	39.4
1–4	25	25.3
5–9	17	17.2
10–19	12	12.1
20 or More	6	6.1
Total	99	100.0
Mean Slaveholding		4.84 slaves
Median Slaveholding		2 slaves

Source: Census of 1860, Slave Schedules.

TABLE A.6 Census data for seated delegates to the Maryland
state convention, February 18, 1861

	Mean	Median
Age	44.8	44.0
Real Estate	$23,958	$14,550
Personal Estate	$19,216	$10,000
Slaveholdings	8.4	2.0

Place of Birth		
State or Region	Number	Percentage
Maryland	137	90.1
Border South	139	91.4
Upper South	2	1.3
Lower South	0	0.0
Free States	8	5.3
Foreign Born	2	1.3
Not Listed	1	0.7

(continued)

TABLE A.6 (continued)

Occupation		
Grouping	Number	Percentage
Agriculture	71	46.7
Legal	38	25.0
Entrepreneurial	24	15.8
Professional	13	8.6
None Listed	6	3.9

Sources: Baltimore Sun, Feb. 18–19, 1861; U.S. Census, 1860; U.S. Census, Slave Schedules, 1860.

TABLE A.7 Census data for legislators attending the Missouri legislative session in Neosho, October 1861

	Mean	Median
Age	39.4	39.0
Real Estate	$11,200	$7,400
Personal Estate	$11,599	$6,150
Slaveholdings	7.6	5.0

Place of Birth		
State or Region	Number	Percentage
Missouri	0	0.0
Border South	5	35.7
Upper South	7	50.0
Lower South	0	0.0
Free States	1	7.1
Foreign Born	1	7.1

Occupation		
Grouping	Number	Percentage
Agriculture	5	35.7
Legal	7	50.0
Entrepreneurial	1	7.1
Professional	1	7.1

Sources: Missouri General Assembly, House of Representatives (Confederate), Journal, 1861, SHS-MO; Dwight H. Brown, *State of Missouri: Official Manual for Years Nineteen-Thirty-Five and Nineteen-Thirty-Six,* 204–5; U.S. Census, 1860; U.S. Census, Slave Schedules, 1860.

TABLE A.8 Census data for delegates to the Kentucky
secession convention, November 1861

	Mean	Median
Age	37.6	35.0
Real Estate	$8,169	$3,000
Personal Estate	$8,265	$3,000
Slaveholdings	6.1	2.0

	Place of Birth	
State or Region	*Number*	*Percentage*
Kentucky	57	65.5
Border South	61	70.1
Upper South	21	24.1
Lower South	0	0.0
Free States	5	5.7

	Occupation	
Grouping	*Number*	*Percentage*
Agriculture	32	36.8
Legal	25	28.7
Entrepreneurial	15	17.2
Other	2	2.3
None Listed	5	5.7

Sources: *Declaration of Independence and Constitution of Provisional Government of Kentucky*, 9–11; U.S. Census, 1860; U.S. Census, Slave Schedules, 1860.

TABLE A.9 Slaveholdings of seated delegates of the Maryland
state convention, February 18, 1861

Slaves Owned	Number	Percentage
0	57	37.5
1–5	39	25.7
6–9	13	8.6
10–19	21	13.8
20 or More	22	14.5
Total	152	100.0
Mean Slaveholding		8.4
Median Slaveholding		2.0

Sources: Baltimore Sun, Feb. 18–19, 1861; U.S. Census, 1860; U.S.
Census, Slave Schedules, 1860.

TABLE A.10 Slaveholdings of legislators attending the
Missouri legislative session in Neosho, October 1861

Slaves Owned	Number	Percentage
0	4	28.6
1–5	3	21.4
6–9	5	35.7
10–19	1	7.1
20 or More	1	7.1
Total	14	100.0
Mean Slaveholding		7.6
Median Slaveholding		5.0

Sources: Missouri General Assembly, House of Representatives
(Confederate), Journal, 1861, SHS-MO; Dwight H. Brown, *State
of Missouri: Official Manual for Years Nineteen-Thirty-Five and
Nineteen-Thirty-Six*, 204–5; U.S. Census, 1860; U.S. Census, Slave
Schedules, 1860.

TABLE A.11 Slaveholdings of delegates to the Kentucky
secession convention, November 1861

Slaves Owned	Number	Percentage
0	38	43.7
1–5	17	19.5
6–9	15	17.2
10–19	8	9.2
20 or More	9	10.3
Total	87	100.0
Mean Slaveholding		6.1
Median Slaveholding		2.0

Sources: *Declaration of Independence and Constitution of Provisional Government of Kentucky*, 9–11; U.S. Census, 1860; U.S. Census, Slave Schedules, 1860.

TABLE A.12 Troop enlistments in the Border South

	Total Enlistment Estimates			% of Male Population, Age 20–59		
	Union			Union		
State	White	Black	Confederate	White	Black	Confederate
Delaware	10,000	1,000	1,000	48.5	23.8	4.8
Kentucky	50,000	24,000	35,000	25.0	54.0	17.5
Maryland	34,000	9,000	20,000	28.9	26.4	17.0
Missouri	80,000	8,000	30,000	31.6	37.1	11.8
Border South Total	174,000	42,000	86,000	29.4	40.3	14.5

Sources: Joseph G. G. Kennedy, *Population of the United States in 1860*; OR, Series III, vol. 4, 1269–70; Gienapp, "Abraham Lincoln and the Border States," 39, table 3; William W. Freehling, *The South vs. the South*, 61.

Notes

Abbreviations

Bates Diary   Bates, Edward. *The Diary of Edward Bates, 1859–1866.* Edited by
                   Howard K. Beale. Washington, DC: Government Printing
                   Office, 1933.
CG   *Congressional Globe,* Thirty-Sixth and Thirty-Seventh
                   Congresses.
CWL   Lincoln, Abraham. *The Collected Works of Abraham Lincoln.*
                   Edited by Roy P. Basler. 8 vols. New Brunswick, NJ: Rutgers
                   University Press, 1953–55.
DHS   Delaware Historical Society, Manuscripts Division, Wilmington,
                   Delaware.
DU   Special Collections, David M. Rubenstein Rare Book
                   and Manuscript Library, Duke University, Durham, North
                   Carolina.
EPFL   Enoch Pratt Free Library, Archives of the Peabody Institute,
                   Baltimore, Maryland.
FHS   Filson Historical Society, Louisville, Kentucky.
Hagley   Hagley Museum and Library, Wilmington, Delaware.
HSP   Historical Society of Pennsylvania, Philadelphia, Pennsylvania.
KDLA   Kentucky Department for Libraries and Archives, Frankfort,
                   Kentucky.
KHS   Kentucky Historical Society, Frankfort, Kentucky.
LOC   Division of Manuscripts, Library of Congress, Washington, DC.
MDHS   Maryland Historical Society, Baltimore, Maryland.
MO-MH   Missouri Museum of History, Saint Louis, Missouri.
MSA   Missouri State Archives, Jefferson City, Missouri.
OR   *The War of the Rebellion: A Compilation of the Official Records of
                   the Union and Confederate Armies.* 128 vols. Washington, DC:
                   Government Printing Office, 1880–1901.
Rebellion Record   Moore, Frank, ed. *The Rebellion Record: A Diary of American
                   Events, with Documents, Narratives, Illustrative Incidents, Poetry,
                   Etc.* 11 vols. New York: D. Van Norstrand, 1861–68.
SHC-UNC   Southern Historical Collection, Wilson Library, University of
                   North Carolina, Chapel Hill, North Carolina.
SHS-MO   State Historical Society of Missouri, Columbia, Missouri.

UC   Special Collections Research Center, University of Chicago
                Library, Chicago, Illinois.
UR   Rush Rhees Library, Department of Rare Books, Manuscripts
                and Archives, University of Rochester, Rochester, New York.
UVA Browser   University of Virginia Geospatial and Statistical Data Center.
                "University of Virginia Historical Census Browser."
                http://mapserver.lib.virginia.edu/collections.

Introduction

1. *Report of the Ceremonies on the Fourth of July*, 3–6.

2. Remini, *Henry Clay*, 740 (quote), 781–85.

3. *Report of the Ceremonies on the Fourth of July*, 47–48.

4. Klotter, *Breckinridges of Kentucky*, 36–91; Tallant, *Evil Necessity*; Harlow, "Religion, Race, and Robert J. Breckinridge"; Harlow, *Religion, Race, and the Making of Confederate Kentucky*.

5. For the best treatment of the political turbulence of the 1850s, see Potter, *Impending Crisis*.

6. *Report of the Ceremonies on the Fourth of July*, 4, 49 (quote).

7. The term *Lower South* refers to the seven states that seceded before Lincoln's inauguration: South Carolina, Mississippi, Florida, Alabama, Georgia, Louisiana, and Texas. Throughout this work, the terms *Deep South*, *Cotton South*, and *Gulf South* are used interchangeably to refer to these states. The label *Upper South* refers to the four slaveholding states that seceded after the April 1861 firing on Fort Sumter and the issuance of Lincoln's Proclamation for seventy-five thousand troops to quell the rebellion: Virginia, Arkansas, North Carolina, and Tennessee. The term *Border South* refers to the four slaveholding states that remained in the Union: Delaware, Maryland, Kentucky, and Missouri. These terms are analytical and employed by modern historians, most notably William Freehling, in an effort to showcase the complexity and diversity of the Old South. See William W. Freehling, *Road to Disunion*, 1:13–36. Contemporary observers often lumped the Upper and Border South together and called them the border states. To avoid confusion I utilize the label *Border South* and have throughout the narrative noted when an observer applied the term *border states* to more than the four states under consideration in this study. Christopher Phillips contends that a Border South identity was created in Kentucky and Missouri during, not before, the Civil War; see Phillips, " 'The Chrysalis State,' " and Phillips, *Rivers Ran Backward*.

8. "Speech of Francis Thomas at the Front Street Theater, in Baltimore, Md., October 29, 1861," in *Rebellion Record*, 3:250. For a similar viewpoint from a transplanted Kentuckian, see William Clark to Dear Son [James Clark], Jan. 22, 1861, Clark-Strater-Watson Family Papers, FHS. For proslavery Unionism, see Degler, *Other South*; McKenzie, "Contesting Secession"; Astor, *Rebels on the Border*; Christopher Phillips, *Civil War in the Border South*; Harlow, *Religion, Race, and the Making of Con-*

federate Kentucky; Lewis, *For Slavery and Union;* and Rockenbach, *War upon Our Border.*

9. Samuel Haycraft to Abraham Lincoln, Oct. 26, 1860, Abraham Lincoln Papers, LOC, http://memory.loc.gov/ammem/alhtml/alhome.html.

10. For Clay's Unionist legacy, see especially Mering, "The Slave-State Constitutional Unionists"; Forgie, *Patricide in the House Divided;* Crofts, *Reluctant Confederates;* Knupfer, *The Union As It Is;* Ayers, *In the Presence of Mine Enemies;* Link, *Roots of Secession;* Cooper, *We Have the War upon Us;* and Paulus, "America's Long Eulogy for Compromise."

11. Speech of Lazarus Powell, Jan. 22, 1861, *CG,* 36th Congress, 2nd Session, appendix 95.

12. *Philadelphia Inquirer,* Feb. 9, 1861.

13. Judah Benjamin to James A. Bayard, Mar. 19, 1861, Callery Collection of the Bayard Family Papers, DHS; R. R. Welford, "The Loyalty of the Border States," *DeBow's Review* 32 (January–February 1862): 87. See also Robert A. Toombs to Dear Stephens, July 5, 1861, Robert Augustus Toombs Correspondence, DU; Thomas F. Bayard to Rodmond Gibbons, Feb. 24, 1861, Gibbons Family Papers, DHS. For Lower South secessionists and their dreams of Southern unity in secession, see Bonner, *Mastering America,* 231–36.

14. Gienapp, "Lincoln and the Border States," 13–15; William W. Freehling, *The South vs. the South;* Towers, *Urban South and the Coming of the Civil War,* 8–9, 22.

15. *Louisville Daily Journal,* Dec. 24, 1860.

16. A few recent studies of the region stand out: Harrold, *Border War;* William C. Harris, *Lincoln and the Border States;* Christopher Phillips, *Civil War in the Border South;* and Christopher Phillips, *Rivers Ran Backward.* While these books are valuable contributions, none focuses solely on the secession crisis. A few older studies deal with portions of the Border South. See Edward Conrad Smith, *Borderland in the Civil War;* Rawley, *Turning Points of the Civil War,* 9–45; and William C. Wright, *Secession Movement in the Middle Atlantic States.*

17. For Delaware, consult Hancock, *Delaware during the Civil War,* and McClanahan, "Lonely Opposition." For Kentucky, see Coulter, *Civil War and Readjustment in Kentucky;* Volz, "Party, State, and Nation"; Paine, " 'Kentucky Will Be the Last to Give Up the Union' "; Boyd, "Neutrality and Peace"; Marshall, *Creating a Confederate Kentucky;* Ramage and Watkins, *Kentucky Rising;* Finck, *Divided Loyalties;* Matthews, *More American Than Southern;* and Craig, *Kentucky Confederates.* For Maryland, refer to Baker, *Politics of Continuity;* Evitts, *Matter of Allegiances;* Denton, *Southern Star for Maryland;* and Cannon, "Lincoln's Divided Backyard." For Missouri, see Ryle, *Missouri;* Parrish, *Turbulent Partnership;* Parrish, *Frank Blair;* Christopher Phillips, *Missouri's Confederate;* and Geiger, *Financial Fraud and Guerrilla Violence.*

18. For slavery's importance to the Border South, see Wagandt, *Mighty Revolution;* Oakes, *Ruling Race;* Fields, *Slavery and Freedom on the Middle Ground;* Essah, *House Divided;* Burke, *On Slavery's Border;* Grivno, *Gleanings of Freedom;* Schermerhorn, *Money over Mastery;* Astor, *Rebels on the Border;* Salafia, *Slavery's Borderland;* and Epps, *Slavery on the Periphery.*

19. For Crittenden as a failure, see Stampp, *And the War Came*; Nevins, *Ordeal of the Union*, vol. 5; Hyman, "Narrow Escape from a 'Compromise of 1860'"; and Ledbetter, "Crittenden and the Compromise Debacle."

20. Works that doubt the possibility of compromise include Stampp, *And the War Came*; Nevins, *Ordeal of the Union*, vol. 5; Foner, *Free Soil, Free Labor, Free Men*; Levine, *Half Slave and Half Free*; Egnal, *Clash of Extremes*; Ashworth, *Republic in Crisis*; and Oakes, *Freedom National*. Accounts that view compromise as realistic include Scrugham, *Peaceable Americans*; Potter, *Lincoln and His Party*; Sowle, "The Conciliatory Republicans"; Crofts, "Union Party of 1861"; Crofts, *Reluctant Confederates*; McClintock, *Lincoln and the Decision for War*; Cooper, *We Have the War upon Us*; and Crofts, *Lincoln and the Politics of Slavery*.

21. See especially Taylor, *Divided Family in Civil War America*, and Bridget Ford, *Bonds of Union*.

22. For other accounts of Southern Unionism, see Current, *Lincoln's Loyalists*; Dyer, *Secret Yankees*; Bynum, *Free State of Jones*; Storey, *Loyalty and Loss*; McKenzie, *Lincolnites and Rebels*; and Browning, *Shifting Loyalties*.

23. Alison Goodyear Freehling, *Drift toward Dissolution*; Crofts, *Reluctant Confederates*; Shade, *Democratizing the Old Dominion*; and Curry, *House Divided*.

24. Anderson, *Abolitionizing Missouri*.

Chapter One

1. Salmon P. Chase to Abraham Lincoln, Nov. 7, 1860, Abraham Lincoln Papers, LOC; Grinspan, "'Young Men for War'"; Egerton, *Year of Meteors*, 208–10.

2. For the fire-eaters, see Walther, *Fire-Eaters*, and Heidler, *Pulling the Temple Down*.

3. Journal entries for Nov. 11, 1860, and Dec. 16, 17, 20, 1860, John Pendleton Kennedy Papers, EPFL. Kennedy sent his essay to the *Washington, D.C. National Intelligencer*, the *Richmond Whig*, and the *Louisville Journal*.

4. John Pendleton Kennedy, "The Border States," in Wakelyn, *Southern Pamphlets on Secession*, 218, 220–21. Kennedy's pamphlet was published in December 1860, and he included Virginia, North Carolina, and Tennessee under the umbrella of the border states. See also Black, *John Pendleton Kennedy*, 227–32; and Nesenhöner, "Maintaining the Center."

5. John Pendleton Kennedy, "Border States," 230–31.

6. For antebellum violence along the border, see Campbell, *Slave Catchers*; Slaughter, *Bloody Dawn*; Etcheson, *Bleeding Kansas*; Oertel, *Bleeding Borders*; Harrold, *Border War*; and Sinha, *Slave's Cause*, ch. 12.

7. Christopher Phillips, *Rivers Ran Backward*; Salafia, *Slavery's Borderland*; Potter, *Impending Crisis*, 217–24; and Ratner and Teeter, *Fanatics and Fire-Eaters*, 27–33.

8. For amicable border relations, see Edward Conrad Smith, *Borderland in the Civil War*; Etcheson, *Emerging Midwest*; and Salafia, *Slavery's Borderland*. Edward L. Ayers

traces similar relations between southern Pennsylvania and Virginia's Shenandoah Valley; see Ayers, *In the Presence of Mine Enemies*, 1–92.

9. Figures compiled from Joseph C. G. Kennedy, *Population of the United States in 1860*, xxxiv, 104, 130, 156, 166, 398, 439; *Louisville Daily Courier*, Jan. 26, 1860; Christopher Phillips, *Rivers Ran Backward*, 25–26.

10. Paskoff, *Troubled Waters*, 69–73; Thomas, *Iron Way*, 17–36. For Baltimore and Saint Louis, see Towers, *Urban South and the Coming of the Civil War*, ch. 2.

11. The bold claim about shifting trade patterns is found in Smith, *Borderland in the Civil War*, 22–24. Smith underestimates the vitality of river trade and neglects the interstate slave trade, one of the most important trade connections between the Border South and the rest of the South. More recently, Marc Egnal has made a similar claim about a redirection of trade; see Egnal, *Clash of Extremes*, ch. 7.

12. United States Census Bureau, "Rank by Population of the 100 Largest Urban Places"; Joseph C. G. Kennedy, *Population of the United States in 1860*, xxxiv, 104, 130, 156, 166, 398, 439; Towers, *Urban South and the Coming of the Civil War*, 22.

13. Scholarship that portrays a dynamic antebellum Southern economy includes Goldfield, *Urban Growth in the Age of Sectionalism*; Thornton, *Politics and Power in a Slave Society*; Lacy K. Ford Jr., *Origins of Southern Radicalism*; DeCredico, *Patriotism for Profit*; Wells, *Origins of the Southern Middle Class*; Schoen, *Fragile Fabric of Union*; and Barnes, Schoen, and Towers, *Old South's Modern Worlds*.

14. Department of the Interior, *Manufactures of the United States in 1860*, 53–54, 178–80, 220–22, 310–12.

15. Data compiled from the census of 1850 and 1860, UVA Browser.

16. Grimstead, *American Mobbing*, 232–34; William Preston Johnston to Mrs. Susan P. Christy, Aug. 4, 1859, Preston Family Papers—Joyes Collection, 1780–1963, FHS. For the impact of German and Irish populations on these cities, see Towers, *Urban South and the Coming of the Civil War*; Gerteis, *Civil War St. Louis*; Arenson, *Great Heart of the Republic*; Anderson, *Abolitionizing Missouri*; and Bridget Ford, *Bonds of Union*. For nativism, see Holt, *Political Crisis of the 1850s*, and Anbinder, *Nativism and Slavery*.

17. Lacy K. Ford Jr., *Deliver Us from Evil*, 19–77.

18. Census of 1850 and 1860, UVA Browser.

19. Census of 1850 and 1860, UVA Browser; Berlin, *Generations of Captivity*, 225. For the hardships faced by free blacks in antebellum America, see Litwack, *North of Slavery*; Berlin, *Slaves without Masters*; Michael P. Johnson and James L. Roark, *Black Masters*; Christopher Phillips, *Freedom's Port*; Etcheson, *Generation at War*; Hudson, "'Upon This Rock'"; and Bridget Ford, *Bonds of Union*, 90–120.

20. Agricultural Schedules, Census of 1850 and 1860, UVA Browser; Towers, *Urban South and the Coming of the Civil War*, 46–47; Litwack, *North of Slavery*, 34–39; Forbes, *Missouri Compromise and Its Aftermath*, 106–18. My understanding of this process has been influenced by Lacy K. Ford Jr., *Deliver Us from Evil*; Fields, *Slavery and Freedom on the Middle Ground*; Hurt, *Agriculture and Slavery in Missouri's Little Dixie*; Aron, *How*

the West Was Lost; Essah, *House Divided*; Morgan, *Slave Counterpoint*; and Aron, *American Confluence*.

21. William W. Freehling, *Road to Disunion*, 1:23–24. Freehling expands on this slave drain theory in *The South vs. the South* and *Road to Disunion*, vol. 2. For Benning's comments, see Reese, *Proceedings of the Virginia State Convention*, 1:65–66.

22. John Pendleton Kennedy, "The Border States," 234, 230.

23. Joseph C. G. Kennedy, *Population of the United States in 1860*, 48–49, 186–87, 216–17, 302–3. Aggregate grouping of the data might lead to a category like professionals (doctors, lawyers, teachers, and so on) surpassing the category of laborer, but these groupings would not come close to the percentage of workers involved in agriculture.

24. Agricultural Schedules, Census of 1850 and 1860, UVA Browser. The Far West (California and Oregon) has been excluded since the census of 1850 included no information for Oregon, but it stands to reason that this region witnessed a massive increase in the number of farms that likely outpaced the Border South.

25. Joseph C. G. Kennedy, *Agriculture of the United States in 1860*, xcvi.

26. Hurt, *Agriculture and Slavery in Missouri's Little Dixie*, 100–102; Coulter, *Civil War and Readjustment in Kentucky*, 9; J. Winston Coleman, *Slavery Times in Kentucky*, 42–44; Burke, *On Slavery's Border*, 100.

27. Joseph C. G. Kennedy, *Agriculture of the United States in 1860*, xxix–xxx.

28. The implications of Lower South monoculture are explored in Gavin Wright, *Political Economy of the Cotton South*, and Coclanis, *Shadow of a Dream*.

29. Agricultural Schedules, Census of 1860, UVA Browser.

30. Joseph C. G. Kennedy, *Population of the United States in 1860*, 48, 185, 215, 301.

31. Speech of E. H. Norton, Mar. 12, 1861, in *Journal and Proceedings of the Missouri State Convention, March 1861*, Proceedings, 78 (quote); Beckie Steuart to Charley Steuart, Apr. 19, 1861, George Hume Steuart Papers, DU.

32. Joseph C. G. Kennedy, *Population of the United States in 1860*, 48, 185, 215, 301.

33. *Louisville Daily Courier*, Jan. 25, 1860.

34. Census of 1850 and 1860, UVA Browser; Christopher Phillips, *Rivers Ran Backward*, 85–86.

35. Lacy K. Ford Jr., *Deliver Us from Evil*, 387–88; William W. Freehling, *Road to Disunion*, 1:462–73, 537–44, 2:222–50; Harrold, *Abolitionists and the South*, 132–48.

36. Census of 1850 and 1860, UVA Browser; Fields, *Slavery and Freedom on the Middle Ground*, 20–21; Baker, *Politics of Continuity*, 4; Evitts, *Matter of Allegiances*, 39–41.

37. Dubin, *Party Affiliations in the State Legislatures*, 86–87; 1860 U.S. Census, Slave Schedules, www.ancestry.com; Fields, *Slavery and Freedom on the Middle Ground*, 76–82; Evitts, *Matter of Allegiances*, 102–105, 136–37.

38. Volz, "Party, State, and Nation," 69–77; Tallant, *Evil Necessity*, 158, 159, 95–97, 49.

39. Dubin, *Party Affiliations in the State Legislatures*, 71–72; *Louisville Daily Courier*, Nov. 2, 1859.

40. Christopher Phillips, *Missouri's Confederate*, 150–53, 165–80, 170–71; Mueller, *Senator Benton and the People*, 229–54; Parrish, *Frank Blair*, 39–42, 45, 54–56; Ryle, *Missouri*, 65, 71–74, 99.

41. Parrish, *Frank Blair*, 86–87; Address of John D. Coalter, Mar. 5, 1861, *Journal and Proceedings of the Missouri State Convention, March 1861*, Proceedings, 26; Ryle, *Missouri*, 103–104.

42. In the last decade of the eighteenth century, the Delaware legislature forbade the sale of enslaved persons outside the state, a restriction that was largely ignored by the 1820s; see Schermerhorn, *Money over Mastery*, 24–40.

43. Essah, *House Divided*, 158–61; Hancock, *Delaware during the Civil War*, 2–3, 11–12, 18–20; McClanahan, "Lonely Opposition," 22–26; Sam Townsend to Stephen A. Douglas, Mar. 28, 1860, quoted in Hancock, *Delaware during the Civil War*, 14.

44. Parrish, *Frank Blair*, 63–64; Dubin, *United States Congressional Elections*, 176, 182; Arenson, *Great Heart of the Republic*, 45, 59–60; Foner, *Fiery Trial*, 17–22, 124–26; Anderson, *Abolitionizing Missouri*, 60–69.

45. Harrold, *Abolitionists and the South*, 28–29; Tallant, *Evil Necessity*, 120–21; James S. Rollins to Cassius M. Clay, Jan. 19, 1861, James S. Rollins Papers, SHS-MO.

46. William W. Freehling, *Road to Disunion*, 2:230–35; Tallant, *Evil Necessity*, 186–87.

47. For the commitment of smaller slaveholders to slavery, see Oakes, *Ruling Race*; Burke, *On Slavery's Border*; and Astor, *Rebels on the Border*.

48. Slave Schedules, Census of 1860, UVA Browser; Huston, "Pregnant Economies of the Border South."

49. Tadman, *Speculators and Slaves*; Walter Johnson, *Soul by Soul*; Gudmestad, *Troublesome Commerce*; Deyle, *Carry Me Back*; Marrs, *Railroads in the Old South*; and Gudmestad, *Steamboats and the Rise of the Cotton Kingdom*.

50. Speech of Henry L. Benning, Feb. 18, 1861, in Reese, *Proceedings of the Virginia State Convention*, 1:66. For racial control and herrenvolk democracy, see Essah, *House Divided*, and Fredrickson, *Black Image in the White Mind*, ch. 2.

51. For the dimensions of proslavery Unionism in Tennessee, see McKenzie, "Prudent Silence and Strict Neutrality," 79–80.

52. Joseph C. G. Kennedy, *Population of the United States in 1860*, xv–xvi; Baker, *Politics of Continuity*, 10; Harrold, *Border War*, 40–41; William W. Freehling, *The South vs. the South*, 27; Sinha, *Slave's Cause*, 382.

53. "Joseph Holt's Letter on the Pending Revolution," May 31, 1861, in *Rebellion Record*, Document 197½, 288, 290.

54. Cooper, *South and the Politics of Slavery*.

55. Thornton, *Politics and Power in a Slave Society*, ch. 6; Lacy K. Ford Jr., *Origins of Southern Radicalism*, ch. 10; Oakes, *Freedom National*, 60-62.

56. *Baltimore Sun*, Mar. 23, 1860.

57. W. S. Bodley to A. Burwell, Nov. 22, 1860, Bodley Family Papers, FHS.

58. Crofts, *Reluctant Confederates*; Knupfer, *The Union as It Is*.

Chapter Two

1. "Edward Bates," in Allen Johnson, *Dictionary of American Biography*, 1:48; Goodwin, *Team of Rivals*, 22–23; Edward Bates to J. Philips Phoenix et al., Feb. 24, 1859, printed in *New York Daily Tribune*, Apr. 16, 1859.

2. Cain, *Lincoln's Attorney General*, 99–100; Abbott, *Republican Party and the South*, 14.

3. Luthin, "Organizing the Republican Party in the 'Border Slave' Regions," 143; Edward Bates to J. Philips Phoenix et al., Feb. 24, 1859, printed in *New York Daily Tribune*, Apr. 16, 1859; Cain, *Lincoln's Attorney General*, 95–98; Entry for Apr. 27, 1859, *Bates Diary*, 11–12.

4. Entries for Apr. 27, May 27, and July 5, 1859, *Bates Diary*, 12, 19, 29–30.

5. Potter, *Impending Crisis*, 211–13; Oates, *To Purge This Land with Blood*, 287–89; McGlone, *John Brown's War against Slavery*, 7–11, 111–12; Peter Wallenstein, "Incendiaries All: Southern Politics and the Harpers Ferry Raid," in Finkelman, *His Soul Goes Marching On*, 166.

6. Morrison, *Slavery and the American West*; Childers, *Failure of Popular Sovereignty*; Landis, *Northern Men with Southern Loyalties*.

7. Potter, *Impending Crisis*, 211–13; *St. Louis Daily Missouri Republican*, June 6, 1856.

8. McGlone, *John Brown's War against Slavery*, 239–45; Potter, *Impending Crisis*, 364–68; Nevins, *Ordeal of the Union*, 4:70–72.

9. Potter, *Impending Crisis*, 369–71; Nevins, *Ordeal of the Union*, 4:71, 83–85; *Baltimore Sun*, Oct. 19, 1859.

10. John J. Crittenden to Orlando Brown, June 7, 1850, John Jordan Crittenden Papers, DU.

11. Salafia, *Slavery's Borderland*, ch. 8; Christopher Phillips, *Rivers Ran Backward*, ch. 3.

12. *Columbus Daily Ohio Statesman*, Oct. 20, 1859; Nathan Appleton to John J. Crittenden, Dec. 14, 1859, Papers of John Jordan Crittenden, LOC; Peter Knupfer, "A Crisis in Conservatism: Northern Unionism and the Harpers Ferry Raid," in Finkelman, *His Soul Goes Marching On*, 119–48.

13. *Baltimore Sun*, Nov. 28, 1859.

14. Entries for Oct. 18, 24, and 25, 1859, Hester Ann [Wilkins] Davis Diary, 1859–1861, Allen Bowie Davis Papers, MDHS. Her husband, Allen Bowie Davis, was a wealthy farmer, but the slave schedule does not list him as a slave owner in 1860. This seems to be an error, for Davis owned twenty-seven slaves in 1850. There is an Allen B. Dorsey who owned thirty slaves listed in the 1860 slave schedules for Montgomery County. No Allen B. Dorsey is listed in the 1850 slave schedules, so perhaps the census taker erroneously recorded Davis's name in 1860. See U.S. Census of 1860, UVA Browser; Manuscript U.S. Census of 1860, District 1, Montgomery County, MD, 234, www.ancestry.com; 1850 U.S. Census, Slave Schedules, District 1, Montgomery County, MD, 457–58, www.ancestry.com; 1860 U.S. Census, Slave Schedules, District 1, Montgomery County, MD, 7, www.ancestry.com.; George Washington Howard, *Monumental City*, 646–50.

15. George Fitzhugh, "Disunion within the Union," *DeBow's Review* 28 (January 1860): 1.

16. James H. Rollins to Dear Father [James S. Rollins], Dec. 3, 1859, James S. Rollins Papers, SHS-MO. James S. Rollins was a Unionist and the owner of thirty-four slaves in 1860; see 1860 U.S. Census, Slave Schedules, Columbia Township, Boone County, MO, 37, www.ancestry.com.

17. McCandless, *History of Missouri*, 2:286–87; Parrish, *Turbulent Partnership*, 37–38.

18. Jeremy Neely, *Border between Them*, 60–63, 76–77; Fitzhugh, "Disunion within the Union," 1; Sinha, *Slave's Cause*, 388–89.

19. Beriah Magoffin, "Message of Governor Magoffin to the General Assembly of Kentucky, December Session, 1859" (Frankfort, KY: John B. Major Printer, 1859), 28, 30–31, Governor's Correspondence, 1859–1861, Governor Beriah Magoffin, KDLA.

20. Coulter, *Civil War and Readjustment in Kentucky*, 82–83; Harrold, *Border War*, 192.

21. Ramage and Watkins, *Kentucky Rising*, 273–76; Fee quoted in Harrold, *Border War*, 193; *New Lisbon, Ohio Anti-Slavery Bugle*, Jan. 14, 1860; J. M. Harris to T. F. Marshall, Jan. 27, 1860, Governor's Correspondence, KDLA; *Louisville Daily Courier*, Jan. 6, 1860.

22. Evitts, *Matter of Allegiances*, 126–27; 1860 U.S. Census, UVA Browser; *Baltimore Sun*, Oct. 22, Nov. 2, 1859.

23. Towers, *Urban South and the Coming of the Civil War*, 171–72; Brugger, *Maryland*, 267–69.

24. Frank P. Blair Jr. to Dear Judge [Montgomery Blair], Oct. 20, 1859, Papers of the Blair Family, LOC.

25. Entries for May 27 and Oct. 25, 1859, *Bates Diary*, 19, 51.

26. Dubin, *Party Affiliations in the State Legislatures*, 39–40, 71–72, 86–87, 108–9.

27. Ibid., 16, 23, 43–44, 48–49, 76, 105–6, 140, 172, 176, 180–81, 192; Dubin, *United States Gubernatorial Elections*, xli–xlii; Evitts, *Matter of Allegiances*, 100–105.

28. Dubin, *Party Affiliations in the State Legislatures*, 87. In the legislature chosen in 1857, non-Democrats held an eight-seat majority in the Senate and a fourteen-seat majority in the House.

29. Dubin, *United States Congressional Elections*, 178–79, 184.

30. *Baltimore Sun*, Dec. 3, 1859; M. Jeff Thompson, "This Is the Story of the War Experiences of Brig. Gen. M. Jeff Thompson, Written by Himself, and Edited by His Youngest Daughter, Marcie A. Bailey," undated memoir, M. Jeff Thompson Papers, SHS-MO. The memoir has been transcribed and typed. The references in the text come from pp. 2, 11.

31. Quoted in Walther, *Fire-Eaters*, 259. See also A Traveller [sic] to Henry A. Wise, Oct. 22, 1859, Mary Horner to Dear William, Oct. 20, 1859, Lawrence Thatcher to Captn J. Brown, Oct. 3, 1859, Governor's Correspondence, KDLA.

32. M. Jeff Thompson, "An Address to the Citizens of the State of Missouri," n.d., M. Jeff Thompson Papers, SHC-UNC. References within the speech indicate the speech was given after the Republican National Convention of May 1860 but before

the outbreak of war in April 1861. For similar instances of paranoia about possible slave insurrections in the Lower South, see Reynolds, *Texas Terror*, 18–21.

33. Potter, *Impending Crisis*, 376–78; *Marshall (Missouri) Democrat*, Nov. 4, 1859. For reports of rescues, see *Baltimore Sun*, Nov. 5, 1859; *St. Louis Daily Missouri Republican*, Nov. 9, Dec. 2, 1859; James H. Rollins to Dear Father [James S. Rollins], Dec. 3, 1859, James S. Rollins Papers, SHS-MO; Journal Entry for Dec. 2, 1859, William Canby Journals, Book #3, DHS.

34. Crofts, *Reluctant Confederates*, 70–72; William Bigler to James Buchanan, Oct. 22, 1859 (quote), James Buchanan Papers, HSP; Johannsen, *Stephen A. Douglas*, 581–97; Stampp, *America in 1857*, 289–93.

35. Charles H. Ray to Abraham Lincoln (quote), Oct. 31, 1859, Hawkins Taylor to Abraham Lincoln, Nov. 8, 1859, Abraham Lincoln Papers, LOC; *St. Louis Daily Missouri Republican*, Nov. 4, 1859.

36. Entry for Dec. 2, 1859, Hester Ann [Wilkins] Davis Diary, Davis Papers, MDHS; John Pendleton Kennedy to My Dear Uncle [P. C. Pendleton], Dec. 4, 1859, Journal Entry for Jan. 8, 1860, John Pendleton Kennedy Papers, EPFL. Kennedy's contact was David Hunter Strother, a journalist who wrote under the pseudonym Porte Crayon. Kennedy encouraged Strother to submit his account of Brown for publication; *Harper's Weekly* turned down the submission. Strother was a committed Unionist and became a brigadier general in the Union Army during the Civil War. See Charles Joyner, "'Guilty of Holiest Crime': The Passion of John Brown," in Finkelman, *His Soul Goes Marching On*, 328–29n1.

37. Entry for Dec. 5, 1859, Hester Ann [Wilkins] Davis Diary, Davis Papers, MDHS; Bond, Entry for Dec. 12, 1859, in Harrison, *Maryland Bride in the Deep South*, 133; *Louisville Daily Courier*, Dec. 2, 1859.

38. *Baltimore Sun*, Dec. 7, 1859.

39. Samuel F. Du Pont to Henry Winter Davis, Dec. 19, 1859, Henry Winter Davis to Samuel F. Du Pont, Dec. 25, 1859, Samuel Francis Du Pont Papers, Hagley; James O. Broadhead to Wm. Newland, Dec. 6, 1859, James O. Broadhead Papers, MO-MH; C. Gibson to James S. Rollins, Oct. 28, 1859, James S. Rollins Papers, SHS-MO.

40. *Marshall (Missouri) Democrat*, Dec. 29, 1859.

41. Dubin, *United States Congressional Elections*, 182, 185, 187; "Biographical Directory of the United States Congress."

42. "Biographical Directory of the United States Congress." The House expelled Clark on July 13, 1861, and Burnett on Dec. 3, 1861.

43. William C. Davis, *Breckinridge*, 167–68, 198–205.

44. Rhodes, *History of the United States*, 2:417–18.

45. Crenshaw, "Speakership Contest," 323–28, 332–33; Grimes quoted in Rhodes, *History of the United States*, 2:424.

46. Speaker Vote, Dec. 5, 1859, *CG*, 36th Congress, 1st Session, 2.

47. Ibid., 3; Helper quoted in Craven, *Growth of Southern Nationalism*, 250; Crenshaw, "Speakership Contest," 323–25; William W. Freehling, *Road to Disunion*, 2:246–53.

48. Speech of John B. Clark, Dec. 6, 1859, *CG*, 36th Congress, 1st Session, 17–18.

49. Ibid., 18; John White Stevenson to Lewis Sanders, Dec. 15, 1859, Sanders Family Papers, FHS.

50. Speaker Vote, Jan. 4, 1861, *CG*, 36th Congress, 1st Session, 338; D. H. Hamilton to William Porcher Miles, Dec. 9, 1859, William Porcher Miles Papers, SHC-UNC; Martin J. Crawford to Alexander Stephens, Dec. 13, 1859, in Crenshaw, "Speakership Contest," 329n18.

51. John White Stevenson to Lewis Sanders, Dec. 15, 1859, Sanders Family Papers, FHS; George Caleb Bingham to James S. Rollins, Jan. 9, 1860, James S. Rollins Papers, SHS-MO.

52. Speaker Vote, Jan. 30, 31, and Feb. 1, 1860, *CG*, 36th Congress, 1st Session, 634, 641, 650; *New York Herald*, Feb. 1, 1860; Henig, *Henry Winter Davis*, 120–25; Henig, "Henry Winter Davis and the Speakership Contest."

53. Henig, *Henry Winter Davis*, 123–26; *Baltimore American*, Feb. 2, 1860; Explanation of William Barksdale's Vote, Feb. 2, 1860, *CG*, 36th Congress, 1st Session, 653; Samuel F. Du Pont to Henry Winter Davis, Feb. 4, 1860, Samuel Francis Du Pont Papers, Hagley.

54. William Burrell to Alexander Boteler, Oct. 24, 1859, Alexander Robinson Boteler Papers, DU; George Pattison to Stephen A. Douglas, Jan. 26, 1860, Stephen A. Douglas Papers, UC.

55. James Moffett to Dear Cousins James and Martha, Dec. 29, 1859, James Moffett Letters, KHS.

56. Potter, *Impending Crisis*, 306–31; Fehrenbacher, *Dred Scott Case*, 516–23.

57. James A. J. Frost to Mr. Burbridge, July 2, 1860, Frost Family Papers, FHS; Joseph C. Bradley to Stephen Douglas, Nov. 10, 1859, Brutus to Stephen Douglas, Dec. 14, 1859, Douglas Papers, UC.

58. William Preston to R. T. Durrett, Dec. 22, 1858, Preston Family Papers—Davie Collection, FHS; Speech of James S. Green, Jan. 10–11, 1860, *CG*, 36th Congress, 1st Session, appendix, 74; Thomas Hand et al. to Stephen Douglas, Nov. 27, 1859, Howard Everett to Stephen Douglas, Dec. 14, 1859, James D. Eads to Stephen Douglas, Jan. 15, 1860, Douglas Papers, UC; Robert Tyler to James Buchanan, Mar. 20, 1860, Levi K. Bowen to James Buchanan, July 12, 1860, Buchanan Papers, HSP; Samuel Ralston to C. F. Jackson, Apr. 24, 1860, John Sappington Papers, SHS-MO.

59. J. W. Bryce to Alexander Boteler, Dec. 2, 1859, Boteler Papers, DU; Journal Entries for Jan. 25 and Feb. 20, 1860, John Crittenden to John Pendleton Kennedy, Jan. 24, 1860, John Pendleton Kennedy to R. C. Winthrop, Jan. 18, 1860, Kennedy Papers, EPFL; George P. Fisher to John Crittenden, Jan. 7, 1860, Crittenden Papers, LOC.

60. William Schley to John Crittenden, Mar. 6, 1860, Crittenden Papers, DU (first quote); John Pendleton Kennedy to Sir Richard Pakenham, Feb. 19, 1860, Kennedy Papers, EPFL (second quote); Alexander H. H. Stuart to John Crittenden, Jan. 26, 1860, Alexander Hugh Holmes Stuart Letter, FHS.

61. Henry Winter Davis to Samuel F. Du Pont, Dec. 20, 27, 1859, Samuel F. Du Pont to Henry Winter Davis, Jan. 13, 1860, Samuel Francis Du Pont Papers, Hagley; J. W. Bryce to Alexander Boteler, Dec. 2, 1859, Boteler Papers, DU; Lindy McConihaigh to James S. Rollins, Feb. 3, 1860, James S. Rollins Papers, SHS-MO; James S. Rollins to James Broadhead, Feb. 1, 1860, Broadhead Papers, MO-MH.

62. *St. Louis Daily Missouri Republican*, Mar. 1, 1860; D. D. Mitchell to Stephen Douglas, Mar. 2, 1860, Douglas Papers, UC; Entry for Feb. 28, 1860, *Bates Diary*, 104; Henry P. H. Bromwell to Abraham Lincoln, Nov. 13, 1859, Mark Delahay to Abraham Lincoln, Dec. 23, 1859, Hawkins Taylor to Abraham Lincoln, Dec. 27, 1859, Samuel Galloway to Abraham Lincoln, Mar. 15, 1860, Abraham Lincoln Papers, LOC.

63. Cain, *Lincoln's Attorney General*, 103–5; Edward Bates to James S. Rollins, Feb. 7, 1860, James H. Rollins to Dear Father, Apr. 22, 1860, James S. Rollins Papers, SHS-MO; *St. Louis Daily Missouri Republican*, Mar. 22, 1860; A. Randall to John Pendleton Kennedy, Apr. 7, 1860, Kennedy Papers, EPFL; E. M. Finch to Abraham Lincoln, Apr. 16, 1860, Abraham Lincoln Papers, LOC.

64. Lewis Sanders to J. H. Harney, Feb. 4, 1860, Sanders Family Papers, FHS.

Chapter Three

1. James A. Bayard to Thomas Bayard, Nov. 6, 1859 (quote), Feb. 22, 1860, Thomas F. Bayard to James A. Bayard, Jan. 15, 1860, Papers of Thomas F. Bayard, LOC; Peter Wallenstein, "Incendiaries All: Southern Politics and the Harpers Ferry Raid," in Finkelman, *His Soul Goes Marching On*, 159–62.

2. McClanahan, "Lonely Opposition," 18, 22–23; Nichols, *Disruption of American Democracy*, ch. 1; Hancock, *Delaware during the Civil War*, 13–14; Samuel Townsend to Stephen Douglas, Feb. 2, 1860, Stephen A. Douglas Papers, UC; *Wilmington Delaware Inquirer*, Jan. 20, 1860.

3. Samuel Townsend to Stephen Douglas, Feb. 20, 1860, Douglas Papers, UC; James A. Bayard to Thomas Bayard, Mar. 24, 1860, Bayard Papers, LOC.

4. Samuel Townsend to Stephen Douglas, Feb. 20, 1860, Douglas Papers, UC.

5. Manuscript U.S. Census of 1860, 4th Ward, City of Wilmington, New Castle County, DE, 147, www.ancestry.com; James A. Bayard to Thomas Bayard, Jan. 21, 1860, Bayard Papers, LOC; Essah, *House Divided*, 166, 168–70.

6. Dubin, *United States Presidential Elections*, 135; McPherson, *Battle Cry of Freedom*, 161–62; Abbott, *Republican Party and the South*, ch. 1; Silbey, *Respectable Minority*, 14–23.

7. Nichols, *Disruption of American Democracy*, 12–20, 288–303; Landis, *Northern Men with Southern Loyalties*, 222–25; E. M. Huntington to Stephen Douglas, Mar. 18, 1860, Douglas Papers, UC. For Charleston as a center of radical sectionalist thought, see William W. Freehling, *Prelude to Civil War*; Barnwell, *Love of Order*; Channing, *Crisis of Fear*; Sinha, *Counterrevolution of Slavery*; Walther, *Fire-Eaters*.

8. Jno. Merritt to Thomas F. Bayard, Feb. 26, 1860, James A. Bayard to Thomas Bayard, Mar. 12, 1860, Bayard Papers, LOC; James C. Van Dyke to James Buchanan, Nov. 10, 1859, James Buchanan Papers, HSP.

9. Samuel Townsend to Stephen Douglas, Mar. 28, 1860, Douglas Papers, UC; James A. Bayard to Thomas Bayard, Mar. 24, 1860, Bayard Papers, LOC; Hancock, *Delaware during the Civil War*, 13; Halstead, *Three against Lincoln*, appendix A, 282.

10. James Guthrie to P. G. Washington, Dec. 22, 1858, Feb. 4, 1859, Sept. 24, 1859, James Guthrie Letters, SHC-UNC; *Louisville Daily Courier*, Oct. 20, 22, Nov. 26, Dec. 1, 3, 1859, Jan. 11, 1860; William Preston to Dear Susan, Apr. 19, 1860, Preston Family Papers—Davie Collection, FHS; E. F. Holloway to Stephen Douglas, Jan. 18, 1860, William W. Bush to Stephen Douglas, Jan. 25, 1860, Lewis Sanders to Beriah Magoffin, Feb. 4, 1860, R. R. Bolling to Stephen Douglas, Feb. 15, 1860, Robert M. Baird to Stephen Douglas, Mar. 27, 1860, Douglas Papers, UC; Lewis Sanders to J. H. Harney, Feb. 4, 1860, Sanders Family Papers, FHS; Halstead, *Three against Lincoln*, appendix A, 283.

11. George P. Lane to James A. Pearce, Nov. 19, 1859, James Alfred Pearce Papers, MDHS; Baker, *Politics of Continuity*, 40; Evitts, *Matter of Allegiances*, 144.

12. A Southern Citizen [Reverdy Johnson], *Remarks on Popular Sovereignty*, 47.

13. See Cooper, *South and the Politics of Slavery*, and Cooper, *Liberty and Slavery* for this important aspect of Southern politics.

14. *Baltimore Sun*, Mar. 3, 1860; Robert M. Magraw to James Buchanan, Feb. 7, 24, 1860, Buchanan Papers, HSP; John Carroll Jr. to James A. Pearce, Mar. 1, 1860, John H. B. Latrobe to James A. Pearce, Mar. 4, 1860, John Lee to James A. Pearce, Pearce Papers, MDHS. Pearce took an active part in a slaveholders' convention in July 1859 that discussed the possibility of expelling free blacks from Maryland and loudly condemned antislavery agitation, which comforted ultra-Democrats in the state; see Fields, *Slavery and Freedom on the Middle Ground*, 65–66; Baker, *Politics of Continuity*, 25.

15. *Baltimore Sun*, Mar. 24, 1860; Levi K. Bowen to James Buchanan, Mar. 21, 22, 23, 1860, Buchanan Papers, HSP; Reverdy Johnson to Stephen Douglas, Mar. 24, 1860, Douglas Papers, UC.

16. Thomas Devecmon to Stephen Douglas, Mar. 24, 1860, Henry May to Stephen Douglas, Mar. 24, 1860, Douglas Papers, UC. The delegate was John J. Morrison, owner of fourteen enslaved persons in 1860; see 1860 U.S. Census, Slave Schedules, Districts 4, 8, 9, Allegany County, MD, 5, www.ancestry.com.

17. Christopher Phillips, *Missouri's Confederate*, 165–80; Ryle, *Missouri*, 88–94, 99–100; Hurt, *Agriculture and Slavery in Missouri's Little Dixie*, 100–102; McCandless, *History of Missouri*, vol. 2, ch. 9; George Caleb Bingham to James S. Rollins, June 3, 1857, in *"But I Forget That I Am a Painter and Not a Politician,"* 186.

18. James D. Eads to Stephen Douglas, Nov. 21, 1859, Howard Everett to Stephen Douglas, Nov. 25, 1859, L. A. Lowe to Stephen Douglas, Jan. 7, 1860, Thomas Allin to Stephen Douglas, Jan. 16, 1860, N. W. Letton to Stephen Douglas, Feb. 8, 1860 (first quote), Douglas Papers, UC; Dubin, *United States Gubernatorial Elections*, xlii; Samiville Weller to the Democrats in the Legislature in Particular and of the State in General, n.d. [ca. early 1860], Samiville Weller Letter, SHS-MO; Waldo P. Johnson to Brother Mortimer, July 28, 1860 (second quote), Waldo P. Johnson Letters, SHS-MO.

19. *St. Louis Daily Missouri Republican*, Apr. 10, 11, 12, 1860; Samuel Ralston to C. F. Jackson, Apr. 24, 1860, John Sappington Papers, SHS-MO.

20. *St. Louis Daily Missouri Republican*, Apr. 13, 1860; Johannsen, *Stephen A. Douglas*, 738, 743–44; James D. Eads to Stephen Douglas, Apr. 13, 1860, Douglas Papers, UC. *Doughface* referred to Northern politicians who subserviently catered to Southern interests; see Richards, *Slave Power*, 85–86; Landis, *Northern Men with Southern Loyalties*, 4, 12.

21. Halstead, *Three against Lincoln*, 9, 16–18; Nichols, *Disruption of American Democracy*, 294; *New York Herald*, Apr. 23, 1860; William M. Browne to James Buchanan, Apr. 22, 1860, Levi K. Bowen to James Buchanan, Apr. 23, 1860, Buchanan Papers, HSP; Walther, *William Lowndes Yancey*, 237–38.

22. *New York Herald*, Apr. 23, 1860.

23. Nichols, *Disruption of American Democracy*, 297–99; Halstead, *Three against Lincoln*, 45–46.

24. George N. Sanders to James Buchanan, Apr. 27, 1860 (telegram), Buchanan Papers, HSP; Halstead, *Three against Lincoln*, 48, 51-52.

25. D. H. Hamilton to William Porcher Miles, Apr. 26, Feb. 2, 1860, William Porcher Miles Papers, SHC-UNC.

26. The contrasting intraregional views about secession are discussed at length in William W. Freehling, *Road to Disunion*, and William W. Freehling, *The South vs. the South*.

27. Nichols, *Disruption of American Democracy*, 301–3; *Louisville Daily Courier*, Apr. 28, May 1, 1860 (quote).

28. Nichols, *Disruption of American Democracy*, 303–5; Halstead, *Three against Lincoln*, 72–77, 82–85, 88. The quote about Stuart's speech is found on p. 73.

29. James A. Bayard to Thomas F. Bayard, May 2, 1860, Bayard Papers, LOC; Halstead, *Three against Lincoln*, 111–12; *New York Herald*, May 3, 1860; *Louisville Daily Courier*, May 1, 1861.

30. Egerton, *Year of Meteors*, 79; Halstead, *Three against Lincoln*, 99, 108–109; *Baltimore Sun*, May 3, 1860.

31. Hancock, *Delaware during the Civil War*, 16. Upon retiring from Institute Hall, Bayard explained he was leaving because "I do not consider it within the scope of my authority to fetter my constituents by the decision of a Convention which no longer is a unit." See National Democratic Executive Committee, *Proceedings of the Conventions at Charleston and Baltimore*, 127.

32. Samuel F. Du Pont to Henry Winter Davis, July 12, 1860, Samuel Francis Du Pont Papers, Hagley. For a Delawarean who supported Bayard's decision, see M. G. Kinlock to James A. Bayard, May 5, 1860, Callery Collection of the Bayard Family Papers, DHS.

33. Eric Walther argues that this is precisely what Yancey hoped for at Charleston; see Walther, *William Lowndes Yancey*, 243–44.

34. *New York Herald*, May 2, 4, 1860; *Baltimore Sun*, May 4, 1860; Halstead, *Three against Lincoln*, 115; Nichols, *Disruption of American Democracy*, 308–9; Egerton, *Year of Meteors*, 81.

35. S. S. English to Stephen Douglas, May 5, 1860, Frank Walers to Stephen Douglas, May 14, 1860, James Monaghan to Stephen Douglas, May 26, 1860, Oscar F. Potter to Stephen Douglas, May 8, 1860 (quote), Douglas Papers, UC.

36. William C. Rives to John J. Crittenden, May 5, 1860, John Crittenden to Washington Hunt, Apr. 25, 1860, Papers of John Jordan Crittenden, LOC.

37. The power of antebellum partisan identification is explained in Howe, *Political Culture of the American Whigs*; Gienapp, "'Politics Seem to Enter into Everything'"; Baker, *Affairs of Party*; Mark E. Neely Jr., *Boundaries of American Political Culture*.

38. Henry Winter Davis to Samuel F. Du Pont, Sept. [no day] 1860, Samuel Barron to Samuel F. Du Pont, Mar. 21, 1861 (quote), Samuel Francis Du Pont Papers, Hagley; Henig, *Henry Winter Davis*, 131–34; W. L. Marshall to Montgomery Blair, May 27, 1860, Papers of the Blair Family, LOC; Worthington Snethen to Abraham Lincoln, Oct. 31, 1860, Abraham Lincoln Papers, LOC.

39. William C. Rives to John Crittenden, May 4, 1860, William C. Rives Papers, LOC.

40. John Crittenden to John Pendleton Kennedy, Feb. 8, 9, 28, 1860, John Pendleton Kennedy to Sir Richard Pakenham, Feb. 19, 1860, John Pendleton Kennedy Papers, EPFL; Washington Hunt to John Crittenden, Apr. 9, 1860, Logan Hunton to John Crittenden, Apr. 10, 1860, John Jordan Crittenden Papers, DU.

41. Edward Everett to John Pendleton Kennedy, May 7, 1860, Kennedy Papers, EPFL.

42. Diary entry for Feb. 20, 1860, Kennedy Papers, EPFL.

43. For the nonpartisanship thesis, see Kelly, "Crittenden and the Constitutional Union Party"; Altschuler and Blumin, *Rude Republic*; Voss-Hubbard, *Beyond Party*; Bensel, *American Ballot Box*; cf. Mering, "Slave-State Constitutional Unionists."

44. Forgie, *Patricide in the House Divided*, ch. 3; Widmer, *Young America*; Eyal, *Young America Movement*.

45. *Louisville Daily Courier*, May 18, 1860. These potential candidates included John McLean, John Crittenden, Sam Houston, Edward Everett, John Bell, and John Minor Botts; see Halstead, *Three against Lincoln*, 121, 123.

46. John Crittenden to Logan Hunton, Apr. 15, 1860, Crittenden Papers, DU; Edward Everett to John Pendleton Kennedy, May 17, 1860, Kennedy Papers, EPFL; Halstead, *Three against Lincoln*, 134–35.

47. Halstead, *Three against Lincoln*, 130–37; Edward Everett to John Crittenden, May 28, 1860, John Crittenden to Edward Everett, May 30, 1860, Crittenden Papers, LOC; Diary entries for May 19, 20, 21, 23, 1860, John Pendleton Kennedy to Edward Everett, May 23, 1860, Kennedy Papers, EPFL.

48. Van Deusen, *William Henry Seward*, 193–94; James H. Rollins to James S. Rollins, Mar. 25, 1860, James S. Rollins Papers, SHS-MO.

49. Fehrenbacher, *Prelude to Greatness*; Holzer, *Lincoln at Cooper Union*; William C. Harris, *Lincoln's Rise to the Presidency*.

50. James S. Rollins to James Broadhead, Feb. 1, 1860, James O. Broadhead Papers, MO-MH.

51. Halstead, *Three against Lincoln*, 144; C. F. Burnam to James S. Rollins, Feb. 14, 1860 (quote), James S. Rollins Papers, SHS-MO; Nathaniel Albertson to Stephen Douglas, Feb. 13, 1860, D. A. Veitch to Stephen Douglas, Mar. 29, 1860, Douglas Papers, UC; James Broadhead to James S. Rollins, Jan. 29, 1860 [misdated 1861], Frank P. Blair Jr. to James S. Rollins, Apr. 7, 1860, James S. Rollins Papers, SHS-MO; James S. Rollins to James Broadhead, Feb. 17, 1860, Broadhead Papers, MO-MH.

52. Charles W. Johnson, *Proceedings of the First Three Republican National Conventions*, 111 (first quote), 113; Halstead, *Three against Lincoln*, 150–51 (second quote); Abbott, *Republican Party and the South*, 14–15; Egerton, *Year of Meteors*, 133.

53. Halstead, *Three against Lincoln*, 156–57; Oakes, *Scorpion's Sting*, 28–50.

54. Jno. Richardson to Abiel Leonard, May 24, 1860, Abiel Leonard Papers, SHS-MO; Entry for May 19, 1860, *Bates Diary*, 129; Francis P. Blair Sr. to Abraham Lincoln, May 26, 1860, Abraham Lincoln Papers, LOC.

55. Halstead, *Three against Lincoln*, 167–71, 175–76; Cassius Clay to Abraham Lincoln, May 21, 1860, Abraham Lincoln Papers, LOC.

56. C. F. Burnam to James S. Rollins, May 22, 1860, James S. Rollins Papers, SHS-MO; James S. Rollins to James Broadhead, June 5, 1860, Broadhead Papers, MO-MH.

57. Edward Bates to James S. Rollins, June 2, 1860, James S. Rollins to Edward Bates, June 6, 1860, James S. Rollins Papers, SHS-MO.

58. Entries for June 16, 22, 1860, *Bates Diary*, 136–38; James O. Broadhead to James S. Rollins, June 26, July 8, 1860, James S. Rollins Papers, SHS-MO; Dubin, *United States Congressional Elections*, 187–88. Rollins narrowly defeated Democrat John B. Henderson in the election.

59. James A. Bayard to Thomas F. Bayard, May 8, June 8, 19, 1860, Bayard Papers, LOC; James A. Bayard to My Dear Child, June 9, 1860, James A. Bayard, Jr., Family Letters, DHS; Hancock, *Delaware during the Civil War*, 16; Nichols, *Disruption of American Democracy*, 310–14.

60. Nichols, *Disruption of American Democracy*, 316–22; Halstead, *Three against Lincoln*, 242 (quotes), 267; James A. Bayard to Thomas F. Bayard, June 24, 1860, Bayard Papers, LOC.

61. Leslie Combs to Abraham Lincoln, May 22, 1860, William B. Todd to Abraham Lincoln, June 27, 1860, Abraham Lincoln Papers, LOC.

62. J. C. Richardson to Abiel Leonard, July 10, 1860, Leonard Papers, SHS-MO.

63. Sophie M. Du Pont to Dear Henry, May 21, 1860, Sophie Madeleine Du Pont Papers, Hagley. For similar sentiments from Kentucky, see Samuel Haycraft to Abraham Lincoln, Oct. 26, 1860, Abraham Lincoln Papers, LOC.

64. Dubin, *United States Gubernatorial Elections*, 146.

65. Christopher Phillips, *Missouri's Confederate*, 227–28; Ryle, *Missouri*, 143–52; Waldo P. Johnson to Brother Mortimer, July 28, 1860, Johnson Letters, SHS-MO.

66. Dubin, *United States Gubernatorial Elections*, 145; Ryle, *Missouri*, 155.

67. *Louisville Daily Journal*, Aug. 17, 1860; *Liberty (Missouri) Weekly Tribune*, Aug. 3, 1860; *Louisville Daily Courier*, Aug. 3, 7, 8, 1860; Volz, "Party, State, and Nation," 381–88.

68. Samuel F. Du Pont to Henry Winter Davis, July 12, 1860, Henry Winter Davis to Samuel F. Du Pont, July [no day] 1860, Samuel Francis Du Pont Papers, Hagley; "Speech of Hon. Humphrey Marshall, of Ky.," in National Democratic Executive Committee, *Speeches of Hon. Humphrey Marshall & Hon. B. F. Hallett*, 3–4.

69. Crofts, *Lincoln and the Politics of Slavery*, 68–77; Henry Winter Davis to David Davis, Sept. [no day] 1860, Jeremiah Snider to Abraham Lincoln, Oct. 3, 1860, Abraham Lincoln Papers, LOC; Crofts, *Reluctant Confederates*, 79–81; Johannsen, *Stephen A. Douglas*, 778–803; J. H. N. Cundiff to Stephen Douglas, Sept. 1, 1860, James T. Donaldson to Stephen Douglas, Sept. 1, 1860, Alexander H. Stephens to Stephen Douglas, Sept. 20, 1860, A. W. Simpson to Stephen Douglas, Oct. 9, 1860, Douglas Papers, UC.

70. *Louisville Daily Courier*, Nov. 6, 1860; Frank P. Blair Jr. et al. to Abraham Lincoln, Oct. 31, 1860, George W. Howard to Abraham Lincoln, Nov. 2, 1860, Worthington G. Snethen to Abraham Lincoln, Nov. 3, 1860, Abraham Lincoln Papers, LOC; Entry for Oct. 22, 1860, *Bates Diary*, 155; A. Roane, "The South, in the Union or Out of It," *DeBow's Review* 29 (October 1860), 452–54; Mering, "Constitutional Union Campaign of 1860."

71. Richard W. Thompson to Abraham Lincoln, June 12, 1860, David Davis to Abraham Lincoln, Aug. 14, 1860, Abraham Lincoln Papers, LOC; Johannsen, *Stephen A. Douglas*, 787–88.

72. W. T. H. to J. Warren Grigsby, Nov. 5, 1860, Grigsby Collection, FHS; Charles Gibson to Orville H. Browning, Oct. 28, 1860, S. W. Spencer to Thomas Corwin, Oct. 29, 1860, Abraham Lincoln Papers, LOC; John Bell to Alexander Boteler, July 2, 30, 1860, Alexander Robinson Boteler Papers, DU; Patrick Henry to J. Morrison Harris, Aug. 6, 1860, J. Morrison Harris Papers, MDHS.

73. McPherson, *Battle Cry of Freedom*, 231–33; Dubin, *Unites States Presidential Elections*, 159; Crenshaw, *Slave States in the Presidential Election of 1860*, 193–97.

74. Dubin, *United States Presidential Elections*, 159; W. H. Sutton to Orlando Brown, Dec. 20, 1860, Papers of Orlando Brown, FHS.

75. Abiel Leonard to Robert Wilson, Jan. 21, 1861 [typescript], Leonard Papers, SHS-MO; (Lexington) *Kentucky Statesman*, Oct. 5, 1860, in Dumond, *Southern Editorials on Secession*, 175 (quote); John C. Breckinridge to A. Dudley Mann, Aug. 8, 1860, Breckinridge Papers, DU; Roed, "Secessionist Strength in Missouri"; Denton, *Southern Star for Maryland*, 32–35.

76. U.S. Census of 1860, UVA Browser; Dubin, *United States Presidential Elections*, 161.

77. James A. Bayard to Thomas F. Bayard, Aug. 5, 17, 1860, William Lowndes Yancey to James A. Bayard, Sept. 23, 1860, James A. Bayard to Thomas F. Bayard, Dec. 4, 1860 (quote), Bayard Papers, LOC.

Chapter Four

1. Mrs. Chapman Coleman, *Life of John J. Crittenden*, 1:42–43.

2. Entry for Oct. 22, 1860, *Bates Diary*, 154; John J. Crittenden to Logan Hunton, Apr. 15, 1860, John Jordan Crittenden Papers, DU; Kirwan, *John J. Crittenden*, 360–63.

3. Cooper, *We Have the War upon Us*, 125; *Louisville Daily Courier*, Nov. 8, 1860; *Daily Chronicle and Sentinel* (Augusta, GA), Nov. 13, 1860, quoted in Dumond, *Southern Editorials on Secession*, 232.

4. Remini, *Henry Clay*, 172–92, 413–35, 730–61.

5. *Louisville Daily Journal*, Nov. 8, 1860, quoted in Dumond, *Southern Editorials on Secession*, 218; J. C. Riffe to Alexander Stephens, Dec. 14, 1860, Alexander H. Stephens Papers, DU.

6. Journal entry for Nov. 9, 1860, John Pendleton Kennedy Papers, EPFL; William W. Freehling, *Road to Disunion*, 2:395–423; Channing, *Crisis of Fear*, 252–93; Sinha, *Counterrevolution of Slavery*, ch. 8.

7. Dumond, *Secession Movement*, 113–21; Entry for Nov. 22, 1861, *Bates Diary*, 157; *Louisville Daily Journal*, Jan. 16, 1861.

8. Dumond, *Secession Movement*, 121–31; W. H. Johnson to George Johnson, Dec. 2, 1860, George W. Johnson Papers, KHS; Potter, *Impending Crisis*, 486–89.

9. [Thomas A. R.] Nelson to William Porcher Miles, Nov. 18, 1860, William Porcher Miles Papers, SHC-UNC.

10. Crofts, *Reluctant Confederates*, ch. 5; Frank Steel to My Dear Sister, Dec. 8, 1860, Frank F. Steel Letters, SHC-UNC; McKenzie, *Lincolnites and Rebels*, 61–63, 125–26.

11. Samuel T. Glover to Abraham Lincoln, Feb. 5, 1861, Abraham Lincoln Papers, LOC.

12. George B. Kinkead to John Pendleton Kennedy, Dec. 31, 1860 (first quote), John Pendleton Kennedy to Robert C. Winthrop, Oct. 20, 1860, Kennedy Papers, EPFL; John P. Gillis to My Dear Son, Nov. 6, 1860, John P. Gillis Papers, DHS; W. S. Bodley to A. Burwell, Nov. 26, 1860 (second quote), Bodley Family Papers, FHS; James M. Mason to William Porcher Miles, Nov. 9, 1860, William E. Martin to William Porcher Miles, Nov. 14, 1860, Miles Papers, SHC-UNC.

13. "George N. Sanders on the Sequences of Southern Secession," Oct. 30, 1860, Sanders Family Papers, FHS; W. S. Bodley to A. Burwell, Nov. 26, 1860, Bodley Family Papers, FHS; James M. Mason to William Porcher Miles, Nov. 9, 1860, William E. Martin to William Porcher Miles, Nov. 14, 1860, Miles Papers, SHC-UNC.

14. See Degler, *Other South*; William W. Freehling, *The South vs. the South*.

15. Worthington G. Snethen to Abraham Lincoln, Nov. 26, 1860, W. T. Early to Abraham Lincoln, Oct. 30, 1860, Abraham Lincoln Papers, LOC; R. W. Thompson to J. Morrison Harris, Aug. 12, 1860, J. Morrison Harris Papers, MDHS; Crofts, *Lincoln and the Politics of Slavery*, 83–141.

16. James Porter to Abraham Lincoln, Nov. 2, 1860, Samuel Haycraft to Abraham Lincoln, Nov. 13, 1860, Nathaniel P. Paschall to Abraham Lincoln, Nov. 18, 1860, Thomas Corwin to Abraham Lincoln, Dec. 10, 1860, Isaac Newton to Abraham Lincoln, Dec. 13, 1860, Abraham Lincoln Papers, LOC; Blanton Duncan to Stephen Douglas, Feb. 6, 1861, Stephen A. Douglas Papers, UC; Edward Bates to James S. Rollins, Oct. 25, 1860, James S. Rollins Papers, SHS-MO.

17. George D. Prentice to Abraham Lincoln, Oct. 26, 1860, Nathaniel P. Paschall to Abraham Lincoln, Nov. 18, 1860, Abraham Lincoln Papers, LOC.

18. Abraham Lincoln to George D. Prentice, Oct. 29, 1860, Abraham Lincoln to Nathaniel Paschall, Nov. 16, 1860, *CWL*, 4:134–35, 139–40.

19. William C. Harris, *Lincoln and the Border States*, 19–21; Holzer, *Lincoln President-Elect*, 75–76.

20. Robert C. Winthrop to John Pendleton Kennedy, Nov. 14, 1860, Kennedy Papers, EPFL; Cooper, *We Have the War upon Us*, 17, 87; Fehrenbacher, *Dred Scott Case*, 284, 574; Supreme Court of the United States, "Members of the Supreme Court"; John Crisfield to Henry Page, Nov. 11, 1860, Henry Page Papers, SHC-UNC. The composition of the Supreme Court had changed slightly since *Dred Scott*. Benjamin Curtis of Massachusetts resigned in 1858 and Peter V. Daniel of Virginia died in May 1860. Both seats were filled *after* the secession of eleven Southern states, which allowed Lincoln to place additional Republicans on the bench.

21. John Pendleton Kennedy to George S. Bryan, Dec. 27, 1860, Kennedy Papers, EPFL; Isaac H. Sturgeon to James Buchanan, Nov. 19, 1860, James Buchanan Papers, HSP. For the disparate elements of the Republicans, see Gienapp, *Origins of the Republican Party*; Sowle, "Conciliatory Republicans"; Holt, *Political Crisis of the 1850s*; Silbey, "'The Surge of Republican Power,'" in *Partisan Imperative*, 166–89; Crofts, *Reluctant Confederates*; and Cooper, *We Have the War upon Us*. For the argument that antislavery politics smoothed over Republican factionalism, see Anbinder, *Nativism and Slavery*; Levine, "'The Vital Element of the Republican Party'"; and Robinson, "Seward and the Onset of the Secession Crisis."

22. Adams, *Charles Francis Adams*, 69–70; Potter, "Why the Republicans Rejected Both Compromise and Secession," in *The South and the Sectional Conflict*, 243–62.

23. James O. Broadhead to My Dear Tom, Dec. 2, 1860, James O. Broadhead Papers, MO-MH; Crofts, *Reluctant Confederates*, 104–6; McClintock, *Lincoln and the Decision for War*, 40–53.

24. George S. Bryan to John Pendleton Kennedy, Jan. 25, 1861, Kennedy Papers, EPFL; Thomas H. Hicks to James L. Dorsey, Dec. 15, 1860, Thomas H. Hicks Papers, MS 1263, MDHS; Stephen S. Nicholas to John Crittenden, Dec. 27, 1860, Thos. W. Riley to John Crittenden, Feb. 8, [1861] (quote), Papers of John Jordan Crittenden, LOC.

25. Jeremy Neely, *Border between Them*, 91–94; Tucker, "'Ho, for Kansas'"; Robert M. Stewart to J. F. Snyder, Nov. 20, 1860, Petition of Citizens of Henry Township, Vernon County, to Governor Robert M. Stewart, Nov. 21, 1860, Petition of Citizens of Jackson County, n.d., Daniel M. Frost to Robert M. Stewart, Nov. 27, 1860, David M. Fox to Robert M. Stewart, Nov. 27, 1860, Missouri-Kansas Border War Collection, MSA; Thornton Marshall and L. J. Bradford to Beriah Magoffin, Dec. 17, 1860, Governor's Correspondence, 1859–1861, Governor Beriah Magoffin, KDLA.

26. *Louisville Daily Journal*, Nov. 9, 10 (first quote), 16, 20, and 21 (second quote), 1860.

27. *Louisville Daily Courier*, Jan. 9, 1861; Journal entry for Nov. 11, 1860, Kennedy Papers, EPFL; B. T. Lacy to Robert J. Breckinridge, Dec. 22, 1860, Breckinridge Family Papers, LOC; Klotter, *Breckinridges of Kentucky*, 79–81; Harlow, *Religion, Race, and the Making of Confederate Kentucky*, 142–49; Zacharias, "John J. Crittenden Crusades."

28. John Pendleton Kennedy, "The Border States: Their Power and Duty in the Present Disordered Condition of the Country," in Wakelyn, *Southern Pamphlets on Secession*, 246.

29. Wooster, *Secession Conventions of the South*, 14, 28, 51, 68, 82, 103, 123–24; R. B. Brabson to Alexander Boteler, Oct. 15, 1860 (quote), Alexander Robinson Boteler Papers, DU; N. W. Watkins to James S. Rollins, Jan. 9, 1861, James S. Rollins Papers, SHS-MO.

30. Kennedy, "The Border States," 227–29; Hancock, *Delaware during the Civil War*, 42; James F. Noble to John Crittenden, Dec. 3, 1860, Crittenden Papers, LOC; William C. Rives to Alexander Boteler, Dec. 8, 1860, Boteler Papers, DU; Jno. H. B. Latrobe to William C. Rives, Dec. 15, 1860 (quote), William C. Rives Papers, LOC.

31. Nathaniel Pitcher Tallmadge to John J. Crittenden, Dec. 17, 1860, Crittenden Papers, LOC; Kennedy, "The Border States," 244; Robert J. Breckinridge, "Discourse Delivered on the Day of National Humiliation, January 4, 1861, at Lexington, Kentucky," in Wakelyn, *Southern Pamphlets on Secession*, 259. For an alternate interpretation of intersectional relations that emphasizes dissonance and conflict, see Harrold, *Border War*; cf. Salafia, *Slavery's Borderland*, and Christopher Phillips, *Rivers Ran Backward*.

32. C. B. Jones to Stephen Douglas, Mar. 11, 1861 (quote), Douglas Papers, UC; Thomas H. Hicks to John J. Crittenden, Dec. 13, 1860, Hicks Papers, MS 2104, MDHS.

33. Thomas H. Hicks to John J. Crittenden, Dec. 13, 1860, Hicks Papers, MS 2104, MDHS; D. P. Henderson to Stephen Douglas, Jan. 30, 1860, Joe V. Meigs to Stephen Douglas and John Crittenden, Jan. 17, 1861, Douglas Papers, UC; Samuel F. Du Pont to Henry Winter Davis, Dec. 12, 1860, Samuel Francis Du Pont Papers, Hagley; Paulus, "America's Long Eulogy for Compromise."

34. Jno. Bransford to W. C. P. Breckinridge, Dec. 7, 1860, B. T. Lacy to Robert J. Breckinridge, Dec. 22, 1860, Breckinridge Family Papers, LOC; Amos Kendall to James L. Orr, Sept. 17, 1860, in *Rebellion Record*, 2:131; Jno. H. Latrobe to William C. Rives, Dec. 28, 1860, Rives Papers, LOC.

35. For the relationship between Southern honor and politics, see Wyatt-Brown, *Southern Honor*; Cooper, *Liberty and Slavery*; Greenberg, *Masters and Statesmen*; Olsen, *Political Culture and Secession in Mississippi*.

36. Abiel Leonard to Robert Wilson, Jan. 21, 1861 (first quote), typescript copy, Abiel Leonard Papers, SHS-MO; Uncle Billie to J. W. Duncan, Jan. 1, 1861 (second and third quotes), Uncle Billie Letter, FHS.

37. A. Roane, "The South, in the Union or out of It," *DeBow's Review* 29 (October 1860): 457, 461. For the initial confidence of fire-eaters, see Reynolds, *Editors Make War*, ch. 8. Senator James Chesnut of South Carolina made the prediction about blood filling a lady's thimble; see McPherson, *Battle Cry of Freedom*, 238.

38. John Pendleton Kennedy, "An Appeal to Maryland," in *Rebellion Record*, 1:368. For the sanctity of the Union among the Northern populace, see Gallagher, *Union War*.

39. Amos Kendall to James L. Orr, Sept. 17, 1860, in *Rebellion Record*, 2:131.

40. Joseph Holt, "Joseph Holt's Letter on the Pending Revolution," May 31, 1861, in *Rebellion Record*, 1:290 (quote); Thomas P. Fitzpatrick to William C. Rives, Feb. 11, 1861, Rives Papers, LOC; Raney Ward to Dear Father, Brothers, and Sisters, Feb. 10, 1861, Shadrach Ward Correspondence, DU.

41. S. Guiteau to Robert Breckinridge, Dec. 10, 1860, Breckinridge Family Papers, LOC. For the power of slave flight, see Franklin and Schweninger, *Runaway Slaves*; Link, *Roots of Secession*; Hahn, *A Nation under Our Feet*; Kaye, *Joining Places*; Ashworth, *Republic in Crisis*.

42. "Views of Winfield Scott," memorandum dated Oct. 29, 1860 (quote), Winfield Scott to John J. Crittenden, Nov. 12, 1860, F. A. Rice to John J. Crittenden, Dec. 22, 1860, Crittenden Papers, LOC; W. S. Bodley to A. Burwell, Nov. 22, 1860, Bodley Family Papers, FHS; Francis P. Blair Sr. to John J. Crittenden, Jan. 30, 1861, Papers of the Blair Family, LOC.

43. Kennedy, "The Border States," 229–30; Breckinridge, "Discourse," 258; Oakes, *Freedom National*, 78–83.

44. Robert C. Winthrop to John Pendleton Kennedy, Dec. 22, 1860, Kennedy Papers, EPFL.

45. Thomas C. Reynolds to William Porcher Miles, Dec. 15, 1860, Howell Cobb to William Porcher Miles, Jan. 10, [1861], Miles Papers, SHC-UNC; *New Orleans Bee*, Nov. 23, 1860, in Dumond, *Southern Editorials on Secession*, 264–65. Daniel Crofts argues that Upper South Unionists were initially on the defensive and did not begin their offensive until January 1861, but in the Border South the Unionist offensive began in November; see Crofts, *Reluctant Confederates*, 90–163. William Freehling and Craig Simpson note that Unionists in Georgia were quick to act in November but soon thereafter became inert, which allowed fire-eaters to gain the upper hand; see Freehling and Simpson, *Secession Debated*, xix.

46. *Washington, D.C., Constitution*, Dec. 4, 1860; *Washington, D.C., National Republican*, Dec. 3, 1860.

47. James Guthrie to P. G. Washington, Dec. 9, 1860, James Guthrie Letters, SHC-UNC; James A. Bayard to Thomas F. Bayard, Dec. 14, 1860, Papers of Thomas F. Bayard, LOC; C. S. Jones to Stephen Douglas, Dec. 29, 1860, Douglas Papers, UC; *Albany Evening Journal*, Nov. 24, 1860; Sowle, "Conciliatory Republicans," 18–21; Crofts, *Reluctant Confederates*, 217–19; McClintock, *Lincoln and the Decision for War*, 57–58; Cooper, *We Have the War upon Us*, 56–60.

48. *CG*, 36th Congress, 2nd Session, appendix, 1–4. All references to the *Congressional Globe* in this chapter refer to this session unless otherwise noted.

49. *Cincinnati Daily Enquirer*, Dec. 6, 1860, *Boston Daily Advertiser*, Dec. 7, 1860, in Perkins, *Northern Editorial on Secession*, 1:141–42, 147; *New Orleans Bee*, Dec. 10, 1860, in Dumond, *Southern Editorials on Secession*, 317; John J. Crittenden to Orlando Brown, Dec. 6, 1860 (quote), Papers of Orlando Brown, FHS; John J. Crittenden to Thomas Hicks, Dec. 15, 1860, Crittenden Papers, DU.

50. Francis P. Blair Sr. to Frank Blair Jr., Jan. 2, [1861], Blair Family Papers, LOC; *CG*, 28 (quote), 19, 24.

51. *CG*, 6, 22, 36–37, 38, 39–40; *Journal of the Committee of Thirty-Three*, in U.S. Congress, House, *Report of the Select Committee of Thirty-Three*, 1–2, hereinafter cited as *Journal of the Committee of 33*; Henry Winter Davis to Samuel F. Du Pont, Dec. 10, 1860, Samuel Francis Du Pont Papers, Hagley; Crofts, *Lincoln and the Politics of Slavery*, 125–33.

52. Cooper, *We Have the War upon Us*, 52–55; *Louisville Daily Journal*, Dec. 10, 1860; *CG*, 76–79, 96, 105–11; *Journal of the Committee of 33*, 3–4; Potter, *Lincoln and His Party in the Secession Crisis*, 100; Crofts, *Reluctant Confederates*, 197–200.

53. Henry Winter Davis to Samuel F. Du Pont, Dec. 18, 1860, Samuel Francis Du Pont Papers, Hagley; *Journal of the Committee of 33*, 5–6; Fehrenbacher, *Slaveholding Republic*, 282; Lubet, *Fugitive Justice*, 50–52.

54. *Journal of the Committee of 33*, 7–8; *Philadelphia Inquirer*, Dec. 17, 1860.

55. *CG*, 112–14.

56. Henry Winter Davis to Samuel F. Du Pont, Dec. 18, 1860, Samuel Francis Du Pont Papers, Hagley; James A. Bayard to Thomas F. Bayard, Dec. 22, 1860, Bayard Papers, LOC; James L. Pugh to William Porcher Miles, Jan. 24, 1861, Miles Papers, SHC-UNC.

57. *CG*, 114.

58. Nevins, *Ordeal of the Union*, 4:385–413; Stampp, *And the War Came*; Hyman, "Narrow Escape from a 'Compromise of 1860' "; Ledbetter, "John J. Crittenden and the Compromise Debacle"; Towers, "Another Look at Inevitability."

59. Abraham Lincoln to Elihu Washburne, Dec. 13, 1860, *CWL*, 4:151; John Sherman to Charles Devens, Dec. 26, 1860, John Sherman Papers, DU; *Boston Daily Advertiser*, Dec. 22, 1860, in Stegmaier, *Henry Adams in the Secession Crisis*, 37.

60. *CG*, 116–17, 158.

61. Dew, *Apostles of Disunion*, 22–23; George Hume Steuart Sr. to W. J. Steuart, Dec. 18, 1860, George Hume Steuart Papers, DU; Thomas H. Hicks to Beriah Magoffin, Dec. 10, 1860, Hicks Papers, MS 2104, MDHS; Thomas H. Hicks to James L. Dorsey, Dec. 15, 1860, Hicks Papers, MS 1263, MDHS; Thomas H. Hicks to A. H. Handy, Dec. 19, 1860, A. H. Handy to John J. Pettus, Jan. 10, 1861, in *Journal of the [Mississippi] State Convention*, 180–83; *Baltimore Sun*, Dec. 20, 1860.

62. S. F. Hale to B. Magoffin, Dec. 27, 1860, B. Magoffin to S. F. Hale, Dec. 28, 1860, in *OR*, Series 4, 1:4–11, 11–15; *St. Louis Daily Missouri Republican*, Dec. 31, 1860; W. Cooper to A. B. Moore, Jan. 7, 1861, in William R. Smith, *History and Debates of the Convention of the People of Alabama*, 405–6 (quote); Dwight H. Brown, *State of Missouri*, 204–5. Dwight Dumond contends that the visit from the commissioner prompted Magoffin to call the legislature into special session, but Magoffin's reply suggests he had already made the decision; see Dumond, *Secession Movement*, 224.

63. *Journal of the Proceedings of the Special Committee under the Resolution of the Senate of the 18th of December, 1860*, in U.S. Congress, Senate, *Report of the Select Committee of Thirteen*, 1–8, hereinafter cited as *Journal of the Committee of 13*. For indications that the Lower South senators were prepared to acquiesce in the settlement, see Cooper, *We Have the War upon Us*, 105–106; and Cooper, *Jefferson Davis, American*, 319–20. Seward was absent from the committee on December 22, but upon his return on December 24 he registered a negative vote with the rest of the Republicans.

64. *Journal of the Committee of 13*, 7; Robert Toombs to the People of Georgia, Dec. 23, 1860 (telegram), in Ulrich Bonnell Phillips, *Correspondence of Toombs, Stephens, and Cobb*, 525.

65. *Journal of the Committee of 13*, 8–11, 16–17; McClintock, *Lincoln and the Decision for War*, 91–95, 103–4; Robinson, "Seward and the Onset of the Secession Crisis," 55–59; Crofts, *Lincoln and the Politics of Slavery*, 117–20.

66. *Louisville Daily Journal*, Dec. 28, 1860 (quote); Duberman, *Charles Francis Adams*, 233–34; *Journal of the Committee of 33*, 11–21; Daniel Lord to John J. Crittenden, Dec. 29, 1860, J. R. Farrar to John J. Crittenden, Dec. 31, 1860, J. Hulme to John J. Crittenden, Dec. 31, 1860, Crittenden Papers, LOC.

67. Call for a Meeting of Congressmen and Senators of the Border States, Dec. 27, 1860, Minutes of the Border State Committee, Dec. 28, 1860, J. Morrison Harris Papers, MDHS; Crofts, *Reluctant Confederates*, 201; John J. Crittenden and Stephen Douglas, Telegram Draft, Dec. 29, 1860, Douglas Papers, UC; Johannsen, *Stephen A. Douglas*, 818–19; J. W. Paine to John J. Crittenden, Jan. 5, 1861, Crittenden Papers, LOC.

68. *Journal of the Committee of 13*, 19; *CG*, 211, 237; *CG*, appendix, 42.

69. Delaware General Assembly, *Journal of the House of Representatives of the State of Delaware*, 15, 17–18, 80, 83–84, 96, 98–99, 101–3, 105, 132, 141–42; Delaware General Assembly, *Journal of the Senate of the State of Delaware*, 42, 44–45, 65.

70. W. Cooper to A. B. Moore, Jan. 7, 1861, C. F. Jackson to Dear Shields, [December 1860], *OR*, Series 4, 1:23, 26–28; Inaugural Address of Claiborne Fox Jackson, Jan. 3, 1861, in Leopard and Shoemaker, *Messages and Proclamations of the Governors of the State of Missouri*, 3:328–39.

71. Ryle, *Missouri*, 176–77, 181–82; Thomas C. Reynolds to N. Paschall, Dec. 31, 1860, printed in *St. Louis Daily Missouri Republican*, Jan. 1, 1861.

72. *St. Louis Daily Missouri Republican*, Jan. 6, 7, 8, 9, 14 (quotes), 1861; Rash, *Painting and Politics of George Caleb Bingham*, 165–74; Bingham, *"But I Forget That I Am a Painter and Not a Politician,"* 1–31; George Caleb Bingham to James S. Rollins, Dec. 9, 1860, Jan. 12, 1861, James S. Rollins Papers, SHS-MO.

73. George Caleb Bingham to James S. Rollins, Nov. 27, 1860, James S. Rollins Papers, SHS-MO; *St. Louis Daily Missouri Republican*, Jan. 14, 1861; Edward Bates to Robert Wilson, Jan. 16, 1861, typescript copy, Leonard Papers, SHS-MO.

74. *St. Louis Daily Missouri Republican*, Jan. 10, 13, 16, 18, 19, 1861; *Journal of the House of Representatives of the State of Missouri*, 106–7; Ryle, *Missouri*, 182–83. The convention bill passed the House 105–18 and the Senate 30–2.

75. Minutes of the Border State Committee, Jan. 3, 4, 1861, J. Morrison Harris Papers, MDHS; James T. Hale to Abraham Lincoln, Jan. 6, 1861, Abraham Lincoln Papers, LOC; Sowle, "Conciliatory Republicans," 223–24; Crofts, *Reluctant Confederates*, 201–4.

76. *New York Herald*, Jan. 6, 7, 1861; James T. Hale to Abraham Lincoln, Jan. 6, 1861, Abraham Lincoln Papers, LOC; Abraham Lincoln to James T. Hale, Jan. 11, 1861, *CWL*, 4:172.

77. *CG*, 265–67, 279–80; A. L. Saunders to Cole Saunders, Jan. 7, 1861, *OR*, Series 1, Vol. 52, Part 2, 3.

78. Current, *Lincoln and the First Shot*, 23–24; *CG*, 267.

79. Wooster, *Secession Conventions of the South*, 36–37; *CG*, 283, 289–90.

80. *CG*, 290, 403–4; *CG*, appendix, 95.

81. McClintock, *Lincoln and the Decision for War*, 117–18; *Daily Palladium* (New Haven), Jan. 16, 1861, in Perkins, *Northern Editorials on Secession*, 1:220–21; Samuel F. Du Pont to William Whetten, Feb. 4, 1861, Samuel Francis Du Pont Papers, Hagley; *New York Herald*, Jan. 10, 1861.

82. Journal entry for Jan. 14, 1861, Kennedy Papers, EPFL; *CG*, 362, 378, 409.

83. Message to the Legislature, Jan. 17, 1861, in *Journal of the Called Session of House of Representatives of Kentucky* (Jan. 17), 6–9; *St. Louis Daily Missouri Republican*, Jan. 18, 19, 1861; Thomas Hicks to John J. Crittenden, Jan. 9, 1861, Crittenden Papers, LOC.

84. John J. Crittenden to S. S. Nicholas, n.d., Crittenden Papers, LOC.

Chapter Five

1. Launius, *Alexander William Doniphan*, 24–71, 127–28, 245.

2. Ibid., 98–117, 134–99; Johannsen, *To the Halls of the Montezumas*, 39–43, 123.

3. Launius, *William Alexander Doniphan*, 220–24, 236–37, 240–45.

4. Link, *Roots of Secession*, 224; Gunderson, *Old Gentlemen's Convention*, 24–27; Crapol, *John Tyler*, 259, 261–64; Alexander W. Doniphan to John Doniphan, Jan. 28, 1861, Alexander W. Doniphan Letters, C1926, SHS-MO.

5. Alexander W. Doniphan to John Doniphan, Jan. 28, 1861, Doniphan Letters, C1926, SHS-MO.

6. Lat. Ogden to John J. Crittenden, Jan. 19, 1861, E. Fanaken to John J. Crittenden, Jan. 19, 1861, Thomas Hicks to John J. Crittenden, Jan. 19, 1861, Papers of John Jordan Crittenden, LOC.

7. Delaware General Assembly, *Journal of the House of Representatives of Delaware*, 141–42; Delaware General Assembly, *Journal of the Senate of Delaware*, 65; Sophie M. Du Pont to Samuel F. Du Pont, Jan. 8, 1861, Sophie M. Du Pont to Ella Breck, Jan. 10, 1861, Sophie Madeleine Du Pont Papers, Hagley; *CG*, 36th Congress, 2nd Session, 378–79. All references to the *Congressional Globe* in this chapter refer to this session unless otherwise noted.

8. *Journal of the Called Session of the House of Representatives of Kentucky* (Jan. 17), 42–45, 52–53, 78–79, 85–87; *Journal of the Called Session of the Senate of Kentucky* (Jan. 17), 42–46, 51, 77, 95.

9. *Louisville Daily Courier*, Jan. 21, 1861; *Journal of the Called Session of the House of Representatives of Kentucky* (Jan. 17), 53–55, 64–66; *Journal of the Called Session of the Senate of Kentucky* (Jan. 17), 50, 62, 83. The House journal indicates a vote of fifty-four to thirty-five to table the Leach Resolution for a state convention, but by my tabulation thirty-six representatives voted against tabling; see the roll call on pp. 64–65.

10. For exceptions, see Volz, "Party, State, and Nation"; Paine, "'Kentucky Will Be the Last to Give Up the Union'"; and Boyd, "Neutrality and Peace."

11. C. F. Burnam to James S. Rollins, Feb. 20, 1861, James S. Rollins Papers, SHS-MO; *Louisville Daily Courier*, Jan. 19, 21, 1861; Blanton Duncan to William Porcher Miles, Jan. 22, 1861, William Porcher Miles Papers, SHC-UNC.

12. Crofts, *Reluctant Confederates*, 144–46; *Louisville Daily Courier*, Jan. 25, 1861; Blanton Duncan to William Porcher Miles, Jan. 22, 24, 1861, Miles Papers, SHC-UNC.

13. Stampp, *And the War Came*, 92–94; *Journal of the Called Session of the House of Representatives of Kentucky* (Jan. 17), 68–71.

14. Blanton Duncan to William Porcher Miles, Jan. 22, 1861, Miles Papers, SHC-UNC; *Louisville Daily Courier*, Jan. 22, 1861; Leslie Combs to John J. Crittenden, Jan. 22, 1861, Crittenden Papers, LOC.

15. *St. Louis Daily Missouri Republican*, Jan. 13 (first, second, and third quotes), 14, 15 (fourth quote), 17, 20, 1861.

16. Thomas Hicks to Thomas G. Pratt et al., Nov. 27, 1860, printed in *Baltimore Sun*, Nov. 29, 1860; Anthony Kimmel to Thomas H. Hicks, Jan. 26, 1861, James C. Welling to Thomas H. Hicks, Dec. 1, 1860, Thomas H. Hicks Papers, MS 1313, MDHS; "Extract from Gov. Hicks' Address," in *Rebellion Record*, 1:18. Section 7 of the Declaration of Rights in Maryland's 1851 Constitution stated "that no power of suspending laws, or the execution of laws, unless by or derived from the legislature, ought to be exercised or allowed." See "Maryland Constitution of 1851," NBER/Maryland State Constitutions Project, last modified Jan. 1, 2003, www.stateconstitutions.umd.edu/Search/results .aspx?srch=1&state=%27MD%27&CID=164&art=&sec=&amd=&key=&Yr=.

17. Thomas Hicks to John J. Crittenden, Jan. 25, 1861, Crittenden Papers, LOC; Henry Lowe to J. R. Blossom, Jan. 12, 1861, John Judge Papers, SHC-UNC.

18. Anonymous to Thomas H. Hicks, ca. 1861, Hicks Papers, MS 2104, MDHS; Alexander McClure to Abraham Lincoln, Jan. 15, 1861, Abraham Lincoln Papers, LOC; *Baltimore Sun*, Jan. 19, 1861 (quote); Radcliffe, *Governor Thomas Hicks*, 33–34.

19. Beriah Magoffin to the Governors of the South, Dec. 9, 1860, in *Journal of the Called Session of the House of Representatives of Kentucky* (Jan. 17), 17, 19; John J. Crittenden et al. to Beriah Magoffin, Jan. 12, 1861 (telegram), in *OR*, Series 1, Vol. 52, Part 2, 6; William C. Rives to T. J. Wertenbaker et al., Jan. 23, 1861, William C. Rives Papers, LOC.

20. Gunderson, *Old Gentlemen's Convention*, 25; Delaware General Assembly, *Journal of the House of Representatives of Delaware*, 235–37; Delaware General Assembly, *Journal of the Senate of Delaware*, 98, 105–6; *Journal of the Called Session of the House of Representatives of Kentucky* (Jan. 17), 109–12, 133–35, 138–40; *Journal of the Called Session of the Senate of Kentucky* (Jan. 17), 95–98, 102; *Journal of the House of Representatives of Missouri, First Session of the Twenty-First General Assembly*, 202–6; Radcliffe, *Governor Thomas Hicks*, 36–37. The governors of Connecticut, Indiana, Kansas, New Hampshire, North Carolina, and Vermont also appointed delegates to the Washington Peace Conference.

21. Date for the twenty-three delegates compiled from Manuscript Census of 1860 and Slave Schedules, Census of 1860, www.ancestry.com; "Biographical Directory of the United States Congress"; Launius, *Alexander William Doniphan*, 182–99; Nichols, *Disruption of American Democracy*, 278–79, 307: Fehrenbacher, *Dred Scott Case*, 282; Remini, *Henry Clay*, 624, 719–21.

22. *CG*, 443; Severn Teackle Wallis to Reverdy Johnson, Jan. 3, 1861, Reverdy Johnson Collection, MDHS.

23. *CG*, 489–90, 493–95, 518–21, 661 (quote), 822; *Philadelphia Inquirer*, Feb. 9, 1861; *CG*, appendix, 93; McClintock, *Lincoln and the Decision for War*, 122–24.

24. *St. Louis Daily Missouri Republican*, Jan. 19, 1861; Potter, *Lincoln and His Party*, 299; *CG*, appendix, 117–18; Sowle, "Conciliatory Republicans," 362–65; *CG*, 690, 697; A. P. Bartlett to Lyman Trumbull, Feb. 9, 1861, quoted in McClintock, *Lincoln and the Decision for War*, 162–63.

25. Nathan Sargent to Abraham Lincoln, Dec. 12, 1860 (quote), Isaac Newton to Abraham Lincoln, Dec. 13, 1860, Abraham Lincoln Papers, LOC; Holzer, *Lincoln President-Elect*, 174–75; Cooper, *We Have the War upon Us*, 107–9.

26. Duff Green to James Buchanan, Dec. 28, 1860, James Buchanan Papers, HSP; Abraham Lincoln to Duff Green, Dec. 28, 1860, Abraham Lincoln to Lyman Trumbull, Dec. 28, 1860, *CWL*, 4:162–63.

27. Abraham Lincoln to Duff Green, Dec. 28, 1860, Abraham Lincoln to Lyman Trumbull, Dec. 28, 1860, *CWL*, 4:162–63; Duff Green to Abraham Lincoln, Jan. 7, 1861, Abraham Lincoln Papers, LOC; *New York Herald*, Jan. 8, 1861. It seems likely that Green read the letter or was made aware of its contents by Trumbull; see Holzer, *Lincoln President-Elect*, 175–76, 533n109.

28. Crofts, "Union Party of 1861 and the Secession Crisis"; Daniel W. Crofts, "The Southern Opposition and the Crisis of the Union," in Gallagher and Shelden, *Political Nation*, 85–111.

29. Entries for Dec. 16, 30, 31, 1860, *Bates Diary*, 164–67 (first quote), 170–72; Basil Manly Jr. to Basil Manly Sr., Jan. 3, 1861, Basil Manly Papers, SHC-UNC; Blanton Duncan to Stephen Douglas, Feb. 6, 1861 (second quote), Stephen A. Douglas Papers, UC; George S. Bryan to John Pendleton Kennedy, Dec. 30, 1860, John Pendleton Kennedy Papers, EPFL; Cain, *Lincoln's Attorney General*, 121; Worthington G. Snethen to Abraham Lincoln, Dec. 21, 1860, Francis S. Corkran to Abraham Lincoln, Dec. 31, 1860, Abraham Lincoln Papers, LOC.

30. Francis Preston Blair to Frank P. Blair Jr., Oct. 27, 1860, David Davis to Abraham Lincoln, Nov. 19, 1860, Leonard Swett to Abraham Lincoln, Nov. 30, 1860, Cassius M. Clay to Abraham Lincoln, Jan. 10, 1861, John T. Graham to Abraham Lincoln, Jan. 25, 1861, Francis T. Corkran to Abraham Lincoln, Feb. 26, 1861, Abraham Lincoln Papers, LOC; George Robertson to John J. Crittenden, Dec. 16, 1860, Jones Family Papers, FHS; C. F. Burnam to James S. Rollins, Feb. 20, 1861, James S. Rollins Papers, SHS-MO; Elbert B. Smith, *Francis Preston Blair*, 218–24; Frank P. Blair Jr. to Francis Preston Blair, Nov. 8, 1860, Papers of the Blair Family, LOC; Foner, *Fiery Trial*, 124–26.

31. William C. Harris, *Lincoln's Rise to the Presidency*, ch. 9; William C. Harris, *Lincoln and the Border States*, 31.

32. George Robertson to John J. Crittenden, Dec. 16, 1860, Jones Family Papers, FHS; James A. Bayard to Thomas F. Bayard, Jan. 28, 1861, Papers of Thomas F. Bayard, LOC; *CG*, 397.

33. Parrish, *Turbulent Partnership*, 15; Gerteis, *Civil War St. Louis*, 79–86; Frank P. Blair Jr. to Dear Judge [Montgomery Blair], Jan. 18, 1861, Blair Family Papers, LOC; Edward Bates to Abraham Lincoln, Jan. 30, 1861, Abraham Lincoln Papers, LOC; Isaac

Sturgeon to James Buchanan, Jan. 5, 1861, Buchanan Papers, HSP; Geiger, *Financial Fraud and Guerrilla Violence*, 9–10, 13.

34. Gerteis, *Civil War St. Louis*, 83–85; Piston and Hatcher, *Wilson's Creek*, 28–30; Parrish, *Turbulent Partnership*, 15–17; *CG*, 344, 352.

35. *CG*, 855–57; *Daily Commercial* (Cincinnati), quoted in *Weekly (Frankfort) Kentucky Yeoman*, Feb. 8, 1861, quoted in Craig, "Henry Cornelius Burnett," 268.

36. Edward Conrad Smith, *Borderland in the Civil War*, 116–17; William E. Simms to the People of the Eighth Congressional District, Dec. 25, 1860, printed in *Louisville Daily Courier*, Jan. 5, 1861; Letter fragment, n.d., John Machir Papers, SHS-MO.

37. Samuel F. Du Pont to William Whetten, Feb. 4, 1861, Samuel Francis Du Pont Papers, Hagley.

38. Gunderson, *Old Gentlemen's Convention*, 41–43, 55–56; Chittenden, *Report of the Debates and Proceedings of the Conference Convention*, 465–66; Woods, *Rebellion and Realignment*, 129–32.

39. Oliver P. Morton to Abraham Lincoln, Jan. 29, 1861, Abraham Lincoln Papers, LOC; Gunderson, *Old Gentlemen's Convention*, 46; Chittenden, *Report of the Debates and Proceedings of the Conference Convention*, 456, 458–64; Dubin, *Party Affiliations in the State Legislatures*, 57, 61, 136, 148, 158.

40. Gunderson, *Old Gentlemen's Convention*, 49–61; Reuben Hitchcock to Peter Hitchcock Jr., Feb. 10, 1861, in Gunderson, "Letters from the Washington Peace Conference of 1861," 387; Henry Winter Davis to Samuel F. Du Pont, Feb. 14, 20, 1861, March 12, 1861, Samuel Francis Du Pont Papers, Hagley. In addition to Guthrie, the committee included Daniel Bates of Delaware, Reverdy Johnson of Maryland, and Alexander Doniphan of Missouri.

41. Speech from the Balcony of the Bates House at Indianapolis, Indiana, Feb. 11, 1861, Speech at Cincinnati, Ohio, Feb. 12, 1861, *CWL*, 4:195, 198–99.

42. Blanton Duncan to William Porcher Miles, Feb. 11, 12, 1861, Miles Papers, SHC-UNC; *Journal of the Called Session of the House of Representatives of Kentucky* (Jan. 17), 45–46, 195–97, 209–10, 214–18; *Louisville Daily Courier*, Feb. 13, 19, 1861; *Baltimore Sun*, Feb. 15, 1861; *St. Louis Daily Missouri Republican*, Feb. 15, 1861; Alexander W. Doniphan to Dear Jno., Feb. 22, 1861, Alexander W. Doniphan Letter, C1935, SHS-MO; Fragment of Speech Intended for Kentuckians, ca. Feb. 12, 1861, *CWL*, 4:200–201.

43. Gunderson, *Old Gentlemen's Convention*, 62–63; Crofts, *Reluctant Confederates*, 209–10; E. W. H. Ellis to Oliver P. Morton, Feb. 9, 1861, in Stampp, "Letters from the Washington Peace Conference," 399.

44. Chittenden, *Report of the Debates and Proceedings of the Conference Convention*, 90, 322; Alexander W. Doniphan to Dear Jno., Feb. 22, 1861, Doniphan Letter, C1935, SHS-MO; Crofts, *Reluctant Confederates*, 211–12; William Baker Reston to Reverdy Johnson, Feb. 18, 1861, Johnson Collection, MDHS.

45. Charles P. Stone Memorandum, Feb. 21, 1861, William L. Schley to Abraham Lincoln, Feb. 23, 1861, Abraham Lincoln Papers, LOC; Stahr, *Seward*, 237–38; John Crisfield to Henry Page, Feb. 24, 1861, Henry Page Papers, SHC-UNC; Chittenden, *Recollections of President Lincoln*, 68–78.

46. Chittenden, *Report of the Debates and Proceedings of the Conference Convention*, 438; *Journal and Proceedings of the Missouri State Convention, March 1861*, Proceedings, 24; Gunderson, *Old Gentlemen's Convention*, 87–88.

47. Charles S. Morehead to John J. Crittenden, Feb. 23, 1862, in Mrs. Chapman Coleman, *Life of John J. Crittenden*, 2:337–38; Holzer, *Lincoln President-Elect*, 425–28; Cooper, *We Have the War upon Us*, 200–201. Morehead recollected this meeting, even though he assured Crittenden he immediately took notes after the visit with Lincoln. His outlook of the events may have been impacted by the fact that U.S. authorities in September 1861 arrested him and charged him with disloyalty. For an explanation of Morehead's recollection, see Cooper, *We Have the War upon Us*, 305n78.

48. Chittenden, *Report of the Debates and Proceedings of the Conference Convention*, 440–45; Gunderson, *Old Gentlemen's Convention*, 89–92; *Evening Star* (Washington), Feb. 27, 1861, quoted in Gunderson, *Old Gentleman's Convention*, 91; Entry for Feb. 28, 1861, William Canby Journals, Book #3, DHS.

49. George S. Bryan to John Pendleton Kennedy, Jan. 16, 1861, Kennedy Papers, EPFL.

50. W. T. Stewart to Stephen Douglas, Feb. 24, 1861 (quote), J. R. Howard to Stephen Douglas, Feb. 19, 1861, Douglas Papers, UC; S. M. Breckinridge to W. C. P. Breckinridge, Feb. 20, 1861, S. M. Breckinridge to R. J. Breckinridge, Feb. 21, 1861, Breckinridge Family Papers, LOC; Wooster, *Secession Conventions of the South*, 226. William Roed points out that most of the official returns for the election were destroyed and historians have relied on a speech made by a Missouri politician in 1863 for this number. See Roed, "Secessionist Strength in Missouri," 419.

51. For the first estimate, see Webb, *Battles and Biographies of Missourians*, 47; Roed, "Secessionist Strength in Missouri," 418–19, 421. The second estimation is found in Viles, "Sections and Sectionalism in a Border State," 21. In April 2012 the author examined the election returns in Records of the 1861 Missouri Convention, MSA, but found too many of the returns damaged by fire or incomplete to derive any new estimates.

52. *CG*, 1001, 1032–33; Frank P. Blair Jr. to Montgomery Blair, Jan. 18, 1861, Blair Family Papers, LOC; Henry Winter Davis to Samuel F. Du Pont, Feb. 28 or Mar. 1, 1861, Samuel Francis Du Pont Papers, Hagley.

53. Sophie M. Du Pont to Samuel F. Du Pont, Feb. 28, 1861, Samuel Francis Du Pont Papers, Hagley; *CG*, 969, 1229–30, 1231; Stampp, *And the War Came*, 117–19.

54. *CG*, 1246–47, 1255, 1258–61, 1263–64, 1269–73, 1283, 1285, 1305–11, 1316–17, 1331–33, 1364–65, 1403; Potter, *Lincoln and His Party*, 302.

55. J. P. Gillis to Samuel F. Du Pont, Mar. 2, 1861 (first quote), Samuel Francis Du Pont Papers, Hagley; *CG*, 37th Congress, Special Session of the Senate, 1507 (second quote); J. P. Kennedy to George S. Bryan, Mar. 15, 1861 (third quote), Kennedy Papers, EPFL; *CG*, 1317 (fourth quote).

56. Kirwan, *John J. Crittenden*, 415–20; *CG*, 1374–79; Entry for Mar. 2, 1861, Hester Ann [Wilkins] Davis Diary, 1859–1861, Allen Bowie Davis Papers, MDHS; Crofts, *Lincoln and the Politics of Slavery*, 225–33.

57. Donald, *Lincoln*, 282–84; Stahr, *Seward*, 239–41; First Inaugural Address—Final Text, *CWL*, 4:266 (first quote), 270–71; C. F. Burnam to James S. Rollins, Mar. 15, 1861 (second quote), James S. Rollins Papers, SHS-MO; Entry for Mar. 4, 1861 (third quote), Samuel Haycraft Journal, FHS. For negative reactions, see James A. Bayard to Thomas F. Bayard, Mar. 5, 1861, Bayard Papers, LOC; Blanton Duncan to Stephen Douglas, Mar. 7, 1861, W. Kimmel to Stephen Douglas, Mar. 16, 1861, Douglas Papers, UC; William Mathews to George B. Boyles, Mar. 5, 1861, Eliza Hall Ball Gordon Boyles Papers, DU. For positive reactions, see Samuel F. Du Pont to Henry Winter Davis, Mar. 7, 1861, Samuel Francis Du Pont Papers, Hagley; Zebulon Vance to J. Morrison Harris, Mar. 12, 1861, John S. Millson to J. Morrison Harris, Apr. 6, 1861, J. Morrison Harris Papers, MDHS; Entry for Mar. 5, 1861, Canby Journals, Book #3, DHS.

58. *CG*, 37th Congress, Special Session of the Senate, 1466–69; Klotter, *Breckinridges of Kentucky*, 118–19; William C. Davis, *Breckinridge*, 248–64.

59. Wooster, *Secession Conventions of the South*, 230–31; Data for the ninety-nine delegates compiled from Manuscript U.S. Census of 1860 and Slave Schedules, Census of 1860, www.ancestry.com; *Journal and Proceedings of the Missouri State Convention, March 1861*, 5–7.

60. Launius, *Alexander William Doniphan*, 248–49; *Journal and Proceedings of the Missouri State Convention, March 1861*, Journal, 19–22, 23–30 (first quote on p. 30), 32, 50–52, 56–57; *Journal and Proceedings of the Missouri State Convention, March 1861*, Proceedings, 217 (second and third quotes). The resolution of thanks passed eighty-three to zero.

61. *Journal and Proceedings of the Missouri State Convention, March 1861*, Proceedings, 35–36, 46–48 (quote on p. 46), 53; *Journal and Proceedings of the Missouri State Convention, March 1861*, Journal, 32–34.

62. *Journal and Proceedings of the Missouri State Convention, March 1861*, Journal, 34–37 (quotes on p. 35).

63. Ibid., 46–47; *Journal and Proceedings of the Missouri State Convention, March 1861*, Proceedings, 76 (first quote), 134 (second quote), 127 (third quote), 169 (fourth and fifth quotes).

64. *Journal and Proceedings of the Missouri State Convention, March 1861*, Journal, 48–49; *Journal and Proceedings of the Missouri State Convention, March 1861* (quote), Proceedings, 245.

65. *Journal and Proceedings of the Missouri State Convention, March 1861*, Journal, 46–61; Link, *Roots of Secession*, 229; Reese, *Proceedings of the Virginia State Convention of 1861*, 1:227–30; S. M. Breckinridge to Robert J. Breckinridge, Mar. 22, 1861, Breckinridge Family Papers, LOC (quote).

66. John Pendleton Kennedy to Sir Charles Wood, Apr. 6, 1861, Kennedy Papers, EPFL; Ethan A. Hitchcock to Winfield Scott, Mar. 1861, Abraham Lincoln Papers, LOC.

67. Thomas Shackelford, "Paper Presented to the Missouri Historical Society in Regard to the Shackelford Amendment of 1861," 1907, Thomas Shackelford to Mary Louise Dalton, May 6, 1907, Thomas Shackelford Papers, SHS-MO; L. B. Harwood to Mr. B. Sappington, Mar. 11, 1861, John Sappington Papers, SHS-MO.

68. *Journal and Proceedings of the Missouri State Convention, March 1861,* Proceedings, 24; Alexander W. Doniphan to Dear Jno., Apr. 10, 1861, Doniphan Letters, C1926, SHS-MO; M. Jeff Thompson, "War Experiences," 13, M. Jeff Thompson Papers, SHS-MO.

Chapter Six

1. Speech of Abraham Comingo, Mar. 15, 1861, *Journal and Proceedings of the Missouri State Convention, March 1861,* Proceedings, 150.

2. Symonds, *Confederate Admiral,* 129–31, 134–36; Franklin Buchanan to Samuel F. Du Pont, Dec. 26, 1860, Samuel Francis Du Pont Papers, Hagley.

3. Franklin Buchanan to Samuel F. Du Pont, Jul. 9, 1861, Samuel Francis Du Pont Papers, Hagley; Symonds, *Confederate Admiral,* 136–38.

4. Andrew A. Harwood to Samuel F. Du Pont, May 2, 1861, Samuel Francis Du Pont Papers, Hagley.

5. *Journal of the Called Session of the Senate of Kentucky* (Jan. 17), 249; *Journal of the Called Session of the House of Representatives of Kentucky* (Jan. 17), 321–22; C. J. Blackburn to John J. Crittenden, Feb. 21, 1861, Orlando Brown to John J. Crittenden, Mar. 7, 1861, Papers of John Jordan Crittenden, LOC; John J. Crittenden to Joseph Wrightman, Mar. 13, 1861, John J. Crittenden Letters, FHS; Kirwan, *John J. Crittenden,* 430–31, 438.

6. For the period between Lincoln's election and Fort Sumter, the term *border slave state* normally referred to any of the eight slaveholding states in the Upper and Border South.

7. J. R. Thompson to John Pendleton Kennedy, Feb. 26, 1861, John Pendleton Kennedy Papers, EPFL; James E. Harvey to Abraham Lincoln, March 1861 [no day], Abraham Lincoln Papers, LOC; David Walker to Beriah Magoffin, Mar. 29, 1861, Governor's Correspondence, 1859–1861, Governor Beriah Magoffin, KDLA; Zebulon B. Vance to J. Morrison Harris, Apr. 8, 1861, J. Morrison Harris Papers, MDHS; A. Whittle to Samuel F. Du Pont, Mar. 15, 1861 (quote), Samuel Francis Du Pont Papers, Hagley.

8. *Journal of the Called Session of the House of Representatives of Kentucky* (Jan. 17), 334, 356; *Louisville Daily Courier,* Mar. 27, 1861; "Speech of the Hon. John J. Crittenden, before the Legislature of Kentucky, on Tuesday, 26th of March, 1861," in Mrs. Chapman Coleman, *Life of John J. Crittenden,* 2:304, 305.

9. "Speech before the Legislature," 2:306–7, 312–14. For interregional kinship networks, see Taylor, *Divided Family in Civil War America,* ch. 4.

10. C. F. Burnam to James S. Rollins, Mar. 28, 1861, James S. Rollins Papers, SHS-MO; Entry for Mar. 29, 1861, Samuel Haycraft Journal, FHS; *Journal of the Called Session of the Senate of Kentucky* (Jan. 17), 314–15, 365–69, 427–28, 450–51, 467–75.

11. *Journal of the Called Session of the House of Representatives of Kentucky* (Jan. 17), 330–32, 391–93, 423–24, 427–28, 443–46, 457–59 (quote on p. 427); *Journal of the Called Session of the Senate of Kentucky* (Jan. 17), 253, 269, 407; *Acts of the Kentucky General Assembly,* 51–52; *Louisville Daily Courier,* Mar. 20, 1861; Coulter, *Civil War and Readjustment in Kentucky,* 36–37; Crofts, *Lincoln and the Politics of Slavery,* 245–46.

12. *Louisville Daily Courier,* Mar. 13, 21, 1861; Blanton Duncan to Stephen Douglas, Mar. 7, 1861, Stephen A. Douglas Papers, UC; Coulter, *Civil War and Readjustment in Kentucky,* 37; Boyd, "Neutrality and Peace," 147.

13. C. F. Burnam to James S. Rollins, Mar. 15, 1861 (first quote), James S. Rollins Papers, SHS-MO; Klotter, *Breckinridges of Kentucky,* 112; *Louisville Daily Courier,* Apr. 4, 1861 (second, third, and fourth quotes).

14. *Louisville Daily Courier,* Apr. 2, 1861; Kirwan, *John J. Crittenden,* 438–39; "Speech before the Legislature," 2:316; D. P. Bedinger to John J. Crittenden, Apr. 11, 1861, D. C. Wickliffe to John J. Crittenden, May 9, 1861, Garrett Davis to John J. Crittenden, May 11, 1861, Crittenden Papers, LOC.

15. Gerteis, *Civil War St. Louis,* 77, 86–91; Duke, *Reminiscences of General Basil W. Duke,* 34–43; *St. Louis Daily Missouri Republican,* Apr. 2, 1861. Taylor won approximately 56 percent of the vote in the Saint Louis mayoral election.

16. CG, 37th Congress, Special Session of the Senate, 1511–13; *Journal and Proceedings of the Missouri State Convention, March 1861,* Proceedings, 235–37, 243–46; *Journal of the Called Session of the House of Representatives of Kentucky* (Jan. 17), 323; Samuel F. Du Pont to William Whetten, Mar. 26, 1861, Samuel Francis Du Pont Papers, Hagley.

17. CG, 37th Congress, Special Session of the Senate, 1507; William C. Davis, *Breckinridge,* 260–64; Sophie M. Du Pont to Samuel F. Du Pont, Jan. 16, 1861, Sophie Madeleine Du Pont Papers, Hagley; *Louisville Daily Courier,* Feb. 1, 1861.

18. For Lincoln's approach to Fort Sumter, see Potter, *Lincoln and His Party;* Stampp, *And the War Came;* Swanberg, *First Blood;* Current, *Lincoln and the First Shot;* Crofts, *Reluctant Confederates;* Klein, *Days of Defiance;* Lankford, *Cry Havoc!;* McClintock, *Lincoln and the Decision for War;* Goodheart, *1861: The Civil War Awakening;* and Cooper, *We Have the War upon Us.*

19. Crofts, *Reluctant Confederates,* 274–75; Crofts, "Secession Winter"; Cooper, *We Have the War upon Us,* 228–40.

20. Entry for Mar. 16, 1861, *Bates Diary,* 179; McPherson, *Tried by War,* 16; Elbert B. Smith, *Francis Preston Blair,* 192–99; Frank P. Blair Jr. to Dear Judge [Montgomery Blair], Dec. 14, 1860, Jan. 18, Feb. 14, 1861, Montgomery Blair to the President, Mar. 15, 1861, Papers of the Blair Family, LOC.

21. McPherson, *Tried by War,* 16–20; Current, *Lincoln and the First Shot,* 103–25; Crofts, *Reluctant Confederates,* 313; Cooper, *We Have the War upon Us,* 242–55; Journal entry for Apr. 14, 1861, Kennedy Papers, EPFL.

22. Entry for Apr. 18, 1861, Haycraft Journal, FHS; *Wilmington Delaware Republican,* May 9, 1861; Henry Du Pont to Samuel F. Du Pont, n.d., Henry Du Pont Papers, Hagley.

23. Joseph Breckinridge to Robert J. Breckinridge, Apr. 21, 1861, Breckinridge Family Papers, LOC; James Guthrie to P. G. Washington, Apr. 13, 1861, James Guthrie Letters, SHC-UNC; J. R. Brent to Stephen Douglas, Apr. 23, 1861, Douglas Papers, UC; William Nelson to John B. S. Todd, Apr. 18, 1861, Orville Hickman Browning to Abraham Lincoln, Apr. 18, 1861, Abraham Lincoln Papers, LOC.

24. Sidney Smith Lee to Samuel F. Du Pont, Jan. 26, 1861 (first quote), Samuel Francis Du Pont Papers, Hagley; James S. Flanagan to Abraham Lincoln, Jan. 25, 1861 (second

quote), Abraham Lincoln Papers, LOC; James Guthrie to P. G. Washington, Mar. 7, 1861 (third quote), Apr. 25, 1861, Guthrie Letters, SHC-UNC; "Waitman Willey's and Jubal Early's Alarm," in Freehling and Simpson, *Showdown in Virginia*, 184.

25. Glenn, Entry for Apr. 17, 1861, in *Between North and South*, 27; Stickles, *Simon Bolivar Buckner*, 54; Shaler, "Border State Men of the Civil War," 255.

26. Crofts, *Reluctant Confederates*, 340–41; Woods, *Rebellion and Realignment*, 153–60; Atkins, *Parties, Politics, and the Sectional Conflict in Tennessee*, 246–47.

27. Beriah Magoffin to Simon Cameron, Apr. 15, 1861, Claiborne Fox Jackson to Simon Cameron, Apr. 17, 1861, William Burton to Simon Cameron, Apr. 25, 1861, *OR*, Series 3, 1:70, 83, 114.

28. *St. Louis Daily Missouri Republican*, Apr. 19, 16, 1861.

29. James Speed to Abraham Lincoln, Dec. 22, 1861, Abraham Lincoln Papers, LOC.

30. For Magoffin as a secessionist, see Harrison, *Civil War in Kentucky*; Thomas C. Mackey, "Not a Pariah, but a Keystone: Kentucky and Secession," in Dollar, Whiteaker, and Dickinson, *Sister States, Enemy States*, 25–45; and Leonard, *Lincoln's Forgotten Ally*. For the opposing interpretation, see Coulter, *Civil War and Readjustment in Kentucky*; Dues, "The Pro-secessionist Governor of Kentucky"; Boyd, "Neutrality and Peace"; and Matthews, *More American than Southern*, 235–39.

31. Beriah Magoffin to William Dennison, n.d. (telegram), Beriah Magoffin to William Dennison, Apr. 26, 1861 (telegram), Beriah Magoffin to Lazarus Powell, Apr. 26, 1861 (telegram), Beriah Magoffin to Oliver Morton, Apr. 28, 1861 (telegram), Beriah Magoffin to Thomas L. Crittenden, Apr. 29, 1861 (telegram) (both quotes), Governor's Correspondence, KDLA.

32. For Fort Sumter's unifying impact in the North, see McPherson, *Battle Cry of Freedom*, 274–75; Bowman, *At the Precipice*, 8–9, 284–87; and Gallagher, *Union War*, ch. 2. For the concept of *rage militaire* I have relied heavily on Charles Royster's analysis of the American people at the beginning of the Revolutionary War; see Royster, *Revolutionary People at War*, ch. 1. See also Goodheart, *1861: The Civil War Awakening*.

33. Sophie M. Du Pont to Henry Du Pont, Apr. 28, 1861, Sophie Madeleine Du Pont Papers, Hagley; Jno. H. B. Latrobe to William C. Rives, Apr. 20, 1861, William C. Rives Papers, LOC; William Dennison to Thomas L. Crittenden, May 1, 1861, Oliver P. Morton to Beriah Magoffin, Apr. 21, May 1, 1861, reprinted in *Journal of the Called Session of the House of Representatives of Kentucky* (May 6), 14–16.

34. Ramage and Watkins, *Kentucky Rising*, 290; Beriah Magoffin to M. O. H. Norton, Apr. 29, 1861 (telegram), M. O. H. Norton to Beriah Magoffin, Apr. 30, 1861 (telegram), Robert A. Johnson to Beriah Magoffin, May 1, 1861 (telegram), Governor's Correspondence, KDLA; C. F. Beyland et al. to Simon Cameron, May 10, 1861, *OR*, Series 1, Vol. 52, Part 1, 141 (quote); Garrett Davis to George Prentice, Apr. 28, 1861, printed in *CG*, 37th Congress, 2nd Session, appendix, 82–83; Stickles, *Simon Bolivar Buckner*, 12–20, 51–91.

35. A. W. Gilpin to Henry Du Pont, Apr. 23, 1861, Henry Du Pont Papers, Hagley; *CG*, 37th Congress, Special Session of the Senate, 1477–79; James A. Bayard to Flor-

ence Bayard, Mar. 13, 1861, James A. Bayard, Jr., Family Letters, DHS; James A. Bayard to Thomas F. Bayard, Apr. 17, 1861, Papers of Thomas F. Bayard, LOC.

36. Henry Eckel to Abraham Lincoln, Apr. 9, 1861, Abraham Lincoln Papers, LOC; Henry Du Pont to Simon Cameron, Apr. 19, 1861, *OR*, Series 1, Vol. 51, Part 1, 328–29; Simon Cameron to Henry Du Pont, Apr. 27, 1861, Henry Du Pont to Henry A. Du Pont, May 27, 1861, Henry Du Pont Papers, Hagley.

37. Kirkpatrick, "Missouri in the Early Months," 235–37.

38. Woods, *Rebellion and Realignment*, 146; Claiborne F. Jackson to David Walker, Apr. 19, 1861, Claiborne Fox Jackson Papers, MSA.

39. *Missouri Statesman* (Columbia), Apr. 19, 1861, quoted in Kirkpatrick, "Missouri in the Early Months," 236.

40. Henry Lowe to John Judge, Feb. 9, Apr. 18, 1861 (quote), John Judge Papers, SHC-UNC; Evitts, *Matter of Allegiances*, 175–76; Radcliffe, *Governor Thomas Hicks*, 51–52; Thomas Hicks to Simon Cameron, Apr. 17, 1861, *OR*, Series 1, Vol. 51, Part 1, 326–27; Journal entry for Apr. 16, 1861, Kennedy Papers, EPFL.

41. Evitts, *Matter of Allegiances*, 185–86; John F. Dent to Thomas Hicks, Apr. 17, 1861, Thomas H. Hicks Papers, MS 1313, MDHS; Thomas H. Hicks to Winfield Scott, Mar. 18, 1861, Thomas H. Hicks Papers, MS 2104, MDHS.

42. Evitts, *Matter of Allegiances*, 186–87; Henry Lowe to John Judge, July 30, 1861, Judge Papers, SHC-UNC; Journal entry for Sept. 10, 1861, Kennedy Papers, EPFL.

43. Towers, *Urban South and the Coming of the Civil War*, 166; George William Brown, *Baltimore and the Nineteenth of April*, 36–39; George W. Brown and Thomas Hicks to Abraham Lincoln, Apr. 18, 1861, George W. Brown to Abraham Lincoln, Apr. 18, 1861, Abraham Lincoln Papers, LOC.

44. Everett, "The Baltimore Riots," 333–35; Mitchell, " 'The Whirlwind Now Gathering' "; James Dorsey to Levin Richardson, Apr. 19, 1861, Levin Richardson Papers, MDHS; Henry Lowe to John Judge, Apr. 26, 1861, Judge Papers, SHC-UNC; George William Brown, *Baltimore and the Nineteenth of April*, 45 (first quote); Towers, *Urban South and the Coming of the Civil War*, 166; Evitts, *Matter of Allegiances*, 179–80; A Supplicant for Peace to Abraham Lincoln, Apr. 22, 1861 (second quote), Abraham Lincoln Papers, LOC. Evitts and Everett contend that four Massachusetts soldiers died, while Towers counts thirteen killed.

45. *Baltimore Sun*, Apr. 20, 1861 (first quote); Radcliffe, *Governor Thomas Hicks*, 54–58; George William Brown, *Baltimore and the Nineteenth of April*, 56 (second quote), 58; Evitts, *Matter of Allegiances*, 180–81. Hicks later denied granting approval for the burning of the bridges, but Brown testified otherwise; see "Communication from the Mayor of Baltimore with the Mayor and Board of Police of Baltimore City," House Document G, in Maryland General Assembly, *House and Senate Documents, 1861*, 2–5.

46. Radcliffe, *Governor Thomas Hicks*, 62–63; *Baltimore Sun*, Apr. 23, 25, 1861; Baker, *Politics of Continuity*, 57, 68–70. In the 1860 presidential election, 30,151 votes were cast by Baltimoreans; Evitts counted 9,244 votes cast in the April 24 election, while Towers tallied 9,578 votes. For these numbers, see Dubin, *United States Presidential Elections*, 171;

Evitts, *Matter of Allegiances*, 188n169; and Towers, *Urban South and the Coming of the Civil War*, 170. Maryland's Southern Rights Party was also branded the States' Rights Party.

47. George William Brown, *Baltimore and the Nineteenth of April*, 71–73, 76; Radcliffe, *Governor Thomas Hicks*, 58–60; Evitts, *Matter of Allegiances*, 187–88; Benjamin F. Butler to Robert Patterson, Apr. 24, 1861, *OR*, Series 1, Vol. 51, Part 1, 1273–75.

48. Joseph C. Booth to Michael, Apr. 21, 1861 (first quote), Phebe Wood Coburn Daugherty Papers, FHS; Beckie Steuart to Charley Steuart, Apr. 19, 1861, George Hume Steuart Papers, DU; Andrew H. Reeder to Simon Cameron, Apr. 24, 1861 (second and third quotes), Abraham Lincoln Papers, LOC; Harris, *Lincoln and the Border States*, 57–58; Denton, *Southern Star for Maryland*, 90–94; Cannon, "Lincoln's Divided Backyard," 103–9; C. F. Burnam to James S. Rollins, Apr. 22, 1861 (fourth quote), James S. Rollins Papers, SHS-MO.

49. "Message of the Governor of Maryland to the General Assembly in Extra Session, 1861," House Document A, in Maryland General Assembly, *House and Senate Documents, 1861*, 3–7; Maryland General Assembly, *Journal of the Proceedings of the House of Delegates*, 9, 24–25.

50. Dubin, *Party Affiliations in the State Legislatures*, 87; Radcliffe, *Governor Thomas Hicks*, 73; William Kimmell to Stephen Douglas, Mar. 9, 1861, W. Kimmell to Stephen Douglas, Apr. 3, 1861 (first quote), R. T. Brent to Stephen Douglas, May 4, 1861 (second quote), Douglas Papers, UC; John Gilmer to William Seward, Apr. 21, 1861, Papers of William Henry Seward, UR. For the Union Party movement, see Crofts, "Union Party of 1861 and the Secession Crisis"; Daniel W. Crofts, "The Southern Opposition and the Crisis of the Union," in Gallagher and Shelden, *Political Nation*, 85–111; Harris, *Lincoln and the Border States*, 75–76, 92.

51. Maryland General Assembly, *Journal of the Proceedings of the House of Delegates*, 10, 15–16, 19, 20–23; Maryland Senate, *Journal of the Proceedings of the Senate of Maryland*, 8–9; "Address to the People of Maryland by the General Assembly, in Extra Session," Senate Document B, in Maryland General Assembly, *House and Senate Documents, 1861*, 3–4. For the party affiliations of the committee, I have relied on a list of attendees to a Southern Rights Caucus held in August 1861 that can be found in the *Baltimore Sun*, Aug. 9, 1861.

52. Journal entry for Apr. 29, 1861, Kennedy Papers, EPFL; George Hume Steuart to W. J. Steuart, May 1, 1861, Steuart Papers, DU; Winfield Scott to Benjamin Butler, Apr. 26, 1861, in Butler, *Private and Official Correspondence of Gen. Benjamin F. Butler*, 1:43; Lyman Trumbull to Montgomery Blair, Apr. 21, 1861, Blair Family Papers, LOC; Christopher Phillips, "Lincoln's Grasp of War"; Lockwood and Lockwood, *Siege of Washington*, 175–237.

53. Radcliffe, *Governor Thomas Hicks*, 76–77; Maryland Senate, *Journal of the Proceedings of the Senate of Maryland*, 29; *Baltimore Sun*, May 3, 4, 1861; Henry Winter Davis to Samuel F. Du Pont, May 5, 1861, Samuel Francis Du Pont Papers, Hagley; Journal entry for May 3, 1861 (quote), Kennedy Papers, EPFL. The author counted forty-four petitions and memorials opposing the Public Safety Bill in Maryland Senate, *Journal of the Proceedings of the Senate of Maryland*, 63, 67, 72–4, 80, 83, 92, 120, and Maryland General

Assembly, *Journal of the Proceedings of the House of Delegates*, 70, 72-3, 83, 95, 104, 111-12. The Senate also received at least 5 petitions in opposition to the body holding secret sessions; Maryland Senate, *Journal of the Proceedings of the Senate of Maryland*, 61, 66, 73.

54. Maryland Senate, *Journal of the Proceedings of the Senate of Maryland*, 29–33, 39–61, 67; *Baltimore Sun*, May 6, 1861.

55. "Report of the Committee on Federal Relations in Regard to the Calling of a Sovereign Convention," House Document F, in Maryland General Assembly, *House and Senate Documents, 1861*, 4–6, 8–9, 16–20 (first quote on p. 8, second quote on p. 16, third quote on p. 20); Maryland General Assembly, *Journal of the Proceedings of the House of Delegates*, 117–22; Maryland Senate, *Journal of the Proceedings of the Senate of Maryland*, 131–35; Radcliffe, *Governor Thomas Hicks*, 84–85.

56. George Hume Steuart Sr. to W. J. Steuart, May 2, 1861, Steuart Papers, DU; George William Brown, *Baltimore and the Nineteenth of April*, 85–86; Entry for May 17, 1861, Mrs. Benjamin Gwinn Harris Diary, MDHS.

57. Harris, *Lincoln and the Border States*, 58–59; George William Brown, *Baltimore and the Nineteenth of April*, 94; Radcliffe, *Governor Thomas Hicks*, 95–96; Joseph Sinnott to William Brobson, May 22, 1861, Brobson Family Papers, DHS; Thomas Davis to Thomas Hicks, May 16, 1861, Johnson, Findley, and Co. to Thomas H. Hicks, n.d. [ca. May 1861], Hicks Papers, MS 1313, MDHS; Mark E. Neely Jr., *Lincoln and the Triumph of the Nation*, ch. 2.

58. Sophie M. Du Pont to My Dear Friend [Sarah], May 4, 1861, Sophie Madeleine Du Pont Papers, Hagley; R. Patterson to Henry Du Pont, Apr. 30, 1861, Henry Du Pont Papers, Hagley; Charles Layton to A. H. Grimshaw, May 1, 1861, J. S. Prettyman to A. H. Grimshaw, May 4, 1861, Franklin E. Smith Papers, DU.

59. General Orders No. 1, May 11, 1861, General Orders No. 2, May 11, 1861, E. Spruance to Henry Du Pont, May 23, 1861, William Burton to Henry Du Pont, June 6, 1861, Henry Du Pont Papers, Hagley.

60. Hancock, *Delaware during the Civil War*, 103–4; Richard Brindley to William Brobson, May 7, 1861, Brobson Family Papers, DHS; John P. Gillis to My Dear Boys, May 7, 1861, John P. Gillis Papers, DHS; Henry Du Pont to Henry A. Du Pont, May 27, 1861, Henry Du Pont Papers, Hagley.

61. Thomas F. Bayard to James A. Bayard, Apr. 29, 1861, William S. Reed to Thomas F. Bayard, May 8, 1861, W. C. Lodge to Thomas F. Bayard, June 19, 1861, Bayard Papers, LOC; James Bayard to Samuel F. Du Pont, May 11, 1861, Samuel F. Du Pont to Henry Winter Davis, May 8, 1861, Samuel Francis Du Pont Papers, Hagley; Henry Du Pont to Henry A. Du Pont, May 27, 1861, Henry Du Pont Papers, Hagley; James Bayard to Florence Bayard Lockwood, June 23, 1861, Bayard Family Letters, DHS; "Senator Bayard on Secession," in *Rebellion Record*, 1:240–42; Hancock, *Delaware during the Civil War*, 67–69.

62. *Louisville Daily Courier*, Apr. 27, 1861; Blanton Duncan to W. C. P. Breckinridge, Apr. 6, 1861, Breckinridge Family Papers, LOC; James S. Grigsby to J. Warren Grigsby, Apr. 14, 1861, Grigsby Collection, FHS; Coulter, *Civil War and Readjustment in Kentucky*, 51–52.

63. Harry Volz estimates that 111,000 Kentuckians voted in the May election, and of that number 107,000 votes went to Unionists. In the November 1860 presidential election, 146,217 votes were cast. Thus, turnout in the May election was 75.9 percent of the November election. See Volz, "Party, State, and Nation," 443–45; Dubin, *United States Presidential Elections*, 169.

64. Ben M. Anderson to Leroy P. Walker, Apr. 12, 1861, Blanton Duncan to Leroy P. Walker, Apr. 13, 1861, John Hunt Morgan to Jefferson Davis, Apr. 16, 1861, Jno. C. Burch to Leroy P. Walker, Apr. 19, 1861, Blanton Duncan to Leroy P. Walker, Apr. 20, 1861, St. George Croghan to Leroy P. Walker, Apr. 24, 1861, *OR*, Series 1, Vol. 52, Part 2, 44, 46, 56–57, 68; Leroy P. Walker to Beriah Magoffin, Apr. 22, 1861, *OR*, Series 4, 1:231–32; William C. Davis, *Orphan Brigade*, 13–22.

65. George H. Gondy to Jno. E. Kimball, June 3, 1861, George Gondy Letter, FHS; John J. Crittenden to George Crittenden, Apr. 30, 1861, Crittenden Letters, FHS; William Nelson to John B. S. Todd, Apr. 22, 1861, Abraham Lincoln Papers, LOC; Father to My Darling Johnnie, May 12, 1861, Green Family Papers, FHS; W. T. H. to Sue Grigsby, May 6, 1861 (second quote), Grigsby Collection, FHS.

66. Message of Beriah Magoffin, May 7, 1861, *Journal of the Called Session of the House of Representatives of Kentucky* (May 6), 6, 8–9; Gideon J. Pillow to Leroy P. Walker, Apr. 24, 1861, *OR*, Series 1, Vol. 52, Part 2, 68–70.

67. Petition from Bracken County Women, in *Journal of the Called Session of the Senate of Kentucky* (May 6), 20–23. No fewer than forty-one petitions or memorials in favor of armed neutrality reached the Senate, while no fewer than twenty-three were introduced in the House.

68. *Journal of the Called Session of the House of Representatives of Kentucky* (May 6), 91–97; John J. Crittenden to Winfield Scott, May 17, 1861, Abraham Lincoln Papers, LOC; Proclamation of Neutrality, May 20, 1861, printed in Speed, *Union Cause in Kentucky*, 47–49; *Journal of the Called Session of the Senate of Kentucky* (May 6), 144–45; Coulter, *Civil War and Readjustment in Kentucky*, 54–56.

69. Unknown, Memorandum on Situation in Kentucky, Apr. 11, 1861, Abraham Lincoln Papers, LOC. This anonymous memorandum almost certainly was penned by Nelson; the handwriting appears similar to that in later reports he filed for Lincoln.

70. Speed, *Union Cause in Kentucky*, 33–34; Coulter, *Civil War and Readjustment in Kentucky*, 86–87; Harrison, *Civil War in Kentucky*, 10; *Louisville Daily Courier*, May 25, 1861.

71. Coulter, *Civil War and Readjustment in Kentucky*, 88–90; Joshua Speed to Abraham Lincoln, May 27, 1861, Robert Anderson to Abraham Lincoln, May 19, 1861, Allan A. Burton to William Henry Seward, May 24, 1861, Charles A. Wickliffe et al. to Abraham Lincoln, May 28, 1861, Joshua F. Speed to Abraham Lincoln, May 29, 1861, Abraham Lincoln Papers, LOC; Christopher Phillips, "Lincoln's Grasp of War," 190–91.

72. Claiborne F. Jackson to J. W. Tucker, Apr. 28, 1861, James O. Broadhead Papers, MO-MH; Jefferson Davis to Claiborne Jackson, Apr. 23, 1861, Claiborne Jackson to Leroy P. Walker, May 5, 1861, *OR*, Series 1, 1:688, 690; Parrish, *Turbulent Partnership*, 20–21; Gerteis, *Civil War St. Louis*, 92–96.

73. Allen P. Richardson to James Broadhead, Apr. 30, 1861 (first quote), Broadhead Papers, MO-MH; O. D. Felley to Montgomery Blair, Apr. 19, 1861, Frank Blair to A. G. Curtin, Apr. 21, 1861, Frank Blair to Montgomery Blair, Apr. 25, 1861, Frank Blair to Montgomery Blair, Apr. 28, 1861 (second and third quotes), William Bishop to Samuel Glover, May 10, 1861, Blair Family Papers, LOC; Gerteis, *Civil War St. Louis*, 92–96.

74. Kirkpatrick, "Missouri in the Early Months," 238–39; Harris, *Lincoln and the Border States*, 122–30; *St. Louis Daily Missouri Republican*, May 8, 1861.

75. Edward Bates to James Broadhead, May 3, 1861, Broadhead Papers, MO-MH; G. Price to W. M. Paxton, Apr. 30, 1861, William McClung Paxton Papers, SHS-MO.

76. Duke, *Reminiscences of General Basil W. Duke*, 49–50; Snead, *Fight for Missouri*, 166–70; H. L. Bodley to W. S. Bodley, May 11, 1861, Bodley Family Papers, FHS; Report of Capt. Nathaniel Lyon, May 11, 1861, *OR*, Series 1, 3:4–5; Gerteis, *Civil War St. Louis*, 102–10; Towers, *Urban South and the Coming of the Civil War*, 190. Duke and Snead contend that Lyon led a force of 7,000 Unionists against a state militia encampment of no more than 700 men; in his official report, Lyon estimated his numbers at about 3,500 soldiers.

77. Kirkpatrick, "Missouri in the Early Months," 239–40; Christopher Phillips, *Missouri's Confederate*, 251–55; Geiger, *Financial Fraud and Guerrilla Violence*, 65–68. Geiger has found that after the Camp Jackson affair, pro-Southern bankers in Missouri signed at least 2,900 promissory notes (for a sum of nearly $3 million) to assist the state militia.

78. Proclamation of Price and Harney, May 21, 1861, William Harney to Sterling Price, May 27, 1861, General Orders No. 5, Department of the West, May 31, 1861, *OR*, Series 1, 3:375, 379–381; Parrish, *Turbulent Partnership*, 30–31.

79. Alexander W. Doniphan to John Doniphan, June 2, 1861, Alexander W. Doniphan Letters, C1926, SHS-MO; Snead, *Fight for Missouri*, 199–200.

80. James O. Broadhead to Edwin Draper, May 21, 1861 (first quote), Broadhead Papers, MO-MH; George Caleb Bingham to James S. Rollins, May 16, 1861 (second quote), James S. Rollins Papers, SHS-MO; Hamilton R. Gamble and James Yeatman to Abraham Lincoln, May 15, 1861, Samuel T. Glover to Abraham Lincoln, May 20, 1861, Abraham Lincoln Papers, LOC; J. G. F. to Thomas Bayard, June 1, 1861 [misdated as 1860], Bayard Papers, LOC; John M. Richardson to Frank Blair Jr., June 4, 1861, Blair Family Papers, LOC; Rorvig, "Significant Skirmish."

81. Christopher Phillips, *Rivers Ran Backward*, 125–26. Anne E. Marshall estimates that 71 percent of Kentucky's eligible white males chose not to fight for the Union or the Confederacy, a strong indication of the prevalence of the neutral mind-set; see Marshall, *Creating a Confederate Kentucky*, 20.

82. Symonds, *Confederate Admiral*, 138–46.

Chapter Seven

1. Manuscript U.S. Census of 1860, Ward 10, Baltimore (Independent City), MD, 953, www.ancestry.com Johnson, *Dictionary of American Biography*, 10:385–86; Steiner, "Severn Teackle Wallis: First Paper," 58–59; Steiner, "Severn Teackle Wallis: Second Paper," 135, 138–40.

2. Steiner, "Severn Teackle Wallis: Second Paper," 143 (first quote), 142 (second quote), 146 (fourth quote); Charles Morris Howard, *Personal Recollections of Severn Teackle Wallis*, 3–4 (third quote); Severn Teackle Wallis, "Speech at the Maryland Institute, February 1, 1861," in *Writings of Severn Teackle Wallis*, 2:130–35.

3. *Journal and Proceedings of the Convention of the Border Slave States*, 4–7; *Louisville Daily Courier*, May 28, 30, 1861.

4. *Journal and Proceedings of the Convention of the Border Slave States*, 4, 7–10, 14–17, 22.

5. *Louisville Daily Courier*, June 3, 1861; Garrett Davis to George Prentice, Apr. 28, 1861, printed in *CG*, 37th Congress, 2nd Session, appendix, 82–83; *Frankfort Commonwealth*, May 3, 1861; *Baltimore Sun*, May 6, 1861; John B. Henderson to James Broadhead, June 10, 1861, James O. Broadhead Papers, MO-MH.

6. *Baltimore Sun*, May 24, 1861.

7. Dubin, *United States Congressional Elections*, 189; Henry Winter Davis to Samuel F. Du Pont, June 13 or 14, 1861, Henry Winter Davis to Samuel F. Du Pont, June 14 or 15, 1861, Samuel Francis Du Pont Papers, Hagley.

8. Dubin, *United States Congressional Elections*, 189; Craig, *Kentucky Confederates*, 99–101; *St. Louis Daily Missouri Republican*, June 25, 1861.

9. Dubin, *United States Congressional Elections*, 184, 189; Sophie M. Du Pont to Samuel F. Du Pont, June 4, 1861, Sophie Madeleine Du Pont Papers, Hagley.

10. James May to John J. Crittenden, June 30, 1861, C. S. Morehead to John J. Crittenden, June 30, 1861, John Hugg to John J. Crittenden, July 1, 1861, Orlando Brown to John J. Crittenden, July 5, 1861, J. B. Underwood to John J. Crittenden, July 13, 1861, Papers of John Jordan Crittenden, LOC.

11. *Cincinnati Daily Gazette*, June 25, 1861, in Perkins, *Northern Editorials on Secession*, 2:890; T. Ewing to John J. Crittenden, June 25, 1861, in Mrs. Chapman Coleman, *Life of John J. Crittenden*, 2:322–23; Johannsen, *Stephen A. Douglas*, 870–73; *CG*, 37th Congress, 1st Session, 36, 35.

12. Donald, *Lincoln*, 302–5; *CG*, 37th Congress, 1st Session, 72–76, 376–78; *CG*, 37th Congress, 1st Session, appendix, 12–19.

13. Enoch T. Carson to Salmon P. Chase, July 9, 1861 (quote), Abraham Lincoln Papers, LOC; Jo. Fallon to Montgomery Blair, June 24, 1861, Papers of the Blair Family, LOC. Republicans had an advantage of 102 to 72 in the House in July 1861, and in the Senate the Republicans held 32 of the 48 seats; see Dubin, *United States Congressional Elections*, 191; Donald, *Lincoln*, 305.

14. *CG*, 37th Congress, 1st Session, 209, 222–23, 265. Crittenden worked with Senator Andrew Johnson, a Tennessee Unionist who had not abandoned his seat, to steer these resolutions through Congress; McPherson, *Battle Cry of Freedom*, 312.

15. Garrett Davis to Abraham Lincoln, Aug. 4, 1861, Charles Calvert to Abraham Lincoln, July 10, 1861, Abraham Lincoln Papers, LOC.

16. Charles Calvert to Abraham Lincoln, Aug. 3, 1861, Abraham Lincoln Papers, LOC; McPherson, *Battle Cry of Freedom*, 355–56; *CG*, 37th Congress, 1st Session, 431, 454; *St. Louis Daily Missouri Republican, Evening Edition*, Aug. 7, 1861; Siddali, *From Property to Person*, 70–77, 84.

17. Sophie M. Du Pont to Samuel F. Du Pont, Aug. 5, 1861 (first quote), Sophie Madeleine Du Pont Papers, Hagley; Alexander Farnsley to Dear Miss Bettie [Mary Elizabeth Thurman], n.d., Alexander Pericles Farnsley Letters, FHS; *Louisville Daily Courier*, Aug. 13, 1861 (second quote). For the importance of war powers in eradicating slavery, see Oakes, *Freedom National*.

18. *Journal of the Missouri State Convention, July, 1861*, 3–5, 9–12; Boman, *Lincoln's Resolute Unionist*, 112. William E. Parrish counts thirty-two absentees when the convention opened, but by the end of the proceedings seventeen of these men had arrived; see Parrish, *Turbulent Partnership*, 212n6.

19. *Journal of the Missouri State Convention, July, 1861*, 17–18, 20–22, 25; William M. McPherson to Hamilton Gamble, July 26, 1861 (quote), Hamilton R. Gamble Papers, MO-MH; Parrish, *Turbulent Partnership*, 27–43. The convention voted fifty-six to twenty-five to vacate the executive offices; fifty-two to thirty-eight to depose the legislature; and fifty-four to twenty-seven to give the convention the power to fill the executive offices.

20. *Proceedings of the Missouri State Convention, July, 1861*, 135; *St. Louis Daily Missouri Republican*, Aug. 1, 1861.

21. Gerteis, *Civil War St. Louis*, 130–31; Charles Gibson to Hamilton Gamble, Aug. 2, 1861, Samuel Conway to Hamilton Gamble, Aug. 9, 1861, Gamble Papers, MO-MH.

22. "Lt. Gov. Reynolds' Proclamation," July 31, 1861, Document 148, *Rebellion Record*, 2:455–56; C. F. Jackson to E. F. Cabell, Aug. 5, 1861, *OR*, Series 1, 3:639; Christopher Phillips, *Missouri's Confederate*, 264–65.

23. Parrish, *Turbulent Partnership*, 49; Elihu P. Washburne to Abraham Lincoln, Oct. 21, 1861, Abraham Lincoln Papers, LOC; L. W. Burris to Hamilton Gamble, Aug. 8, 1861, Gamble Papers, MO-MH.

24. John C. Frémont to Abraham Lincoln, July 29, 1861 (first quote), John Poyner to Abraham Lincoln, Aug. 27, 1861 (second quote), Henry T. Blow to Abraham Lincoln, Sept. 20, 1861, Abraham Lincoln Papers, LOC; Piston and Hatcher, *Wilson's Creek*, 268–69, 306–8, 323. For the emerging guerrilla war in Missouri, see Fellman, *Inside War*; Sutherland, *Savage Conflict*; Geiger, *Financial Fraud and Guerrilla Violence*; and Astor, *Rebels on the Border*.

25. Frank Blair Jr. to Montgomery Blair, Aug. 29, Sept. 1, 1861, Peter L. Foy to Montgomery Blair, Sept. 17, 1861, William Jones to Montgomery Blair, Oct. 14, 1861, Blair Family Papers, LOC.

26. Proclamation, Aug. 30, 1861, *OR*, Series 1, 3:466–67.

27. *Louisville Daily Courier*, Sept. 2, 1861; John B. Henderson to James O. Broadhead, Sept. 7, 1861, Abraham Lincoln Papers, LOC; S. J. to Montgomery Blair, Sept. 3, 1861, Blair Family Papers, LOC.

28. Dubin, *Party Affiliations in the State Legislature*, 72; E. F. Drake to Salmon Chase, Aug. 29, 1861, printed in Hart, "Letters to Secretary Chase," 343; N. J. Eaton to Edward Bates, Sept. 16, 1861, Abraham Lincoln Papers, LOC.

29. Garrett Davis to Salmon Chase, Sept. 3, 1861, printed in Hart, "Letters to Secretary Chase," 346–47; James Guthrie to P. G. Washington, Sept. 3, 1861, James Guthrie Letters,

SHC-UNC; Joshua F. Speed to Abraham Lincoln, Sept. 1, 1861, Green Adams and James Speed to Abraham Lincoln, Sept. 2, 1861 (telegram), Leslie Combs to Abraham Lincoln, Sept. 6, 1861, Joseph C. G. Kennedy to Abraham Lincoln, Sept. 6, 1861, Joseph Holt to Abraham Lincoln, Sept. 12, 1861, Robert Anderson to Abraham Lincoln, Sept. 13, 1861, Montgomery Blair to Abraham Lincoln, Sept. 14, 1861, Abraham Lincoln Papers, LOC.

30. J. F. Bullitt, C. Ripley, and W. E. Hughes to Joshua F. Speed, Sept. 13, 1861 (telegram), Joshua F. Speed to Abraham Lincoln, Sept. 3, 1861, Abraham Lincoln Papers, LOC; Garrett Davis to John J. Crittenden, Aug. 12, 1861, J. F. Robinson to John J. Crittenden, Aug. 13, 1861, William Nelson to John J. Crittenden, Aug. 12, 1861, Crittenden Papers, LOC; William C. Bullitt to Dear Tom, Dec. 31, 1861, Bullitt Family Papers—Oxmoor Collection, FHS; Coulter, *Civil War and Readjustment in Kentucky*, 101–4; Harrison, *Civil War in Kentucky*, 11–12; U.S. Census of 1860, Slave Schedules, 4th Ward, City of Louisville, Jefferson County, KY, 3, www.ancestry.com.

31. J. G. Roberts to Abraham Lincoln, Sept. 17, 1861 (quote), John L. Scripps to Abraham Lincoln, Sept. 23, 1861, Abraham Lincoln Papers, LOC; Harris, *Lincoln and the Border States*, 102.

32. Parrish, *Turbulent Partnership*, 61–76; Harris, *Lincoln and the Border States*, 102–8; Abraham Lincoln to Orville H. Browning, Sept. 22, 1861, *CWL*, 4:531–32.

33. William Preston Johnston to My Dear Rosa, Dec. 24, 1861, Johnston Family Papers, FHS.

34. Coulter, *Civil War and Readjustment in Kentucky*, 108–10, 114–15; Woodworth, "'The Indeterminate Quantities'"; Cooper, *Jefferson Davis, American*, 356–58; Orlando Brown to John J. Crittenden, July 9, 1861, Crittenden Papers, LOC; J. O. Davis to Hamilton Gamble, Aug. 22, 1861, Gamble Papers, MO-MH.

35. Kirkpatrick, "Missouri's Secessionist Government," 124–27.

36. *Journal of the Senate, Extra Session of the Rebel Legislature*, 1–12, 38, 41; Typescript, 2, Missouri General Assembly, House of Representatives (Confederate), Journal, 1861, SHS-MO; Christopher Phillips, *Rivers Ran Backward*, 143. The author wishes to thank Joan E. Stack, curator of art collections, and Amy L. Waters, reference specialist, both of the State Historical Society of Missouri, Columbia, for their assistance with locating the names of the attendees at this session of the legislature.

37. The House journal does not record the actual tally of the vote on secession, but merely states that the measure passed with only Isaac N. Shambaugh of DeKalb County casting a negative vote; see Typescript, 10, Missouri General Assembly, House of Representatives (Confederate), Journal, SHS-MO.

38. Kirkpatrick, "Missouri's Secessionist Government," 127–31; Christopher Phillips, *Missouri's Confederate*, 273.

39. Craig, "Henry Cornelius Burnett," 271–73; Coulter, *Civil War and Readjustment in Kentucky*, 137–38; *Declaration of Independence and the Constitution of the Provisional Government of Kentucky*, 5–9.

40. C. F. Mitchell to Abraham Lincoln, Jan. 27, 1861, Abraham Lincoln Papers, LOC.

41. Underwood, Entry for Mar. 10, 1861, in *Josie Underwood's Civil War Diary*, 4, 68.

42. Isaac H. Sturgeon to James Buchanan, Jan. 10, 1861, James Buchanan Papers, HSP; *CG*, 37th Congress, 2nd Session, 2297.

43. "Tellula" to Abraham Lincoln, May 27, 1861, Abraham Lincoln Papers, LOC.

44. Copeland, "Where Were the Kentucky Unionists and Secessionists?"

45. Roed, "Secessionist Strength in Missouri."

46. Towers, *Urban South and the Coming of the Civil War*, 169–70.

47. Harrison, *Civil War in Kentucky*, 20.

48. These findings confirm Robert E. May's contention that even though secessionists sought a radical political solution to the sectional conflict, in general they were not estranged outsiders in Southern society. See May, "Psychobiography and Secession."

49. Wooster, *Secession Conventions of the South*, 244–47.

50. For data on slaveholding at the Missouri state convention, see Table A.5.

51. Wooster, *Secession Conventions of the South*, 209–12.

52. George William Brown, *Baltimore and the Nineteenth of April, 1861*, 100–108; Glenn, Entry for Sept. 13, 1861, in *Between North and South*, 36–37; Cannon, "Lincoln's Divided Backyard," 110–23; Harris, *Lincoln and the Border States*, 70–71; Cusey to Joseph Williams, Sept. 16, 1861, Joseph S. Williams Letters, DU.

53. Severn Teackle Wallis to the Public, Sept. 22, 1861, Abraham Lincoln Papers, LOC; Severn Teackle Wallis to John Sherman, Jan. 3, 1863, in *Writings of Severn Teackle Wallis*, 2:276, 282.

54. Quoted in Stahr, *Seward*, 288; Abiel Leonard to James Broadhead, July 29, 1861, Broadhead Papers, MO-MH; Christopher Phillips, *Rivers Ran Backward*, 188–89.

Conclusion

1. *Report of the Ceremonies on the Fourth of July*, 48; National Park Service, "Lexington Cemetery and Henry Clay Monument"; Klotter, *Breckinridges of Kentucky*, 80–81; Breckinridge, *Civil War*, 646. For a similar metamorphosis, compare "Rough Draft of Suggestions to Mr. Lincoln," Jan. 9, 1861, and "Memo of E. Bates, in Cabinet," Apr. 15, 1861, Papers of Edward Bates, LOC, to Entry for Sept. 30, 1861, *Bates Diary*, 194–95.

2. Joseph Holt to J. Buchanan Henry, May 26, 1884, quoted in Crofts, "Joseph Holt, James Buchanan, and the Secession Crisis," 229; Christopher Phillips, "Lincoln's Grasp of War," 199; M. J. Church to My Dear Brother, July 22, 1861, Bodley Family Papers, FHS; Mrs. Augusta [Maria] Holyoke to My Dear Mother and Sister, Aug. 18, 1861, Holyoke Family Papers, FHS. For other examples of family divisions, see M. T. B. to My Dear Tom, Feb. 9, 1861, Mildred T. Bullitt to My Dear Tom, June 18, 1861, M. T. B. to My Dear John, Nov. 14, 1861, Bullitt Family Papers—Oxmoor Collection, FHS; *Tuesday Evening Post*, June 3, 1861, Pattie A. Curd Papers, KHS; James M. Woods to Dear Sister Zelia, June 24, 1861, Woods-Holman Family Papers, SHS-MO; James Headly to Miss Rebecca Atchison, Sept. 16, 1861, David Rice Atchison Papers, SHS-MO. For the evaporation of proslavery Unionism during the war, see Astor, *Rebels on the Border*; Christopher Phillips, *Civil War in the Border South*; Harlow, *Religion, Race, and the Making of Confederate Kentucky*; and Lewis, *For Slavery and Union*.

3. George W. Johnson to My Dear Ann, Oct. 20, 1861, George W. Johnson Papers, KHS; Harrison, "George W. Johnson and Richard Hawes"; Daniel, *Shiloh*, 276–77.

4. Duke, *Reminiscences of General Basil W. Duke*, 36; Speed, *Union Cause in Kentucky*, 44; George McClellan to E. D. Townsend, May 17, 1861 (Davis quote), *OR*, Series 1, Vol. 51, Part 1, 381; George D. Prentice to Richard Yates, Aug. 30, 1861, Richard Yates Papers, FHS.

5. See Harris, *Lincoln and the Border States*.

6. William S. Harney to John O'Fallon, May 1, 1861 (copy), James S. Rollins Papers, SHS-MO.

7. Foner, *Fiery Trial*, 181–84; Harris, *Lincoln and the Border States*, 159–62; Essah, *House Divided*, 162–72; Fladeland, "Compensated Emancipation"; Hamilton Gamble to David K. Pitman, Dec. 14, 1861, Hamilton R. Gamble Papers, MO-MH.

8. Henry Winter Davis to Sophie M. Du Pont, May 20, 1862, Samuel Francis Du Pont Papers, Hagley.

9. Breckinridge, *Two Speeches of Rev. Robert J. Breckinridge*, 10; Essah, *House Divided*, 189–90; Ramage and Watkins, *Kentucky Rising*, 347. During the war Republicans managed to gain control of the state governments of Maryland and Missouri and enacted emancipation programs in their states. See Wagandt, *Mighty Revolution*, 246–68; Parrish, *Turbulent Partnership*, 200–201; Anderson, *Abolitionizing Missouri*, 110–42.

10. *Journal and Proceedings of the Convention of the Border Slave States*, 22.

Bibliography

Primary Sources

MANUSCRIPT COLLECTIONS

Baltimore, Maryland
 Enoch Pratt Free Library, Archives of the Peabody Institute
  John Pendleton Kennedy Papers (microfilm)
 Maryland Historical Society
  Allen Bowie Davis Papers
  Mrs. Benjamin Gwinn Harris Diary
  J. Morrison Harris Papers
  Thomas H. Hicks Papers, 1821–1881, MS 1263
  Thomas H. Hicks Papers, 1860–1862, MS 1313
  Thomas H. Hicks Papers, 1860–1865, MS 2104
  Reverdy Johnson Collection
  James Alfred Pearce Papers
  Levin Richardson Papers
Chapel Hill, North Carolina
 Southern Historical Collection, Wilson Library, University of North Carolina at
   Chapel Hill
  James Guthrie Letters
  John Judge Papers
  Basil Manly Papers
  William Porcher Miles Papers (microfilm)
  Henry Page Papers
  Frank F. Steel Letters
  M. Jeff Thompson Papers
Chicago, Illinois
 Special Collections Research Center, University of Chicago Library
  Stephen A. Douglas Papers
Columbia, Missouri
 State Historical Society of Missouri
  David Rice Atchison Papers
  Alexander W. Doniphan Letters, 1861–1873, C1926
  Alexander W. Doniphan Letter, 1861, C1935
  Waldo P. Johnson Letters
  Abiel Leonard Papers

John Machir Papers
Missouri Confederate Archives, 1861
Missouri General Assembly, House of Representatives (Confederate),
    Journal, 1861
William McClung Paxton Papers
James S. Rollins Papers
John Sappington Papers
Thomas Shackelford Papers
M. Jeff Thompson Papers
Samiville Weller Letter
Woods-Holman Family Papers
Durham, North Carolina
    Special Collections, David M. Rubenstein Rare Book and Manuscript Library,
        Duke University
        Alexander Robinson Boteler Papers
        Eliza Hall Ball Gordon Boyles Papers
        John C. Breckinridge Papers
        John Jordan Crittenden Papers
        Valerius Ebert Papers
        John H. Gould Correspondence
        William Henry Seward Papers
        John Sherman Papers
        Franklin E. Smith Papers
        Alexander H. Stephens Papers
        George Hume Steuart Papers
        Robert Augustus Toombs Correspondence
        Shadrach Ward Correspondence
        Joseph S. Williams Letters
        Wright-Harris Papers
Frankfort, Kentucky
    Kentucky Department for Libraries and Archives
        Governor's Correspondence, 1859–1861, Governor Beriah Magoffin
    Kentucky Historical Society
        Pattie A. Curd Papers
        George W. Johnson Papers
        James Moffett Letters
Jefferson City, Missouri
    Missouri State Archives
        Claiborne Fox Jackson Papers, 1861, Office of the Governor, Record Group 3.15
        Missouri-Kansas Border War Collection, 1858–1862, Office of the Secretary of
            State, Record Group 5
        Records of the 1861 Missouri Convention, Office of the Secretary of State,
            Record Group 5.23

Louisville, Kentucky
  Filson Historical Society
    Bodley Family Papers
    Papers of Orlando Brown
    Bullitt Family Papers—Oxmoor Collection
    Clark-Strater-Watson Family Papers
    John J. Crittenden Letters
    Phebe Wood Coburn Daugherty Papers
    Alexander Pericles Farnsley Letters
    Frost Family Papers
    George Gondy Letter
    Green Family Papers
    Grigsby Collection
    James Guthrie Miscellaneous Papers
    Samuel Haycraft Journal
    Holyoke Family Papers
    Johnson Family Papers
    Johnston Family Papers
    Jones Family Papers
    Humphrey Marshall Miscellaneous Papers
    Moxley-Offutt Papers
    Preston Family Papers—Davie Collection
    Preston Family Papers—Joyes Collection
    Sanders Family Papers
    Alexander Hugh Holmes Stuart Letter
    Uncle Billie Letter
    Yandell Family Papers
    Richard Yates Papers
Philadelphia, Pennsylvania
  Historical Society of Pennsylvania
    James Buchanan Papers (microfilm)
Rochester, New York
  Rush Rhees Library, Department of Rare Books, Manuscripts and Archives,
      University of Rochester
    Papers of William Henry Seward (microfilm)
Saint Louis, Missouri
  Missouri Museum of History
    James O. Broadhead Papers
    Hamilton R. Gamble Papers
Washington, DC
  Division of Manuscripts, Library of Congress
    Papers of Edward Bates (microfilm)
    Papers of Thomas F. Bayard

Papers of the Blair Family (microfilm)

Breckinridge Family Papers

Papers of John Jordan Crittenden (microfilm)

Abraham Lincoln Papers (available at https://memory.loc.gov/ammem/alhtml
/malhome.html)

William C. Rives Papers

Wilmington, Delaware

Delaware Historical Society, Manuscripts Division

James A. Bayard, Jr., Family Letters

Brobson Family Papers

Callery Collection of the Bayard Family Papers

William Canby Journals

Gibbons Family Papers

John P. Gillis Papers

Hagley Museum and Library

Henry Du Pont Papers, Winterthur Manuscripts, Group 7

Samuel Francis Du Pont Papers, Winterthur Manuscripts, Group 9

Sophie Madeleine Du Pont Papers, Winterthur Manuscripts, Group 9

GOVERNMENT DOCUMENTS

*Acts of the General Assembly of the Commonwealth of Kentucky, Passed at the Called
Session Which Was Begun and Held in the City of Frankfort, on Thursday, the 17th Day
of January, 1861, and Ended on Friday, the Fifth Day of April, 1861.* Frankfort, KY:
Jno. B. Major, 1861.

Congressional Globe, 36th–37th Congresses.

*The Declaration of Independence and the Constitution of the Provisional Government of
the State of Kentucky, Together with the Messages of the Governor.* Bowling Green,
KY: 1861.

Delaware General Assembly. *Journal of the House of Representatives of the State of
Delaware, at a Session of the General Assembly, Convened and Held at Dover, on
Tuesday, the First of January, in the Year of Our Lord One Thousand Eight Hundred
and Sixty-One, and of the Independence of the United States the Eighty-Fifth.*
Wilmington, DE: Henry Eckel Printer, 1861.

———. *Journal of the Senate of the State of Delaware, at a Session of the General
Assembly, Commenced and Held at Dover, on Tuesday, the First Day of January, in the
Year of Our Lord One Thousand Eight Hundred and Sixty-One, and of the Indepen-
dence of the United States the Eighty-Fifth.* Dover, DE: James Kirk Printer, 1861.

Department of the Interior. *Manufactures of the United States in 1860; Compiled from
the Original Returns of the Eighth Census, under the Direction of the Secretary of the
Interior.* Washington, DC: Government Printing Office, 1865.

*Journal and Proceedings of the Convention of the Border Slave States, Begun and Held in
the City of Frankfort, State of Kentucky, on the 27th Day of May, 1861.* Frankfort:
Kentucky Yeoman Office, 1861.

Journal and Proceedings of the Missouri State Convention, Held at Jefferson City and St. Louis, March 1861. Saint Louis: George Knapp, 1861.

Journal of the Called Session of the House of Representatives of the Commonwealth of Kentucky, Begun and Held in the Town of Frankfort, on Monday, the Sixth Day of May, in the Year of Our Lord 1861, and of the Commonwealth the Sixty-Ninth. Frankfort, KY: John B. Major Printer, 1861.

Journal of the Called Session of the House of Representatives of the Commonwealth of Kentucky, Begun and Held in the Town of Frankfort, on Thursday the Seventeenth Day of January, in the Year of Our Lord 1861, and of the Commonwealth the Sixty-Ninth. Frankfort: Kentucky Yeoman Office, 1861.

Journal of the Called Session of the Senate of the Commonwealth of Kentucky, Begun and Held in the Town of Frankfort, on Monday, the Sixth Day of May, in the Year of Our Lord 1861, and of the Commonwealth the Sixty-Ninth. Frankfort, KY: Jno. B. Major, 1861.

Journal of the Called Session of the Senate of the Commonwealth of Kentucky, Begun and Held in the Town of Frankfort, on Thursday the Seventeenth Day of January, in the Year of Our Lord 1861, and of the Commonwealth the Sixty-Ninth. Frankfort: Kentucky Yeoman Office, 1861.

Journal of the House of Representatives of the State of Missouri, at the First Session of the Twenty-First General Assembly. Jefferson City, MO: W.G. Cheeney, 1861.

Journal of the [Mississippi] State Convention and Ordinances and Resolutions, Adopted in January 1861, with an Appendix. Jackson, MS: E. Barksdale State Printer, 1861.

Journal of the Missouri State Convention, Held at Jefferson City, July, 1861. Saint Louis: George Knapp, 1861.

Journal of the Senate, Extra Session of the Rebel Legislature, Called Together by a Proclamation of C. F. Jackson, Begun and Held at the Town of Neosho, Newton County, Missouri, on the Twenty-First Day of October, Eighteen Hundred and Sixty-One. Washington, DC: Statute Law Book Company, 1916.

Kennedy, Joseph C. G. *Agriculture of the United States in 1860; Compiled from the Original Returns of the Eighth Census.* Washington, DC: Government Printing Office, 1864.

———. *Population of the United States in 1860: Compiled from the Original Returns of the Eighth Census.* Washington, DC: Government Printing Office, 1864.

Maryland General Assembly. *House and Senate Documents, 1861.* Frederick, MD: E. S. Riley Printer, 1861.

———. *Journal of the Proceedings of the House of Delegates, in Extra Session.* Frederick, MD: Elihu S. Riley, 1861.

Maryland Senate. *Journal of Proceedings of the Senate of Maryland, in Extra Session, April 1861.* Frederick, MD: Beale H. Richardson, 1861.

Proceedings of the Missouri State Convention, Held at Jefferson City, July, 1861. Saint Louis: George Knapp, 1861.

United States Census, 1830–60.

U.S. Congress. House. *Report of the Select Committee of Thirty-Three on the Disturbed Condition of the Country.* 36th Cong., 2nd Sess., Volume I, Number 31.

U.S. Congress. Senate. *Report of the Select Committee of Thirteen on the Disturbed Condition of the Country*. 36th Cong., 2nd Sess., Number 288.

The War of the Rebellion: A Compilation of the Official Records of the Union and Confederate Armies. 128 vols. Washington, DC: Government Printing Office, 1880–1901.

PRINTED POLITICAL DOCUMENTS AND REFERENCE SOURCES

Brown, Dwight H. *State of Missouri: Official Manual for Years Nineteen-Thirty-Five and Nineteen-Thirty-Six*. Jefferson City, MO: Midland, n.d.

Chittenden, L. E. *A Report of the Debates and Proceedings in Secret Sessions of the Conference Convention for Proposing Amendments to the Constitution of the United States, Held at Washington, D.C., in February, A.D. 1861*. New York: D. Appleton, 1864.

Dubin, Michael J. *Party Affiliations in the State Legislatures: A Year by Year Summary, 1796–2006*. Jefferson, NC: McFarland, 2007.

———. *United States Congressional Elections, 1787–1997: The Official Results of the Elections of the 1st through the 105th Congresses*. Jefferson, NC: McFarland, 1998.

———. *United States Gubernatorial Elections, 1776–1860*. Jefferson, NC: McFarland, 2003.

———. *United States Presidential Elections, 1788–1860: The Official Results by County and State*. Jefferson, NC: McFarland, 2002.

Dumond, Dwight Lowell, ed. *Southern Editorials on Secession*. New York: Century, 1931.

Freehling, William W., and Craig M. Simpson, eds. *Secession Debated: Georgia's Showdown in 1860*. New York: Oxford University Press, 1992.

———. *Showdown in Virginia: The 1861 Convention and the Fate of the Union*. Charlottesville: University of Virginia Press, 2010.

Hall, Clayton Coleman. *Baltimore: Its History and Its People*. 3 vols. New York: Lewis Historical, 1912.

Halstead, Murat. *Three against Lincoln: Murat Halstead Reports the Caucuses of 1860*. Edited by William B. Hesseltine. Baton Rouge: Louisiana State University Press, 1960.

Howard, George Washington. *The Monumental City: Its Past History and Present Resources*. Baltimore: J. D. Ehlers, 1873.

Johnson, Allen, ed. *Dictionary of American Biography*. 22 vols. New York: Charles Scribner's Sons, 1928–58.

Johnson, Charles W., ed. *Proceedings of the First Three Republican National Conventions of 1856, 1860, and 1864, including Proceedings of the Antecedent National Convention Held at Pittsburg, in February, 1856, as Reported by Horace Greeley*. Minneapolis: Harrison and Smith, 1893.

Leopard, Buel, and Floyd C. Shoemaker, eds. *The Messages and Proclamations of the Governors of the State of Missouri*. 12 vols. Columbia: State Historical Society of Missouri, 1922–.

National Democratic Executive Committee. *Proceedings of the Conventions at Charleston and Baltimore*. Washington, DC: National Democratic Executive Committee, 1860.

Parsons, Stanley B., William W. Beach, and Michael J. Dubin. *United States Congressional Districts and Data, 1843–1883*. New York: Greenwood, 1986.

Perkins, Howard Cecil, ed. *Northern Editorials on Secession*. 2 vols. New York: D. Appleton, 1942.

Reese, George H., ed. *Proceedings of the Virginia State Convention of 1861, February 13–May 1*. 4 vols. Richmond: Virginia State Library, 1965.

Smith, William R. *The History and the Debates of the Convention of the People of Alabama, Begun and Held in the City of Montgomery, on the Seventh Day of January, 1861, in Which Is Preserved the Speeches of the Secret Sessions, and Many Valuable State Papers*. Montgomery, AL: Atlanta, White, Pfister, 1861.

Stegmaier, Mark J., ed. *Henry Adams in the Secession Crisis: Dispatches to the "Boston Daily Advertiser": December 1860–March 1861*. Baton Rouge: Louisiana State University Press, 2012.

Warner, Ezra J., and W. Buck Yearns. *Biographical Register of the Confederate Congress*. Baton Rouge: Louisiana State University Press, 1975.

NEWSPAPERS AND MAGAZINES

Albany Evening Journal (New York)
Baltimore American
Baltimore Sun
Columbus Daily Ohio Statesman
DeBow's Review
Frankfort Commonwealth (Kentucky)
Liberty Weekly Tribune (Missouri)
Louisville Daily Courier
Louisville Daily Journal
Marshall Democrat (Missouri)

New Lisbon Anti-slavery Bugle (Ohio)
New York Daily Tribune
New York Herald
Philadelphia Inquirer
St. Louis Daily Missouri Republican
Washington D.C. Constitution
Washington D.C. National Republican
Wilmington Delaware Inquirer
Wilmington Delaware Republican

PRINTED DIARIES, LETTER COLLECTIONS, MEMOIRS, REMINISCENCES, AND SPEECHES

Adams, Charles Francis, Jr. *Charles Francis Adams, 1835–1915: An Autobiography*. Boston: Houghton Mifflin, 1916.

Bates, Edward. *The Diary of Edward Bates, 1859–1866*. Edited by Howard K. Beale. Washington, DC: Government Printing Office, 1933.

Bingham, George Caleb. *"But I Forget That I Am a Painter and Not a Politician": The Letters of George Caleb Bingham*. Edited by Lynn Wolf Gentzler and Roger E. Robinson. Columbia: State Historical Society of Missouri, 2011.

Bond, Priscilla. *A Maryland Bride in the Deep South*. Edited by Kimberly Harrison. Baton Rouge: Louisiana State University Press, 2006.

Breckinridge, Robert J. *The Civil War: Its Nature and End*. Cincinnati: Office of the Danville Review, 1861.

———. *Two Speeches of Rev. Robert J. Breckinridge, D.D., LL.D., on the State of the Country*. Cincinnati: E. Morgan, 1862.

Brown, George William. *Baltimore and the Nineteenth of April, 1861: A Study of the War*. 1887. Reprint, Baltimore: Johns Hopkins University Press, 2001.

Butler, Benjamin F. *Private and Official Correspondence of Gen. Benjamin F. Butler during the Period of the Civil War.* Edited by Benjamin F. Butler and Jessie Ames Marshall. 5 vols. Norwood, MA: Plimpton, 1917.

Chittenden, L. E. *Recollections of President Lincoln and His Administration.* New York: Harper and Brothers, 1891.

Coleman, Mrs. Chapman, ed. *The Life of John J. Crittenden, with Selections from His Correspondence and Speeches.* 2 vols. Philadelphia: J. B. Lippincott, 1871.

Davis, Jefferson. *The Papers of Jefferson Davis.* Edited by Lynda Lasswell Crist and Mary Seaton Dix. 11 vols. Baton Rouge: Louisiana University Press, 1971–.

Duke, Basil W. *Reminiscences of General Basil W. Duke, C.S.A.* Garden City, NY: Doubleday, Page, 1911.

Glenn, William Watkins. *Between North and South: A Maryland Journalist Views the Civil War.* Edited by Bayly Ellen Marks and Mark Norton Schatz. Rutherford, NJ: Fairleigh Dickinson, 1976.

Gunderson, Robert Gray, ed. "Letters from the Washington Peace Conference of 1861." *Journal of Southern History* 17 (August 1951): 382–92.

Hart, Albert Bushnell, ed. "Letters to Secretary Chase from the South, 1861." *American Historical Review* 4 (January 1899): 331–47.

Howard, Charles Morris. *Personal Recollections of Severn Teackle Wallis.* Baltimore: Daily Record, 1939.

Kennedy, John Pendleton. *The Border States: Their Power and Duty in the Present Disordered Condition of the Country.* Philadelphia: J. B. Lippincott, 1861.

———. *The Great Drama: An Appeal to Maryland.* Baltimore: J. D. Toy, 1861.

Lincoln, Abraham. *The Collected Works of Abraham Lincoln.* Edited by Roy P. Basler. 8 vols. New Brunswick, NJ: Rutgers University Press, 1953–55.

Moore, Frank, ed. *The Rebellion Record: A Diary of American Events, with Documents, Narratives, Illustrative Incidents, Poetry, Etc.* 11 vols. New York: D. Van Norstrand, 1861–68.

National Democratic Executive Committee. *Speeches of Hon. Humphrey Marshall & Hon. B. F. Hallett, in the City of Washington, on the Nomination of Breckinridge and Lane.* Washington, DC: National Democratic Executive Committee, 1860.

Phillips, Ulrich Bonnell, ed. *The Correspondence of Robert Toombs, Alexander Stephens, and Howell Cobb.* Washington, DC: Government Printing Office, 1913.

Report of the Ceremonies on the Fourth of July, 1857, at the Laying of the Corner Stone of a Nation Monument, to be Erected near Lexington, Kentucky, to the Memory of Henry Clay; Together with the Oration Delivered on the Occasion, by the Rev. Robert J. Breckinridge, D.D., L.L.D. Lexington, KY: Clay Monument Association, 1857.

Rowan, Steve, trans. *Germans for a Free Missouri: Translations from the St. Louis Radical Press, 1857–1862.* Columbia: University of Missouri Press, 1983.

Shaler, Nathaniel Southgate. "The Border State Men of the Civil War." *Atlantic Monthly* 69 (February 1892): 245–57.

Snead, Thomas L. *The Fight for Missouri: From the Election of Lincoln to the Death of Lyon.* New York: Charles Scribner's Sons, 1886.

A Southern Citizen [Reverdy Johnson]. *Remarks on Popular Sovereignty, as Maintained and Denied Respectively by Judge Douglas, and Attorney-General Black.* Baltimore: Murphy, 1859.

Speed, Thomas. *The Union Cause in Kentucky, 1860–1865.* New York: G. P. Putnam's Sons, 1911.

Stampp, Kenneth M., ed. "Letters from the Washington Peace Conference of 1861." *Journal of Southern History* 9 (August 1943): 394–403.

Underwood, Josie. *Josie Underwood's Civil War Diary.* Edited by Nancy Disher Baird. Lexington: University Press of Kentucky, 2009.

Wakelyn, Jon, ed. *Southern Pamphlets on Secession, November 1860–April 1861.* Chapel Hill: University of North Carolina Press, 1996.

————, ed. *Southern Unionist Pamphlets and the Civil War.* Columbia: University of Missouri Press, 1999.

Wallis, Severn Teackle. *Writings of Severn Teackle Wallis.* 4 vols. Baltimore: John Murphy, 1896.

Webb, W. L. *Battles and Biographies of Missourians, or the Civil War Period of Our State.* Kansas City: Hudson-Kimberly, 1900.

ONLINE SOURCES

"Biographical Directory of the United States Congress, 1774–Present." Accessed February 25, 2013. http://bioguide.congress.gov.

"Indexed United States Manuscript Census Records." Accessed March 18, 2013. www .ancestry.com.

National Park Service. "Lexington Cemetery and Henry Clay Monument." Accessed February 20, 2013. www.nps.gov/nr/travel/lexington/lce.htm.

Supreme Court of the United States. "Members of the Supreme Court of the United States." Accessed November 14, 2012. www.supremecourt.gov/about/members.aspx.

United States Census Bureau. "Quick Facts." Accessed May 31, 2012. www.quickfacts .census.gov/qfd/index.html.

————. "Rank by Population of the 100 Largest Urban Places, Listed Alphabetically by State: 1790–1990." Accessed February 11, 2013. www.census.gov/population /www/documentation/twps0027/tab01.txt.

University of Virginia Geospatial and Statistical Data Center. "University of Virginia Historical Census Browser." Accessed May 11, 2012. http://mapserver.lib.virginia .edu/collections/. Site discontinued.

Wallis, John Joseph. "NBER/University of Maryland State Constitutions Project." Accessed May 20, 2014. www.stateconstitutions.umd.edu.

Secondary Sources

BOOKS

Abbott, Richard H. *The Republican Party and the South, 1855–1877: The First Southern Strategy.* Chapel Hill: University of North Carolina Press, 1986.

Altschuler, Glenn C., and Stuart M. Blumin. *Rude Republic: Americans and Their Politics in the Nineteenth Century*. Princeton, NJ: Princeton University Press, 2000.

Anbinder, Tyler. *Nativism and Slavery: The Northern Know Nothings and the Politics of the 1850s*. New York: Oxford University Press, 1992.

Anderson, Kristen Layne. *Abolitionizing Missouri: German Immigrants and Racial Ideology in Nineteenth-Century America*. Baton Rouge: Louisiana State University Press, 2016.

Arenson, Adam. *The Great Heart of the Republic: St. Louis and the Cultural Civil War*. Cambridge, MA: Harvard University Press, 2011.

Aron, Stephen. *American Confluence: The Missouri Frontier from Borderland to Border State*. Bloomington: Indiana University Press, 2006.

———. *How the West Was Lost: The Transformation of Kentucky from Daniel Boone to Henry Clay*. Baltimore: Johns Hopkins University Press, 1996.

Ashworth, John. *The Republic in Crisis, 1848–1861*. Cambridge: Cambridge University Press, 2012.

Astor, Aaron. *Rebels on the Border: Civil War, Emancipation, and the Reconstruction of Kentucky and Missouri*. Baton Rouge: Louisiana State University Press, 2012.

Atkins, Jonathan M. *Parties, Politics, and the Sectional Conflict in Tennessee, 1832–1861*. Knoxville: University of Tennessee Press, 1997.

Ayers, Edward L. *In the Presence of Mine Enemies: War in the Heart of America, 1859–1863*. New York: W. W. Norton, 2003.

Baker, Jean H. *Affairs of Party: The Political Culture of Northern Democrats in the Mid-Nineteenth Century*. Ithaca, NY: Cornell University Press, 1983.

———. *Ambivalent Americans: The Know-Nothing Party in Maryland*. Baltimore: Johns Hopkins University Press, 1977.

———. *The Politics of Continuity: Maryland Political Parties from 1858 to 1870*. Baltimore: Johns Hopkins University Press, 1973.

Barnes, L. Diane, Brian Schoen, and Frank Towers, eds. *The Old South's Modern Worlds: Slavery, Region, and Nation in the Age of Progress*. New York: Oxford University Press, 2011.

Barnwell, John. *Love of Order: South Carolina's First Secession Crisis*. Chapel Hill: University of North Carolina Press, 1982.

Bensel, Richard Franklin. *The American Ballot Box in the Mid-Nineteenth Century*. Cambridge: Cambridge University Press, 2004.

Berlin, Ira. *Generations of Captivity: A History of African-American Slaves*. Cambridge, MA: Belknap Press of Harvard University Press, 2003.

———. *Slaves without Masters: The Free Negro in the Antebellum South*. New York: Pantheon, 1974.

Black, Andrew R. *John Pendleton Kennedy: Early American Novelist, Whig Statesman, and Ardent Nationalist*. Baton Rouge: Louisiana State University Press, 2016.

Bohner, Charles H. *John Pendleton Kennedy: Gentleman from Baltimore*. Baltimore: Johns Hopkins University Press, 1961.

Boman, Dennis K. *Lincoln's Resolute Unionist: Hamilton Gamble, Dred Scott Dissenter and Missouri's Civil War Governor.* Baton Rouge: Louisiana State University Press, 2006.

Bonner, Robert E. *Mastering America: Southern Slaveholders and the Crisis of American Nationhood.* Cambridge: Cambridge University Press, 2009.

Bowman, Shearer Davis. *At the Precipice: Americans North and South during the Secession Crisis.* Chapel Hill: University of North Carolina Press, 2010.

Brown, Thomas. *Politics and Statesmanship: Essays on the American Whig Party.* New York: Columbia University Press, 1985.

Browning, Judkin. *Shifting Loyalties: The Union Occupation of Eastern North Carolina.* Chapel Hill: University of North Carolina Press, 2011.

Brugger, Robert J. *Maryland: A Middle Temperament, 1634–1980.* Baltimore: Johns Hopkins University Press, 1988.

Burke, Diane Mutti. *On Slavery's Border: Missouri's Small-Slaveholding Households, 1815–1865.* Athens: University of Georgia Press, 2010.

Bynum, Victoria E. *The Free State of Jones: Mississippi's Longest Civil War.* Chapel Hill: University of North Carolina Press, 2001.

Cain, Marvin R. *Lincoln's Attorney General Edward Bates of Missouri.* Columbia: University of Missouri Press, 1965.

Campbell, Stanley W. *The Slave Catchers: Enforcement of the Fugitive Slave Law, 1850–1860.* Chapel Hill: University of North Carolina Press, 1968.

Channing, Steven A. *Crisis of Fear: Secession in South Carolina.* New York: Simon and Schuster, 1970.

Childers, Christopher. *The Failure of Popular Sovereignty: Slavery, Manifest Destiny, and the Radicalization of Southern Politics.* Lawrence: University Press of Kansas, 2012.

Coclanis, Peter A. *The Shadow of a Dream: Economic Life and Death in the South Carolina Low Country, 1670–1920.* New York: Oxford University Press, 1989.

Coleman, J. Winston. *Slavery Times in Kentucky.* Chapel Hill: University of North Carolina Press, 1940.

Cooper, William J., Jr. *Jefferson Davis, American.* New York: Alfred A. Knopf, 2000.

———. *Liberty and Slavery: Southern Politics to 1860.* New York: Alfred A. Knopf, 1983.

———. *The South and the Politics of Slavery, 1828–1856.* Baton Rouge: Louisiana State University Press, 1978.

———. *We Have the War upon Us: The Onset of the Civil War, November 1860–April 1861.* New York: Alfred A. Knopf, 2012.

Coryell, Janet L. *Neither Heroine nor Fool: Anna Ella Carroll of Maryland.* Kent, OH: Kent State University Press, 1990.

Coulter, E. Merton. *The Civil War and Readjustment in Kentucky.* Chapel Hill: University of North Carolina Press, 1926.

Craig, Berry F. *Kentucky Confederates: Secession, Civil War, and the Jackson Purchase.* Lexington: University Press of Kentucky, 2014.

Crapol, Edward P. *John Tyler: The Accidental President.* Chapel Hill: University of North Carolina Press, 2006.

Craven, Avery. *The Coming of the Civil War*. Chicago: University of Chicago Press, 1942.

———. *The Growth of Southern Nationalism, 1848–1861*. Baton Rouge: Louisiana State University Press, 1953.

Crenshaw, Ollinger. *The Slave States in the Presidential Election of 1860*. Baltimore: Johns Hopkins University Press, 1943.

Crofts, Daniel W. *Lincoln and the Politics of Slavery: The Other Thirteenth Amendment and the Struggle to Save the Union*. Chapel Hill: University of North Carolina Press, 2016.

———. *Reluctant Confederates: Upper South Unionists in the Secession Crisis*. Chapel Hill: University of North Carolina Press, 1989.

Current, Richard Nelson. *Lincoln and the First Shot*. New York: Harper and Row, 1963.

———. *Lincoln's Loyalists: Union Soldiers from the Confederacy*. Boston: Northeastern University Press, 1992.

Curry, Richard O. *A House Divided: A Study of Statehood Politics and the Copperhead Movement in West Virginia*. Pittsburgh: University of Pittsburgh Press, 1964.

Daniel, Larry J. *Shiloh: The Battle That Changed the Civil War*. New York: Simon and Schuster, 1997.

Davis, William C. *Breckinridge: Statesman, Soldier, Symbol*. Baton Rouge: Louisiana State University Press, 1974.

———. *The Orphan Brigade: The Kentucky Confederates Who Couldn't Go Home*. Garden City, NY: Doubleday, 1980.

DeCredico, Mary A. *Patriotism for Profit: Georgia's Urban Entrepreneurs and the Confederate War Effort*. Chapel Hill: University of North Carolina Press, 1990.

Degler, Carl N. *The Other South: Southern Dissenters in the Nineteenth Century*. New York: Harper and Row, 1974.

Denton, Lawrence M. *A Southern Star for Maryland: Maryland and the Secession Crisis, 1860–1861*. Baltimore: Publishing Concepts, 1995.

Dew, Charles B. *Apostles of Disunion: Southern Secession Commissioners and the Causes of the Civil War*. Charlottesville: University of Virginia Press, 2001.

Deyle, Steven. *Carry Me Back: The Domestic Slave Trade in American Life*. New York: Oxford University Press, 2005.

Dollar, Kent T., Larry H. Whiteaker, and W. Calvin Dickinson, eds. *Sister States, Enemy States: The Civil War in Kentucky and Tennessee*. Lexington: University Press of Kentucky, 2009.

Donald, David Herbert. *Lincoln*. New York: Simon and Schuster, 1995.

Duberman, Martin. *Charles Francis Adams, 1807–1886*. Stanford, CA: Stanford University Press, 1960.

Dumond, Dwight Lowell. *The Secession Movement, 1860–1861*. New York: Macmillan, 1931.

Dyer, Thomas G. *Secret Yankees: The Union Circle in Confederate Atlanta*. Baltimore: Johns Hopkins University Press, 1999.

Egerton, Douglas R. *Year of Meteors: Stephen Douglas, Abraham Lincoln, and the Election That Brought on the Civil War*. New York: Bloomsbury, 2010.

Egnal, Marc. *Clash of Extremes: The Economic Origins of the Civil War*. New York: Hill and Wang, 2009.

Epps, Kristen. *Slavery on the Periphery: The Kansas-Missouri Border in the Antebellum and Civil War Eras.* Athens: University of Georgia Press, 2016.

Essah, Patience. *A House Divided: Slavery and Emancipation in Delaware, 1638–1865.* Charlottesville: University Press of Virginia, 1996.

Etcheson, Nicole. *Bleeding Kansas: Contested Liberty in the Civil War Era.* Lawrence: University Press of Kansas, 2004.

———. *The Emerging Midwest: Upland Southerners and the Political Culture of the Old Northwest, 1787–1861.* Bloomington: Indiana University Press, 1996.

———. *A Generation at War: The Civil War Era in a Northern Community.* Lawrence: University Press of Kansas, 2011.

Evitts, William J. *A Matter of Allegiances: Maryland from 1850 to 1861.* Baltimore: Johns Hopkins University Press, 1974.

Eyal, Yonatan. *The Young America Movement and the Transformation of the Democratic Party, 1828–1861.* Cambridge: Cambridge University Press, 2007.

Fehrenbacher, Don E. *The Dred Scott Case: Its Significance in American Law and Politics.* New York: Oxford University Press, 1978.

———. *Prelude to Greatness: Lincoln in the 1850s.* Stanford, CA: Stanford University Press, 1962.

———. *The Slaveholding Republic: An Account of the United States Government's Relations to Slavery.* Completed and edited by Ward M. McAfee. New York: Oxford University Press, 2001.

Fellman, Michael. *Inside War: The Guerrilla Conflict in Missouri during the American Civil War.* New York: Oxford University Press, 1989.

Fields, Barbara Jeanne. *Slavery and Freedom on the Middle Ground: Maryland during the Nineteenth Century.* New Haven, CT: Yale University Press, 1985.

Finck, James W. *Divided Loyalties: Kentucky's Struggle for Armed Neutrality in the Civil War.* El Dorado Hills, CA: Savas Beatie, 2012.

Finkelman, Paul, ed. *His Soul Goes Marching On: Responses to John Brown and the Harpers Ferry Raid.* Charlottesville: University Press of Virginia, 1995.

Foner, Eric. *The Fiery Trial: Abraham Lincoln and American Slavery.* New York: W. W. Norton, 2010.

———. *Free Soil, Free Labor, Free Men: The Ideology of the Republican Party before the Civil War.* New York: Oxford University Press, 1970.

Forbes, Robert Pierce. *The Missouri Compromise and Its Aftermath.* Chapel Hill: University of North Carolina Press, 2007.

Ford, Bridget. *Bonds of Union: Religion, Race, and Politics in a Civil War Borderland.* Chapel Hill: University of North Carolina Press, 2016.

Ford, Lacy K., Jr. *Deliver Us from Evil: The Slavery Question in the Old South.* New York: Oxford University Press, 2009.

———. *Origins of Southern Radicalism: The South Carolina Upcountry, 1800–1860.* New York: Oxford University Press, 1988.

Forgie, George B. *Patricide in the House Divided: A Psychological Interpretation of Lincoln and His Age.* New York: W. W. Norton, 1979.

Franklin, John Hope, and Loren Schweninger. *Runaway Slaves: Rebels on the Plantation.* New York: Oxford University Press, 1999.

Fredrickson, George M. *The Black Image in the White Mind: The Debate on Afro-American Character and Destiny, 1817–1914.* New York: Harper and Row, 1971.

Freehling, Alison Goodyear. *Drift toward Dissolution: The Virginia Slavery Debate of 1831–1832.* Baton Rouge: Louisiana State University Press, 1982.

Freehling, William W. *Prelude to Civil War: The Nullification Controversy in South Carolina, 1816–1836.* New York: Oxford University Press, 1965.

———. *The Road to Disunion.* 2 vols. New York: Oxford University Press, 1990–2007.

———. *The South vs. the South: How Anti-Confederate Southerners Shaped the Course of the Civil War.* New York: Oxford University Press, 2001.

Gallagher, Gary W. *The Union War.* Cambridge: Harvard University Press, 2011.

Gallagher, Gary W., and Rachel A. Shelden, eds. *A Political Nation: New Directions in Mid-Nineteenth-Century American Political History.* Charlottesville: University of Virginia Press, 2012.

Geiger, Mark. *Financial Fraud and Guerrilla Violence in Missouri's Civil War, 1861–1865.* New Haven, CT: Yale University Press, 2010.

Gerteis, Louis S. *Civil War St. Louis.* Lawrence: University Press of Kansas, 2001.

Gienapp, William E. *The Origins of the Republican Party, 1852–1856.* New York: Oxford University Press, 1987.

Goldfield, David R. *Urban Growth in the Age of Sectionalism: Virginia, 1847–1861.* Baton Rouge: Louisiana State University Press, 1977.

Goodheart, Adam. *1861: The Civil War Awakening.* New York: Alfred A. Knopf, 2011.

Goodwin, Doris Kearns. *Team of Rivals: The Political Genius of Abraham Lincoln.* New York: Simon and Schuster, 2005.

Greenberg, Kenneth S. *Masters and Statesmen: The Political Culture of American Slavery.* Baltimore: Johns Hopkins University Press, 1985.

Grimstead, David. *American Mobbing, 1828–1861: Toward Civil War.* New York: Oxford University Press, 1998.

Grivno, Max. *Gleanings of Freedom: Free and Slave Labor along the Mason-Dixon Line, 1790–1860.* Urbana: University of Illinois Press, 2011.

Gudmestad, Robert H. *Steamboats and the Rise of the Cotton Kingdom.* Baton Rouge: Louisiana State University Press, 2011.

———. *A Troublesome Commerce: The Transformation of the Interstate Slave Trade.* Baton Rouge: Louisiana State University Press, 2003.

Gunderson, Robert Gray. *Old Gentlemen's Convention: The Washington Peace Conference of 1861.* Madison: University of Wisconsin Press, 1961.

Hahn, Steven. *A Nation under Our Feet: Black Political Struggles in the Rural South from Slavery to the Great Migration.* Cambridge, MA: Belknap Press of Harvard University Press, 2003.

Hancock, Harold Bell. *Delaware during the Civil War: A Political History.* Wilmington: Historical Society of Delaware, 1961.

Harlow, Luke E. *Religion, Race, and the Making of Confederate Kentucky, 1830–1880.* New York: Cambridge University Press, 2014.

Harris, William C. *Lincoln and the Border States: Preserving the Union.* Lawrence: University Press of Kansas, 2011.

———. *Lincoln's Rise to the Presidency.* Lawrence: University Press of Kansas, 2007.

Harrison, Lowell H. *The Civil War in Kentucky.* Lexington: University Press of Kentucky, 1975.

Harrison, Lowell H., and James C. Klotter. *A New History of Kentucky.* Lexington: University Press of Kentucky, 1997.

Harrold, Stanley. *The Abolitionists and the South, 1831–1861.* Lexington: University Press of Kentucky, 1995.

———. *Border War: Fighting over Slavery before the Civil War.* Chapel Hill: University of North Carolina Press, 2010.

Heidler, David S. *Pulling the Temple Down: The Fire-Eaters and the Destruction of the Union.* Mechanicsburg, PA: Stackpole, 1994.

Henig, Gerald S. *Henry Winter Davis: Antebellum and Civil War Congressman from Maryland.* New York: Twayne, 1973.

Holt, Michael F. *The Fate of Their Country: Politicians, Slavery Extension, and the Coming of the Civil War.* New York: Hill and Wang, 2004.

———. *The Political Crisis of the 1850s.* New York: John Wiley and Sons, 1978.

Holzer, Harold. *Lincoln at Cooper Union: The Speech That Made Abraham Lincoln President.* New York: Simon and Schuster, 2004.

———. *Lincoln President-Elect: Abraham Lincoln and the Great Secession Winter, 1860–1861.* New York: Simon and Schuster, 2008.

Howe, Daniel Walker. *The Political Culture of the American Whigs.* Chicago: University of Chicago Press, 1979.

Hurt, R. Douglas. *Agriculture and Slavery in Missouri's Little Dixie.* Columbia: University of Missouri Press, 1992.

Johannsen, Robert W. *Stephen A. Douglas.* New York: Oxford University Press, 1973.

———. *To the Halls of the Montezumas: The Mexican War in the American Imagination.* New York: Oxford University Press, 1985.

Johnson, Michael P. *Toward a Patriarchal Republic: The Secession of Georgia.* Baton Rouge: Louisiana State University Press, 1977.

Johnson, Michael P., and James L. Roark. *Black Masters: A Free Family of Color in the Old South.* New York: W. W. Norton, 1984.

Johnson, Walter. *Soul by Soul: Life inside the Antebellum Slave Market.* Cambridge, MA: Harvard University Press, 1999.

Kaye, Anthony E. *Joining Places: Slave Neighborhoods in the Old South.* Chapel Hill: University of North Carolina Press, 2007.

Kirwan, Albert D. *John J. Crittenden: The Struggle for the Union.* Lexington: University Press of Kentucky, 1962.

Klein, Maury. *Days of Defiance: Sumter, Secession, and the Coming of the Civil War.* New York: Alfred A. Knopf, 1997.

Klotter, James C. *The Breckinridges of Kentucky, 1760–1981.* Lexington: University Press of Kentucky, 1986.

Knoles, George Harmon, ed. *The Crisis of the Union, 1860–1861*. Baton Rouge: Louisiana State University Press, 1965.

Knupfer, Peter B. *The Union as It Is: Constitutional Unionism and Sectional Compromise, 1787–1861*. Chapel Hill: University of North Carolina Press, 1991.

Landis, Michael Todd. *Northern Men with Southern Loyalties: The Democratic Party and the Sectional Crisis*. Ithaca, NY: Cornell University Press, 2014.

Lankford, Nelson D. *Cry Havoc! The Crooked Road to Civil War, 1861*. New York: Viking, 2007.

Launius, Roger D. *Alexander William Doniphan: Portrait of a Missouri Moderate*. Columbia: University of Missouri Press, 1997.

Leonard, Elizabeth D. *Lincoln's Forgotten Ally: Judge Advocate General Joseph Holt of Kentucky*. Chapel Hill: University of North Carolina Press, 2011.

Levine, Bruce. *Half Slave and Half Free: The Roots of the Civil War*. New York: Hill and Wang, 1992.

Lewis, Patrick A. *For Slavery and Union: Benjamin Buckner and Kentucky Loyalties in the Civil War*. Lexington: University Press of Kentucky, 2015.

Link, William A. *Roots of Secession: Slavery and Politics in Antebellum Virginia*. Chapel Hill: University of North Carolina Press, 2003.

Litwack, Leon F. *North of Slavery: The Negro in the Free States, 1790–1860*. Chicago: University of Chicago Press, 1961.

Lockwood, John, and Charles Lockwood. *The Siege of Washington: The Untold Story of the Twelve Days That Shook the Union*. New York: Oxford University Press, 2011.

Lubet, Steven. *Fugitive Justice: Runaways, Rescuers, and Slavery on Trial*. Cambridge, MA: Belknap Press of Harvard University Press, 2010.

Marrs, Aaron. *Railroads in the Old South: Pursuing Progress in a Slave Society*. Baltimore: Johns Hopkins University Press, 2009.

Marshall, Anne E. *Creating a Confederate Kentucky: The Lost Cause and Civil War Memory in a Border State*. Chapel Hill: University of North Carolina Press, 2010.

Matthews, Gary R. *More American than Southern: Kentucky, Slavery, and the War for an American Ideology, 1828–1861*. Knoxville: University of Tennessee Press, 2014.

McCandless, Perry. *A History of Missouri*. Vol. 2, *1820–1860*. Columbia: University of Missouri Press, 1972.

McClintock, Russell. *Lincoln and the Decision for War: The Northern Response to Secession*. Chapel Hill: University of North Carolina Press, 2008.

McCormick, Richard P. *The Second American Party System: Party Formation in the Jacksonian Era*. Chapel Hill: University of North Carolina Press, 1966.

McGlone, Robert E. *John Brown's War against Slavery*. Cambridge: Cambridge University Press, 2009.

McKenzie, Robert Tracy. *Lincolnites and Rebels: A Divided Town in the American Civil War*. New York: Oxford University Press, 2006.

McPherson, James M. *Battle Cry of Freedom: The Civil War Era*. New York: Oxford University Press, 1988.

—————. *Tried by War: Abraham Lincoln as Commander in Chief.* New York: Penguin, 2008.

Mering, John Vollmer. *The Whig Party in Missouri.* Columbia: University of Missouri Press, 1967.

Morgan, Philip D. *Slave Counterpoint: Black Culture in the Eighteenth-Century Chesapeake and Lowcountry.* Chapel Hill: University of North Carolina Press, 1998.

Morrison, Michael A. *Slavery and the American West: The Eclipse of Manifest Destiny and the Coming of the Civil War.* Chapel Hill: University of North Carolina Press, 1997.

Mueller, Ken S. *Senator Benton and the People: Master Race Democracy on the Early American Frontiers.* DeKalb: Northern Illinois University Press, 2014.

Munroe, John A. *History of Delaware.* 2nd ed. Newark: University of Delaware Press, 1984.

Neely, Jeremy. *The Border between Them: Violence and Reconciliation on the Kansas-Missouri Line.* Columbia: University of Missouri Press, 2007.

Neely, Mark E., Jr. *The Boundaries of American Political Culture in the Civil War Era.* Chapel Hill: University of North Carolina Press, 2005.

—————. *Lincoln and the Triumph of the Nation: Constitutional Conflict in the American Civil War.* Chapel Hill: University of North Carolina Press, 2011.

Nevins, Allan. *The Ordeal of the Union.* 8 vols. New York: Charles Scribner's Sons, 1947–71.

Nichols, Roy Franklin. *The Disruption of American Democracy.* New York: Macmillan, 1948.

Oakes, James. *Freedom National: The Destruction of Slavery in the United States, 1861–1865.* New York: W. W. Norton, 2013.

—————. *The Ruling Race: A History of American Slaveholders.* New York: Alfred A. Knopf, 1982.

—————. *The Scorpion's Sting: Antislavery and the Coming of the Civil War.* New York: W. W. Norton, 2014.

Oates, Stephen B. *To Purge This Land with Blood: A Biography of John Brown.* New York: Harper and Row, 1970.

Oertel, Kristen Tegtmeier. *Bleeding Borders: Race, Gender, and Violence in Pre-Civil War Kansas.* Baton Rouge: Louisiana State University Press, 2009.

Olsen, Christopher J. *Political Culture and Secession in Mississippi: Masculinity, Honor, and the Antiparty Tradition, 1830–1860.* New York: Oxford University Press, 2000.

Parrish, William E. *Frank Blair: Lincoln's Conservative.* Columbia: University of Missouri Press, 1998.

—————. *Turbulent Partnership: Missouri and the Union, 1861–1865.* Columbia: University of Missouri Press, 1963.

Paskoff, Paul F. *Troubled Waters: Steamboat Disasters, River Improvements, and American Public Policy, 1821–1860.* Baton Rouge: Louisiana State University Press, 2007.

Phillips, Christopher. *The Civil War in the Border South.* Santa Barbara, CA: Praeger, 2014.

——. *Damned Yankee: The Life of General Nathaniel Lyon*. Columbia: University of Missouri Press, 1990.

——. *Freedom's Port: The African American Community of Baltimore, 1790–1860*. Urbana: University of Illinois Press, 1997.

——. *Missouri's Confederate: Claiborne Fox Jackson and the Creation of Southern Identity in the Border West*. Columbia: University of Missouri Press, 2000.

——. *The Rivers Ran Backward: The Civil War and the Remaking of the American Middle Border*. New York: Oxford University Press, 2016.

Piston, William Garrett, and Richard W. Hatcher III. *Wilson's Creek: The Second Battle of the Civil War and the Men Who Fought It*. Chapel Hill: University of North Carolina Press, 2000.

Potter, David M. *The Impending Crisis, 1848–1861*. Completed and edited by Don E. Fehrenbacher. New York: Harper and Row, 1976.

——. *Lincoln and His Party in the Secession Crisis*. 1942. Reprint, Baton Rouge: Louisiana State University Press, 1995.

——. *The South and the Sectional Conflict*. Baton Rouge: Louisiana State University Press, 1968.

Radcliffe, George L. *Governor Thomas H. Hicks of Maryland and the Civil War*. Baltimore: Johns Hopkins University Press, 1902.

Ramage, James A., and Andrea S. Watkins. *Kentucky Rising: Democracy, Slavery, and Culture from the Early Republic to the Civil War*. Lexington: University Press of Kentucky, 2011.

Randall, J. G. *Lincoln and the South*. Baton Rouge: Louisiana State University Press, 1946.

Rash, Nancy. *The Painting and Politics of George Caleb Bingham*. New Haven, CT: Yale University Press, 1991.

Ratner, Lorman A., and Dwight L. Teeter Jr. *Fanatics and Fire-Eaters: Newspapers and the Coming of the Civil War*. Urbana: University of Illinois Press, 2003.

Rawley, James A. *Turning Points of the Civil War*. New Bison Book Edition. Lincoln: University of Nebraska Press, 1989.

Remini, Robert V. *Henry Clay: Statesman for the Union*. New York: W. W. Norton, 1991.

Reynolds, Donald E. *Editors Make War: Southern Newspapers in the Secession Crisis*. Nashville: Vanderbilt University Press, 1966.

——. *Texas Terror: The Slave Insurrection Panic of 1860 and the Secession of the Lower South*. Baton Rouge: Louisiana State University Press, 2007.

Rhodes, James Ford. *History of the United States from the Compromise of 1850 to the Restoration of Home Rule in the South in 1877*. 8 vols. New York: Macmillan, 1906–19.

Richards, Leonard L. *The Slave Power: The Free North and Southern Domination, 1780–1860*. Baton Rouge: Louisiana State University Press, 2000.

Rockenbach, Stephen I. *War upon Our Border: Two Ohio Valley Communities Navigate the Civil War*. Charlottesville: University of Virginia Press, 2016.

Royster, Charles. *A Revolutionary People at War: The Continental Army and American Character, 1775–1783*. Chapel Hill: University of North Carolina Press, 1979.

Ruffner, Kevin Conley. *Maryland's Blue and Gray: A Border State's Union and Confederate Junior Officer Corps*. Baton Rouge: Louisiana State University Press, 1997.

Ryle, Walter Harrington. *Missouri: Union or Secession*. Nashville: George Peabody College for Teachers, 1931.

Salafia, Matthew. *Slavery's Borderland: Freedom and Bondage along the Ohio River*. Philadelphia: University of Pennsylvania Press, 2013.

Schermerhorn, Calvin. *Money over Mastery, Family over Freedom: Slavery in the Antebellum Upper South*. Baltimore: Johns Hopkins University Press, 2011.

Schoen, Brian. *The Fragile Fabric of Union: Cotton, Federal Politics, and the Global Origins of the Civil War*. Baltimore: Johns Hopkins University Press, 2009.

Scrugham, Mary. *The Peaceable Americans of 1860–1861: A Study in Public Opinion*. 1921. Reprint, New York: Octagon, 1976.

Shade, William G. *Democratizing the Old Dominion: Virginia and the Second Party System, 1824–1861*. Charlottesville: University of Virginia Press, 1996.

Shalhope, Robert E. *Sterling Price: Portrait of a Southerner*. Columbia: University of Missouri Press, 1971.

Siddali, Silvana R. *From Property to Person: Slavery and the Confiscation Acts, 1861–1862*. Baton Rouge: Louisiana State University Press, 2005.

Silbey, Joel H. *The Partisan Imperative: The Dynamics of American Politics before the Civil War*. New York: Oxford University Press, 1985.

———. *A Respectable Minority: The Democratic Party in the Civil War Era, 1860–1868*. New York: W. W. Norton, 1977.

———. *Storm over Texas: The Annexation Controversy and the Road to Civil War*. New York: Oxford University Press, 2005.

Sinha, Manisha. *The Counterrevolution of Slavery: Politics and Ideology in Antebellum South Carolina*. Chapel Hill: University of North Carolina Press, 2000.

———. *The Slave's Cause: A History of Abolition*. New Haven, CT: Yale University Press, 2016.

Slaughter, Thomas P. *Bloody Dawn: The Christiana Riot and Racial Violence in the Antebellum North*. New York: Oxford University Press, 1991.

Smiley, David L. *Lion of White Hall: The Life of Cassius M. Clay*. Madison: University of Wisconsin Press, 1962.

Smith, Edward Conrad. *The Borderland in the Civil War*. New York: Macmillan, 1927.

Smith, Elbert B. *Francis Preston Blair*. New York: Free Press, 1980.

Smith, William E. *The Francis Preston Blair Family in Politics*. 2 vols. New York: Macmillan, 1933.

Stahr, Walter. *Seward: Lincoln's Indispensable Man*. New York: Simon and Schuster, 2012.

Stampp, Kenneth M. *America in 1857: A Nation on the Brink*. New York: Oxford University Press, 1990.

———. *And the War Came: The North and the Secession Crisis, 1860–1861.* Baton Rouge: Louisiana State University Press, 1950.

Stickles, Arndt M. *Simon Bolivar Buckner: Borderland Knight.* Chapel Hill: University of North Carolina Press, 1940.

Storey, Margaret M. *Loyalty and Loss: Alabama's Unionists in the Civil War and Reconstruction.* Baton Rouge: Louisiana State University Press, 2004.

Sutherland, Daniel E., ed. *Guerrillas, Unionists, and Violence on the Confederate Home Front.* Fayetteville: University of Arkansas Press, 1999.

———. *A Savage Conflict: The Decisive Role of Guerrillas in the American Civil War.* Chapel Hill: University of North Carolina Press, 2009.

Swanberg, W. A. *First Blood: The Story of Fort Sumter.* New York: Charles Scribner's Sons, 1957.

Symonds, Craig L. *Confederate Admiral: The Life and Wars of Franklin Buchanan.* Annapolis: Naval Institute Press, 1999.

Tadman, Michael. *Speculators and Slaves: Masters, Traders, and Slaves in the Old South.* Madison: University of Wisconsin Press, 1989.

Tallant, Harold D. *Evil Necessity: Slavery and Political Culture in Antebellum Kentucky.* Lexington: University Press of Kentucky, 2003.

Taylor, Amy Murrell. *The Divided Family in Civil War America.* Chapel Hill: University of North Carolina Press, 2005.

Thomas, William G. *The Iron Way: Railroads, the Civil War, and the Making of Modern America.* New Haven, CT: Yale University Press, 2011.

Thornton, J. Mills, III. *Politics and Power in a Slave Society: Alabama, 1800–1860.* Baton Rouge: Louisiana State University Press, 1978.

Towers, Frank. *The Urban South and the Coming of the Civil War.* Charlottesville: University of Virginia Press, 2004.

Townsend, William H. *Lincoln and the Bluegrass: Slavery and Civil War in Kentucky.* Lexington: University Press of Kentucky, 1955.

Van Cleve, George William. *A Slaveholders' Union: Slavery, Politics, and the Constitution in the Early American Republic.* Chicago: University of Chicago Press, 2010.

Van Deusen, Glyndon G. *William Henry Seward.* New York: Oxford University Press, 1967.

Varon, Elizabeth R. *Disunion! The Coming of the American Civil War, 1789–1859.* Chapel Hill: University of North Carolina Press, 2008.

Voss-Hubbard, Mark. *Beyond Party: Cultures of Antipartisanship in Northern Politics before the Civil War.* Baltimore: Johns Hopkins University Press, 2002.

Wagandt, Charles Lewis. *The Mighty Revolution: Negro Emancipation in Maryland, 1862–1864.* Baltimore: Johns Hopkins University Press, 1964.

Waldstreicher, David. *Slavery's Constitution: From Revolution to Ratification.* New York: Hill and Wang, 2009.

Walther, Eric H. *The Fire-Eaters.* Baton Rouge: Louisiana State University Press, 1992.

———. *William Lowndes Yancey and the Coming of the Civil War.* Chapel Hill: University of North Carolina Press, 2006.

Wells, Jonathan Daniel. *The Origins of the Southern Middle Class: 1800–1861*. Chapel Hill: University of North Carolina Press, 2004.

Widmer, Edward. *Young America: The Flowering of Democracy in New York City*. New York: Oxford University Press, 1999.

Wilentz, Sean. *The Rise of American Democracy: Jefferson to Lincoln*. New York: W. W. Norton, 2005.

Woods, James M. *Rebellion and Realignment: Arkansas's Road to Secession*. Fayetteville: University of Arkansas Press, 1987.

Wooster, Ralph A. *The People in Power: Courthouse and Statehouse in the Lower South, 1850–1860*. Knoxville: University of Tennessee Press, 1969.

———. *Politicians, Planters, and Plain Folk: Courthouse and Statehouse in the Upper South, 1850–1860*. Knoxville: University of Tennessee Press, 1975.

———. *The Secession Conventions of the South*. Princeton, NJ: Princeton University Press, 1962.

Wright, Gavin. *The Political Economy of the Cotton South: Households, Markets, and Wealth in the Nineteenth Century*. New York: W. W. Norton, 1978.

Wright, William C. *The Secession Movement in the Middle Atlantic States*. Rutherford, NJ: Fairleigh Dickinson, 1973.

Wyatt-Brown, Bertram. *Southern Honor: Ethics and Behavior in the Old South*. New York: Oxford University Press, 1982.

ARTICLES AND ESSAYS

Alexander, Thomas B. "The Civil War as Institutional Fulfillment." *Journal of Southern History* 47 (February 1981): 3–32.

Avillo, Philip J., Jr. "The Oath and the Emergence of Slave State Republican Congressmen, 1861–1867." *Civil War History* 22 (June 1976): 164–74.

Calbert, Jack. "The Jackson Purchase and the End of the Neutrality Policy in Kentucky." *Filson Club History Quarterly* 38 (July 1964): 206–23.

Calderhead, William. "How Extensive Was the Border State Slave Trade? A New Look." *Civil War History* 18 (March 1972): 42–55.

Carroll, Stephen. "Loyalty or Secession? Missouri Politics and Sentiment before the Civil War." *Missouri Historical Society Bulletin* 19 (1972): 20–31.

Copeland, James E. "Where Were the Kentucky Unionists and Secessionists?" *Register of the Kentucky Historical Society* 71 (October 1973): 344–63.

Craig, Berry F. "Henry Cornelius Burnett: Champion of Southern Rights." *Register of the Kentucky Historical Society* 77 (Autumn 1979): 266–74.

———. "Kentucky's Rebel Press: The Jackson Purchase Newspapers in 1861." *Register of the Kentucky Historical Society* 75 (January 1977): 20–27.

Crenshaw, Ollinger. "The Speakership Contest of 1859–1860: John Sherman's Election a Cause of Disruption?" *Mississippi Valley Historical Review* 29 (December 1942): 323–38.

Crofts, Daniel W. "Joseph Holt, James Buchanan, and the Secession Crisis." In *James Buchanan and the Coming of the Civil War*, edited by John W. Quist and Michael J. Birkner, 208–36. Gainesville: University Press of Florida, 2013.

———. "Secession Winter: William Henry Seward and the Decision for War." *New York History* 65 (July 1984): 229–56.

———. "The Union Party of 1861 and the Secession Crisis." *Perspectives in American History* 11 (1977–1978): 327–76.

Dorsett, Lyle W., and Arthur H. Shaffer. "Was the Antebellum South Antiurban? A Suggestion." *Journal of Southern History* 38 (February 1972): 93–100.

Dues, Michael T. "The Pro-secessionist Governor of Kentucky: Beriah Magoffin's Credibility Gap." *Register of the Kentucky Historical Society* 67 (July 1969): 221–31.

Eidson, William G. "Louisville, Kentucky during the First Year of the Civil War." *Filson Club History Quarterly* 38 (July 1964): 224–38.

Everett, Edward G. "The Baltimore Riots, April, 1861." *Pennsylvania History* 24 (October 1957): 331–42.

Fladeland, Betty L. "Compensated Emancipation: A Rejected Alternative." *Journal of Southern History* 42 (May 1976): 169–86.

Gienapp, William E. "Abraham Lincoln and the Border States." *Journal of the Abraham Lincoln Association* 13 (1992): 13–46.

———. " 'Politics Seem to Enter into Everything': Political Culture in the North, 1840–1860." In *Essays on American Antebellum Politics, 1840–1860*, edited by Stephen E. Maizlish and John J. Kushma, 15–69. College Station: Texas A&M University Press, 1982.

Gilliam, Will D., Jr. "Kansas and Slavery in Two Lexington, Kentucky Newspapers: 1857." *Register of the Kentucky Historical Society* 49 (July 1951): 225–30.

———. "Party Regularity in Three Kentucky Elections and Union Volunteering." *Journal of Southern History* 16 (November 1950): 511–18.

———. "Robert J. Breckinridge: Kentucky Unionist." *Register of the Kentucky Historical Society* 69 (October 1971): 362–85.

Goldfield, David R. "The Urban South: A Regional Framework." *American Historical Review* 86 (December 1981): 1009–34.

Grinspan, Jon. " 'Young Men for War': The Wide Awakes and Lincoln's 1860 Presidential Campaign." *Journal of American History* 96 (September 2009): 357–78.

Gunderson, Robert Gray. "William C. Rives and the Old Gentlemen's Convention." *Journal of Southern History* 22 (November 1956): 459–76.

Hancock, Harold Bell. "Civil War Comes to Delaware." *Civil War History* 2 (December 1956): 29–46.

Harlow, Luke E. "Religion, Race, and Robert J. Breckinridge: The Ideology of an Antislavery Slaveholder, 1830–1860." *Ohio Valley History* 6 (Fall 2006): 1–24.

Harrison, Lowell H. "George W. Johnson and Richard Hawes: The Governors of Confederate Kentucky." *Register of the Kentucky Historical Society* 79 (Winter 1981): 3–39.

———. "Governor Magoffin and the Secession Crisis." *Register of the Kentucky Historical Society* 72 (April 1974): 91–110.

———. "John C. Breckinridge: Nationalist, Confederate, Kentuckian." *Filson Club History Quarterly* 47 (April 1973): 125–44.

Heck, Frank H. "John C. Breckinridge in the Crisis of 1860–61." *Journal of Southern History* 21 (August 1955): 317–30.

Henig, Gerald S. "Henry Winter Davis and the Speakership Contest of 1859–1860." *Maryland Historical Magazine* 68 (Spring 1973): 1–19.

Hitchcock, William S. "Southern Moderates and Secession: Senator Robert M. T. Hunter's Call for Union." *Journal of American History* 59 (March 1973): 871–84.

Hudson, J. Blaine. "'Upon This Rock': The Free African American Community of Antebellum Louisville, Kentucky." *Register of the Kentucky Historical Society* 109 (Summer/Autumn 2011): 295–326.

Huston, James L. "The Pregnant Economies of the Border South, 1840–1860: Virginia, Kentucky, Tennessee, and the Possibilities of Slave-Labor Expansion." In *The Old South's Modern Worlds: Slavery, Region, and Nation in the Age of Progress*, edited by L. Diane Barnes, Brian Schoen, and Frank Towers, 120–41. New York: Oxford University Press, 2011.

———. "Southerners against Secession: The Arguments of the Constitutional Unionists in 1850–1851." *Civil War History* 46 (December 2000): 281–99.

Hyman, Harold M. "The Narrow Escape from a 'Compromise of 1860': Secession and the Constitution." In *Freedom and Reform: Essays in Honor of Henry Steele Commager*, edited by Harold M. Hyman and Leonard W. Levy, 149–66. New York: Harper and Row, 1967.

Johannsen, Robert W. "The Douglas Democracy and the Crisis of Disunion." *Civil War History* 9 (September 1963): 229–47.

Kelly, Jack. "John J. Crittenden and the Constitutional Union Party." *Filson Club History Quarterly* 48 (July 1974): 265–76.

Kirkpatrick, Arthur Roy. "Missouri in the Early Months of the Civil War." *Missouri Historical Review* 55 (April 1961): 235–66.

———. "Missouri on the Eve of the Civil War." *Missouri Historical Review* 55 (January 1961): 98–108.

———. "Missouri's Secessionist Government, 1861–1865." *Missouri Historical Review* 45 (January 1951): 124–37.

Kornblith, Gary J. "Rethinking the Coming of the Civil War: A Counterfactual Exercise." *Journal of American History* 90 (June 2003): 76–105.

Ledbetter, Patsy S. "John J. Crittenden and the Compromise Debacle." *Filson Club History Quarterly* 51 (April 1977): 125–42.

Lee, Jacob F. "Between Two Fires: Cassius M. Clay, Slavery, and Antislavery in the Kentucky Borderlands." *Ohio Valley History* 6 (Fall 2006): 50–70.

Levine, Bruce. "'The Vital Element of the Republican Party': Antislavery, Nativism, and Abraham Lincoln." *Journal of the Civil War Era* 1 (December 2011): 481–505.

Long, E. B. "The Paducah Affair: Bloodless Action That Altered the Civil War in the Mississippi Valley." *Register of the Kentucky Historical Society* 70 (October 1972): 253–76.

Luthin, Reinhard H. "Organizing the Republican Party in the 'Border Slave' Regions: Edward Bates's Presidential Candidacy in 1860." *Missouri Historical Review* 38 (January 1944): 138–61.

Mathias, Frank F. "Slavery, the Solvent of Kentucky Politics." *Register of the Kentucky Historical Society* 70 (January 1972): 1–16.

May, Robert E. "Psychobiography and Secession: The Southern Radical as Maladjusted 'Outsider.'" *Civil War History* 34 (March 1988): 46–69.

McCrary, Peyton, Clark Miller, and Dale Baum. "Class and Party in the Secession Crisis: Voting Behavior in the Deep South, 1856–1861." *Journal of Interdisciplinary History* 8 (Winter 1978): 429–57.

McKenzie, Robert Tracy. "Contesting Secession: Parson Brownlow and the Rhetoric of Proslavery Unionism, 1860–1861." *Civil War History* 48 (December 2002): 294–312.

———. "Prudent Silence and Strict Neutrality: The Parameters of Unionism in Parson Brownlow's Knoxville, 1860–1863." In *Enemies of the Country: New Perspectives on Unionists in the Civil War South*, edited by John C. Inscoe and Robert C. Kenzer, 73–96. Athens: University of Georgia Press, 2001.

Mering, John Vollmer. "The Constitutional Union Campaign of 1860: An Example of the Paranoid Style." *Mid-America* 60 (April–July 1978): 95–106.

———. "The Slave-State Constitutional Unionists and the Politics of Consensus." *Journal of Southern History* 43 (August 1977): 395–410.

Mitchell, Charles W. "'The Whirlwind Now Gathering': Baltimore's Pratt Street Riot and the End of Maryland Secession." *Maryland Historical Magazine* 97 (Summer 2002): 203–32.

Moore, James Tice. "Secession and the States: A Review Essay." *Virginia Magazine of History and Biography* 94 (January 1986): 60–76.

Najar, Monica. "'Meddling with Emancipation': Baptists, Authority, and the Rift over Slavery in the Upper South." *Journal of the Early Republic* 25 (Summer 2005): 157–86.

Nesenhöner, Stefan. "Maintaining the Center: John Pendleton Kennedy, the Border States, and the Secession Crisis." *Maryland Historical Magazine* 89 (Winter 1994): 413–26.

Paulus, Sarah Bischoff. "America's Long Eulogy for Compromise: Henry Clay and American Politics, 1854–1858." *Journal of the Civil War Era* 4 (March 2014): 28–52.

Phillips, Christopher. "'The Chrysalis State': Slavery, Confederate Identity, and the Creation of the Border South." In *Inside the Confederate Nation: Essays in Honor of Emory M. Thomas*, edited by Lesley J. Gordon and John C. Inscoe, 147–64. Baton Rouge: Louisiana State University Press, 2005.

———. "'The Crime against Missouri': Slavery, Kansas, and the Cant of Southernness in the Border West." *Civil War History* 48 (March 2002): 60–81.

———. "Lincoln's Grasp of War: Hard War and the Politics of Neutrality and Slavery in the Western Border States, 1861–1862." *Journal of the Civil War Era* 3 (June 2013): 184–210.

Robertson, James R. "Sectionalism in Kentucky from 1855 to 1865." *Mississippi Valley Historical Review* 4 (June 1917): 49–63.

Robinson, Michael D. "William Henry Seward and the Onset of the Secession Crisis." *Civil War History* 59 (March 2013): 32–66.

Roed, William. "Secessionist Strength in Missouri." *Missouri Historical Review* 72 (July 1978): 412–23.

Rorvig, Paul. "The Significant Skirmish: The Battle of Boonville, June 17, 1861." *Missouri Historical Review* 86 (January 1992): 127–48.

Schwalm, Leslie A. "'Overrun with Free Negroes': Emancipation and Wartime Migration in the Upper Midwest." *Civil War History* 50 (June 2004): 145–74.

Shortridge, Wilson Porter. "Kentucky Neutrality in 1861." *Mississippi Valley Historical Review* 9 (March 1923): 283–301.

Sowle, Patrick Michael. "Cassius Clay and the Crisis of the Union." *Register of the Kentucky Historical Society* 65 (April 1967): 144–49.

Steiner, Bernard C. "Severn Teackle Wallis: First Paper." *Sewanee Review* 15 (January 1907): 58–74.

———. "Severn Teackle Wallis: Second Paper." *Sewanee Review* 15 (April 1907): 129–47.

Towers, Frank. "Another Look at Inevitability: The Upper South and the Limits of Compromise in the Secession Crisis." *Tennessee Historical Quarterly* 70 (Summer 2011): 108–25.

Tucker, Phillip T. "'Ho, for Kansas': The Southwest Expedition of 1860." *Missouri Historical Review* 86 (October 1991): 22–36.

Turner, Wallace B. "The Secession Movement in Kentucky." *Register of the Kentucky Historical Society* 66 (July 1968): 259–78.

Viles, Jonas. "Sections and Sectionalism in a Border State." *Mississippi Valley Historical Review* 21 (June 1934): 3–22.

Waldrep, Christopher. "Rank-and-File Voters and the Coming of the Civil War: Caldwell County, Kentucky, as Test Case." *Civil War History* 35 (March 1989): 59–72.

Wallace, Doris Davis. "The Political Campaign of 1860 in Missouri." *Missouri Historical Review* 70 (January 1976): 162–83.

Woodworth, Steven E. "'The Indeterminate Quantities': Jefferson Davis, Leonidas Polk, and the End of Kentucky Neutrality, September 1861." *Civil War History* 38 (December 1992): 289–97.

Zacharias, Donald W. "John J. Crittenden Crusades for the Union and Neutrality in Kentucky." *Filson Club History Quarterly* 38 (July 1964): 193–205.

THESES AND DISSERTATIONS

Boyd, John A. "Neutrality and Peace: Kentucky and the Secession Crisis of 1861." Ph.D. diss., University of Kentucky, 1999.

Cannon, Jessica Ann. "Lincoln's Divided Backyard: Maryland in the Civil War Era." Ph.D. diss., Rice University, 2010.

Goebel, Robert W. "'Casualty of War': The Governorship of Beriah Magoffin, 1859–1862." M.A. thesis, University of Louisville, 2005.

Hoskins, Patricia Ann. "'The Old First Is with the South': The Civil War, Reconstruction, and Memory in the Jackson Purchase Region of Kentucky." Ph.D. diss., Auburn University, 2008.

Jenness, Timothy Max. "Tentative Relations: Secession and War in the Central Ohio River Valley, 1859–1862." Ph.D. diss., University of Tennessee, 2011.

McClanahan, Brion T. "A Lonely Opposition: James A. Bayard, Jr. and the American Civil War." Ph.D. diss., University of South Carolina, 2006.

Paine, Christopher M. "'Kentucky Will Be the Last to Give Up the Union': Kentucky Politics, 1844–1861." Ph.D. diss., University of Kentucky, 1998.

Parmley, Curtis Lushan. "'The Greatest Evil That Can Befall Us': Unionism in Antebellum Era Kentucky." M.A. thesis, University of Louisville, 2012.

Sowle, Patrick Michael. "The Conciliatory Republicans during the Winter of Secession." Ph.D. diss., Duke University, 1963.

Volz, Harry August, III. "Party, State, and Nation: Kentucky and the Coming of the American Civil War." Ph.D. diss., University of Virginia, 1982.

Index